BODY IMAGE: NEW RESEARCH

BODY IMAGE: NEW RESEARCH

MARLENE V. KINDES
EDITOR

Nova Biomedical Books
New York

NOTICE TO THE READER
The Publisher has taken reasonable care in the preparation of this book, but makes no expressed or implied warranty of any kind and assumes no responsibility for any errors or omissions. No liability is assumed for incidental or consequential damages in connection with or arising out of information contained in this book. The Publisher shall not be liable for any special, consequential, or exemplary damages resulting, in whole or in part, from the readers' use of, or reliance upon, this material.

Independent verification should be sought for any data, advice or recommendations contained in this book. In addition, no responsibility is assumed by the publisher for any injury and/or damage to persons or property arising from any methods, products, instructions, ideas or otherwise contained in this publication.

This publication is designed to provide accurate and authoritative information with regard to the subject matter cover herein. It is sold with the clear understanding that the Publisher is not engaged in rendering legal or any other professional services. If legal, medical or any other expert assistance is required, the services of a competent person should be sought. FROM A DECLARATION OF PARTICIPANTS JOINTLY ADOPTED BY A COMMITTEE OF THE AMERICAN BAR ASSOCIATION AND A COMMITTEE OF PUBLISHERS.

Library of Congress Cataloging-in-Publication Data
Body image : new research / Marlene V. Kindes, editor.
     p. cm.
Includes bibliographical references and index.
ISBN 1-60021-059-7
1. Body image. I. Kindes, Marlene V.
BF697.5.B63B6185   2006
306.4'613--dc22   2006004648

Published by Nova Science Publishers, Inc. ✤*New York*

CONTENTS

PREFACE

Western culture has increasingly valued physical appearance and in particular slenderness in the last 20 years. Unrealistic targets of thinness and excessive weight loss have led to eating disorders, the idea of obligatory exercise and other mental health problems. The concept of dissatisfaction with one's body image is driven home by images of ultra-thin models appearing in newspapers, magazines and television. This new book brings together leading international research in this alarming and growing field.

The drive for muscularity, which reflects the desire to achieve a muscular mesomorphic physique, is emerging as an important area of inquiry within the field of male body image. The purpose of this chapter was to review published literature examining the drive for muscularity and, in so doing, delineate researchers' current knowledge about the construct. Four key areas were reviewed: 1) the psychometric properties of measures designed to assess the drive for muscularity; 2) the dominant theoretical frameworks that have been used to explain the emergence of this drive and the role it potentially plays in body dissatisfaction; 3) the psychological and behavioural correlates of the drive for muscularity; and 4) muscle dysmorphia, a clinical condition which thus far possesses an unclear association with the drive for muscularity. Stated briefly, chapter I suggests there are critical measurement, theoretical, and methodological issues that must be addressed if we are to understand this drive more fully.

Evolutionary psychologists have argued that there exist universally shared criteria of attractiveness, which are potent cues to a person's potential reproductive success. Chapter II reviews the current state of evolutionary psychology's study of female and male physical attractiveness. The former focuses on body shape as measured by the waist-to-hip ratio (WHR) and body weight scaled for height, or the body mass index (BMI), whereas the latter examine the waist-to-chest ratio (WCR). The evidence seems to point to BMI being the dominant cue for female physical attractiveness, with WHR playing a more minor role. The opposite is true for male attractiveness, with WCR playing a more important role than either the WHR or BMI. Importantly, cross-cultural studies have suggested that there are significant differences for physical attractiveness in terms of body shape and weight, which evolutionary psychological arguments have difficulty in explaining. Alternative explanations and the future of the field are discussed in conclusion.

The studies in chapter III examined the effects of sport-related advertising on body image. In Study 1, two hundred and twenty four collegiate females were categorised into regular exercisers and non-exercisers. In the pre-test and post-test (i.e., before and after exposure to advertising), each participant completed the Silhouette Measure of Body Image, the 9-item Social Physique Anxiety Scale and the Attitudes Towards Sport Advertisements, and the exercisers completed the 7-subscale Reasons for Exercise Inventory. They were then assigned to the model or product-related advertising condition. Participants were shown 15 sport-related advertisements either showing models (model condition) or workout shoes (product condition). Participants were given five minutes to view the advertisements, and then completed the questionnaires again. The results showed that the exercisers who were exposed to the model condition scored significantly ($p<.01$) higher on all measures in the post-test compared to the pre-test. The non-exercisers exposed to the model condition increased significantly ($p<.05$) on all measures from pre- to post-test but scored significantly ($p<.05$) lower on all post-test measures than the exerciser group. The product condition groups did not increase significantly on any measure ($p>.05$ in all cases). In Study 2, two hundred and forty nine sedentary undergraduates (126 males, 123 females) completed the SPAS, the SMBI and the ATSA. Following the pre-test, participants were shown 15 sport-related same-sex advertisements. Participants were given five minutes to view the advertisements, before completing the measures again. Group x test ANOVAs revealed that, in both the pre-test and the post-test, females scored significantly ($p<.05$) higher than males on the SMBI and SPAS. The SMBI, SPAS and ATSA scores of the female participants, and the SPAS and ATSA scores of the males, increased significantly ($p<.05$) from pre- to post-test. Males' SMBI scores were higher in the post-test than the pre-test but the difference was not statistically significant ($p>.05$). These results show that the use of very fit and toned models in the advertising of sport-related products can have a detrimental effect upon body image of both males and females.

Body image knowledge and its cognitive organization within the self concept were studied, in chapter IV, in four partial replicating experiments using young women with bulimic tendencies. The authors used a choice decision reaction time methodology to establish an empirical foundation for measuring body image schemas and then expanded the paradigm to accommodate the investigation of other facets and dynamics of the self. The classical self-referencing paradigm was first applied to index responses of body image to an actual self, and was adapted to allow for sentence stems to cue the relevant self components of interest such as those of a possible self. The reaction time paradigm was further elaborated to measure encoding to complete sentences by using a letter-word-sentence unfolding method allowing for the study of decisional information processing to self statements of the kind found in psychometrically derived self concept scales. The first study established baseline data and confirmed the presence of body image schemas when self-referencing to body shape vs. trait words in women preoccupied or not preoccupied with their body shape. In the second study information processing to "dreamed-of" and "feared-of" facets of possible selves revealed that words representing body image concerns are processed as schemas or knowledge structures only if they are referenced to the self, and that actual self and possible self facets can co-exist as constructs within the same person. Body image words in bulimic women activate cognitive schemas only when referenced to an aspect of the self. The third experiment replicated the latter findings with women with bulimic behaviors and found that in addition to being schematic for body image words these women tended to be aschematic for attributes that described social and personality traits. The fourth experiment presented items from Physical, Social, and Academic self concept scales and found that negative body image schemas "spill over" and influence social and academic self concepts. Women, distinguished by the presence or absence of bulimic tendencies processed body shape words more quickly when describing themselves, their dreamed-of and feared-of body image, and their Physical and Social self concept. The findings that bulimic women aspire more to be thin more than to be socially or academically competent, or to describe themselves positively in terms of personality traits were consistent with the view that self and identity eccentricities in bulimic women originate with socially constructed standards.

The current knowledge base that serves as a foundation for diagnosing and treating eating disorders, disorders grouped due to ill behavior sets with regards to food and nutrition, recognizes EDS as an adolescent or post adolescent phenomenon, with specific overt indicators. As a corollary with eating disorders, also presenting in adolescence (though trending younger) body image and body image distortion (as overt expression) is identified as one of these indicators. However, when researchers and clinicians explore beyond presenting behavioral sets, and beyond the age bracket associated with those behaviors, it becomes clear that these disorders, and bosy image itself, express a much deeper, and more challenging pathology, what is more, exploration may indicate that the eating disorders are related one to another only superficially. In chapter V, current research on BI is used to illustrate a developmental approach for improved recognition and efficacious treatment aimed at ED prevention.

In chapter VI, the authors describe the manifestations of body image disturbance in individuals with borderline personality disorder as they might appear in psychiatric and medical settings. In psychiatric settings, body image disturbances may be one of several mediators for self-harm behavior, which is commonly observed in patients with borderline personality. In medical settings, body image disturbances may play a meaningful role in ill-defined somatic complaints or somatic preoccupation in patients as well as medically self-harming behavior. In either setting, the body image disturbances encountered in borderline personality disorder are likely to be due to the effects of childhood trauma. If so, then the body image disturbances encountered in borderline personality are not necessarily due to the disorder, itself, but rather to one of the proposed etiological substrates—childhood trauma.

Body image aberration in schizophrenia was earlier conceived as delusional and hallucinatory symptoms. However, perceptions of schizophrenia have changed dramatically, especially with the concept of negative symptoms in the 1980s and in the 1990s, to include the neurocognitive aspects of schizophrenia. Deviations in schizophrenics' body image from the standard underlying various behaviors or allegations concerning the body should be now refocused. In chapter VII, using the Body Image Questionnaire (BIQ), comprised of three hypothetical components, anatomical, functional and psychological, attempts were made to resolve some primary questions. They were (1) whether or not there is any related clinical characteristics to schizophrenic body image abberation, (2) whether there are aberrant components of body image specific to schizophrenia, (3) whether or not there is unique link between depression and body image in schizophrenia. In study 1, correlations between body image assessed by the BIQ and clinical characteristics as positive and negative symptoms assessed by SAPS and SANS, insight assessed by SAI, and daily dose of conventional antipsychotic drugs were examined. In study 2, three components of body image, that is, anatomical, functional and psychological, were compared between schizophrenic and non-schizophrenic groups. In study 3, the correlation between depression assessed by SDS and body image assessed by the BIQ was examined. In these studies, 93 chronic schizophrenics, 177 normal adults, and 43 patients with anxiety disorders according to DSM-IV criteria, were examined. In studies 4-5, the additional finding of Rorschach percepts concerning body image in schizophrenia was reported. Schizophrenics' body image aberration proved to be independent of symptoms and medication. It was also shown that the aberration proved to be limited to functional imageries, and that the anatomical component remained intact. As to depression, a specific link of body image, especially with functional imageries, with the depression characteristic to schizophrenia was found. All these results showed that body image aberration in schizophrenics is not the result of symptoms or effects of conventional neuroleptic medications, but they are germane to schizophrenia, which is comprised of aberration mainly in functional body imageries. This body image deviation proved to be linked to some serious depressive signs and symptoms in schizophrenia. The subsidiary findings, that is, the Rorschach percepts as a mass of flesh quite often seen in schizophrenia, are congruent with the main findings that schizophrenic patients showed an anticipation of becoming unmovable.

The main characteristic of body dysmorphic disorder (BDD) is a preoccupation with an imagined defect in appearance in a normally appearing person or an excessive preoccupation with appearance in a person with a small physical defect. In chapter VIII, the objective was to describe the socio-demographic and phenomenological characteristics of a Brazilian sample of 28 patients with BDD from two university clinics. The combined sample was characterized by a predominance of female (n=15; 53.6%), single or divorced (n=23; 82.1%), and economically unproductive patients (n=23; 82.1%). The authors found an average of 2.4 current imagined defects per patient. The most frequently reported body parts of excessive current concern were the overall appearance, size or shape of the face (n=10; 35.7%), the hair (n=8; 28.7%); the nose (n=8; 28.7%); skin (n=7; 25%), and the body build and the weight (n=7; 25%). Most individuals exhibited a chronic condition (n=20; 71.4%) and had the same concerns during the course of the disorder (n=20; 71.4%). All patients displayed compulsive behaviors, including recurrent mirror checking (n=18; 64.3%), camouflaging (n=16; 57.1%), reassurance seeking by means of repetitive questioning of others (n=16; 57.1%) and excessive use of cosmetics (n=7; 25%). Two patients reported "do-it-yourself" surgeries. Ten patients had current suicidal ideation (37.5%). Eight patients (28.6%) showed no insight over their dysmorphic beliefs. Twenty-five patients (89.3%) exhibited psychiatric comorbidities, mostly obsessive-compulsive disorder (OCD) [n=14, 50%] and major depressive disorder (n=15; 53.6%). The results are consistent with the characterization of BDD as a true trans-cultural disorder.

Obesity has been considered by WHO as the epidemic of XXI century, affecting a considerable amount of persons in developed countries, being associated to an increase in cardiovascular risk. Morbid obesity, defined by a BMI > 40 Kg/m^2 is the extreme type of obesity associated with a great number of diseases: mellitus diabetes type 2, arterial hypertension, cardiovascular disease, arthropathy and sleep apnoea syndrome. It's a fact that western society emphasizes thinness and denigrates excess weight, stigmatising obese people, and determining a poor body image in obese individuals. The objective of chapter IX is to establish the degree of body image dissatisfaction in morbid obese individuals and how it's modified by bariatric surgery with a result of significant weight loss. In the first part the authors will make a review of current literature on the relationship between obesity and body image, the body image dissatisfaction and distortion that experience obese individuals and apparent risk factors (degree of overweight, being female, binge eating, early age of onset of obesity and race). The second part shows the results of a group, using the Body Dissatisfaction and Drive for Thinness subscales of EDI (Eating Disorder Inventory) in 100 morbid obese candidates for bariatric surgery, appreciating a high body image dissatisfaction and a significant drive for thinness, finding as the only indicator associated to a higher body image dissatisfaction, an age greater than 40 years; and in 31 operated morbid obese persons (evaluated at a mean postoperative period of 16 months) with a statistically significant reduction in body dissatisfaction. Finally the authors present a discussion of our results and tentative conclusions.

Due to the trendy emphasis on the slimmer body in which not only women or adults are suffering with different weight related sickness, our young Chinese children in this generation is also facing a huge challenge in their weight and appearance concern. In last decades, clinical eating disorders have been documented in Hong Kong and commercial body slimming products are very common in the Chinese society. Little is known in the literature if the western lifestyle (physical inactivity and diet) has already influenced the Chinese children regarding the psychological and sociological perspectives. Chapter X intended to examine the associations between Chinese children's body rating, actual fatness, gender and age impact, and the cultural issue regarding the weight and body weight issue.

In chapter XI, in order to figure out how normal healthy children actually regard their own bodies, the Human Figure Drawing test: Goodenough-Harris Drawing test (also called Draw-A-Man test, or DAM test) was used as one resource tool, and body image in children was scored from the development process of human figure drawingsquantitatively. Since the body is the key to both motor ability and sports activities, they have an intimate relationship with body image, thus suggesting that physical exercise changes body image. For this reason, a survey of motor ability was performed to reveal its mutual relationships with the DAM test, which is thought to hold a relationship with body image. For the human figure drawing scoring, based on Goodenough's handbook of human intelligence testing, one point was awarded for each of 15 body parts that met achievement criteria for that drawing component (for a maximum of 15 points). In our study, the total score is the body image score, and the higher the score, the greater the child's awareness of body parts, and that child can be considered to have a more developed body image. Since previous research has shown that motor ability in children from 4.0 to 6.5 years of age is comprised of the lower range of power, flexibility, muscle strength, balance, and endurance, the four categories of 25-meter dash, standing jump, softball throw, and body support time were surveyed. With regards to the relationship between DAM test and motor ability, in 4-year olds, while a significant correlation could not be determined between body image score as a score of 15 body parts that could be drawn correctly in the human figure drawing, and the total score of the four motor ability tests (using T scores), a significant positive correlation was observed for 5-year olds ($r = .284$). These results showed that the higher the child's motor ability, the greater the change in body image, the higher the awareness of body parts, and the more firmly established body image held by the child. Also, that individual differences for human figure drawing and motor ability were smaller and more stable for 5-year olds than 4-year olds was indicated as one factor affecting the correlation between body image and motor ability.

As medical and surgical treatments become ever more invasive and complicated, people today are living with treated illnesses, which would have resulted in death only a matter of years ago. Increasingly intense use of technology can often complicate the rehabilitation of such patients who must adapt to radical changes in body appearance and/or function. If the patient survives the illness and treatment, but his/her quality of life is never restored, how can one call the treatment successful? The author has used three specific intervention strategies to assist patients who are recovering from such experiences: interactive guided imagery, empty chair work, and therapeutic letter-writing. All three can be effective methods to assist patients to adjust mentally, emotionally and spiritually to perceived attacks on their physical bodies. Interactive guided imagery is conceptually described as a tool from the school of Psychosynthesis. This form of guided imagery is verbally interactive, and used to assist patients to employ their visualization skills to "dis-identify from" and therefore "relate to" changing body parts and functions. The purpose of this technique is help them to grieve their losses and reintegrate the altered parts/functions back into a cohesive whole once again. Empty chair work is derived from the Gestalt school and takes the imagery work a bit farther as the therapist invites the patient to "put the affected body part in the chair" and proceed with a dialogue, again to work through attendant grief issues and to work towards re-integration. The literature recommends the use of journaling as an adjunct to treatment. More specifically, therapeutic letter-writing moves the locus of attention from "writing about" to "writing to/from" the affected body part, always the more evocative, more powerful form of therapy. Chapter XII describes the conceptual frameworks and techniques of each of the above intervention strategies. Case illustrations are offered to describe their use with patients who experience medical and/or surgical alterations to their bodies as a result of illness and/or its treatment.

A healthy normal skin is essential for a person's physical and mental well being. It is an important aspect of their sexual attractiveness, a sense of well being and a sense of self confidence. The skin is the largest and most visible organ of the human body. Hence any discoloration on the skin visibly affects the witness and thus the person affected extremely. Vitiligo is an important skin disease having major impact on the quality of life of sufferers. Although the disease does not produce direct physical impairment, it may considerably influence the psychological well-being of the patients. It has been suggested that patients suffer from low self-esteem, poor body image and a poor quality of life. A negative body image is directly related to self esteem. The more negative the perception of our bodies, the more negative we feel about ourselves. Vitiligo can also result in problems in interpersonal relations particularly as a result of depression and dissatisfaction. The men and women with vitiligo do not promote self- esteem or positive self image. In chapter XIII, the impact of vitiligo on patient's body image in consideration of interpersonal relationship, psychological, and social aspects regarding cultural and geographical differences is reviewed.

In: Body Image: New Research
Editor: Marlene V. Kindes, pp. 1-34

ISBN 1-60021-059-7
© 2006 Nova Science Publishers, Inc.

Chapter I

STRIVING FOR BODILY PERFECTION? AN OVERVIEW OF THE DRIVE FOR MUSCULARITY

Todd G. Morrison[1]*, Melanie A. Morrison[2] and Leigh McCann[1]
[1]Department of Psychology, National University of Ireland, Galway, Ireland;
[2]Department of Psychology, University of Saskatchewan,
Saskatoon, SK, S7N 5K5, Canada.

ABSTRACT

The drive for muscularity, which reflects the desire to achieve a muscular mesomorphic physique, is emerging as an important area of inquiry within the field of male body image. The purpose of this chapter was to review published literature examining the drive for muscularity and, in so doing, delineate researchers' current knowledge about the construct. Four key areas were reviewed: 1) the psychometric properties of measures designed to assess the drive for muscularity; 2) the dominant theoretical frameworks that have been used to explain the emergence of this drive and the role it potentially plays in body dissatisfaction; 3) the psychological and behavioural correlates of the drive for muscularity; and 4) muscle dysmorphia, a clinical condition which thus far possesses an unclear association with the drive for muscularity. Stated briefly, this review suggests there are critical measurement, theoretical, and methodological issues that must be addressed if we are to understand this drive more fully.

Keywords: Muscularity, Male Body Image, Physical Appearance, Body Attitudes.

---

* Correspondence concerning this article should be addressed to Dr. Todd G. Morrison, Department of Psychology, National University of Ireland, Galway, Ireland. E-mail: Todd.Morrison@nuigalway.ie.

INTRODUCTION

Research suggests that the ideal male physique is muscular mesomorphic, characterized by broad shoulders, a muscular stomach, chest and arms, and a narrow waist (Kimmel & Mahalik, 2004; Labre, 2005b; Ridgeway & Tylka, 2005). Studies indicate that male participants often express the desire to attain this body ideal, even though it is far removed from the physique they possess currently (Grieve, Newton, Kelley, Miller, & Kerr, 2005; Morrison, Morrison & Hopkins, 2003; Morrison, Morrison, Hopkins, & Rowan, 2004b; Olivardia, Pope, Borowiecki, & Cohane, 2004). For example, in a study conducted with undergraduate students in the Midwestern United States, Vartanian, Giant, and Passino (2001) found that 85% of male participants wanted to be more muscular. These authors also noted that, in comparison to women, the men reported a greater discrepancy between their desired versus current level of muscularity. Olivardia et al. (2004) instructed a sample of 154 American college men to select their perceived and ideal images using the somatomorphic matrix, which is a computerized programme that presents 100 body drawings organized in a 10 x 10 matrix and representing 10 levels of musculature and adiposity. The authors concluded that there was a "striking gulf between men's actual and desired muscularity" (p. 117), with study participants selecting an ideal that was approximately 25lbs greater in muscularity and 8lbs lower in body fat than their current physique. Similar findings were reported by Pope et al. (2000) in a study examining body image perceptions among men residing in Austria, France, and the United States (i.e., participants' ideal body was, on average, 28lbs more muscular).

The popularity of the muscular mesomorphic ideal is not surprising given its predominance in cultural artefacts such as toys, advertisements, motion pictures, and music videos (Rohlinger, 2002). An additional incentive for some men to pursue a muscular mesomorphic physique may reside in the positive characteristics ascribed to this body type; ascriptions that include strong, brave, adventurous, physically healthy, and good-looking (Ryckman, Butler, Thornton, & Lindner, 1997). Further, it is possible that some men wish to achieve this build for reasons that are highly utilitarian. For example, in a recent qualitative study, male participants reported that "people who look fit [i.e., muscular] are treated better by others and are more likely to be successful in their careers" (Labre, 2005b, p. 226).

The drive for muscularity is an individual difference variable formulated to account for variations in the desire to achieve an idealized, muscular physique (McCreary & Sasse, 2000; Morrison et al., 2003). While this construct does not represent a drive in the traditional sense, it was labelled as such for the purpose of creating a term parallel to the drive for thinness, which is a well researched concept in the literature on female body image (e.g., Davis, Karvinen, & McCreary, 2005). The parallelism of these terms is important as both reflect the determination to achieve a culturally idealized, albeit gender-specific, body.

An additional point concerning the definition of the drive for muscularity warrants consideration at this juncture. Morrison and associates (2003, 2004b) contend that this drive is evident primarily, though not exclusively, in men because, according to Kimmel and Mahalik (2004), it reflects a masculine body ideal, the core features of which revolve around adjectival descriptors such as "thick," "big," "strong," "chiselled," and "buff" (Ridgeway &

Tylka, 2005). With the possible exception of the word "strong," these adjectives do not reflect the physical ideal for women in Western culture.

A corollary to this point is the argument that scales designed to measure the drive for muscularity must be gender specific (Morrison et al., 2004b); in other words, as the construct manifests itself differentially for men and women, a single scale cannot assess this drive in both groups[1]. Some researchers concur with this line of reasoning, and have developed measures that specifically target men (e.g., Swansea Muscularity Attitudes Questionnaire [SMAQ]: Edwards & Launder, 2000; the Drive for Muscularity subscale of the Male Eating Behaviour and Body Image Evaluation [MEBBIE] inventory: Kaminski, Chapman, Haynes, & Own, 2005; and the Drive for Muscularity subscale of the Male Body Attitudes Scale [MBAS]: Tylka, Bergeron, & Schwartz, 2005). However, other researchers seemingly disagree with this position, and have constructed instruments that they believe are suitable for both genders (e.g., the Drive for Muscularity Scale: McCreary & Sasse, 2000).

Irrespective of definitional issues, burgeoning interest in the drive for muscularity has occurred since the term was introduced by McCreary and Sasse (2000). Thus, a review of the available literature is worthwhile at this point, as it would serve to consolidate what researchers do and, importantly, do not know about the drive for muscularity.

The current chapter[2] is partitioned into four sections[3]. The first section provides a review of the construction and validation of measures designed to assess the drive for muscularity. Following this, major theoretical frameworks that may be applied to the drive for muscularity are presented. The third and fourth sections focus on the psychological and behavioural correlates of the drive for muscularity and on muscle dysmorphia, respectively. In each section, avenues for future inquiry are highlighted, where appropriate.

Measurement of the Drive for Muscularity

Cafri and Thompson (2004) report that "the growing interest in the assessment of muscle appearance attitudes, particularly among men, makes it imperative that researchers attend to the methodological issues related to assessment of this construct" (p. 229). We agree with this recommendation, and would add that reliance on measures of the drive for muscularity that are psychometrically poor or tested inappropriately hinders the development of research in this area.

To date, four scales designed to measure the drive for muscularity have had elements of their psychometric properties (i.e., scale score reliability, factor structure, and/or validity) tested in more than one published study. These are: the Drive for Muscularity Scale (DMS: McCreary & Sasse, 2000); another measure also entitled the Drive for Muscularity scale (DM: Yelland & Tiggemann, 2003); the Drive for Muscularity Attitudes Questionnaire

---

[1]   Based on anecdotal information, we believe that, among women, the drive for muscularity is more accurately labelled the drive for tone. Choi (2003) reiterates this observation by suggesting "female muscular development must remain at the level of muscle tone, not muscle size or bulk as the female muscular body is generally considered unattractive because it symbolizes masculinity" (p. 72).

[2]   It should be noted that this review focuses on methodological and theoretical issues pertaining to the drive for muscularity. For a more clinical overview, the interested reader is directed to Cafri and associates (2005).

[3]   Given that the four categories are not orthogonal, overlap in the literature reviewed may be evident.

(DMAQ: Morrison et al., 2003); and the Swansea Muscularity Attitudes Questionnaire (SMAQ: Edwards & Launder, 2000). Each of these measures will be outlined briefly, with particular attention being paid to indicants of psychometric soundness.

Drive for Muscularity Scale (DMS)

The DMS consists of 15 items (e.g., "1 think that I would look better if I gained 10 pounds in bulk") and uses a six-point Likert-type response format (*never* to *always*). In the original study detailing the measure's construction and validation, McCreary and Sasse (2000) formulated a list of motivations to become muscular using information gathered from "weight-training enthusiasts" (p. 298) as well as a content analysis of weight-training magazines. The face validity of these motivations was assessed by men and women involved in weight-training, and the DMS was subsequently created. Contrary to routine psychometric practice, the authors did not over-sample content domain by generating a large number of items, and then employing stringent item reduction criteria. Thus, one must assume that the authors felt these 15 items were the best exemplars of the drive for muscularity.

Copies of the DMS and other instruments (e.g., the Rosenberg Self-esteem Scale, RSE; Rosenberg, 1989) were distributed to 197 Canadian high-school students. Results indicated that the scale score reliability coefficients for the DMS were satisfactory (α = .84 for boys; α = .78 for girls). In addition, as predicted, the authors found that boys' scores on the DMS correlated negatively with scores on the self-esteem measure and positively with scores on a measure of depression. None of these correlations were significant for girls, which the authors used as evidence to support their prediction of differential salience (i.e., the drive for muscularity is more pertinent to boys than girls; thus, correlations between this drive and variables of interest such as depression should be stronger for the former than the latter). Results concerning the scale's discriminant validity were mixed. No significant correlations were obtained between girls' drive for muscularity and two indices of the drive for thinness (the Eating Attitudes Test and the Body Dissatisfaction subscale of the Eating Disorders Inventory). For boys, contrary to the authors' prediction, a significant positive correlation was obtained between scores on the Eating Attitudes Test and the DMS (r = .37)[4].

The authors stated that they conceptualised the drive for muscularity as a unidimensional construct and hence expected the DMS to be unidimensional (p. 302). An exploratory factor analysis was not conducted on the grounds that the sample size was too small. However, it should be noted that rules of thumb concerning $N{:}p$ ratios, where N equals number of participants and p equals number of variables, have been criticized for being ad hoc rather than empirically driven, and for failing to consider other important issues such as the estimation method used and the clarity of the factor solution (Hogarty, Hines, Kromrey, Ferron, & Mumford, 2005; MacCallum, Widaman, Zhang, & Hong, 1999). Indeed, research suggests that the influence of sample size diminishes as item communalities and factor overdetermination increase (Hogarty et al., 2005).

---

[4] Despite this correlation being contrary to their hypothesis, it is not conceptually problematic as it merely suggests simultaneous desires for greater musculature and lower body fat. Similar statistically significant positive correlations have been reported by Duggan and McCreary (2004) for their sample of gay men and Tylka et al. (2005).

More recently, McCreary, Sasse, Saucier, and Dorsch (2004) conducted a principal components analysis (PCA) with varimax rotation on DMS data provided by 630 Canadian high-school and university students. Findings for the "lower-order" component analysis revealed a two-component solution for male participants, with the first component representing "muscularity-oriented body image" (p. 52) and the second one appearing to focus on behaviours engaged in by men to become more muscular[5]. A question measuring contemplation of anabolic steroid use did not load on either component and was deleted. Thus, the DMS was regarded as a 14-item measure, with each subscale possessing 7 items.

For females, a four-component solution was obtained. However, based on the scree test and factor interpretability, the authors suggested a two-component solution provided the best representation of the data. Inspection of the component loadings revealed that a body-image/behaviour division was suitable for the women. As noted with the male participants, the steroid item did not load on either component and was removed.

Due to incompatibilities in component loadings across male and female participants, the authors reported that gender comparisons on the DMS were untenable. To rectify this problem, a "higher-order" principal components analysis with varimax rotation was utilised, with averaged scores on the "muscularity-oriented body image (MBI)" and "muscularity-oriented behaviours (MB)" components serving as input variables. A one-component solution was obtained for both genders.

Key statistical decisions made by McCreary and associates (2004) to assess the scale's dimensionality are questionable. First, the authors used PCA rather than exploratory factor analysis (EFA). The former is recommended for data reduction and the latter for structure detection because PCA does not distinguish between common and unique variance and, thus, does not recognise random error (Fabrigar, Wegener, MacCallum, & Strahan, 1999).

Second, the authors used varimax rotation, which constrains factors or, given their use of PCA, components to be uncorrelated (Finch & West, 1997). Such a constraint would appear to be inappropriate when applied to a scale whose items (purportedly) assess a common latent construct: namely, the drive for muscularity. Indeed, for male participants, McCreary and associates (2004) reported a moderate correlation ($r = .43$) between the two lower-order components. (This analysis was not conducted for women.) As oblique rotation permits, but does not require factors to be intercorrelated, it affords "a more accurate and realistic representation of how constructs are likely to be related to one another" (Fabrigar et al., 1999, p. 282) and hence would have been the preferable choice of rotation.

---

[5] Inspection of the items loading onto the behavioural component of the DMS suggests that this label may not be entirely accurate, as some items are cognitive in nature (e.g., "I think that my weight-training schedule interferes with other aspects of my life"; "I feel guilty if I miss a weight-training session"; and "Other people think I work out with weights too often"). Additionally, these three items appear to be more symptomatic of measures designed to assess muscle dysmorphia (e.g., Hildebrandt, Langenbucher, & Schlundt, 2004; Mayville, Williamson, White, Netemeyer, & Drab, 2002) than a *non-pathological* drive for muscularity. The existence of behavioural items on the DMS also is problematic because researchers have simultaneously used behavioural indicants such as self-reported participation in weight-training to test the scale's convergent validity (see McCreary & Sasse, 2000, p. 300). In such cases, the same indicants are being measured twice.

Table 1. Reliability Information for Various Indicants of the Drive for Muscularity.

Scale	Type of Reliability	Author(s)
Drive for Muscularity Scale (DMS)	*Cronbach's Alpha*	
Total Scale	.89 (76 M)	Cafri & Thompson (2004)[1]
	.81 (103 W)	
	.91 (101 M)	Duggan & McCreary (2004)[1]
	.91 (100 M)	Davis, Karvinen, & McCreary (2005)[1]
	.87 (276 M)	McCreary, Sasse, Saucier, & Dorsch
	.82 (354 W)	(2004)[2]
	.91 (157 M)	McCreary, Saucier, & Courtenay
	.83 (343 W)	(2005)[1]
	.89 (527 M)	
MBI Subscale	.88 (76 M)	Cafri & Thompson (2004)[3]
	.88 (276 M)	McCreary et al. (2004)[2,4]
	.89 (294 M)	Tylka, Bergeron, & Schwartz (2005)[2]
MB Subscale	.86 (76 M)	Cafri & Thompson (2004)[3]
	.81 (276 M)	McCreary et al. (2004)[2,4]
	.86 (294 M)	Tylka et al. (2005)[2]
	Test-Retest	
	Reliability	
	(7-10 day interval)	
Total Scale	.93 (76 M)	Cafri & Thompson (2004)[3]
MBI Subscale	.84 (76 M)	
MB Subscale	.96 (76 M)	
Drive for Muscularity Scale (DM)	*Cronbach's Alpha*	
	.87 (103 M)	Yelland & Tiggemann (2003)
	(55 W)[5]	
	.85 (83 M)[6]	Hallsworth, Wade, & Tiggemann
		(2005)
	.85 (652 M)	Tiggemann (2005)
Drive for Muscularity Attitudes Questionnaire (DMAQ)	*Cronbach's Alpha*	
	.84 (412 M)	Morrison, Morrison, Hopkins, &
	.82 (304 M)[7]	Rowan (2004)
	.80 (250 M)	
	.82 (202 M)	Morrison & Harriman (2005)
Swansea Muscularity Attitudes Questionnaire (SMAQ)	*Cronbach's Alpha*	
DFM	.97 (89 M)	Hatoum & Belle (2004)[8]
	.92 (294 M)	Tylka et al. (2005)
PAM	.97 (89 M)	Hatoum & Belle (2004)[8]
	.92 (294 M)	Tylka et al. (2005)

Note: M = men; W = women

1. The 15-item version of the DMS was used. With one exception (McCreary, Saucier, & Courtenay [2005]), none of the remaining authors mention whether item 10 (I think about taking anabolic steroids) was excluded.

2. The 14-item version of the DMS was used.

3. Cafri and Thompson (2004) appeared to use the 15-item version, but also computed MBI and MB totals. Although not specified, one would assume that the item measuring steroid contemplation was not included in subscale totals, as this item did not load on either subscale (see McCreary et al., 2004).

4. McCreary et al. (2004) did not recommend computation of subscale scores for women and, thus, did not provide alpha coefficients for female participants.

5. This reliability coefficient should be interpreted with caution, as it appears the authors computed alpha using combined data from gay men, heterosexual men, and heterosexual women.

6. This reliability coefficient should be interpreted with caution, as it appears the authors computed alpha using combined data from bodybuilders, competitive weightlifters, and controls (first-year psychology students).

7. The same sample was used in a published study by Morrison, Morrison, and Hopkins (2003).

8. Hatoum and Belle (2004) created short-form versions of the DFM and the PAM (5 items each). The criteria used for item selection were not specified.

Third, the suitability of using PCA (or exploratory factor analysis) to identify higher-order factors has been questioned (Rubio, Berg-Weger, & Tebb, 2001) as has the appropriateness of relying on scree plots and the eigenvalue greater than one "rule" to determine component retention (O'Connor, 2000). Fourth, the authors conducted the PCA on *combined* data for high-school and university participants, without first conducting separate analyses to determine the comparability of their respective component solutions. As a majority of the high-school students were enrolled in grades 9 or 10, one would estimate their ages as being between 14 and 16 years. In contrast, the university students, most of whom were first-year, were likely 18 or 19 years old. Research by Humphreys and Paxton (2004) suggest that such age differences warrant consideration vis-à-vis body attitudes because adolescent boys and young adults are at different developmental stages, with the former possibly being more likely to believe that, as they mature, they will attain the muscular body idealised by Western society. It is possible that these two groups evidence differential response patterns on the DMS which, in turn, would have implications for the factor structure of the measure.

No additional published factor analytic work has been conducted on the DMS or its subscales. Therefore, at present, it is unclear whether the DMS is best represented as a uni- or multidimensional measure.

Although the scale's dimensionality is ambiguous, researchers have provided additional evidence in support of its scale score reliability (see Table 1). Only one study has investigated the test-retest reliability of the DMS and its subscales; however, the resultant r values were good (see Table 1).

Little validation work has been conducted using the MBI and MB subscales of the DMS. Cafri and Thompson (2004) did report a modest correlation ($r = .37$) between scores on the MBI and scores on a silhouette scale containing 9 male figures ranging from very thin to very muscular. Although the authors instructed participants to select both their current and ideal physiques, it is unclear whether the correlation reported is between the MBI and selection of an ideal or the MBI and body dissatisfaction (as determined by the absolute discrepancy between current and ideal body shapes). In a multiple regression analysis, Cafri and Thompson (2004) reported that the MBI accounted for a substantial proportion of variance (approximately 25%) in scores on the MB. None of the other measures of muscle appearance attitudes emerged as significant predictors of this criterion measure leading the authors to optimistically conclude that the MBI may be the scale "best suited for the analysis of behaviours related to the pursuit of a muscular ideal" (p. 228). Given the intercorrelation between the MB and MBI (rs range from .43 [McCreary et al., 2004; Tylka et al., 2005] to .48 [Cafri & Thompson, 2004], and the fact that items were developed to reflect the *same* content domain (i.e., the drive for muscularity), one would anticipate that each measure would account for response variability in the other. The treatment of the MB as a criterion measure of muscle appearance attitudes raises another important question: Are both subscales properly classified as indicants of the drive for muscularity? Or is the behaviour subscale best represented as a putative consequence of the drive (as measured by the MBI)? If the latter, then is revision to the MB warranted, given that it does not currently assess body fat reduction methods (Cafri & Thompson, 2004)?

Finally, Tylka et al. (2005) reported that the MBI correlated positively and substantially with other measures of the drive for muscularity suggesting that this subscale possesses concurrent validity. Far weaker, though still statistically significant, correlations were observed between these indicants of the drive for muscularity and the MB. Neither the MBI nor the MB correlated significantly with a measure of impression management thereby alleviating concerns that responses on these subscales are contaminated by response bias. Finally, contrary to what might be expected, a positive – though small – statistically significant correlation was observed between self-esteem and the MBI. Thus, for the male participants in this study, as their self-esteem increased, so did their drive for muscularity[6].

Evidence of validity is similarly limited for the total DMS. However, several hypotheses investigating associations between the drive for muscularity and specific personality characteristics and indicants of masculinity have been confirmed attesting to its construct validity. This information is detailed in the section focusing on the correlates of the drive for muscularity.

Drive for Muscularity Scale (DM)

The 7-item DM was based on the Drive for Thinness subscale of the Eating Disorders Inventory (EDI)-2, with the same items being used only modified to pertain to muscularity (e.g., "I think about dieting" was modified to read, "I think about building up my muscles"). Although convenient, one may question whether this process of item replacement would establish a measure that offers adequate representation of content domains relevant to male body image (and, more specifically, muscularity). Further, the absence of item generation informed by research and theory relevant to the drive for muscularity increases the DM's susceptibility to construct under-representation[7].

As no published research has investigated the factor structure of the DM, its dimensionality is unknown. With respect to scale score reliability, available studies suggest that alpha coefficients are good (however, see notes 5 and 6).

With respect to the validation of the DM, the scale's criterion-related validity has not been assessed, and evidence of its construct validity is scant. Specifically, Yelland and

---

[6] This finding is congruent with recent evidence suggesting that the motivation to achieve greater muscularity does not ipso facto denote a lower level of self-esteem. For example, Pickett, Lewis, and Cash (2005) found that competitive bodybuilders evidenced higher levels of social self-esteem than active controls (i.e., individuals who did not engage in frequent weight-training, but were involved in other athletic pursuits such as running and basketball).

[7] Hubley and Zumbo (1996) define construct under-representation as a measure's failure "to include important dimensions or facets of [a] construct" (p. 212).

Tiggemann (2003) conducted an assessment of the measure's discriminative validity (Foster & Cone, 1995) and found that, as hypothesized, gay men evidenced a stronger drive for muscularity in comparison to both heterosexual men and women. Hallsworth, Wade, and Tiggemann (2005) provide mixed support for the measure's discriminative validity (i.e., bodybuilders evidenced higher levels of the drive for muscularity in comparison to controls, but not in comparison to competitive weight-lifers, which was contrary to the researchers' hypothesis). A recent study by Tiggemann (2005) investigating exposure to different categories of television programme and body image among adolescents provides another strand of evidence in support of the DM's construct validity. The specific details of this study are provided in the section focusing on theoretical frameworks pertinent to the drive for muscularity. Research by Hallsworth et al. (2005) investigating the association between the drive for muscularity and individual difference variables such as body dissatisfaction, depression, and appearance anxiety similarly provides evidence attesting to the scale's construct validity. These findings are outlined in the section on attitudinal and behavioural correlates of the drive for muscularity.

Drive for Muscularity Attitudes Questionnaire (DMAQ)

The DMAQ contains 8 items (e.g., Muscularity is important to me) and uses a five-point Likert-type response format (*strongly disagree* to *strongly agree*). Two of the items are reverse-scored to control for response set bias; however, the usefulness of this practice has been questioned (e.g., Barnette, 2000).

In developing the DMAQ, Morrison et al. (2004b) generated 41 items designed to assess attitudes toward muscularity. Item generation was informed by a review of the available literature on male body image and by an inspection of items found on extant measures of the drive for muscularity. Distributing the measure to 412 Canadian male undergraduate students, principal components analysis (PCA) with oblique rotation was used for item-reduction purposes. The authors employed fairly stringent retention criteria (i.e., only items that loaded on the first component at .50 or higher, but did not cross-load on any other component at .30 or greater were retained). Scale score reliability analysis then was used to refine the measure (i.e., items having item-total correlation coefficients lower than .30 or higher than .70 were removed) resulting in the final 8-item version.

To gauge whether the scale's unidimensionality was replicable, a PCA was conducted using the sample of 412 as well as an additional sample of 304 Canadian male undergraduate students. No rotation option was specified in either analysis, as it was presumed the scale would be unidimensional. Results indicated that, in both instances, a one-component solution was obtained. As noted earlier with the DMS (McCreary et al., 2004), the authors' decision to conduct PCA for structure detection is questionable. So, too, is the authors' reliance on the eigenvalue greater than one "rule" to assist in determining the number of components to retain. Although it is the default in many statistical packages, this criterion is not recommended as it routinely results in factor over-extraction (Costello & Osborne, 2005; Preacher & MacCallum, 2003). However, given the DMAQ's unidimensionality, this means of component retention did not appear to be problematic (i.e., component over-extraction did not occur).

Concluding that the DMAQ's scale structure had been assessed by EFA [sic]" (p. 35) and found to be unidimensional, the authors then conducted a confirmatory factor analysis (CFA) using a third sample of Canadian male undergraduate students ($N = 250$). Four fit indices were tested, with resultant values supporting the DMAQ's unidimensional structure. This analysis affords a less subjective assessment of dimensionality (Costello & Osborne, 2005) and, thus, provides the most compelling evidence in support of the scale's structure.

Recently, Morrison and Harriman (2005) conducted an exploratory factor analysis (EFA) of the DMAQ using data provided by 202 Canadian male undergraduate students. A one-factor solution was obtained, with factor loadings ranging from .56 to .66. These findings in concert with results from the CFA suggest that the DMAQ is reliably unidimensional.

Published research indicates that the DMAQ's scale score reliability is satisfactory (see Table 1). The concurrent validity of the DMAQ has not been examined in any published research. However, the measure's discriminative validity has been investigated, with results confirming a hypothesised difference between varsity athletes and non-athletes (i.e., the former obtained significantly higher scores on the DMAQ). The construct validity of the measure is reinforced by the confirmation of various hypotheses examining associations between the drive for muscularity and variables such as appearance esteem, vanity and engagement in muscle-building behaviour (e.g., weightlifting and protein consumption). This information is detailed in the section outlining the correlates of the drive for muscularity.

Finally, Morrison and Harriman (2005) reported that scores on the DMAQ were uncorrelated with scores on a measure of social desirability bias. This correlation remained statistically non-significant, even when correcting for attenuation due to measurement error.

Swansea Muscularity Attitudes Questionnaire (SMAQ)

The SMAQ consists of 20 items (e.g., "Being muscular gives me confidence") and uses a seven-point Likert-type response format (*definitely* to *definitely not*). In the published article outlining the scale's development, Edwards and Launder (2000) conducted two preliminary studies ($Ns = 112$ and 152). The specific details of these studies are not provided; however, the resultant findings led to the creation of a "refined" 32-item version, which then was distributed to a third sample ($N = 303$). An unspecified form of factor analysis with varimax rotation was used to assess the dimensionality of the modified scale. In accordance with the authors' expectations, a two-factor solution was deemed appropriate. Twenty items were retained in total, with ten loading on the first factor (Drive for Muscularity [DFM], and ten loading on the second (Positive Attributes of Muscularity [PAM]). The former represents the desire to achieve greater, rather than lesser, muscularity whereas the latter assesses beliefs concerning the putative benefits associated with being muscular. Scale score reliability coefficients on the DFM and PAM were extremely high (αs = .94 and .91, respectively). No additional psychometric testing of the SMAQ or its subscales was conducted.

Similar to the problems highlighted earlier in relation to the principal components analysis of the DMS and the DMAQ, some of the statistical choices made by Edwards and Launder (2000) in their exploratory factor analysis are questionable. First, they used an orthogonal rather than oblique method of rotation. Second, they relied solely on the eigenvalue greater than one "rule" to determine factor retention. Third, they retained items that loaded on more than factor (e.g., "Being muscular gives me confidence" and "It is important to me that I should be more rather than less muscular").

To date, no subsequent published studies have examined the factor structure of the SMAQ. Therefore, in light of the problems associated with the EFA conducted by Edwards and Launder (2000), one must conclude that the dimensionality of this scale is unknown.

Other researchers have examined the scale score reliability of the SMAQ's subscales (DFM and PAM) with alpha coefficients being extremely high (see Table 1). Indeed, the magnitude of these coefficients suggests that item redundancy may be problematic (Coste, Guillemin, Pouchot, & Fermanian, 1997)[8].

To date, only one published study provides evidence of the SMAQ's concurrent validity. Tylka et al. (2005)[9] reported statistically significant correlations between scores on McCreary et al.'s (2004) Muscularity-oriented Body-image (MBI) subscale and both the DFM ($r = .55$) and the PAM ($r = .52$). The correlation between scores on McCreary et al.'s Muscularity-oriented Behaviours (MB) subscale and the DFM was statistically significant, though modest ($r = .22$), while the correlation between the MB and the PAM was non-significant ($r = .14$). It should be noted that the correlation between the MBI and DFM suggests that approximately 30% of the variance in the former may be accounted for by the latter. This proportion denotes a modest level of predictability from one measure to the other, which is surprising given that both the MBI and DFM were developed to assess the *same* content domain. Tylka et al. (2005) also obtained a statistically significant, though small, correlation ($r = -.16$) between scores on the DFM and scores on a measure of impression management suggesting that participants' responses to the former may be nominally influenced by response bias. The correlation was not significant for the PAM. Finally, non-significant correlations were reported between scores on a measure of maladaptive eating attitudes and behaviours (EAT-26) and the DFM and PAM. These findings may be used as evidence of the latter subscales' discriminant validity, although significant positive correlations are not inherently problematic (see footnote 4).

Summary

A review of the published literature detailing various measures of the drive for muscularity suggests that, at present, all are in need of additional validation work. The factor structure of three of the four measures is unclear (DMS and SMAQ) or unknown (DM). To address this issue, EFA using oblique rotation is recommended, with factor retention being determined through parallel analysis (O'Connor, 2000) or use of ML parameter estimation and its attendant estimates of fit (Preacher & MacCallum, 2003). Confirmatory factor

---

[8] Inspection of the items comprising the SMAQ reinforces concerns about redundancy. For example, it is difficult to perceive a meaningful distinction between items such as: "I would like to be bigger in the future," "I would like to be more muscular in the future," and "I want to be more muscular than I am now." The issue of redundancy was raised by Hatoum and Belle (2004) who reported that in a small pilot-study participants "revealed unanimous frustration with the repetitive nature of the questions [on the SMAQ]" (pp. 399-400).

[9] Tylka et al. (2005) use the SMAQ subscales (i.e., the DFM and PAM) in validating their newly developed measure, the Male Body Attitudes Scale (MBAS). Given the absence of documentation concerning the validity of the SMAQ, its use in the validation process of new instruments may be questioned.

analyses also are recommended for all scales. The concurrent validity of the DMAQ and DM needs to be determined and redundancy analysis should be conducted with the SMAQ so as to achieve an optimal level of alpha (.90, according to Streiner, [2003]). As well, attention should be paid to particularizing whether the MB subscale of the DMS is best represented as a component of the drive for muscularity or as a correlate of the drive. The putative gender neutrality of the DMS also should be examined empirically, perhaps by distributing copies of the measure to samples of women and asking them whether they believe its items reflect their muscularity concerns. Finally, there is a need for assessing the psychometric properties of these measures outside the parameters of universities and colleges. Published studies for the two measures having the greatest psychometric support (i.e., the DMS and DMAQ) have focused exclusively on this population.

Theoretical Frameworks Relevant to the Drive for Muscularity

Most of the published research investigating the drive for muscularity has been atheoretical. However, in an effort to explain why men are concerned with and driven to enhance their muscularity, a few studies have employed theories commonly found in the literature on body satisfaction. These are Sociocultural Theory (ST) and Social Comparison Theory (SCT). The core assumptions of each theory – as they apply to male body image – will be reviewed briefly. We should point out that, despite being discussed individually, many researchers contend that these theories operate in tandem. That is, in a cultural context endorsing narrow standards of attractiveness, social comparison processes are the primary mechanism accounting for variations in body perceptions (Thompson, Heinberg, Altabe, & Tantleff-Dunn, 2002).

Sociocultural Theory

The term "sociocultural" broadly refers to exogenous factors such as family, peers, and mass media that have the potential to influence individuals' cognitive, affective, and behavioural orientations toward their bodies (e.g., McCabe & Ricciardelli, 2001; Ricciardelli, McCabe, & Banfield, 2000). Prior to discussing one specific media-oriented version of Sociocultural Theory (Morrison, Kalin, & Morrison, 2004a), two points must be noted. First, the factors underlying promotion of various body ideals have received insufficient attention. Thus, while studies have documented that muscular mesomorphic bodies are more common in cultural artefacts such as magazines (e.g., Law & Labre, 2002) and toys (e.g., Pope, Olivardia, Gruber, & Borowiecki, 1999), it is unclear *why* this change has occurred. Second, although easy to accomplish statistically, disentangling various sources of influence may possess little conceptual sense. Peers and family operate *within* a specific cultural context; thus their endorsement of muscularity, for example, may be attributable to their own awareness and internalization of this ideal, as disseminated by media. It has been argued that "mass media are probably the most powerful conveyors of sociocultural ideals [in terms of appearance]" (Tiggemann & Slater, 2003, p. 49). Thus, within this realm, the idea that peers and family are extensions of, rather than independent from, mass media warrants consideration.

Morrison et al.'s (2004a) version of Sociocultural Theory possesses three core tenets: 1) mass media depict and promote a muscular mesomorphic ideal; 2) coterminous with the presentation and promotion of this ideal is the view that muscularity is desirable and non-muscularity undesirable; and 3) the emphasis placed on the muscular mesomorphic ideal and the imbuement of this physique with properties of desirability and goodness has implications for how individuals view the male body. The latter tenet suggests that men may be inclined to perceive themselves as a constellation of parts that are to be evaluated aesthetically (body-as-object) rather than instrumentally (body-as-process). Further, men who internalise[10] the idealistic body standards promoted by mass media may be particularly likely to adopt a body-as-object orientation.

There is substantial evidence for the first tenet. For example, in a content analysis of pictorials appearing in *Playgirl* magazine between 1973 and 1997, Leit, Pope, and Gray (2001) observed that the bodies of male centrefolds became larger and more muscular over time. In an examination of more mainstream magazines, Law and Labre (2002) analysed for content visual representations of the male body appearing in *GQ*, *Rolling Stone*, and *Sports Illustrated* from 1967 to 1997. Results indicated that, while the proportion of images devoted to male bodies increased nominally during this time period, substantial changes in the *types* of bodies displayed were apparent. Specifically, from 1967 to 1979, 3% of the images reviewed were categorized as "low body fat/very muscular"; for the 1991 to 1997 period, this proportion had increased to 28%. In fact, the total proportion of images classified as "somewhat or very muscular" during the 1990s was 84%, with a majority of images (62%) also being categorized as low in body fat.

A 30-year analysis of variations in the physiques of popular action figures (e.g., *G.I. Joe, Batman, Han Solo*) revealed that modern versions are more muscular than previous ones (Pope et al., 1999). The dramatic nature of this difference is encapsulated by Olivardia's (2004) remark that:

> A G.I. Joe figure in 1964 would have a 32-inch waist, 44-inch chest, and a 12-inch bicep if he were a man 5 feet 10 inches tall. This is a reasonable, attainable physique, similar to that of an ordinary man in …good physical shape. G.I. Joe's 1988 counterpart, however, would have a 55-inch chest, a 27-inch bicep, and a 36-inch waist. Note that the bicep is almost as big as the waist – and bigger than that of the greatest bodybuilders of all time (p. 211).

Recently published investigations of popular men's magazines (e.g., *Men's Health* and *Men's Fitness*) reinforce the view that idealistic male bodies are predominant (Frederick, Fessler, & Haselton, 2005; Labre, 2005a). For example, Labre (2005a) reported that approximately 96% of images ($n = 2,426$) evaluated by two coders were deemed to possess a low level of body fat. The proportion of images deemed to be "very muscular" was approximately 82% ($n = 2,306$). Assessing issues published between 2002 and 2004, Frederick et al. (2005) found that representations of the male body on the cover of magazines

---

[10] In this context, internalization refers to the extent to which messages disseminated by media concerning the muscular mesomorphic ideal are incorporated into men's self-identity (Keery, van den Berg, & Thompson, 2004).

targeting men (e.g., *Men's Health* and *Men's Fitness*) were significantly more muscular than representations of the male body in magazines targeting women (specifically, *Cosmopolitan's* "hunk of the month"). The authors specifically chose the covers of male-oriented magazines because they constitute the "principal source of ...images of shirtless men to which large numbers of [people] are exposed in supermarkets, bookstores, and newsstands" (p. 84). Additionally, covers are designed for the express purpose of enhancing a magazine's saleability. Therefore, the publishers must be operating from the assumption that a substantial proportion of the 1.7 million individuals who read *Men's Health* (Labre, 2005a), for example, are motivated to do so by the body presented on the cover.

There is little published research examining the second tenet of this modified version of Sociocultural Theory. To our knowledge, no researchers have particularized the ways in which mass media characterize non-muscular bodies in comparison to those considered representative of the ideal. However, investigating the relative visibility of men possessing various types of physique may serve as an indirect measure of this tenet; that is, if thin or overweight bodies are less visible in mass media than their muscular counterparts, such a disparity may transmit the message that non-muscular bodies are accorded less attention because they are less desirable.

In a content analysis of 505 commercials presented on three major American television networks (ABC, CBS, and NBC), Lin (1998) found that approximately 30% of the men appearing in prime-time commercials were muscular. In contrast, much smaller proportions were classified as skinny (4.4%) or chunky (8.7%). A content analysis by Kolbe and Albanese (1996) revealed that fewer than 10% of men appearing in solo advertisements in popular male-oriented magazines such as *Business Week*, *Esquire*, *Rolling Stone*, and *Sports Illustrated* were endomorphic (i.e., fat) or ectomorphic (i.e., thin). As noted earlier, research by Law and Labre (2002) also provides evidence attesting to the over-representation of low fat and somewhat or very muscular male bodies in mass media.

Little research has been conducted on the third tenet. However, some studies suggest that men's perceptions of the male body may reflect a greater awareness of, and concern with, its aesthetic properties. In a series of interviews with American male college students ($N = 13$), Labre (2005b) noted that one part of the body served as a locus of concern: the stomach. All of the interviewees reported that "six-pack abs" were a key feature of the ideal male body, with 8 of the 13 stating that they would like to possess this type of abdomen. Labre (2005b) contends that a "sculpted" stomach is aesthetic rather than functional. Thus, participants' desire to achieve this look in conjunction with its apparent status as an indicant of the "ideal" male body suggests that aesthetic considerations are *not* irrelevant.

Research by Hatoum and Belle (2004), using a small sample of American university students ($N = 89$), underscores this point. When instructed to specify the part of the body that they were most likely to notice when looking at a male model, the most common response (32.5%) was the model's abdominal muscles/stomach. Similarly, when participants were asked to identify the part of the body with which they were least satisfied, the most commonly mentioned area was the stomach. The authors' also observed that many participants in this study recommended the researchers investigate other features of male body image such as "body hair, freckles, and penis size" (Hatoum & Belle, 2004, p. 405). Participants' evident awareness that elements such as hirsuteness, skin pigmentation, and genitalia size may have implications for how men perceive themselves physically reinforces the idea that the male body is under increasing scrutiny as an aesthetic object.

In a content analysis of two popular men's magazines (*Men's Health* and *Men's Fitness*), Labre (2005a) found that articles (n = 515) were more likely to focus on leanness and muscularity (25.2%) than on health (17.8%) or fitness (14.5%). Similar findings were obtained in terms of the major benefits promoted by advertisements (n = 496) appearing in these magazines (i.e., leanness/muscularity [23.2%] versus fitness [12.4%] and health [10.6%]). Another common benefit promoted by these advertisements was labelled beauty/style (i.e., the product advertised emphasised that it would enhance aspects of physical appearance or attractiveness other than body build). The proportion of advertisements focusing on this benefit was 22.1%. These findings, among others, led the author to conclude that "the contents of the articles and advertisements in these magazines were more likely to focus on appearance than on fitness or physical performance" (p. 197).

To date, only a few studies have examined the association between exposure to idealistic representations of the male body disseminated by mass media and the drive for muscularity. Hatoum and Belle (2004) examined the correlation between body image variables and male college students' exposure to media in the form of magazines, television, motion pictures, and music videos. Results indicated that the drive for muscularity, as measured by a short-form version of Edwards and Launder's (2000) Drive for Muscularity (DFM) subscale, was significantly associated with the number of male-directed magazines (e.g., *Gear, Details*) participants reported skimming or reading in the past month (r = .40). A similar correlation was observed for their short-form version of the Positive Attitudes toward Muscularity (PAM) subscale (r = .39). No associations were found between number of hours spent watching television, movies, or music videos and scores on either the DFM or PAM. The non-significance of these correlations is not surprising, as the degree to which participants viewed television programmes, for example, containing neutral versus idealistic body image content was not assessed. The authors also found that men's scores on the DFM and PAM correlated significantly with the value they placed on women's thinness, rs = .40 and .36, respectively. This finding suggests that endorsement of cultural stereotypes of ideal male *and* female bodies may be interrelated.

Morrison et al. (2003, N = 310) found that self-reported exposure to a list of popular health and fitness magazines correlated positively with scores on the DMAQ (r = .34). Botta (2003) also reported that a multiplicative index assessing number of hours spent reading fitness/health magazines as well as the amount of attention paid to them was a significant positive predictor of scores on a measure of commitment to muscularity (n = 196 American adolescent males).

Using the DMS, Duggan and McCreary (2004) examined the association between the drive for muscularity and self-reported consumption and purchase of media in the form of muscle/fitness magazines. Participants were gay (n = 67) and heterosexual men (n = 29), a majority of whom likely resided in Canada. Positive correlations between scores on the DMS and a combined viewing/purchasing magazine index emerged for both categories of respondent (i.e., gay, r = .42; heterosexual, r = .54).

In a recent study using 241 American college students, Tylka et al. (2005) reported positive correlations between scores on the Muscularity subscale of the Male Body Attitudes

Scale (MBAS) and the Internalization subscale of the Sociocultural Attitudes toward Appearance Questionnaire-Revised (Thompson et al., 2002) and the Perceived Sociocultural Pressures Scale (PSPS; Stice, Ziemba, Margolis, & Flick, 1996), which was modified to focus on muscularity. The correlation coefficients were .44 and .32, respectively. Thus, the greater men's internalisation of idealistic standards of appearance and the stronger their belief that sociocultural forces (e.g., family and media) place pressure[11] on them to be muscular, the greater was their drive for muscularity.

The putative influence of sociocultural variables on the drive for muscularity is not limited to samples of adult males. For example, Tiggemann (2005) conducted a large-scale study designed to examine the influence of media exposure on male adolescents' body image ($n = 652$). Of interest for this review, is the association between self-reported drive for muscularity, as measured by Yelland and Tiggemann's (2003) DMS, and exposure to various categories of television programming as well as frequency of reading magazines and watching music videos. Total television exposure did not correlate significantly with boys' drive for muscularity. However, when separated into discrete genres, a statistically significant – albeit weak – correlation ($r = .16$) emerged between frequency of soap opera viewing and the drive for muscularity. Further, a significant correlation was noted between boys' drive for muscularity and frequency of viewing music videos ($r = .14$).

In Tiggemann's (2005) study, adolescent males' drive for muscularity along with several other variables such as internalization, appearance schemas (i.e., the extent to which individuals deem physical appearance to have importance and meaning in their lives), and bulimia (i.e., the extent to which individuals engage in bouts of excessive overeating and purging) were related to television exposure when viewing was regarded as a mechanism to reduce negative affect (i.e., boredom, sadness, and disassociation with school). However, Tiggemann (2005) provides only the range of significant correlations ($rs = .20$ to $.34$); thus, the specific correlation for participants' drive for muscularity and television exposure is unknown.[12]

It should be noted that all of the research examining the drive for muscularity and mass media has been correlational. To date, no experimental research has examined whether exposure to images characteristic of the body ideal for men intensifies their motivation to become muscular[13]. It is unclear whether different categories of media image are associated

---

[11] The extent to which men feel pressure or stress as a function of the idealistic representations of the male body warrants attention. For example, in a large qualitative study conducted in the United Kingdom with a diverse sample of men ($N = 140$), Gill, Henwood, and McLean found that discussants' were most likely to frame discussions about media representations of the male body in terms of "feeling under pressure" (p. 107).

[12] Other studies (e.g., McCabe & Ricciardelli, 2003a; McCabe & Ricciardelli, 2003b; McCabe & Ricciardelli, 2004; Ricciardelli & McCabe, 2003) have assessed a number of body image variables among adolescents in relation to sociocultural influences. However, they have been excluded from this review as they do not measure male adolescents' *motivation* to become more muscular. Instead, they focus on what they refer to as "body change strategies." In this context, participants respond to statements such as: "How often do you change your eating/exercise to decrease/increase body size?" and "How often do you change your eating/exercise to decrease/increase muscles?"

[13] Agliata and Tantleff-Dunn (2004) recently conducted an experimental study examining whether exposure to commercials featuring actors denotative of the male ideal influenced scores on a series of visual analogue scales (VAS) assessing satisfaction with parts of the body relevant to men (e.g., biceps, chest, abdomen, and calf muscles). Using 158 American male undergraduate students as participants, results indicated that exposure to appearance-related advertisements increased levels of muscle dissatisfaction in comparison to those viewing

with stronger or weaker "effects" on the drive for muscularity. For example, does exposure to male models exert the same influence as exposure to sports figures?

Social Comparison Theory

Festinger's (1954) theory of social comparison asserts that individuals are driven to make cognitive judgements about their attributes. Further, in the absence of objective criteria, this comparative process typically involves similar others. Since its original formulation, the theory has undergone a number of revisions resulting in its focus expanding from individuals' reliance on targets for the purpose of self-evaluation to "a lively and varied area of research encompassing many different paradigms, approaches, and applications" (Buunk & Mussweiler, 2001).

Modifications of particular importance in terms of the theory's application to male body image include recognition that: a) unsought comparisons often occur (Collins, 1996); b) targets may be dissimilar to oneself on the dimension of interest (Martin & Kennedy, 1993); c) social comparison is not restricted to an individual's opinions and abilities, but occurs on myriad dimensions such as physical appearance and eating habits (Wheeler & Miyake, 1992); and d) social comparisons may take place even in the presence of objective criteria (Thompson et al., 2002).

Researchers have emphasised two broad categories of comparative target: universalistic and particularistic, with Morrison et al. (2004a) defining the former as distant sources of influence such as mass media, and the latter as more immediate sources such as family and peers. It should be noted that, on the dimension of physical appearance, the distinction between these categories may be obscured by the presentation of universalistic targets as "real" people rather than as manufactured images (Morrison, 2001). Agliata and Tantleff-Dunn (2004) contend that "today's media do not distinguish between glorified fiction and reality ... thus, society regards media images as realistic representations of [attractiveness] and as appropriate comparison targets for appearance" (p. 9).

In addition to type of target, the direction of the comparison has received scrutiny. It may be upward (i.e., comparing oneself to a target who is superior on the dimension of interest) or downward (i.e., comparing oneself to a target who is inferior on the dimension of interest), with each comparative direction producing positive or negative affective consequences depending on various moderator variables (Suls, Martin, & Wheeler, 2002). These moderators include perceived self-relevance (i.e., the self-views of aspiring athletes, for example, are more likely to be influenced by high performing athletic targets than by high performing artistic targets) and attainability[14] (i.e., perceiving the target's achievement on the

---

neutral advertisements. A similar experiment could be conducted using the drive for muscularity as the dependent measure. Another recent experimental study (Hargreaves & Tiggemann, 2004) did not find that exposure to muscular-ideal television commercials affected body dissatisfaction among a sample of Australian adolescent boys (n = 285). However, a limitation of this study is that, despite using four VAS measures of body dissatisfaction (i.e., fat, strong, unhappy with face, unhappy with overall appearance), they created a 3-item composite measure which *excluded* strong. Arguably scores on a VAS for strength would be most susceptible to viewing images representing the muscular ideal.

[14] The variable of attainability may prove useful in accounting for discrepancies observed in the literature between adolescent boys' neutral or positive reaction to idealistic male imagery versus young adults' more negative reaction (e.g., Humphreys & Paxton, 2004). The former, by virtue of their developmental phase, may regard the muscular mesomorphic ideal as more attainable than the latter. Indeed, Gill et al. (2000) noted that perceptions of

dimension of interest as attainable will likely engender positive affect in contrast to perceiving the achievement as unattainable) (Lockwood & Kunda, 1997).

Scant research has examined the association between men's drive for muscularity and their engagement in social comparison to targets embodying the muscular mesomorphic ideal. Morrison et al. (2003) investigated the association between the drive for muscularity and scores on a measure of universalistic social comparison (USC; Morrison et al., 2004b) designed to examine individuals' engagement in comparison processes with models and performers on television and in motion pictures. In this study, Canadian male university students' ($N = 310$) drive for muscularity correlated significantly with their scores on the USC, $r = .67$. Tylka et al. (2005) examined the association between self-reported engagement in particularistic social comparison, as measured by the Physical Comparison Scale (Thompson, Heinberg, & Tantleff, 1991) and the drive for muscularity (Muscularity subscale of the MBAS). A statistically significant positive correlation was observed ($r = .43$). Finally, among a sample of 196 American high-school and college males, Botta (2003) reported that scores on a three-item measure of social comparison (focusing on ideal bodies presented in magazines as targets) emerged as a significant predictor of scores on a cumulative index of commitment to muscularity. The direction of the standardized beta weight suggested that as the frequency of social comparison increased so did commitment to becoming muscular.

Summary

This overview clearly suggests that research on the drive for muscularity has paid little attention to the dominant theories used to account for variations in male and female body satisfaction. Given its recent emergence and attendant concerns over measurement issues, the atheoretical nature of literature on the drive for muscularity is not surprising. However, it is recommended that future studies attempt to embed this construct within an appropriate theoretical framework. Research is recommended that manipulates important features of the comparative target (e.g., its attainability and relevance) as are studies measuring individual differences variables that influence the likelihood of engaging in appearance-based comparisons (e.g., social comparison orientation [Buunk & Mussweiler, 2001] and appearance schematicity [Hargreaves & Tiggemann, 2004]). Finally, researchers should consider the viability of other explanatory frameworks which, though they have received little attention, may prove useful in understanding the drive for muscularity. These include: Objectification Theory (Frederickson & Roberts, 1997; Hallsworth et al., 2005) and the theory of Threatened Masculinity (Olivardia, 2004).

Correlates of the Drive for Muscularity

The drive for muscularity among men is now regarded as an increasingly important facet of male body image. As a result, it is not surprising that considerable attention has been

---

media depictions of the male body as inspirational were restricted to male interviewees who saw these images as

devoted to identifying the correlates of this drive. An inspection of published research on this topic suggests that three general categories of correlates have received the most attention. These are psychological, behavioural, and sociocultural. The third category has been addressed earlier in this chapter; thus, the focus is on categories one and two.

Psychological

Morrison et al. (2004b) observed that scores on the DMAQ correlated significantly with the following indicants of body image dissatisfaction: the desire for a more muscular body shape ($r = .46$), and the absolute discrepancy between one's actual and ideal physique ($r = .49$), as determined by Lynch and Zellner's (1999) silhouette drawings. Recently, Morrison and Harriman (2005) documented a statistically significant inverse correlation between scores on the DMAQ and scores on a single-item measure of muscle satisfaction ($r = -.32$).

Additional studies corroborate these findings, as they pertain to the drive for muscularity and desired improvement in musculature. For example, Davis et al. (2005) found that male participants' drive for muscularity, as measured by the DMS, correlated significantly with the Appearance ($r = .41$) and Fitness Orientation ($r = .45$) subscales of the Multidimensional Body Self-Relations Questionnaire (MBSRQ). The orientation measures assess attitudes toward physical appearance and fitness as well as commitment to physical endeavours designed to enhance these components of body image[15]. Tylka et al. (2005) conducted a series of studies detailing the construction and validation of a measure entitled the Male Body Attitudes Scale (MBAS). In Study 1, using a sample of American undergraduate men ($N = 294$), the authors found that scores on the muscularity subscale of the MBAS correlated negatively with indices of body esteem focusing on one's physical condition ($r = -.24$) and upper body strength ($r = -.49$).

Correlations also have been reported between the drive for muscularity and more general indicants of satisfaction with appearance. Specifically, in a sample of Canadian male undergraduate students ($N = 250$), Morrison et al. (2004b) obtained a modest, though statistically significant, negative correlation ($r = -.21$) between the drive for muscularity (DMAQ) and global satisfaction with physical appearance. Duggan and McCreary (2004) also noted a positive association between participants' drive for muscularity (DMS) and self-reported discomfort at the prospect of having others observe their physique (i.e., social physique anxiety). Statistically significant correlations were observed for both the gay ($n = 67$, $r = .32$) and heterosexual ($n = 29$, $r = .42$) men in their sample. Using a sample of Australian bodybuilders, competitive weight-lifers, and university controls ($N = 83$), Hallsworth et al. (2005) similarly found that the drive for muscularity correlated positively with measures of appearance anxiety ($r = .38$), self-objectification ($r = .44$), and body dissatisfaction ($r = .41$).

---

achievable.

[15] Davis et al. (2005) reported that men evidencing a stronger drive for muscularity tended to be higher in neuroticism, perfectionism, and more strongly invested in appearance- and fitness-enhancing behaviours. The adjusted R^2 value was .40 suggesting that these variables accounted for substantial variability in scores on the DMS. However, the R^2 value may be inflated, as the DMS contains items that assess participation in behaviours designed to improve appearance and fitness (e.g., I lift weights to build more muscle).

It should be noted that research investigating the association between the drive for muscularity and global measures of self-esteem has produced equivocal findings. Using a short-form version of the SMAQ, Hatoum and Belle (2004) reported non-significant correlations between the Drive for Muscularity (DFM) and Positive Beliefs about Muscularity (PAM) subscales of the SMAQ and scores on the Rosenberg Self-esteem Scale (RSE, N = 89 American male undergraduate students)[16]. Duggan and McCreary (2004) also found that the drive for muscularity (DMS) did not correlate with self-esteem, as measured by the RSE. This finding was obtained with both the gay and heterosexual subsamples.

Conversely, among a modest sample of adolescent boys (n = 96), McCreary and Sasse (2000) found a significant inverse association between global self-esteem and the drive for muscularity (DMS, r = -.41). Yelland and Tiggemann (2003) also reported a statistically significant negative correlation (r = -.38) between gay men's drive for muscularity (as measured by a scale the authors designed specifically for their study) and Bachman and O'Malley's (1977) revised version of the RSE. Further, Tylka et al. (2005) reported statistically significant negative correlations between scores on the RSE and scores on the Muscularity subscale of the MBAS as well as the PAM subscale of the SMAQ. A non-significant correlation was observed between self-esteem and the DFM subscale of the SMAQ (r = .01), whereas a statistically significant positive correlation (r = .18) was noted between self-esteem and the Muscularity-oriented Body Image subscale of the DMS. Given that the MBAS, SMAQ, and DMS are designed to measure the *same* construct (i.e., the drive for muscularity), such variability within the parameters of a single study is disconcerting. Additional research is needed to clarify the nature of this association.

Of particular importance are variables that potentially serve as moderators. For example, Kimmel and Mahalik (2004) contend that the extent to which one's distance from the muscular mesomorphic ideal constitutes a source of *distress* should be taken into consideration. This is an important point. Discrepancies between current and ideal body shapes and the expression of a desire to become more muscular do not necessarily imply that one is distressed by one's current state of non-muscularity. Indeed, in a qualitative study, male interviewees were able to specify the ideal body for men; reported that they would like to have elements of that body (e.g., "six-pack abs"); but simultaneously acknowledged that this look was too difficult to achieve and they had other priorities in their lives (Labre, 2005b). Such individuals may have fairly high levels of the drive for muscularity, but not evidence low levels of self-esteem, appearance-esteem, and so on. Taking moderators such as distress into consideration may serve to clarify the "muddy" findings observed for general self-esteem.

Associations between the drive for muscularity and maladaptive eating attitudes (as well as behaviours) also have been investigated. For example, Duggan and McCreary (2004) reported a statistically significant positive correlation (r = .31) between gay men's scores on the DMS and the Eating Attitudes Test (EAT). The correlation between the DMS and the EAT was .27 for the heterosexual men in this study, but did not achieve statistical significance due to the small number in this group (n = 29). Tylka et al. (2005) similarly reported a positive correlation between scores on the Eating Attitudes Test-26 and the

---

[16] The correlations between the DFM, PAM, and RSE may have been attenuated due to measurement error (i.e., the

Muscularity subscale of the MBAS ($r = .24$) as well as the MBI ($r = .22$) and MB ($r = .20$) subscales of the DMS. Such findings suggest that the ideal male body is characterised by two inter-related, yet distinct, components: the presence of muscularity and the absence of body fat.

Research examining the association between men's drive for muscularity and personality traits is in its infancy. However, Davis et al. (2005) assessed several potential personality correlates of the drive for muscularity in a sample of Canadian undergraduate men ($N = 100$). These variables were: neuroticism (i.e., presence of emotional reactivity and proneness to anxiety), perfectionism (i.e., presence of setting exceedingly high self-expectations), and narcissism (i.e., presence of excessive self-affirmation and feelings of self-importance). Statistically significant correlations were obtained between scores on the DMS and both neuroticism ($r = .27$) and perfectionism ($r = .31$). Contrary to expectations, however, a non-significant correlation emerged for narcissism. The authors acknowledge that exploring the relationship between the drive for muscularity and a specific element of narcissism (i.e., vanity) may prove more useful. (Indeed, Morrison et al. [2004a] found that scores on a measure of vanity correlated significantly with the drive for muscularity, as measured by the DMAQ [$r = .31$]).

Finally, as noted earlier, McCreary and Sasse (2000) found that adolescent boys' drive for muscularity was significantly related to depression ($r = .32$), as measured by the Centre for Epidemiologic Studies Depression Scale (CES-D). Hallsworth et al. (2005) also noted a statistically significant – though small – correlation between the drive for muscularity and scores on the CES-D ($r = .20$) for their combined sample of bodybuilders, weight-lifters and university controls ($N = 83$).

Falling outside the rubric of psychological traits and more along the lines of individual difference variables, McCreary et al. (2005) examined the drive for muscularity and both endorsement of traditional views about men (i.e., the extent to which men feel they need to "fit" stereotypic prescriptions for being a man) and gender role conflict (i.e., the extent to which men experience conflict in regard to their gender roles and socialization). The former was measured using a scale developed by the authors, and the latter was examined using the Gender Role Conflict Scale (GRCS). Participants were 527 men recruited from an all-male college in the United States. Multiple regression analysis revealed that three predictors were statistically significant. The direction of the beta-weights suggested that as the drive for muscularity increased so did: a) endorsement of traditional beliefs about how men should behave; b) concern about achieving dominance over others (Success, Power, Competition subscale of the GRCS); and c) perceived conflict between balancing the demands of school/work and family (Conflict between Work and Family subscale of the GRCS).

In an additional study ($N = 500$: 157 men, 343 women) published in the same article, these authors investigated the association between the drive for muscularity and subscription to gender-typed personality traits and gender-typed behaviour. Hierarchical multiple regression analysis revealed that scores on a measure of unmitigated agency (i.e., displaying greater concern for self than for others) as well as self-reported engagement in male-valued and male-sex specific behaviour were significant positive predictors of scores on the DMS. It

alpha coefficient for the RSE was .62).

should be noted that gender did not emerge as a moderator suggesting that these associations were applicable to both men and women.

To date, this study constitutes the first quantitative glimpse into the associations between men's drive for muscularity and variables that are related to masculinity and socialization processes salient to men. Greater attention should be paid to these and other individual difference variables that fall outside the arena of body image.

Behavioural

Few studies have examined the behavioural correlates of the drive for muscularity. However, available research suggests that, as might be expected, the drive is associated with various behaviours designed to increase muscle mass. Morrison et al. (2004b) developed the Body Image Investment (BII) scale which was designed to measure consumption of protein and other supplements (3 items), weightlifting (3 items) and cardiovascular training (3 items). Results indicated that men's (N = 304; Study 2) drive for muscularity correlated positively with protein/supplement consumption (r = .40) and with multiplicative indices of weightlifting (r = .25), and cardiovascular training (r = .13). As hypothesized, the correlation between the drive for muscularity and weight training was significantly stronger than the correlation between the drive and cardiovascular training[17]. Finally, Hatoum and Belle (2004) found that scores on a short-form version of the DFM subscale correlated positively with total amount of time participants spent exercising per week (r = .27), whether they were members of a gym (r = .40)[18], as well as their responses to items such as: "I lift weights to build muscle" (r = .73) and "I take dietary supplements to build muscle" (r = .39).

Summary

Research on the attitudinal and behavioural correlates of the drive for muscularity is gaining momentum. As numerous medical and social scientists are now recognizing that a large proportion of men are dissatisfied with their bodies, particular attention is being paid to concerns about men's cognitions surrounding muscularity and the physical pursuits they undertake to achieve increased musculature.

This review illuminates a variety of research streams that must be pursued if we are to consolidate our knowledge of the drive for muscularity. First, much of the research presented in this section relied on male undergraduates as study participants. In fact, with the exception of three studies (Duggan & McCreary, 2004; Hallsworth et al., 2005; Tiggemann, 2005), all of the available research employs male students attending college or university. Due to this restriction, age-related changes in the motivation to become muscular have not been investigated. Second, there is an absence of experimental research on the drive for

---

[17] The magnitude of the correlation between weight training and the drive for muscularity was smaller than anticipated. Upon inspection of the responses to three weight training items, it became apparent that the range for one question (i.e., "number of sets performed") was low. When a correlation was computed between the drive for muscularity and frequency of weightlifting, r increased to .35.

[18] This correlation may be attenuated, as it appears the authors used Pearson's r with a dichotomous variable (gym membership: yes/no).

muscularity which, in turn, has limited the ability of researchers to make causal inferences. Third, cross-cultural investigations of the drive for muscularity and studies using ethnically diverse samples are required.

Muscle Dysmorphia

McCreary et al. (2004) posit that an important stream of research within the realm of the drive for muscularity concerns the possible association between this construct and clinical disorders (i.e., muscle dysmorphia, MD). Therefore, in this section, an overview of the published literature on MD is provided. Of particular importance is the controversy surrounding MD's diagnostic placement, and issues concerning its measurement.

Body dysmorphic disorder (BDD) is characterized by preoccupation with an imagined defect in one's appearance (Veale, 2004). In the case that a minor physical anomaly exists, the concern is regarded as markedly excessive in comparison to the severity of the defect. According to the American Psychiatric Association (1994), another factor which must be present to meet the diagnosis of BDD is that the preoccupation must cause clinically significant distress or impairment in relation to social, occupational or other important areas of functioning. In addition, the preoccupation must not be better accounted for by another disorder (e.g., anorexia nervosa). The fourth edition of the Diagnostic and Statistical Manual of Mental Disorders (DSM-IV) classifies BDD as a separate disorder in the somatoform section, while in the Tenth Revision of the International Classification of Diseases (ICD-10), BDD is classified as a form of hypochondriasis and not as a separate disorder (Phillips & Crino, 2001).

Claiborn and Pedrick (2002) identified two major features which comprise BDD: the preoccupation with the defect and the actions taken to reduce feelings of distress. Veale (2004) argues that people affected by the disorder can display delusions of reference, thinking that those around them observe their imperfection and, consequently, judge them negatively. There is variability in the presentation of BDD, from individuals with borderline personality disorder and self-harming behaviours to those with muscle dysmorphia (Pope, Gruber, Choi, Olivardia, & Phillips, 1997). Research indicates that BDD is relatively common, causes significant distress and impairment in functioning, and is associated with markedly poor quality of life (Phillips & Crino, 2001). In an examination of gender differences in BDD, Phillips and Diaz (1997) found that women were more likely to be concerned with weight and hip size typically thinking that they were too large or too fat. On the other hand, men's concerns were generally with respect to body build, worrying that their body was too small, skinny or not muscular enough.

Muscle dysmorphia is a recently recognized form of BDD that, due to cultural emphasis on the ideal muscular mesomorphic build, predominantly affects men (Olivardia, Pope, & Hudson, 2000; Phillips & Crino, 2001; Pope et al., 1997). This body image disorder, originally termed "reverse anorexia," was first described in a study of male bodybuilders (Pope, Katz, & Hudson, 1993). Of 108 bodybuilders, 8.3% displayed signs of "reverse anorexia" believing that they appeared small and weak, even though they were actually large and muscular. Although their symptoms are diametric, the authors suggest that "reverse anorexia" found in bodybuilders resembles anorexia nervosa as both disorders are characterized by a misperception of current appearance and may be related forms of BDD. Pope and colleagues (1997) proposed to rename the syndrome muscle dysmorphia (MD) in a paper which described the disorder's qualitative features and proposed diagnostic criteria (see Table 2).

Table 2. Proposed Diagnostic Criteria for Muscle Dysmorphia (Pope et al., 1997).

1. The person has a preoccupation with the idea that one's body is not sufficiently lean and muscular. Consequent behaviours may include excessive weightlifting and attention to diet.
2. This preoccupation causes clinically significant distress or impairment in social, occupational or other important areas of functioning.
3. The primary focus of the preoccupation and behaviours is on being too small or inadequately muscular, and not a fear of being fat, or a primary preoccupation with other aspects of appearance.

Individuals with MD were described as being "pathologically preoccupied with the appearance of the body as a whole; they are concerned that they are not sufficiently large or muscular; their lives become consumed by weightlifting, dieting, and associated activities" (Pope et al., 1997, p. 548). The individual's anxiety is focused on being too small or inadequately muscular, not a fear of being fat or on other aspects of appearance (Chung, 2001).

Impaired social and occupational functioning, due to compliance with strict dietary or weightlifting regimes, has been documented (Pope et al., 1997; Pope et al., 1993) and individuals with muscle dysmorphia may experience severe distress if prevented from following these behavioural routines. Such individuals also may evade situations where their bodies would be seen by others, such as beaches, swimming pools, locker rooms and intimate relationships, due to embarrassment about their physique (Pope et al., 1997). Behaviours associated with muscle dysmorphia include weight-lifting, consuming large amounts of food and adopting special diets, mirror checking, constantly comparing themselves to others, reassurance-seeking, camouflaging with clothing, and wearing extra layers of clothing to enhance apparent size (Pope et al., 1997).

While bodybuilders typically partake in extreme amounts of weight training and strict dietary regimes in an attempt to achieve the hyper-mesomorphic ideal (Connan, 1998), Pope and colleagues (1997) warn that ordinary non-pathological dedication to body-building or other sports should not be confused with MD.

This point is critical when considering the possible association between the drive for muscularity and MD. Stated briefly, the motivation to increase one's musculature and attendant involvement in behaviours designed to do so are not tantamount to having a clinical disorder, even when evidenced by groups purportedly at greatest risk of MD such as competitive bodybuilders (e.g., Pickett et al., 2005). However, inspection of a recently published measure designed to assess "symptoms" associated with MD suggests that a lack of precision in terms of the disorder's diagnostic features may be problematic.

Hildebrandt et al.'s (2004) 13-item Muscle Dysmorphic Disorder Inventory (MDDI) contains three subscales: drive for size (i.e., "thoughts of being smaller, less muscular, and weaker than desired or *wishes to increase size and strength*" p. 170 [italics ours]); appearance intolerance (i.e., negative beliefs about one's body, and resultant avoidance of body exposure); and functional impairment (i.e., preoccupation with exercise to the exclusion of other activities and attendant feelings of anxiety when unable to exercise). Item content from these subscales is quite similar to existing measures of the drive for muscularity. For example, "I wish I could get bigger" and "I wish my arms were bigger" (Drive for Size subscale) do not appear to differ meaningfully from "I wish my legs were more muscular" (DMAQ; Morrison et al., 2004), "I would like to be bigger in the future" (SMAQ; Edwards & Launder, 2000), or "I wish that I were more muscular" (DMS; McCreary & Sasse, 2000). Similarly, "I pass up social activities (e.g., watching football games, eating dinner, going to see a movie, etc.) with friends because of my workout schedule" (Functional Impairment subscale) appears similar to "I think that my weight-training interferes with other aspects of my life" and "Other people think I work out with weights too often" (both DMS).

The overlap in content suggests that: a) measures of the drive for muscularity have inadvertently incorporated items that more accurately reflect muscle dysmorphia; or b) the MDDI may be contaminated by construct irrelevant variance (i.e., in its current form, the scale is "too broad and [contains] excess reliable variance associated with other distinct constructs [in the current instance, the drive for muscularity]" (Hubley & Zumbo, 1996, p. 212). We believe that items measuring perceived interference with daily activities due to weightlifting or distress associated with being unable to weight-train may warrant inclusion in scales designed to assess MD. However, we are not convinced that items reflecting the desire or wish to become more muscular are indicants of pathology and should be used in measures of MD[19].

The same concern may be directed toward another instrument assessing MD symptoms (the Muscle Appearance Satisfaction Scale; Mayville et al., 2004). While many of its items appear to reflect the diagnostic elements proposed by Pope et al. (1997), other questions seem more tangentially related to MD. For example, "I am satisfied with my muscle tone/definition" and "I am satisfied with the size of my muscles" do not necessarily denote preoccupation or impairment. We concur with Kimmel and Mahalik's (2004) observation that "dissatisfaction" is not synonymous with "distress."

Therefore, it is imperative that measures developed for the purpose of diagnosing MD clearly assess *profound* body dissatisfaction, *impaired* social and occupational functioning, and subjective feelings of *distress*; symptoms which do not appear to be present in the majority of weightlifters (Olivardia et al., 2000; Pickett et al., 2005; Pope et al., 1997). An exaggerated fear of fat and lifetime occurrence of mood, anxiety, and eating disorders also appear to be prevalent among those evidencing signs of muscle dysmorphia (Choi, Pope, & Olivardia, 2002; Olivardia et al., 2000).

A possible behavioural indicant of muscle dysmorphia is the use of anabolic-androgenic steroids (AAS), which assist men in becoming far leaner and more muscular than would be

---

[19] Content overlap also may suggest that neither the drive for muscularity nor muscle dysmorphia have been operationalized with sufficient clarity.

possible naturally (Pope, 2001)[20]. Yesalis (1992) contends that social fixation on winning and physical appearance is responsible for the demand for these substances. While not all men who use AAS are muscle dysmorphic, it has been suggested that this muscle enhancement strategy is comparable to food restriction amongst eating disordered females given that both represent the adoption of extreme behaviours to obtain a body ideal (Cafri et al., 2005).

Research into the epidemiology of AAS use suggests that between one and three million American males have used these drugs (Pope et al., 2000). Such widespread use is disturbing as AAS poses a variety of health risks. Cafri and colleagues (2005) provide a lengthy description of the physical and psychological consequences of AAS use (see pp. 216-218) and, thus, these will not be reiterated in detail. However, stated briefly, potential psychiatric problems include paranoid jealousy, extreme irritability, delusions, impaired judgement and feelings of invincibility (Claiborn & Pedrick, 2002), in addition to aggressive or manic symptoms during exposure, and depressive symptoms during withdrawal (Pope & Katz, 1994). Steroid use elevates risk of coronary artery disease by reducing levels of low-density lipoproteins which assist in the removal of cholesterol (Cafri et al., 2005). The use of AAS also may increase the risk of developing prostate cancer (Claiborn & Pedrick, 2002).

In addition to maladaptive behaviours such as steroid abuse and restrictive dieting, individuals with muscle dysmorphia often display considerable psychiatric morbidity (Pope et al., 2000). Those with muscle dysmorphia may exhibit other forms of BDD involving a particular part of their body, while the preoccupation with looking muscular remains dominant (Pope et al., 1997). In BDD, generally, frequent co-morbidity is found for major depression, agoraphobia, simple phobia, social phobia, and obsessive compulsive disorder (OCD), as well as an increased past history of anorexia nervosa (Phillips & Diaz, 1997; Pope et al., 1993, 1997).

With respect to the treatment of muscle dysmorphia, Cafri and associates (2005) suggest that it falls within the domain of clinical psychology. While research regarding treatment approaches is in its infancy, emerging evidence indicates that cognitive-behavioural therapy, serotonin-reuptake inhibitors and selective serotonin-reuptake inhibitors are often effective for BDD (Phillips & Crino, 2001). Treatment may be difficult as patients with BDD tend to be secretive and reluctant to reveal their symptoms (Phillips & Diaz, 1997). Additionally, it has been argued that the classification of muscle dysmorphia as either an OCD or a form of BDD has implications for its treatment (Chung, 2001). As an OCD, muscle dysmorphia would be regarded as a behavioural disorder and, thus, addressed using behavioural modification strategies. On the other hand, treatment for BDD may focus on altering one's perception of the physical self and in so doing modifying one's behaviour (Chung, 2001).

While muscle dysmorphia is generally regarded as a form of BDD, there is much debate surrounding its classification and it is not included in the DSM-IV. Chung (2001) questions whether it is justifiable to create an official subcategory of BDD for muscle dysmorphia, and if so, whether that subcategory would fit into the BDD framework in the DSM. Maida and

[20] In recognition that steroid use (or its contemplation) may serve as a possible indicant of muscle dysmorphia, we recommend that measures examining the drive for muscularity do not include items pertaining to steroid use. This recommendation is bolstered by McCreary et al.'s (2004) finding that an item from the DMS assessing whether respondents thought "about using anabolic steroids" did not load on either of the two components identified using PCA.

Armstrong (2005) suggest that muscle dysmorphia does in fact belong on the OCD spectrum. Pope and associates (1997) acknowledge that muscle dysmorphia is similar to OCDs in that the person experiences both obsessive thoughts regarding muscularity and related compulsive behaviours, such as reassurance seeking, comparing, checking and excessive exercise. In an effort to achieve their desired body image, they often adopt an all-consuming lifestyle revolving around their work-out schedule and meticulous diet (Pope et al., 1997). However, these authors contend that it is more apt to classify muscle dysmorphia as a form of BDD, instead of OCD, due to the fact that body image is the locus of the preoccupation.

While Pope and colleagues maintain that muscle dysmorphia is a subcategory of BDD, others prefer to align it with eating disorders. Chung (2001) surmises that muscle dysmorphia is closer to anorexia nervosa which also features specific behaviour motivated by a distorted perception of one's body. Connan (1998) argues that the male focus upon exercise in muscle dysmorphia parallels the focus on weight concern in bulimia nervosa, and that the core psychopathology appears to be strikingly similar in the two disorders. The term "machismo nervosa" (coined by Whitehead, 1994 as cited in Connan, 1998) may be more appropriate as it emphasizes the shared feature of the two disorders, that is, the *nervosa* (Connan, 1998). Connan proposes that in machismo nervosa, body shape and weight excessively influence self-evaluation, and the behavioural manifestations include excessive weight training, abnormal eating behaviours (e.g., dietary and fluid restriction and bingeing) as well as cognitive distortions comparable to bulimia nervosa.

According to Chung (2001), it is the behavioural expression of the preoccupation with body build that should be pathologised and not the preoccupation itself. Thus, the creation of a new DSM subcategory is unnecessary as the criteria of OCDs cover the outward display of symptoms. Chung (2001) further warns that the classification of muscle dysmorphia has many implications: If classified within the BDD realm, the focus is on the preoccupation with one's body build as "abnormal," while if positioned within the OCD spectrum, the attention is on the extreme and repeated behaviours. Such variations will influence the treatment modalities that are pursued.

Summary

Recent research has demonstrated the association between male body image dissatisfaction and distorted cognition and consequent maladaptive health risk behaviours. Muscle dysmorphia is a distressing and debilitating condition resulting from severe body dissatisfaction. Pope (2001) proposes that muscle dysmorphia, AAS abuse, eating disorders and BDD in males may manifest themselves due to the emergence of what has been termed the Adonis Complex, whereby men strive to attain a hyper-mesomorphic physique. It appears there are a variety of culturally-dependent as well as independent factors which contribute to the development of this complex. Further research is necessary to better understand the phenomenology, aetiology and epidemiology of muscle dysmorphia. Body image disturbance is possibly central to the pathophysiology and maintenance of BDD, and so is a particularly important area for future research (Phillips & Crino, 2001). As well, issues concerning precision of measurement with respect to the distinction between MD and the drive for muscularity must be addressed. Greater clarity also is needed concerning the placement of muscle dysmorphia in the diagnostic arena. Does it better correspond with the eating disorder nervosas, with BDD or OCD? Only when greater understanding of muscle dysmorphia is gained can preventative and intervention programs be developed to tackle this incapacitating condition.

CONCLUSION

The drive for muscularity is a relatively new construct developed to account for men's cognitions, affective reactions, and behavioural pursuits surrounding the attainment of a muscular, mesomorphic physique. This chapter presented key considerations for researchers as they engage in ongoing empirical investigations of the drive for muscularity. Of great importance are the psychometric properties of extant measures of the drive for muscularity and their associated limitations. If researchers are developing additional measures of the drive for muscularity, adherence to appropriate scale development and validation procedures is advised. The dominant theoretical frameworks used to understand men's drive for the culturally, ideal body type also were outlined. Upon review of the empirical research conducted to date, it becomes apparent that just as Sociocultural and Social Comparison theories have accounted for substantive variance in women's body image, so these theories possess predictive power when used with the drive for muscularity. It should be noted that additional theoretical frameworks such as Objectification Theory and the theory of Threatened Masculinity should be explored in an effort to better understand this construct. An extensive overview of the psychological and behavioural correlates of the drive for muscularity amassed to date also was presented. There is considerable need for researchers to begin examining correlates beyond indicants of body image dissatisfaction. Finally, a review of muscle dysmorphia and its relation to the drive for muscularity revealed that understanding of the former is in its infancy. A definitive classification of muscle dysmorphia as either a part of BDD or OCD remains unresolved.

Men are reporting progressively more dissatisfaction with their bodies and are actively engaged in the pursuit of a culturally ideal body type (i.e., muscular mesomorphy). Moreover, men perceive that considerable advantages are accrued when in possession of the muscular, mesomorphic build. Given that men are striving for bodily perfection, a pursuit that may, in turn, deleteriously affect their health and well-being, studies investigating this individual difference variable are important. Researchers conducting empirical investigations, however, can ensure that they advance understanding of men's drive for muscularity by attending to the specific empirical considerations, recommendations, and avenues of future inquiry outlined in this chapter.

REFERENCES

Agliata, D., & Tantleff-Dunn, S. (2004). The impact of media exposure on males' body image. *Journal of Social and Clinical Psychology, 23,* 7-22.

American Psychiatric Association. (1994). *Diagnostic & statistical manual of mental disorders* (4th ed.). Washington, DC: Author.

Bachman, J.G., & O'Malley, P.M. (1977). Self-esteem in young men: A longitudinal analysis of the impact of educational and occupational attainment. *Journal of Personality and Social Psychology, 35,* 365-380.

Barnette, J.J. (2000). Effects of stem and Likert response option reversals on survey internal consistency: If you feel the need, there is a better alternative to using those negatively worded items. *Educational & Psychological Measurement, 60,* 361-370.

Botta, R.A. (2003). For your health? The relationship between magazine reading and adolescents' body image and eating disturbances. *Sex Roles, 48,* 389-399.

Buunk, B.P., & Mussweiler, T. (2001). New directions in social comparison research. *European Journal of Social Psychology, 31,* 467-475.

Cafri, G., & Thompson, J.K. (2004). Evaluating the convergence of muscle appearance attitude measures. *Assessment, 11,* 224-229.

Cafri, G., Thompson, J.K., Ricciardelli, L., McCabe, M., Smolak, L., & Yesalis, C. (2005). Pursuit of the muscular ideal: Physical and psychological consequences and putative risk factors. *Clinical Psychology Review, 25,* 215-239.

Choi, P.Y.L. (2003). Muscle matters: Maintaining visible differences between women and men. *Sexualities, Evolution, & Gender, 5,* 71-81.

Choi, P.Y.L., Pope, H.G. Jr., & Olivardia, R. (2002). Muscle dysmorphia: A new syndrome in weightlifters. *British Journal of Sports Medicine, 36,* 375-377.

Chung, B. (2001). Muscle dysmorphia: A critical review of the proposed criteria. *Perspectives in Biology and Medicine, 44,* 565-574.

Claiborn, J., & Pedrick, C. (2002). *The BDD workbook.* Oakland, CA: New Harbinger Publications, Inc.

Collins, R. (1996). For better or worse: The impact of upward social comparison on self-evaluations. *Psychological Bulletin, 119,* 51-69.

Connan, F. (1998). Machismo nervosa: An ominous variant of bulimia nervosa? *European Eating Disorders Review, 6,* 154-159.

Coste, J., Guillemin, F., Pouchot, J., & Fermanian, J. (1997). Methodological approaches to shortening composite measurement scales. *Journal of Clinical Epidemiology, 50,* 247-252.

Costello, A.B., & Osborne, J.W. (2005). Best practices in exploratory factor analysis: Four recommendations for getting the most from your analysis. *Practical Assessment, Research, & Evaluation, 10*(7). Available at: http://pareonline.net/getvn.asp?v=10&n=7

Davis, C., Karvinen, K., & McCreary, D.R. (2005). Personality correlates of a drive for muscularity in young men. *Personality and Individual Differences, 39,* 349-359.

Duggan, S.J., & McCreary, D.R. (2004). Body image, eating disorders, and the drive for muscularity in gay and heterosexual men: The influence of media images. *Journal of Homosexuality, 47,* 45-58.

Edwards, S., & Launder, C. (2000). Investigating muscularity concerns in male body image: Development of the Swansea Muscularity Attitudes Questionnaire. *International Journal of Eating Disorders, 28,* 120-124.

Fabrigar, L.R., Wegener, D.T., MacCallum, R.C., & Strahan, E.J. (1999). Evaluating the use of exploratory factor analysis in psychological research. *Psychological Methods, 4,* 272-299.

Festinger, L. (1954). A theory of social comparison processes. *Human Relations, 7,* 117-140.

Finch, J.F., & West, S.G. (1997). The investigation of personality structure: Statistical models. *Journal of Research in Personality, 31,* 439-485.

Foster, S.L., & Cone, J.D. (1995). Validity issues in clinical assessment. *Psychological Assessment, 7,* 248-260.

Frederick, D.A., Fessler, D.M.T., & Haselton, M.G. (2005). Do representations of male muscularity differ in men's and women's magazines? *Body Image, 2,* 81-86.

Frederickson, B.L., & Roberts, T.A. (1997). Objectification theory: Toward understanding women's lived experiences and mental health risks. *Psychology of Women Quarterly, 21,* 173-206.

Gill, R., Henwood, K., & McLean, C. (2000). The tyranny of the "six-pack"? Understanding men's responses to representations of the male body in popular culture. In C. Squire (Ed.), *Culture in psychology* (pp. 100-117). London, UK: Routledge.

Grieve, F.G., Newton, C.C., Kelley, L.V., Miller, R.C., & Kerr, N.A. (2005). The preferred male body shapes of college men and women. *Individual Differences Research, 3*(3), 188-192.

Hallsworth, L., Wade, T., & Tiggemann, M. (2005). Individual differences in male body-image: An examination of self-objectification in recreational bodybuilders. *British Journal of Health Psychology, 10,* 453-465.

Hargreaves, D.A., & Tiggemann, M. (2004). Idealized media images and adolescent body image: "Comparing" boys and girls. *Body Image, 1,* 351-361.

Hatoum, I.J., & Belle, D. (2004). Mags and abs: Media consumption and bodily concerns in men. *Sex Roles, 51,* 397-407.

Hildebrandt, T., Langenbucher, J., & Schlundt, D.G. (2004). Muscularity concerns among men: Development of attitudinal and perceptual measures. *Body Image, 1,* 169-181.

Hogarty, K.Y., Hines, C.V., Kromrey, J.D., Ferron, J.M., & Mumford, K.R. (2005). The quality of factor solutions in exploratory factor analysis: The influence of sample size, communality, and overdetermination. *Educational and Psychological Measurement, 65,* 202-226.

Hubley, A.M., & Zumbo, B.D. (1996). A dialectic on validity: Where we have been and where we are going. *Journal of General Psychology, 123,* 207-215.

Humphreys, P., & Paxton, S.J. (2004). Impact of exposure to idealized male images on adolescent boys' body image. *Body Image, 1,* 253-266.

Kaminski, P.L., Chapman, B.P., Haynes, S.D., & Own, L. (2005). Body image, eating behaviours, and attitudes toward exercise among gay and straight men. *Eating Behaviours, 6,* 179-187.

Keery, H., van den Berg, P., & Thompson, J.K. (2004). An evaluation of the Tripartite Influence Model of body dissatisfaction and eating disturbance with adolescent girls. *Body Image, 1,* 237-251.

Kimmel, S.B., & Mahalik, J.R. (2004). Measuring masculine body ideal distress: Development of a measure. *International Journal of Men's Health, 3,* 1-10.

Kolbe, R.H., & Albanese, P.J. (1996). Man to man: A content analysis of sole-male images in male-audience magazines. *Journal of Advertising, 25,* 1-20.

Labre, M.P. (2005a). Burn fat, build muscle: A content analysis of *Men's Health* and *Men's Fitness. International Journal of Men's Health, 4,* 187-200.

Labre, M.P. (2005b). The male body ideal: Perspectives of readers and non-readers of fitness magazines. *Journal of Men's Health and Gender, 2,* 223-229.

Law, C., & Labre, M.P. (2002). Cultural standards of attractiveness: A thirty-year look at changes in male images in magazines. *Journalism and Mass Communication Quarterly, 79,* 697-711.

Leit, R.A., Pope, H.G. Jr., & Gray, J.J. (2001). Cultural expectations of muscularity in men: The evolution of *Playgirl* centrefolds. *International Journal of Eating Disorders, 29,* 90-93.

Lin, C.A. (1998). Uses of sex appeals in prime-time television commercials. *Sex Roles, 38,* 461-475.

Lockwood, P., & Kunda, Z. (1997). Superstars and me: Predicting the impact of role models on the self. *Journal of Personality and Social Psychology, 73,* 91-103.

Lynch, S.M., & Zellner, D.A. (1999). Figure preference in two generations of men: The use of figure drawings illustrating differences in muscle mass. *Sex Roles, 40,* 833-843.

MacCallum, R.C., Widaman, K.F., Zhang, S., & Hong, S. (1999). Sample size in factor analysis. *Psychological Methods, 4,* 84-99.

Maida, D.M., & Armstrong, S.L. (2005). The classification of muscle dysmorphia. *International Journal of Men's Health, 4*(1), 73-91.

Martin, M.C., & Kennedy, P.F. (1993). Advertising and social comparison: Consequences for female preadolescents and adolescents. *Psychology and Marketing, 10,* 513-530.

Mayville, S.B., Williamson, D.A., White, M.A., Netemeyer, R.G., & Drab, D.L. (2002). Development of the Muscle Appearance Satisfaction Scale: A self-report measure for the assessment of muscle dysmorphia symptoms. *Assessment, 9,* 351-360.

McCabe, M.P., & Ricciardelli, L.A. (2001). The structure of the Perceived Sociocultural Influence on Body Image and Body Change Questionnaire. *International Journal of Behavioural Medicine, 8,* 19-41.

McCabe, M.P., & Ricciardelli, L.A. (2003a). A longitudinal study of body change strategies among adolescent males. *Journal of Youth and Adolescence, 32,* 105-113.

McCabe, M.P., & Ricciardelli, L.A. (2003b). Sociocultural influences on body image and body changes among adolescent boys and girls. *The Journal of Social Psychology, 143,* 5-26.

McCabe, M.P., & Ricciardelli, L.A. (2004). A longitudinal study of pubertal timing and extreme body change behaviours among adolescent boys and girls. *Adolescence, 39,* 145-165.

McCreary, D.R., & Sasse, D.K. (2000). An exploration of the drive for muscularity in adolescent boys and girls. *Journal of American College Health, 48,* 297-304.

McCreary, D.R., Sasse, D.K., Saucier, D.M., & Dorsch, K.D. (2004). Measuring the drive for muscularity: Factorial validity of the Drive for Muscularity Scale in Men and Women. *Psychology of Men and Masculinity, 5,* 49-58.

McCreary, D.R., Saucier, D.M., & Courtenay, W.H. (2005). The drive for muscularity and masculinity: Testing the associations among gender-role traits, behaviours, attitudes, and conflict. *Psychology of Men and Masculinity, 6,* 83-94.

Morrison, M.A. (2001). *A critical examination of the factors influencing men's body image: A case for theoretical integration.* Unpublished manuscript.

Morrison, T.G., & Harriman, R.L. (2005). Additional evidence for the psychometric soundness of the Drive for Muscularity Attitudes Questionnaire (DMAQ). *Journal of Social Psychology, 145,* 618-620.

Morrison, T.G., Kalin, R., & Morrison, M.A. (2004a). Body image evaluation and investment among adolescents: A test of sociocultural and social comparison theories. *Adolescence, 39,* 573-592.

Morrison, T.G., Morrison, M.A., & Hopkins, C. (2003). Striving for bodily perfection? An exploration of the drive for muscularity in Canadian males. *Psychology of Men and Masculinity, 4,* 111-120.

Morrison, T.G., Morrison, M.A., Hopkins, C., & Rowan, E.T. (2004b). Muscle mania: Development of a new scale examining the drive for muscularity in Canadian males. *Psychology of Men and Masculinity, 5,* 30-39.

O'Connor, B.P. (2000). SPSS and SAS programs for determining the number of components using parallel analysis and Velicer's MAP test. *Behaviour Research Methods, Instruments, & Computers, 32,* 396-402.

Olivardia, R. (2004). Body image and muscularity. In T.F. Cash & T. Pruzinsky (Eds.), *Body image: A handbook of theory, research, and clinical practice* (pp. 210-218). New York, NY: Guilford Press.

Olivardia, R., Pope, H.G., Jr., Borowiecki, J.J., & Cohane, G.H. (2004). Biceps and body image: The relationship between muscularity and self-esteem, depression, and eating disorder symptoms. *Psychology of Men & Masculinity, 5,* 112-120.

Olivardia, R., Pope, H.G. Jr., & Hudson, J.I. (2000). Muscle dysmorphia in male weightlifters: A case control study. *American Journal of Psychiatry, 157,* 1291-1296.

Phillips, K.A., & Crino, R.D. (2001). Body dysmorphic disorder. *Current Opinion in Psychiatry, 14,* 113-118.

Phillips, K.A., & Diaz, S.F. (1997). Gender differences in body dysmorphic disorder. *Journal of Nervous & Mental Disease, 185,* 570-577.

Pickett, T.C., Lewis, R.J., & Cash, T.F. (2005). Men, muscles, and body image: Comparisons of competitive bodybuilders, weight trainers, and athletically active controls. *British Journal of Sports Medicine, 39,* 217-222.

Pope, H.G. Jr. (2001). Unravelling the Adonis Complex. *Psychiatric Times, 18 (3).* Retrieved November 23, 2005, from *http://www.psychiatric times.com/p010353.html*

Pope, H.G., Jr., Gruber, A.J., Choi, P., Olivardia, R., & Phillips, K.A. (1997). Muscle dysmorphia: An under-recognised form of body dysmorphic disorder. *Psychosomatics, 38,* 548-557.

Pope, H.G. Jr., Gruber, A.J., Mangweth, B., Bureau, B., deCol, C., Jouvent, R., & Hudson, J.I. (2000). Body image perception among men in three countries. *The American Journal of Psychiatry, 157,* 1297-1301.

Pope, H.G. Jr., & Katz, D.L. (1994). Psychiatric and medical effects of anabolic-androgenic steroids. A controlled study of 160 athletes. *Archives of General Psychiatry, 51*, 375-382.

Pope, H.G. Jr., Katz, D.L., & Hudson, J.I. (1993). Anorexia nervosa and 'reverse anorexia' among 108 male body builders. *Comparative Psychology, 34*, 406-409.

Pope, H.G. Jr., Olivardia, R., Gruber, A.J., & Borowiecki, J. (1999). Evolving ideals of male body image as seen through action toys. *International Journal of Eating Disorders, 26*, 65-72.

Preacher, K.J., & MacCallum, R.C. (2003). Repairing Tom Swift's electric factor analysis machine. *Understanding Statistics, 2*, 13-43.

Ricciardelli, L.A., & McCabe, M.P. (2003). Sociocultural and individual influences on muscle gain and weight loss strategies among adolescent boys and girls. *Psychology in the Schools, 40*, 209-224.

Ricciardelli, L.A., McCabe, M.P., & Banfield, S. (2000). Body image and body change methods in adolescent boys: Role of parents, friends, and media. *Journal of Psychosomatic Medicine, 49*, 189-197.

Ridgeway, R.T., & Tylka, T.L. (2005). College men's perceptions of ideal body composition and shape. *Psychology of Men & Masculinity, 6*, 209-220.

Rohlinger, D.A. (2002). Eroticising men: Cultural influences on advertising and male objectification. *Sex Roles, 46*, 61-74.

Rosenberg, M. (1989). *Society and the adolescent self-image* (reprint ed.).Middletown, CT: Wesleyan University Press.

Rubio, D.M., Berg-Weger, M., & Tebb, S.S. (2001). Using structural equation modelling to test for multidimensionality. *Structural Equation Modelling, 8*, 613-626.

Ryckman, R.M., Butler, J.C., Thornton, B., & Lindner, M.A. (1997). Assessment of physique subtype stereotypes. *Genetic, Social, and General Psychology Monographs, 123*, 101-128.

Stice, E., Ziemba, C., Margolis, J., & Flick, P. (1996). The dual pathway model differentiates bulimics, subclinical bulimics, and controls: Testing the continuity hypothesis. *Behaviour Therapy, 27*, 531-549.

Streiner, D.L. (2003). Starting at the beginning: An introduction to coefficient alpha. *Journal of Personality Assessment, 80*, 99-103.

Suls, J., Martin, R., & Wheeler, L. (2002). Social comparison: Why, with whom, and with what effect? *Current Directions in Psychological Science, 11*, 159-163.

Thompson, J.K., Heinberg, L.J., Altabe, M., & Tantleff-Dunn, S. (2002). *Exacting beauty: Theory, assessment, and treatment of body image disturbance*. Washington, DC: American Psychological Association.

Thompson, J.K., Heinberg, L.J., & Tantleff, S. (1991). The Physical Appearance Comparison Scale (PACS). *The Behaviour Therapist, 14*, 174.

Thompson, M.A., & Gray, J.J. (1995). Development and validation of a new body image assessment scale. *Journal of Personality Assessment, 64*, 258-269.

Tiggemann, M. (2005). Television and adolescent body image: The role of program content and viewing motivation. *Journal of Social and Clinical Psychology, 24*, 361-381.

Tiggemann, M., & Slater, A. (2003). Thin ideals in music television: A source of social comparison and body dissatisfaction. *International Journal of Eating Disorders, 35,* 48-58.

Tylka, T.L., Bergeron, D., & Schwartz, J.P. (2005). Development and psychometric evaluation of the Male Body Attitudes Scale (MBAS). *Body Image, 2,* 161-175.

Vartanian, L.R., Giant, C.L., & Passino, R.M. (2001). "Ally McBeal vs. Arnold Schwarzenegger": Comparing mass media, interpersonal feedback, and gender as predictors of satisfaction with body thinness and muscularity. *Social Behaviour and Personality, 29,* 711-724.

Veale, D. (2004). Body Dysmorphic Disorder. *Postgraduate Medical Journal, 80,* 67-71.

Wheeler, L., & Miyake, K. (1992). Social comparison in everyday life. *Journal of Personality and Social Psychology, 62,* 760-773.

Yelland, C., & Tiggemann, M. (2003). Muscularity and the gay ideal: Body dissatisfaction and disordered eating in homosexual men. *Eating Behaviours, 4,* 107-116.

Yesalis, C.E. (1992). Epidemiology and patterns of anabolic-androgenic steroid use. *Psychiatry Annals, 22,* 7-18.

In: Body Image: New Research
Editor: Marlene V. Kindes, pp. 35-61

ISBN 1-60021-059-7
© 2006 Nova Science Publishers, Inc.

Chapter II

THE INFLUENCE OF BODY WEIGHT AND SHAPE IN DETERMINING FEMALE AND MALE PHYSICAL ATTRACTIVENESS

*Viren Swami**

Department of Psychology, University College of London.

ABSTRACT

Evolutionary psychologists have argued that there exist universally shared criteria of attractiveness, which are potent cues to a person's potential reproductive success. This article reviews the current state of evolutionary psychology's study of female and male physical attractiveness. The former focuses on body shape as measured by the waist-to-hip ratio (WHR) and body weight scaled for height, or the body mass index (BMI), whereas the latter examine the waist-to-chest ratio (WCR). The evidence seems to point to BMI being the dominant cue for female physical attractiveness, with WHR playing a more minor role. The opposite is true for male attractiveness, with WCR playing a more important role than either the WHR or BMI. Importantly, cross-cultural studies have suggested that there are significant differences for physical attractiveness in terms of body shape and weight, which evolutionary psychological arguments have difficulty in explaining. Alternative explanations and the future of the field are discussed in conclusion.

Keywords: Evolutionary psychology, physical attractiveness, waist-to-hip ratio, body mass index, waist-to-chest ratio.

---

* Correspondence concerning this article should be addressed to Viren Swami, Department of Psychology, University College of London, 26, Bedford Way, London WC1E 6BT. Email: viren.swami@ucl.ac.uk.

INTRODUCTION

Although human beauty has been a topic of debate for poets, philosophers and scientists for centuries, most lay theories of physical attractiveness concur with David Hume's (1757: 208-209) declaration that beauty 'is no quality in things themselves; it exists merely in the mind that contemplates them; and each mind perceives a different beauty.' Recently, however, investigators have claimed that progress in theories of evolutionary psychology and empirical evidence has challenged this conclusion (Buss, 1994, 1999; Buss, & Schmitt, 1993; Symons, 1995). Evolutionary psychologists argue that there exist universally shared criteria of attractiveness, which are potent cues to a person's potential reproductive success. Within this tradition, males and females are said to select partners that will enhance their reproductive success, and there has been a concurrent emphasis on the attractiveness of salient morphological features. The latter are said to honestly signal that one individual is more 'desirable' than another (Buss, 1994, 1999).

Much of the literature within this field has concerned two potentially critical cues in women, namely, body shape and weight scaled for height, or the body mass index (BMI). This chapter begins by reviewing the evidence in support of the thesis that female body *shape* is an important predictor of physical attractiveness, before examining comparable evidence in favour of body *weight*. In addition, some recent studies have begun to look at male physical attractiveness from an evolutionary perspective. This chapter considers evidence in this regard, before finally presenting alternative (but not mutually exclusive) explanations for these findings, and suggests directions for future research.

THE WAIST-TO-HIP RATIO IN WOMEN

Overall body weight is the most noticeable change caused by pubertal onset in women, and the traditional technique for estimating body weight has been the BMI. However, in a series of papers published in the 1990s, Singh (1993a, 1993b, 1994a, 1994b, 1994c, 1994d, 1995a, 1995b; Singh, & Luis, 1995; Singh, & Young, 1995) argued that the increase in BMI observed in women during puberty does not take into account the sex-dependent anatomical distribution of fat deposits. Instead, he made the point that the deposit and utilisation of fat from various anatomical areas is regulated by sex hormones. Oestrogen inhibits fat deposit in the abdominal region and maximally stimulates fat deposit in the gluteofemoral region (buttocks and thighs) more than in any other region of the body. Testosterone, on the other hand, stimulates fat deposit in the abdominal region and inhibits deposits in the gluteofemoral region (Björntorp, 1997). It is this sexually dimorphic body fat distribution that primarily sculpts typical body shape differences between the sexes that become noticeable after pubertal onset.

Before puberty, body shape is more or less similar for both males and females (Pond, 1978). After puberty, however, women have greater amounts of body fat (adipose tissue) in the lower part of the body, thus engendering what is known as gynoid fat distribution, whereas men have greater amounts of fat in the upper body, or what is known as android fat distribution (Björntorp, 1987, 1991; Rebuffé-Scrive, 1988, 1991). This sexually dimorphic fat distribution is most commonly quantified by measuring the ratio of the circumference of the waist (the narrowest portion below the ribs and above the iliac crest) to the circumference of the hips (at the level of the greatest protrusion of the buttocks), that is, the waist-to-hip ratio (WHR).

These differences between the gynoid and the android fat distribution engender a noticeable and typical sex difference (Molarius, Seidell, Sans, Tuomilehto, & Kuulasmaa, 1999). For healthy, pre-menopausal Caucasian women, the range of WHRs has been shown to be between 0.67 and 0.80 (Lanska, Lanska, Hartz, & Rimm, 1985); for healthy Caucasian men, it ranges from 0.85 to 0.95 (Jones, Hunt, Brown, & Norgan, 1986; Marti, *et al.*, 1991). Women typically maintain a lower WHR than men through adulthood, although the WHR approaches the masculine range after menopause (Arechiga, Prado, Canto, & Carmenati, 2001; Kirschner, & Samojlik, 1991). It has been shown that the increase in WHR in menopausal women is caused by the reduction in oestrogen levels.

This interpretation seems to be corroborated by the observation that pre-menopausal women suffering from polycystic ovary syndrome (which is marked by impaired oestrogen production) have higher WHRs than age-matched non-patients (Pasquali, *et al.*, 1999; Pirwany, *et al.*, 2001). Additionally, Pasquali, *et al.* (1999) have shown that when women suffering from polycystic ovary syndrome are administered an oestrogen-progestagen compound, their WHRs become lower over time. Conversely, men suffering from disorders associated with endocrine imbalance (for example, Klinefelter syndrome) or treated with oestrogen for testosterone-dependent cancer of the prostate, develop gynoid fat distribution and lower WHRs that are more typical or normal-weight women (Kirschner, & Samojlik, 1991).

Singh also pointed out that risk for various diseases depends not only on the degree of obesity as measured by BMI, but importantly on anatomical location of fat deposits (Guo, Salisbury, Roche, Chumela, & Siervogel, 1994; Kissebah, & Krakower, 1994), that is, that the WHR is systematically related to a variety of life outcomes. In particular, WHR is a risk factor for cardiovascular disorders, adult-onset diabetes, hypertension, endometrial, ovarian and breast cancer, and gall bladder disease (Folsom, *et al.*, 1993; Huang, Willet, & Colditz, 1999; Misra, & Vikram, 2003). In addition, the WHR signals all the conditions that affect women's reproductive status. Females with higher WHRs have more irregular menstrual cycles (van Hooff, *et al.*, 2000), and WHR becomes significantly lower during ovulation compared to non-ovulatory phases of the menstrual cycle (Singh, Davis, & Randall, 2000). The probability of successful pregnancy induction is also affected by WHR – women participating in donor insemination programmes have a lower probability of conception if their WHR is greater than 0.8, after controlling for age, BMI and parity (Zaadstra, *et al.*, 1993). Married women with a higher WHR and a lower BMI also have more difficulty becoming pregnant and have their first live birth at a later age than married women with lower WHR (Kaye, Folsom, Prineas, & Gapstur, 1990). It has been suggested that the lower pregnancy rate in women with high WHRs, compared to women with low WHRs, may have to do with a problem in embryo development and its viability (Waas, Waldenstrom, Rossner, & Hellberg, 1997).

THE IDEAL WAIST-TO-HIP RATIO

According to Singh, one of the main problems facing our hunter-gatherer ancestors during human evolutionary history was the identification of mate value. To overcome this problem, he argues that males possess 'perceptual mechanisms' to detect and use information conveyed by the WHR in determining a woman's attractiveness as a potential mate. Because of this, it is possible to systematically change men's evaluations of women's attractiveness by manipulating the size of the WHR alone. In support of this idea, Singh amassed evidence for an evolved male preference for a WHR of 0.7, which correspond closely to the optimal in terms of health and fertility.

To begin with, Singh (1993a, 1993b) developed a set of twelve two-dimensional, line drawings of the female figure, which were systematically varied with respect to overall body weight (underweight, normal weight, and overweight) and the WHR. Within each weight category, line drawings represented four levels of the WHR by changing the waist size. In a series of experiments using these drawings, Singh (1993a, 1993b, 1994c; Singh, & Luis, 1995) described a negative correlation between WHR and female attractiveness, with line drawings with gynoid WHRs (0.7 and 0.8) being judged as the most attractive. However, the relationship is not strictly monotone – beyond a certain point, an extremely low WHR may appear grotesque and repelling (Furnham, & Radley, 1989).

The finding that normal weight female figures with a low WHR are judged as most attractive has been replicated with participants in the United States, United Kingdom, Germany and Australia using the twelve line drawings developed from the initial study (Connally, Slaughter, & Mealy, submitted; Furnham, Tan, & McManus, 1997; Henss, 1995, 2000; Singh, 1994c). For Singh (1993a: 304), the WHR 'acts as a wide first-pass filter, which would automatically exclude women who are unhealthy or who have low reproductive capacity.' It is only after this 'culturally invariant' filter is passed that other features such as the face, skin or weight (which may vary between cultures) become utilised in final mate selection.

A BROKEN FILTER?

Reviewing the literature suggests that the evidence may once have supported Singh's conclusions, but that it may not anymore. For one thing, several authors have questioned the validity of Singh's findings based on the use of evidence purporting to show that the WHR 0.7 is optimal for health and reproductive potential. For example, Singh (2002) cites evidence that fat deposits in early pregnancy are primarily localised in the pelvic girdle regions, and hence, an increase in WHR in the absence of any significant weight gain is one of the first signs of pregnancy. Coupled with this is the finding that reproductive history such as parity or lactation can also increase the size of a woman's WHR (Tonkelaar, et al., 1990). Singh uses such data to support his claim that the WHR provides reliable information about mate nulliparousity and female pregnancy induced by other males during human evolutionary history. But he does not present evidence to suggest that nulliparousity and mate pregnancy were important problems for human ancestral populations – the lack of detailed information about hunter-gatherer populations in our evolutionary past precludes any such conjecture. Importantly, Wetsman (1998) reports that obesity is typically presumed to have been more rare in our evolutionary past, especially among reproductive-aged women. If correct, then the consequences of different kinds of obesity could not have been a target of selection.

On the other hand, from a methodological point of view, Tassinary and Hansen (1998) have criticised the fact that research in this area has been almost exclusively restricted to the set of line drawings developed by Singh. They argued that the use of line drawings to depict variations in WHR used by Singh and other researchers lacked ecological validity. As Singh self-critically indicates, line-drawing stimuli are often impoverished and unrealistic, relying on a single original image from which modifications are made. It is thus ecologically unrealistic to show modified versions of the same stimulus and expect each to be rated on its own merits, without any recourse to a comparison with variations that have been presented simultaneously or sequentially.

To examine the issue, Tassinary and Hansen (1998) developed a set of their own line drawings comprising twenty-seven female figures that varied in weight (light, moderate, heavy), waist size (small, medium, large) and hip size (small, medium, large). With this new set of images, the authors found the weight of the figure to be a more potent factor than the WHR. Light- and moderate-weight figures were judged to be much more attractive than the heavy figures, whereas moderate-weight and heavy figures were judged to be much more fecund than the light figures. They thus suggest that the apparent positive association between the WHR, judged attractiveness and judged fecundity is an artefact of a limited stimulus set, and argue that their findings 'demonstrate that weight and hip size are important and independent co-determinants of both relative attractiveness and fecundity, and that the WHR is of marginal importance for predicting relative attractiveness. This pattern of results... constitutes a clear and unambiguous disconfirmation of the WHR hypothesis' (Tassinary, & Hansen, 1998: 154-155). More recently, however, Streeter and McBurney (2003), using stimuli that statistically controlled for body weight, failed to replicate the positive relationship between WHR and attractiveness reported by Tassinary and Hansen.

A number of other studies have also attempted to overcome the ecological invalidity associated with line drawings. Henss (2000), for example, designed a study using full frontal photographs that included the face and breasts of different women with computer-altered WHR. For each photograph, two versions of the WHR were created using morphing techniques – in one picture the waist was tightened (lower WHR), and in the other it was widened (higher WHR). Using this new set of stimuli, Henss found support for Singh's contention that the WHR is an essential attribute of the attractiveness of the female figure. However, Henss also pointed out that when whenever both WHR and overall body weight have been manipulated, it is evident that weight accounts for more variance than WHR. All the evidence, he concludes, underlines the fact that the WHR plays a less potent role than the weight category or the face.

This is also the conclusion of Forestell, Humphrey and Stewart (2004), who used Tassinary and Hansen's line drawings to test the degree to which various body shape characteristics influence women's ratings of attractiveness of female figures. Their results showed that participants preferred figures that had WHRs around 0.7, but that as body size increased, larger WHRs tended to be preferred. Figures with small and medium waists and hips were generally preferred regardless of body weight, but figures with large hips were preferred less regardless of other shape characteristics. In addition, when photographs of women with WHR manipulated either by hip or waist changes are used, attractiveness seems to be more influenced by changes in waist than hip size (Rozmus-Wrzesinska, & Pawlowski, 2005). It seems likely, therefore, that body weight, waist size and hip size all interact to influence women's ratings of attractiveness of other female figures (Furnham, Petrides, & Constantinides, 2005).

FEMALE BODY WEIGHT

Tovée and his colleagues (Tovée, Maisey, Emery, & Cornelissen, 1999; Tovée, Mason, Emery, McClusky, & Cohen-Tovée, 1997; Tovée, Reinhardt, Emery and Cornelissen, 1998) have objected to the extant WHR research on the grounds that none of the previous studies used women with known WHRs. Thus, it may very well be that such a relationship does not generalise to an actual population. In addition, they argue that the assumption held by WHR researchers that the BMI of figures is held constant when narrowing the waist is false (Tovée, & Cornelissen, 2001). When the figures are modified by a altering the width of the torso around the waist, this not only alters the WHR, but also apparent BMI. As the value of the WHR rises, so does that of the apparent BMI, and so it is not possible to say whether changes in attractiveness ratings are made on the basis of WHR or BMI, or both (Tovée, & Cornelissen, 1999; Tovée, et al., 1999). This error is intrinsic to most studies that have used line drawings, including the study by Tassinary and Hansen (1998), but is also duplicated by Henss (2000). In short, Tovée et al. (1999) suggest that the importance attributed to WHR in previous studies is likely to be an artefact of co-varying WHR with apparent BMI.

To investigate the relative importance of BMI and WHR in the perception of female attractiveness, Tovée and his colleagues used images of real women in a standard pose and distance from view. By using images of real women (as opposed to line drawings) both BMI and actual WHR were known precisely and their effects could be estimated separately. A further advantage of these stimuli was the fact that the heads of the women were obscured, so that facial attractiveness would not be a factor in participants' ratings. Multiple regressions of the attractiveness ratings for these images of real women suggests that although both shape and body mass are significant predictors of female attractiveness, weight scaled for height is a far more important factor than WHR (Tovée et al., 1998, 1999; Tovée, & Cornelissen, 2001). BMI is said to account for more than 70 per cent of the variance in their analyses, whereas WHR accounts for little more than 2 per cent. These results also hold when the women are presented in profile, as opposed to a frontal view (Tovée, & Cornelissen, 2001), when computer-generated photographic stimuli are used in a between-subjects design (Puhl, & Boland, 2001) and when three-dimensional images are used (Fan, Liu, Wu, & Dai, 2004).

However, the multivariate analyses by Tovée and his colleagues used the widest range of BMI and WHR values available. One objection to this is that the relative ranges of BMI and WHR are unequal, and that the apparent importance of BMI in such studies is due to greater relative variation in this parameter than in WHR (Singh, 2002). To address this problem, Tovée, Hancock, Mahmoodi, Singleton, and Cornelissen (2002) used images of female bodies where the range of BMI values was strictly controlled (thereby giving WHR an 'advantage'), but WHR still failed to emerge as a strong determinant for attractiveness. In a second experiment, the researchers disturbed the natural relationship between the WHR and BMI. Normally, BMI and WHR tend to be positively correlated in the female population, that is, women with a higher BMI tend to have a less curvaceous shape. Instead, Tovée et al. (2002) deliberately chose a set of photographic images that demonstrated an inverse correlation between BMI and WHR, that is, a group in which as the women become heavier, they also become more curvaceous. Even though the relative ranges of WHR and BMI should favour WHR in this sample of images, BMI again emerged as the dominant predictor. In other words, women with a low BMI and a high WHR were judged as more attractive, rather than women with a high BMI and a low WHR.

The finding that BMI may be the primary determinant of female attractiveness is consistent with the fact that successful female fashion and glamour models all fall within a narrow BMI range (Tovée, et al., 1997), albeit an underweight range. From an evolutionary psychological point of view, Tovée and his colleagues suggest that there are advantages to using BMI as a basis for mate selection, as BMI provides a reliable cue to female health (Manson, et al., 1995; Willet, et al., 1995) and reproductive potential (Frisch, 1988; Lake, Power, & Cole, 1997; Reid, & van Vugt, 1987; Wang, Davies & Norman, 2000). Put together, Tovée and his colleagues suggest that the balance between the optimal BMI for health and fertility is struck at around a value of $19kg/m^2$, which, in their studies, is also the preferred BMI for attractiveness. In addition, Tovée, et al. (2002) suggest that actual WHR may be limited in its utility. For example, there is a considerable overlap in the WHRs of populations of normal women and anorexic patients (Tovée, et al., 1997). The latter group are amenorrhoeic, and so a woman with an effective fertility of zero can have the same WHR as a woman with normal fertility.

Based on these findings, Tovée et al. (2002) have suggested that one simply does not need to be very sensitive to shape cues. In a normal situation, BMI and body shape are linked, which would suggest that, on average, a body with a particular BMI would tend to have a particular shape. An alternative explanation is that there exists a 'hierarchy of cues' used in partner selection. Features such as WHR may be used to discriminate broad categories, such as male from female or pregnant from non-pregnant. Discriminating within the category of potential partners, one may use such cues as BMI and then other cues such as the proportions of the body to discriminate between women of very similar BMI.

FEMALE ATTRACTIVENESS ACROSS CULTURES

Preferences for a low WHR have been replicated in a wide range of countries, including Australia, the UK, Germany, Greece, India and the Azores (Connally, et al., submitted; Furnham, Dias, & McClelland, 1998; Furnham, Lavancy, & McClelland, 2001; Furnham, Moutafi, & Baguma, 2002; Furnham, Tan, & McManus, 1997; Singh, 2000, 2004, 2004; Singh, & Luis, 1995). This has been taken as evidence for the universal and culturally invariant nature of WHR as a signal for mate selection. However, a single factor shared by all these studies, which makes the claim unwarranted, is that they were carried out in industrial societies. What is clear from the literature is that cultures differ widely in their attitudes towards such things as obesity and body shape (Brown, & Konner, 1987; Ford, & Beach, 1952; Sobal, & Stunkard, 1989).

In an early cross-cultural study, Furnham and Alibhai (1983) compared Black Kenyan to White British and British Kenyan participants' ratings of line figures from anorexic to obese, reporting that Black Kenyan participants viewed obese female shapes more positively than either British or British Kenyan participants, both of which were indistinguishably negative in their evaluation. Replication in Uganda also found the native African sample to be much more approving of obese female figures than a British comparison group (Furnham, & Baguma, 1994; Swami, Furnham, Shah, Tovée, & Baguma, submitted).

Ethnographers have also noted the greater positive association between body fat and prestige in the South Pacific, as body fat is more likely to reflect access to food resources (Brewis, & McGarvey, 2000; Craig, Swinburn, Matenga-Smith, Matangi, & Vaughan 1996; Wilkinson, Ben-Tovin, & Walker, 1994). Becker (1995), for example, reported that Fijian men and women were more tolerant of overweight and obese line drawings than a British comparison. This line of evidence is corroborated by a raft of studies (for example, Akan, & Greilo, 1995; Perez, & Joiner, 2003; Poran, 2002; Rucker, & Cash, 1992) and reviews of the literature (Crago, Shisslak, & Estes, 1996; Fitzgibbon, et al., 1998) demonstrating that African Americans have different attitudes about weight, body shape, and attractiveness than Caucasians, with overall less drive for thinness and greater acceptance of larger body proportions.

The argument remains, however, that while preferences for body weight may differ across cultures, preferences for a low WHR do not. What is the evidence for this? Wetsman and Marlowe (1999) elicited WHR preferences from a hunter-gatherer tribe called the Hadza, in Tanzania, who subsist almost exclusively from foraging wild foods. They found that the size of WHR does not affect judgements of attractiveness. Instead, the Hadza preferred heavy to medium and medium to lightweight line drawings when selecting for attractiveness, health and desirability as a wife, regardless of WHR. The authors concluded that the WHR may be more akin to a 'second-pass filter': 'The first-pass filter could consist of partner preferences based on body weight... The influence of WHR may only become relevant when food resources are plentiful enough that the risk of starvation during pregnancy and lactation for women is minimal...' (Wetsman, & Marlowe, 1999: 226).

These results are strikingly similar to that of a previous study conducted amongst a relatively isolated population, the Matsiengka of southern Peru, who practise swidden (slash and burn) agriculture (Yu, & Shepard, 1998). The researchers tested three groups of the same population, differing in their degree of contact (and, therefore, their degree of 'westernisation'). The least westernised group, like the Hadza, ranked figures first by weight (high preferred to low) and then high WHR over low WHR, once again diametrically opposing findings using participants in industrial societies. The second, moderately westernised group differed in that they rated low WHR females as being more attractive and more desirable as spouses, but not more healthy. The third and most westernised group (first contacted 20 to 30 years previously) did not differ from male participants in the United States.

Marlowe and Wetsman (2001) recently returned to Tanzania with a new set of line drawings in which only the WHR was varied. With no weight variation, Hadza men preferred high WHRs, which the authors argue is nevertheless an artefact of the preference for heavier women. They argue that their (as well as Yu and Shepard's) findings can be explained by the fact that exposure to western media is likely to co-vary with dependence on wild versus domesticated foods. That is, the more subsistence-oriented a society is, and the more energetically expensive women's work, the more men will find heavier women attractive. Among foragers, women who are too thin and energetically stressed reach menarche later, ovulate less regularly, and have less capacity to support pregnancy and lactation (Ellison, 1990; Frisch, 1987). They argue that obesity does not exist among the Hadza and probably rarely, if ever, existed prior to agriculture. In the past, therefore, men should have been selected to find heavier women attractive, as indeed they do in many societies. Agriculture led to a more predictable, surplus food supply, the risk of obesity decreased, and men began to prefer low body mass indices. Thus, the more food-rich a society, and the longer it has been food-rich, the more likely a low WHR will be preferred. However, in a stratified society, a low preference might begin among upper strata men and spread to lower strata men, even if lower strata women are too poor to be at risk of obesity.

Furnham, Moutafi and Baguma (2002) have investigated the effect of weight and WHR on attractiveness ratings on subjects from Uganda, Greece and Britain. They too found a clear cultural influence on body size and shape preference – although the European data showed an overall preference for the 0.7 WHR, the Ugandan subjects gave the ratio of 0.5 the highest rating. A monotonic negative relationship between WHR and perceived attractiveness has in fact been proposed by researchers (Singh, 1993a), but using 0.7 as the lowest ratio. An extrapolation of this relationship would yield 0.5 as the most attractive WHR, but the evolutionary psychological hypothesis would also require it to be the most fertile and healthy ratio as well, which is not what has been reported. A possible explanation for the preference of the Ugandan subjects for the 0.5 ratio is that the 0.5 ratio could only be achieved by having a small waist and large hips, and large hips yield the impression of a heavier figure. Therefore, the preference of a 0.5 ratio could be explained by their preference for large figures, which can be seen by looking at the effect of weight on attractiveness ratings. Furnham, et al. (2002) hypothesised that they would find a preference of heavy figures by the Ugandans, in contrast to a preference of light figures by Greeks and the British. The results supported the hypothesis, suggesting that weight matters, sometimes over and above WHR.

This set of results is similar to that reported by Freedman, Carter, Sbrocco, and Gray (2004), who examined ethnic differences in male preferences for ideal body size and shape in women. The researchers found that African American men were more likely to choose heavier figures as ideal than Caucasian men did. Specifically, African American men disliked a low body weight for women more frequently than did their Caucasian counterparts. In addition, both ethnic groups chose figures with a low WHR, but African American men were more likely to choose a very low WHR as ideal. For the authors, the findings emphasized the importance of assessing male preferences for female shape (or WHR), but also showed weight to be a more important cue than WHR in the male selection process. It appears that African American men are more willing to idealise a woman of a heavier body size, with more curves, than do their Caucasian counterparts, and such differences may play a role in the differential messages that get communicated to women about the kinds of bodies that men like.

EXPLAINING CROSS-CULTURAL DIFFERENCES

An early attempt by evolutionary psychologists to explain cross-cultural differences in preferences for WHR rests on WHR acting as a predictor of child gender. A high pre-conceptual WHR is a good predictor of male offspring, and so in cultures that value male children, an androgynous body shape should be judged as more attractive. The predictive value of WHR is based on studies measuring women who already have children and correlating their WHR with the proportion of existing male offspring. Thus, two independent studies (Manning, Anderton, & Washington, 1996; Singh, & Zambarano, 1997) argued that women with high WHRs and thick waists tended to have more sons, and that preference for women with a high WHR might result in selection for increased testosterone levels in children. Similarly, Manning, Trivers, Singh and Thornhill (1999) presented data from a rural Jamaican population which showed that there is a positive association between a woman's waist circumference and her number of sons.

However, this model fails to explain why westernised indigenous populations in South America, for example, should prefer hour-glass-shaped women (Yu, & Shepard, 1999). If it is argued that most traditional societies value strength (or sons), then South America's male-dominated economy should increase, not decrease, the value of males in westernised populations, and, by extension, the value of high WHR females. Yu and Shepard (1999) also argue that such preference changes as suggested by the adaptationist paradigm could not feasibly occur in a single generation from an evolutionary point of view. In addition, carrying a male child may alter the WHR in a different way to carrying a female child, and a high WHR may be an *effect* rather than a cause of offspring. To test the predictive power of pre-conceptual WHR and offspring gender, Tovée, Brown and Jacobs (2001) took WHR measures from 458 women who intended to become pregnant and then correlated with the gender of the subsequent child. Going against the grain of the thesis that WHR acts as a predictor of child gender, they found no significant correlation.

A different explanation for cross-cultural variation in preferences for WHR, but one that nevertheless remains compatible with evolutionary psychology, has been proposed by Sugiyama (2004). He argues that cross-cultural tests of the low-WHR hypothesis have used stimuli that were not scaled to local conditions: forager women have high fecundity, parasite loads and caloric dependence on fibrous foods, all of which increase WHR. Since mate selection should calibrate for local conditions, he argues that WHR-preference mechanisms will assess the local distribution of female WHR in relation to other correlates of mate value, and will recalibrate as conditions change. Instead of expecting uniform cross-cultural preference for a specific WHR value, researchers should anticipate only that values lower than the local average will be attractive, and that the influence of this factor relative to others will vary cross-culturally.

Taking into account the local distribution of Ecuadorian Shiwiar WHR, Sugiyama (2004) found that Shiwiar males use female WHR in a way that is consistent with the hypothesis that

WHR assessment is sensitively calibrated to local parameters. When differences in body weight are minimised, Shiwiar men preferred lower-than-locally-average female WHR. However, the reliability of this study should be questioned: preferences were only elicited from 18 participants, and the stimuli did not completely unconfound body weight and WHR (Shiwiar men prefer higher-body-fat females within locally observed levels). Thus, when WHR and body fat were not independently assessed, Shiwiar men preferred high-WHR figures because they appear to weigh the most among the high-weight figures.

A different evolutionary argument suggests that the reported difference in preferences for WHR in different cultures may instead be based on BMI. Combined with the argument that WHR and body weight are confounded in line drawings, Tovée, and Cornelissen (2001) suggest that the same ideal BMI should not be expected for all racial groups and environments. On the basis of epidemiological evidence that suggests that different ethnic populations may have differing levels of risk for negative health consequences with changing BMI (for example, Kopelman, 2000; McKeigue, Shah, & Marmot, 1991; Shetty, & James, 1994), they suggest that there may be a different optimal BMI for health and longevity in different racial groups. As a consequence, there will be a preferred optimal BMI for each group, which will balance environmental and health factors, but that this optimal BMI may differ between groups and environments (Tovée, & Cornelissen, 2001).

Recently, Swami and his colleagues (for example, Swami, & Tovée, 2005; Swami, Caprario, et al., in press; Swami, Knight, et al., submitted; Swami, Tovée, et al., submitted) have tested this hypothesis in a series of cross-cultural replications of the BMI research. Swami and Tovée (2005), for example, examined preferences for female physical attractiveness along a socio-economic gradient in Britain and Malaysia, from rural to semi-urban to urban. Their results showed that, regardless of the cultural setting, BMI was the primary predictor of attractiveness ratings, whereas WHR failed to emerge as a strong predictor. The authors also found that preferences for physical attractiveness varied with socio-economic setting, with rural observers preferring larger figures than semi-urban observers, who in turn preferred larger figures than urban observers.

Importantly, this study also examined the physical attractiveness preferences of observer groups of different racial origin from the same environment (Malay, Chinese and Indian in Kuala Lumpur). Studies have indicated that ethnic Malays, Chinese and Indians in South East Asia have different optimal BMIs for risk factors for morbidity and mortality (e.g., Deurenberg, Deurenberg-Yap, & Guricci, 2002), which would suggest that these ethnic groups should have different preferences for body weight. However, this was not the case: Malays, Chinese and Indians in Kuala Lumpur all had a similar preference for slender figures. Elsewhere, Swami, Tovée, et al. (submitted) have reported that physical attractiveness preferences can be modified, as attested by the changing preferences of migrants.

All the evidence, therefore, seems to point to body weight, rather than shape, acting as the primary predictor of female physical attractiveness. However, preferences for BMI appear to vary considerably depending on the socio-economic status of observers and, to a lesser degree, the cultural context occupied by observers. If this is true of female physical attractiveness, what of male attractive?

MALE PHYSICAL ATTRACTIVENESS

Although much research concerning physical attractiveness has focussed on the female body, researchers are increasingly paying attention to masculinity and the male body (for example, Stam, 1998). What little work has been done employs an evolutionary psychological perspective and considers different traits to be an indicator of genetic variability. This explanation assumes that a reliable connection exists between body attractiveness and male quality; that male attractiveness is an indicator or some component of fitness such as health and vigour; and that females detect and use this indicator for choosing a mate (Shackelford, *et al.*, 2000). The most obvious case of sexually selected characters in humans concerns features such as beards and body shape that differ conspicuously between the sexes (Barber, 1995). Thus, it has been argued that men with dominance- and masculinity-related facial and body characteristics are considered most physically and sexually attractive. Testosterone and areas of the body indexing testosterone play key roles, as dominant males have higher testosterone levels (Ehrenkantz, Bliss, & Sheard, 1974). It has also been suggested that aspects of male body build, particularly the upper torso, might be sexually selected. The shoulders of men, their upper body musculature and biceps are all more developed than in women, even when differences in stature are accounted for (Ross, & Ward, 1982), and these characteristics are influenced by testosterone levels (Björntorp, 1987).

Using silhouettes as stimuli, a number of studies have shown that females tend to prefer a moderately developed male torso than extremely muscular physiques (Barber, 1995). However, most of these studies have not looked explicitly at male bodily physique, focussing rather on the waist-to-hip ratio (WHR; the ratio of the circumference of the waist to the circumference of the hips). According to Singh (1995), men with WHRs in the 'desirable' range (0.90 to 0.95) should have fared better when competing for mates in evolutionary history. To test this idea, Singh (1995) had participants rate line drawings depicting men with different WHRs and body sizes. Men with WHRs near the desirable range were consistently rated as the healthiest and most attractive mates. They were also rated as being more intelligent and having better leadership qualities. In contrast, men with WHRs lower than 0.90 or higher than 0.95 were rated as less healthy, less attractive and as having less-desirable personality characteristics. This basic pattern of results has been replicated by a number of different researchers (Furnham, *et al.*, 1997; Henss, 1995; Lynch, & Zellner, 1999; Olivardia, *et al.*, 2004).

However, more recent research using photographic stimuli shows that while the WHR, body mass index (BMI) and waist-to-chest ratio (WCR) are all significant contributors to male attractiveness, WCR was the principal determinant and accounted for 56 per cent of the variance (Maisey, Vale, Cornelissen, & Tovée, 1999; see also Fan, Dai, Liu, & Wu, 2005). By contrast, BMI accounted for only 12.7 per cent of the variance and the WHR was not a significant predictor of attractiveness. Maisey, *et al.* (1999) concluded that women's ratings of male attractiveness can be explained by simple physical characteristics that measure body shape (in particular the WCR). Women are said to prefer men whose torso has an 'inverted triangle' shape, that is, a narrow waist and a broad chest and shoulders, which is consistent with physical strength and muscle development in the upper body (for example, Franzoi, &

Herzog, 1987; Horvath, 1979). This finding is comparable with other studies using line drawings which show that women prefer men with a 'V-shape' (wider shoulders than chest, which was again is wider than the hips; Frederick, & Haselton, 2003; Furnham, & Radley, 1989; Hughes, & Gallup, 2003; Lavrakas, 1975).

MALE ATTRACTIVENESS ACROSS CULTURES

If judgements of attractiveness are an innate preference, as evolutionary psychology argues, then it might be suggested that these preferences should be consistent across cultures. Although there is now a growing body of evidence examining body type preferences for the male body, the literature examining these preferences cross-culturally remains limited. Using an undergraduate sample of Caucasian and Asian-American students, Mintz and Kashubeck (1999) found that males aspired for a large, muscular cultural ideal that does not differ between ethnic groups. However, while Mintz and Kashubeck (1999) explored satisfaction with specific body parts, they did not specifically investigate the interaction between ethnicity and gender on overall body figure preference. A more recent study suggests that Asian-American men are more invested in developing a large, muscular body (Barnett, Keel, & Conoscenti, 2001), but to date few studies have examined male physical attractiveness cross-nationally.

One exception to this is a recent study by Swami and Tovée (submitted), which examined preferences for male physical attractiveness in Britain and Malaysia. The results of their study show that a woman's rating of male bodily attractiveness can be explained by simple physical characteristics, in particular the WCR and BMI. However, there are clear cross-cultural differences in the way these characteristics are used. In *urban* settings in Malaysia and Britain, the WCR is the primary component of attractiveness ratings, suggesting that body shape is more important for male attractiveness than body size. Women prefer men whose torso has an 'inverted triangle' shape, but the BMI of the male body is comparatively unimportant. This is distinguishable from investigations of female attractiveness, which show that body weight is the primary predictor of attractiveness ratings (Fan, *et al.*, 2004; Tovée, *et al.*, 1999).

By contrast, BMI is the primary cue for male attractiveness in *rural* Malaysia, with body shape (as measured by the WCR and WHR) playing comparatively minor roles. The preference among rural participants for heavier men is combined with a preference for a more tubular body shape (that is, changing body shape has less of an effect on attractiveness in the rural group, and a less curvaceous shape is regarded as relatively more attractive in the rural group than in the other observer groups). This set of findings is striking given existing cross-cultural evidence suggesting that Asian-American men, like their Caucasian counterparts, are invested in developing a large, muscular body (Barnett, *et al.*, 2001; Mintz, & Kashubeck, 1999). Rather, when ratings are elicited from rural contexts, body size and not shape is the primary cue for male physical attractiveness.

SOCIOCULTURAL THEORY

The results of recent studies examining male and female physical attractiveness across cultures suggests that evolutionary explanations for these findings are problematic. Some evolutionary psychologists have attempted to provide a more rounded theory of attractiveness by combining evolutionary and social explanations of mate choice. (Swami, & Tovée, 2005). Sociocultural theories have typically been shunned by evolutionary psychologists, but nevertheless provides substantial explanatory power for the findings of research regarding physical attractiveness.

Sociocultural theory emphasises the learning of preferences for body sizes in social and cultural contexts (Smolak, & Levine, 1996). With regard to the female body, the results of research within the Euro-American cultural sphere show that prejudice and discrimination against heavyweight people flourishes and remains largely legal and culturally approved (Crandall, 1994). Parental and peer influences have been implicated in the development of ideas concerning what constitutes an 'ideal' female image (for example, Gordon, 2000), but most researchers believe that the mass media plays a more significant role in influencing preferences for thin female figures in western societies by exhibiting underweight female models (for example, Bryant, & Zhilman, 2002; Harrison, 1997).

Research on Miss America contestants and *Playboy* centrefolds, for example, has shown that the ideal became increasingly thinner over a 20 period, between 1959 and 1978, while women actually became 4 per cent heavier (Garner, Garfinkel, Schwartz, & Thompson, 1980). A follow-up study found that this trend continued between 1979 and 1988: Miss America contestants continued to become thinner, whereas *Playboy* centrefolds fell into a plateau of very low BMIs (Wiseman, Gray, Mosimann, & Ahrens, 1992). Others have examined body satisfaction and eating disorder symptamology as correlates of using mass media (for example, Abramson, & Valene, 1991; Baker, Sivyer, & Towell, 1998; Cash, Cash, & Butters, 1983; Posavac, Posavac, & Weigel, 2001), the idea being that the mass media promulgates a slender ideal that elicits negative affect. Thus, the preference for relatively slender ideals in industrialised settings in the current study may be traced back to the emphasis on a slim physique and negative stereotyping of obese figures (Becker, & Hamburg, 1996).

While thin figures are typically regarded as 'ideal' in mainstream, western culture, cross-ethnic and cross-cultural research reveals differing perceptions of attractiveness and healthy body sizes (Miller, & Pumariega, 2001; Powers, 1980). In most traditional, non-western settings, body fat is believed to be an indicator of wealth and prosperity, with obesity as a symbol of economic success, femininity, and sexual capacity (Ghannam, 1997; Nasser, 1988; Rudovksy, 1974). In less affluent societies, there is often a positive relationship between increased socio-economic status and body weight. Only high-status individuals would have been able to put on body weight, which would explain why the majority of the world's cultures had or have ideals of feminine beauty that include plumpness (Anderson, Crawford, Nadeau, & Lindberg, 1992; Brown, & Konner, 1987), as it would have been advantageous for women to be able to store excess food as fat in times of surplus.

The findings reported by Swami and Tovée (2005), therefore, lend credence to the view that physical attractiveness may be linked less to ethnicity than modernity or socio-economic status. Lee and Lee (2000: 324) have argued that economic liberalisation has encouraged the deregulation of mass media, which projects a powerful image that 'rigidly equates success with a young, slender and, glamorously adorned woman' (Lee, & Lee, 2000: 324). For Nasser (1994, 1997), the transculturality of body image disturbance is evidence of the globalisation of fat-phobia due to the emergence of a culturally shrunken world by a virtue of mass communication technology. Studies conducted in less developed countries show an increasing influence of western culture infused through technology, which have been shown to engender a desire on the part of adolescents, particularly women, to be thin (Wang, Popkin, & Thai, 1998).

Of course, it would be wrong to attribute preferences of physical attractiveness to 'westernisation' alone. Rather, the intensification of preferences for slim physiques is embedded in a 'gendered complex of hegemonic forces that accompany global economic change' (Lee, & Lee, 2000: 324). Rapid industrialisation and urbanisation have meant unparalleled changes in women's condition, with regards to education, employment opportunities, mate choice, birth control and legal rights. These changes have created conflicting demands on young women to strive simultaneously for career accomplishment while maintaining their physical attractiveness (Malson, 1998). Along with increasing affluence, there has also been an increase in the prevalence of worldwide obesity that legitimises the pursuit of thinness and a fear of fatness.

SOCIOCULTURAL THEORY AND MALE BODY

In opposition to evolutionary psychological explanations, it has been suggested that society has expectations for ideal male body shapes (Hesse-Biber, 1996; Murray, Touyz, & Beumont, 1996) and that males in urban contexts increasingly compare their bodies to idealised media and cultural images (Davis, & Katzman, 1997; Heinberg, Thompson, & Stormer, 1995; McCreary, & Sasse, 2000). Although gender differences emerge in attitudes toward cultural ideals of attractiveness, with women more motivated to conform to these ideals than men, sociocultural pressures concerning male body image seems to be on the increase. For example, one content analysis found a consistency in the V-shaped standard of male bodily attractiveness presented in US men's magazines between 1960 and 1992 (Petrie, et al., 1996). In a more recent study, Leit, Pope and Gray (2001) examined centrefold models in *Playgirl* from 1973 to 1997, and found that the cultural norm for the ideal male body has become increasingly muscular, especially in the 1990s.

Similarly, in studying the media's portrayal of the ideal body shape for men, Andersen and DiDomenico (1992) found that men's magazines published significantly more advertisements and articles about changing body shape than about losing weight, suggesting that men might be more concerned with overall physique than with body fat. Another study found that boys' action toys have become increasingly muscular over time, with many contemporary figures having physiques more muscular than is humanly attainable (Pope, Olivardia, Gruber, & Borowiecki, 1999). For Pope, Phillips and Olivardia (2000: 36), the contemporary muscular male ideal featured in the media represents a 'hypermale' or 'more male than male' look, characterised by a disproportionate amount of muscularity in the shoulders and upper arms.

The preference for a large, muscular, and mesomorphic body type in industrialised settings develops at a very young age (Staffieri, 1967), and reaches its peak during early adolescence and early adulthood (Collins, & Plahn, 1988; McCreary, & Sasse, 2000). Importantly, the development of such preferences has been linked with media use and exposure (Morry, & Staska, 2001). In a recent study, Botta (2003) surveyed US college students to test the extent to which reading fashion, sports, health or fitness magazines is related to body image and eating disorders. Results indicated that, for men specifically, reading was linked to increased muscularity, which means that the more time they spent reading, the more likely they were to engage in behaviours intended to increase muscle composition. Furthermore, the absence of a strong preference for muscular, V-shaped bodies among rural participants in the present study lends credence to the view that such an ideal is a culturally-influenced phenomenon.

However, it would be overly simplistic to blame media influences alone. Emerging evidence highlights other personal and sociocultural factors, especially parental and peer influences (Field, *et al.*, 2001; Ricciardelli, & McCabe, 2001). For example, adolescent boys gain greater peer acceptance and popularity with both same-gender and other-gender peers by achieving a more muscular body (Eppright, Sanfancon, Beck, & Bradley, 1997; Silbereisen, & Kracker, 1997). Another possibility is that, in most industrialised settings, women have rapidly achieved parity with men in many aspects of life, leaving men with only their bodies as a distinguishing source of masculinity (Faludi, 1999; Leit, *et al.*, 2001). Images of muscular, fit and toned men are argued to represent men seeking to embody the physical strength, hardness and power associated with the traditional muscular ideal, signalling distance from traditional cultural ideas about feminity. The contemporary preoccupation with abdominal stomach muscles has been discussed precisely in these terms by Baker (1997), who argues that this preoccupation is a way for men faced with decline in physical labour and increasing leisure time, and a related increase in girth, to hold on to the outward appearance of masculinity. If the softness and roundness of women's bodies are viewed as the apothesis of assumed femininity, then men's aspiration for abdominal tautness may be offering them a means to affirm a male-female difference. White and Gillet (1994) have, likewise, commented on the muscular body as an attempt at literally embodying traditional masculine ideals. They argue that the presentation of muscular masculinity as a cultural ideal may be a form of resistance to alternative masculinities that contest power hierarchies among men.

A WORKING HYPOTHESIS

The finding that preference for body weight and shape varies according to socio-economic status is in line with earlier ethnographic reports. Until recently, this pattern linking resource availability (as indicated by socio-economic status) and female body weight lacked an obvious psychological mechanism. Nelson and Morrison (2005), however, proposed an implicit psychological mechanism based on the situational influence of environmental conditions, which does not require the invoking of any evolved mechanism. They argue that collective resource scarcity has consequences for individual resources, as individual members of a society in which resources are scarce are likely to lack resources themselves. They further argue that the affective and physiological states associated with individual-level resource availability provide implicit information about collective resource availability, and that this information then plays a role in the construction of preferences.

In a series of studies, Nelson and Morrison (2005) tested this hypothesis by manipulating people's financial satisfaction or hunger (both these being proxies for personal resources in industrialised societies) and measuring their preferences for potential romantic partners. Their studies confirmed that financially dissatisfied and hungry men preferred a heavier mate than did financially satisfied men or satiated men respectively. Swami and Tovée (submitted) have since confirmed the finding manipulating hunger using photographic stimuli, with hungrier men preferring larger figures than satiated men.

These studies provide evidence that *temporary affective states* can produce individual variation in mate preferences that mirrors patterns of cultural differences. In this sense, ratings of attractiveness vary over time. The mood or state of the rater can subtly but significantly influence his or her ratings of the physical attractiveness of a possible mate. This helps explains why preferences for body weight should vary according to socio-economic status, as individual preferences depend on situational feelings of resource scarcity. In rural contexts, where resource scarcity is more likely to be prevalent, affective and physiological states associated with individual-level resource availability provide implicit information about collective resource availability, and this information then plays a role in the construction of preferences for a heavier body weight. This hypothesis appears to have firm grounding in the psychological literature: feelings not only often serve as 'information' about the environment, but can also influence behaviour without the engagement of complex cognitive processes.

Evolutionary theory has proved to be a powerful theoretical tool in exploring male and female bodily attractiveness. Slogans like 'biology is destiny' have been used by both supporters and critics of evolutionary theory, which always attracts both philosophic and socio-political criticism. Some aspects of attractiveness may be ingrained in our biology: characteristics associated with evolutionary advantages (for example, a low WHR) seem to be perceived as attractive, although debate still continues. However, while some aspects of bodily attractiveness appear innate, other aspects are clearly influenced by culture and experience. The existence of culturally incongruent behaviours and attitudes, of course, suggests that cultures are not fully-integrated systems or coherent wholes. Rather, cultures can best be conceptualised as 'constantly changing, open systems of attitudes, norms, behaviors, artifacts, and institutions that people reinforce but also continually modify or even challenge through diverse means of participation and engagement' (Kim, & Markus, 1999: 798). There are, however, a few core ideas and themes that connect different parts of a given cultural context and that are shared by the majority of its participants. It is the latter that helps explain the extant findings of cross-cultural psychology with regards to body weight and shape preferences.

REFERENCES

Abramson, E. E., & Valene, P. (1991). Media use, dietary restraint, bulimia and attitudes toward obesity: A preliminary study. *British Review of Bulimia and Anorexia Nervosa, 5*, 73-76.

Akan, G., & Greilo, C. (1995). Socio-cultural influences on eating attitudes and behaviours, body image and psychological functioning: A comparison of African-American, Asian-American and Caucasian college women. *International Journal of Eating Disorders, 18*, 181-187.

Andersen, A. E., & DiDomenico, L. (1992). Diet versus shape content of popular male and female magazines: A dose-response relationship to the incidence of eating disorders? *International Journal of Eating Disorders, 11*, 283-287.

Anderson, J. L., Crawford, C. E., Nadeau, J., & Lindgberg, T. (1992). Was the Duchess of Windsor right? A cross-cultural view of the socio-biology of ideals of female body shape. *Ethology and Socio-biology, 13*, 197-227.

Arechiga, J., Prado, C., Canto, M., & Carmenati, H. (2001). Women in transition-menopause and body composition in different populations. *Collective Anthropology, 25*, 443-448.

Baker, D., Sivyer, R., & Towell, T. (1998). Body image dissatisfaction and eating attitudes in visually impaired women. *International Journal of Eating Disorders, 24*, 319-322.

Baker, P. (1997). The soft underbelly of the Abdominis: Why men are obsessed with stomach muscles. In *Pictures of Lily: About Men by Men* (pp. 18-23). Exhibition catalogue, Underwood Gallery, London, September.

Barber, N. (1995). The evolutionary psychology of physical attractiveness: Sexual selection and human morphology. *Ethology and Sociobiology, 16*, 395-424.

Barnett, H. L., Keel, P. K., & Conoscenti, L. M. (2001). Body type preferences in Asian and Caucasian college students. *Sex Roles, 45*, 867-878.

Becker, A. E. (1995). *Body, Self and Society: The View From Fiji*. Philadelphia: University of Pennsylvania Press.

Becker, A. E., & Hamburg, P. (1996). Culture, the media, and eating disorders. *Harvard Review of Psychiatry, 4*, 163-167.

Björntorp, P. (1987). Fat cell distribution and metabolism. In R. J. Wurtman & J. J. Wurtman (Eds.), *Human Obesity* (pp. 66-72). New York: New York Academy of Sciences.

Björntorp, P. (1991). Adipose tissue distribution and function. *International Journal of Obesity, 15*, 67-81.

Björntorp, P. (1997). Body fat distribution, insulin resistance and metabolic disease. *Nutrition, 13*, 795-803.

Botta, R. A. (2003). For your health? The relationship between magazine reading and adolescents' body image and eating disturbances. *Sex Roles, 48*, 389-399.

Brewis, A. A., & McGarvey, S. T. (2000). Body image, body size, and Samoan ecological and individual modernisation. *Ecology of Food and Nutrition, 39*, 105-120.

Brown, P., & Konner, M. J. (1987). An anthropological perspective of obesity. *Annals of the New York Academy of Science, 499*, 29.

Bryant, J., & Zhilman, D. (2002). *Media Effects: Advances in Theory and Research*. Mahwah, NJ: Erlbaum.

Buss, D. (1994). *The Evolution of Desire*. New York: Basic Books.

Buss, D. (1999). *Evolutionary Psychology: The New Science of the Mind*. Boston: Allyn & Bacon.

Buss, D., & Schmitt, P. (1993). Sexual strategies theory: An evolutionary perspective on human mating. *Psychological Review, 100,* 204-232.

Cash, T. F., Cash, D. W., & Butters, J. W. (1983). 'Mirror, mirror on the wall...?': Contrast effects and self-evaluations of physical attractiveness. *Personality and Social Psychology Bulletin, 9,* 351-358.

Collins, J. K., & Plahn, M. R. (1988). Recognition accuracy, stereotypic preference, aversion and subjective judgement of body appearance in adolescents and young adults. *Journal of Youth and Adolescence, 17,* 317-332.

Connaly, J., Sluaghter, V., & Mealy, L. (submitted for publication). Children's preference for waist-to-hip ratio: A developmental strategy.

Crago, M., Shisslak, C. M., & Estes, L. S. (1996). Eating disturbances among American minority groups: A review. *International Journal of Eating Disorders, 19,* 239-248.

Crandall, C. (1994). Prejudice against fat people: Ideology and self-interest. *Journal of Personality and Social Psychology, 66,* 882-894.

Davis, C., & Katzman, M. A. (1999) Perfection as acculturation: Psychological correlates of eating problems in Chinese male and female students living in the United States. *International Journal of Eating Disorders, 25,* 65-70.

Deurenberg, P., Deurenberg-Yap, M., & Guricci, S. (2002). Asians are different from Caucasians and from each other in their body mass index/body fat percentage relationship. *Obesity Reviews, 3,* 141-146.

Ehrenkantz, J., Bliss, E., & Sheard, M. H. (1974). Plasma testosterone: Correlation with aggressive behaviour and social dominance in man. *Psychosomatic Medicine, 36,* 469-475.

Ellisson, P. (1990). Human ovarian function and reproductive ecology: New hypotheses. *American Anthropologist, 92,* 933-952.

Eppright, T. D., Sanfancon, J. A., Beck, N. C., & Bradley, J. S. (1997). Sport psychiatry in childhood and adolescence: An overview. *Child Psychiatry and Human Development, 28,* 71-88.

Faludi, S. (1999). *Stiffed: The Betrayal of the American Man*. New York: W. Morrow, & Co.

Fan, J. T., Dai, W., Liu, F., & Wu, J. (2005). Visual perception of male body attractiveness. *Proceedings of the Royal Society of London B, 272,* 219-226.

Fan, J., Liu, F., Wu, J., & Dai, W. (2004). Visual perception of female physical attractiveness. *Proceedings of the Royal Society of London B, 271,* 347-352.

Field, A. E., Carmago, C. A., Taylor, C. B., Berkey, C. S., Roberts, S. B., & Coldizt, G. A. (2001). Peer, parent and media influences on the development of weight concerns and frequent dieting among preadolescent and adolescent girls and boys. *Paediatrics, 107,* 54-60.

Fitzgibbon, M.L., Spring, B., Avellone, M. E., Blackman, L. R., Pingitore, R., & Stolley, M. R. (1998). Correlates of binge eating in Hispanic, black and white women. *International Journal of Eating Disorders, 24,* 43-52.

Ford, C. S., & Beach, F. A. (1952). *Patterns of Sexual Behaviour*. New York: Harper.

Forestell, C. A., Humphrey, T. M., & Stewart, S. H. (2004). Involvement of body weight and shape factors in ratings of attractiveness by women: A replication and extension of Tassinary and Hansen (1998). *Personality and Individual Differences, 36,* 295-305.

Franzoi, S. L., & Herzog, M. E. (1987). Judging physical attractiveness: What body aspects do we use? *Personality and Social Psychology Bulletin, 13,* 19-33.

Frederick, D. A., & Haselton, M. G. (2003). Muscularity as a communicative signal. *Paper presentation at the International Communications Association,* San Diego, California.

Freedman, R. E. K., Carter, M. M., Sbrocco, T., & Gray, J. J. (2004). Ethnic differences in preferences for female weight and waist-to-hip ratio: A comparison of African-American and White American college and community samples. *Eating Behaviors, 5,* 191-198.

Frisch, R. E. (1987). Body fat, menarche, fitness and fertility. *Human Reproduction, 2,* 521-533.

Frisch, R. E. (1988). Fatness and fertility. *Scientific American, 258,* 88-95.

Furnham, A., & Alibhai, N. (1983). Cross-cultural differences in the perception of female body-shapes. *Psychological Medicine, 13,* 829-837.

Furnham, A., & Baguma, P. (1994). Cross-cultural differences in the evaluation of male and female body shapes. *International Journal of Eating Disorders, 15,* 81-89.

Furnham, A. F., & Radley, S. (1989). Sex differences in the perceptions of male and female body shapes. *Personality and Individual Differences, 10,* 653-662.

Furnham, A., Dias, M., & McClelland, A. (1998). The role of body weight, waist-to-hip ratio, and breast size in judgments of female attractiveness. *Sex Roles, 34,* 311-326.

Furnham, A., Lavancy, M., & McClelland, A. (2001). Waist-to-hip ratio and facial attractiveness: A pilot study. *Personality and Individual Differences, 30,* 491-502.

Furnham, A., Moutafi, J., & Baguma, P. (2002). A cross-cultural study on the role of weight and waist-to-hip ratio on judgements of women's attractiveness. *Personality and Individual Differences, 32,* 729-745.

Furnham, A., Petrides, K. V., & Constantinides, A. (2005). The effects of body mass index and waist-to-hip ratio on ratings of female attractiveness, fecundity and health. *Personality & Individual Differences, 38,* 1823-1834.

Furnham, A., Tan, T., McManus, C. (1997). Waist-to-hip ratio and preferences for body shape: A replication and extension. *Personal and Individual Differences, 22,* 539-549.

Folsom, A. R., Kaye, S. A., Sellers, T. A., Hong, C., Cerhan, J. R., Potter, J. D., & Prineas, R. (1993). Body fat distribution and 5-year risk of death in older women. *Journal of the American Medical Association, 269,* 483-487.

Garner, D. M., Garfinkel, P. E., Schwartz, D., & Thompson, M. (1980). Cultural expectations of thinness in women. *Psychological Reports, 47,* 483-491.

Ghannam, F. (1997). Fertile, plump and strong: The social construction of female body in low income Cairo. *Monographs in Reproductive Health Number 3.* Cairo: Population Council Regional Office for West Asia and North Africa.

Gordon, R. A. (2000). *Eating Disorders: Anatomy of a Social Epidemic,* 2nd Edition. Cambridge: Blackwell.

Guo, S., Salisbury, S., Roche, A. F., Chumela, W. C., & Siervogel, R. M. (1994). Cardiovascular disease risk factor and body composition: A Review. *Nutrition Research, 14,* 1721-1777.

Harrison, K. (1997). Does interpersonal attraction to thin media personalities promote eating disorders? *Journal of Broadcasting and Electronic Media, 41*, 478-500.

Heinberg, L. J., Thompson, J. K., & Stormer, S. (1995). Development and validation of the Sociocultural Attitudes Towards Appearance Questionnaire. *International Journal of Eating Disorders, 17*, 81-89.

Henss, R. (1995). Waist-to-hip ratio and attractiveness. Replication and extension. *Personality and Individual Differences, 19*, 479-488.

Henss, R. (2000). Waist-to-hip ratio and female attractiveness. Evidence from photographic stimuli and methodological considerations. *Personality and Individual Differences, 28*, 501-513.

Hesse-Biber, S. (1996). *Am I Thin Enough Yet? The Cult of Thinness and the Commercialisation of Identity*. New York: Oxford University Press.

Horvath, T. (1979). Correlates of physical beauty in men and women. *Social Behaviour and Personality, 7*, 145-151.

Huang, Z., Willet, W. C., & Colditz, G. A. (1999). Waist circumference, waist:hip ratio, and risk of breast cancer in the Nurses' Health Study. *American Journal of Epidemiology, 150*, 1316-1324.

Hughes, S. M., & Gallup, G. G. (2003). Sex differences in morphological predictors of sexual behaviour: Shoulder-to-hip and waist-to-hip ratios. *Evolution and Human Behavior, 24*, 173-178.

Hume, D. (1757). *Four Dissertations. IV: Of the Standard of Taste*. London: Millar.

Jones, P. R. M., Hunt, M. J., Brown, T. P., & Norgan, N. G. (1986). Waist-hip circumference ratio and its relation to age and overweight in British men. *Human Nutrition: Clinical Nutrition, 40C*, 239-247.

Kaye, S. A., Folsom, A. R., Prineas, R. J., & Gapstur, S. M. (1990). The association of body fat distribution with lifestyle and reproductive factors in a population study of post-menopausal women. *International Journal of Obesity, 14*, 583-591.

Kim, H., & Markus, H. R. (1999). Deviance or uniqueness, harmony or conformity? A cultural analysis. *Journal of Personality and Social Psychology, 77*, 785-800.

Kirschner, M. A., & Samojlik, E. (1991). Sex hormone metabolism in upper and lower body obesity. *International Journal of Obesity, 15*, 101-108.

Kissebah, A. H., & Krakower, G. R. (1994). Regional adiposity and mortality. *Physiological Review, 74*, 761-811.

Kopelman, P. G. (2000). Obesity as a medical problem. *Nature, 404*, 635-643.

Lake, J. K., Power, C., & Cole, T. J. (1997). Women's reproductive health: The role of body mass index in early and adult life. *International Journal of Obesity, 21*, 432-438.

Lanska, D. J., Lanska, M. J., Hartz, A. J., & Rimm, A. A. (1985). Factors influencing anatomical location of fat tissue in 52,953 women. *International Journal of Obesity, 9*, 29-38.

Lavrakas, P. J. (1975). Female preferences for male physique. *Journal of Research in Personality, 9*, 324-334.

Leder, H. (1996). *Linienzeichnungen von Gesichtern. Verfremdungen im Gesichtsmodul* (*Line drawings of faces. Distortions in the face module*). Bern: Huber.

Lee, S., & Lee, A. M. (2000). Disordered eating in three communities of China: A comparative study of female high school students in Hong Kong, Shenzhen, and rural Hunan. *International Journal of Eating Disorders, 27,* 317-327.

Leit, R. A., Pope, H. G. Jr., & Gray, J. J. (2001). Cultural expectations of muscularity in men: The evolution of *Playgirl* centrefolds. *International Journal of Eating Disorders, 29,* 90-93.

Lynch, S. M., & Zellner, D. A. (1999). Figure preferences in two generations of men: The use of figure drawings illustrating differences in muscle mass. *Sex Roles, 40,* 833-843.

Maisey, D. M., Vale, E. L. E., Cornelissen, P. L., & Tovée, M. J. (1999). Characteristics of male attractiveness for women. *Lancet, 353,* 1500.

Malson, H. (1998). *The Thin Woman: Feminism, Post-Structuralism and the Social Psychology of Anorexia Nervosa.* London: Routledge.

Manning, J. T., Anderton, K., & Washington, S. M. (1996). Women's waist and the sex ratio of their progeny: Evolutionary aspects of the ideal female body shape. *Journal of Human Evolution, 31,* 41-47.

Manning, J. T., Trivers, R. L., Singh, D., & Thornhill, A. (1999). The mystery of female beauty. *Nature, 399,* 214-215.

Manson, J. E., Willet, W. C., Stampfer, M. J., Colditz, G. A, Hunter, D. J., Hankinson, S. E., Hennekens, C. H., & Speizer, F. E. (1995). Body weight and mortality among women. *New England Journal of Medicine, 333,* 677-685.

Marlowe, F., & Wetsman, A. (2001). Preferred waist-to-hip ratio and ecology. *Personality and Individual Differences, 30,* 481-489.

Marti, B., Tuomilehto, J., Saloman, V., Kartovaara, H. J., & Pietinen, P. (1991). Body fat distribution in the Finnish population: Environmental determinants and predictive power for cardiovascular risk factor level. *Journal of Epidemiological Community Health, 45,* 131-137.

McCreary, D. R., & Sasse, D. K. (2000). An exploration of the drive for muscularity in adolescent boys and girls. *Journal of American College Health, 48,* 297-320.

McKeigue, P. M., Shah, B., Marmot, M. G. (1991). Relation of central adiposity and insulin resistance with high diabetes prevalence and cardiovascular risk in South Asians. *The Lancet, 337,* 382-386.

Miller, M. N., & Pumariega, A. J. (2001). Culture and eating disorders: A historical and cross-cultural review. *Psychiatry, 64,* 93-110.

Mintz, L. B., & Kashubeck, S. (1999). Body image and disordered eating among Asian-American and Caucasian college students: An examination of race and gender differences. *Psychology of Women Quarterly, 23,* 781-796.

Misra, A., & Vikram, N. (2003). Clinical and pathophysiological consequences of abdominal adiposity and abdominal adipose tissue depots. *Nutrition, 19,* 456-457.

Molarius, A., Seidell, J. C., Sans, S., Tuomilehto, J. R., & Kuulasmaa, K. (1999). Waist and hip circumference, and waist-to-hip ratio in 19 populations of WHO MONICA Project. *International Journal of Obesity, 23,* 116-125.

Morry, M. M., & Staska, S. L. (2001). Magazine exposure: Internalization, self-objectification, eating attitudes, and body satisfaction in male and female university students. *Canadian Journal of Behavioural Sciences, 33,* 269-279.

Murray, S. H., Touyz, S. W., & Beumont, P. J. V. (1996). Awareness and perceived influence of body ideals in the media: A comparison of eating disorder patients and the general community. *Eating Disorders: The Journal of Treatment and Prevention, 4*, 33-46.

Nasser, M. (1986). Comparative study of the prevalence of abnormal eating attitudes among Arab female students of both London and Cairo universities. *Psychological Medicine, 16*, 621-625.

Nasser, M. (1994). Screening for abnormal eating attitudes in a population of Egyptian secondary school girls. *Social Sciences and Medicine, 42*, 21-34.

Nasser, M. (1997). *Culture and Weight Consciousness.* London: Routledge.

Nelson, L. D., & Morrison, E. L. (2005). The symptoms of resource scarcity: Judgements of food and finances influence preference for potential partners. *Psychological Science, 16*, 167-173.

Olivardia, R., Pope, H. G. Jr., Borowiecki, J. J., & Cohane, G. H. (2004). Biceps and body image: The relationship between muscularity and self-esteem, depression, and eating disorder symptoms. *Psychology of Men and Masculinity, 5*, 112-120.

Pasquali, R , Gambineri, A., Anconetani, B., Vicennati, V., Colitta, D., Caramelli, E., Casimirri, F., & Morselli-Labali, A. M. (1999). The natural history of the metabolic syndrome in young women with the polycystic ovary syndrome and the effect on long-term oestrogen-progestagen treatment. *Clinical Endocrinology, 50*, 517-527.

Perez, M., & Joiner, T. E., Jr. (2003). Body image dissatisfaction and disordered eating in Black and White women. *International Journal of Eating Disorders, 33*, 342-350.

Petrie, T. A., Austin, L. J., Crowley, B. J., Helmcamp, A., Johnson, C. E., Lester, R., Rogers, R., Turner, J., & Walbrick, K. (1996). Sociocultural expectations of attractiveness for males. *Sex Roles, 35,* 581-602.

Pirwany, I. R., Fleming, R., Greer, C. J., Packard, C. J., & Sattar, N. (2001). Lipids and lipoprotein subfractions in women with PCOS: Relationship to metabolic and endocrine parameters. *Clinical Endocrinology, 54*, 447-453.

Pond, C. M. (1978). Morphological aspects and the ecological and mechanical consequences of fat deposition in wild vertebrates. *Annual Review of Ecology and Systematics, 9*, 519-570.

Pope, H. G. Jr., Olivardia, R., Gruber, A., & Borowiecki, J. (1999). Evolving ideals of male body image as seen through action toys. *International Journal of Eating Disorders, 26*, 65-72.

Pope, H. G. Jr., Phillips, K. A., Olivardia, R. (2000). *The Adonis Complex: How to Identify, Treat, and Prevent Body Obsession in Men and Boys.* New York: Simon & Schuster.

Poran, M. A. (2002). Denying diversity: Perceptions of beauty and social comparison processes among Latina, Black and White women. *Sex Roles, 47*, 65-81.

Posavac, H. D., Posavac, S. S., & Weigel, R. G. (2001). Reducing the impact of media images on women at risk for body image disturbance: Three targeted interventions. *Journal of Social and Clinical Psychology, 20*, 324-340.

Powers, P. S. (1980). *Obesity: The Regulation of Weight.* Baltimore: Williams & Wilkins.

Puhl, R. M., & Boland, F. J. (2001). Predicting female physical attractiveness: Waist-to-hip ratio versus thinness. *Psychology, Evolution and Gender, 3*, 27-46.

Rebuffé-Scrive, M (1988). Metabolic differences in deposits. In C. Bouchhard & F. E. Johnston (Eds.), *Fat Distribution During Growth and Later Health Outcomes* (pp. 163-173). New York: Alan R. Liss.

Rebuffé-Scrive, M. (1991). Neuroregulation of adipose tissue: Molecular and hormonal mechanisms. *International Journal of Obesity, 15*, 83-86.

Reid, R. L. & van Vugt, D. A. (1987). Weight related changes in reproductive function. *Fertility and Sterility, 48*, 905-913.

Ricciardelli, L. A., & McCabe, M. P. (2001). Self-esteem and negative affect as moderators of sociocultural influences on body dissatisfaction, strategies to decrease weight, and strategies to increase muscles among adolescent boys and girls. *Sex Roles, 44*, 189-206.

Ross, W. D., & Ward, R. (1982). Human proportionality and sexual dimorphism. In R. L. Hall (Ed.), *Sexual Dimorphism in Homo Sapiens: A Question of Size* (pp. 317-361). New York: Praeger.

Rozmus-Wrzesinska, M., & Pawłowski, B. (2005). Men's ratings of female attractiveness are influenced more by changes in female waist size compared with changes in hip size. *Biological Psychology, 68*, 299-308.

Rucker III, C. E., & Cash, T. F. (1992). Body images, body-size perceptions, and eating behaviour among African-Americans and white college women. *International Journal of Eating Disorders, 12*, 291-299.

Rudovsky, B. (1974). *The Unfashionable Human Body*. New York: Anchor Books.

Shackelford, T. K., Weekes-Shackelford, V. A., LeBlanc, G. J., Bleske, A. L., Euler, H. A., & Hoier, S. (2000). Female coital orgasm and male attractiveness. *Human Nature: An Interdisciplinary Biosocial Perspective, 11*, 299-306.

Shetty, P. S., & James, W. P. T. (1994). *Body mass index: A measure of chronic energy deficiency in adults*. Rome: Food and Agriculture Organisation of the United Nations, Food and Nutrition Paper 56.

Silbereisen, R. K., & Kracke, B. (1997). Self-reported maturational timing and adaptation in adolescence. In G. Schulenberg (Ed.), *Health Risks and Developmental Transition During Adolescence* (pp. 85-109). Cambridge, UK: Cambridge University Press.

Singh, D. (1993a). Adaptive significance of female physical attractiveness: Role of waist-to-hip ratio. *Journal of Personality and Social Psychology, 65*, 292-307.

Singh, D. (1993b). Body shape and women's attractiveness. The critical role of waist-to-hip ratio. *Human Nature, 4*, 297-321.

Singh, D. (1994a). Is thin really beautiful and good? Relationship between waist-to-hip ratio (WHR) and female attractiveness. *Personality and Individual Differences, 16*, 123-132.

Singh, D. (1994b). Waist-to-hip ratio and judgements of attractiveness and healthiness of females' figures by male and female physicians. *International Journal of Obesity, 18*, 731-737.

Singh, D. (1994c). Body fat distribution and perception of desirable female body shape by young black men and women. *International Journal of Eating Disorders, 16*, 289-294.

Singh, D. (1994d). WHR and judgements of attractiveness and healthiness by male and female physicians. *International Journal of Obesity, 18*, 731-737.

Singh, D. (1995a). Female judgement of male attractiveness and desirability for relationships: Role of waist-to-hip ratio and financial status. *Journal of Personality and Social Psychology*, *69*, 1089-1101.

Singh, D. (1995b). Female health, attractiveness and desirability for relationships: Role of breast asymmetry and WHR. *Ethology and Sociobiology*, *16*, 465-481.

Singh, D. (2000). Waist-to-hip ratio: An indicator of female mate value. Paper presented at the Kyoto Symposium on Human Mate Choice. November 20-24.

Singh, D. (2002). Female mate value at a glance: Relationship of waist-to-hip ratio to health, fecundity and attractiveness. *Human Ethology and Evolutionary Psychology*, *23*, 81-91.

Singh, D. (2004). Mating strategies of young women: Role of physical attractiveness. *Journal of sex Research*, *41*, 43-54.

Singh, D. & Luis, S. (1995). Ethnic and gender consensus for the effect of waist-to-hip ratio on judgements of women's attractiveness. *Human Nature*, *6*, 51-65.

Singh, D., & Young, R. K. (1995). Body weight, waist-to-hip ratio, breasts, and hips: Role in judgements of female attractiveness and desirability for relationships. *Ethology and Sociobiology*, *16*, 483 507.

Singh, D., & Zambarano, R. J. (1997). Offspring sex ratio in women with android body fat distribution. *Journal of Human Biology*, *69*, 545-556.

Singh, D., Davis, M., & Randall, P. (2000, June). Fluctuating ovulation: Lower WHR, enhanced self-perceived attractiveness, and increased sexual desire. Paper presented at Human Evolution and Behaviour Society meeting, London.

Smolak, L., & Levine, M. P. (1996). Developmental transitions at middle school and college. In L. Smolak, M. P. Levine & R. H. Strigel-Moore (Eds.), *The Developmental Psychopathology of Eating Disorders: Implications for Research, Prevention and Treatment* (pp. 207-233). Hillsdale, New Jersey: Erlbaum.

Sobal, J., & Stunkard, A. J. (1989). Socio-economic status and obesity: A review of the literature. *Psychological Bulletin*, *105*, 260-275.

Staffieri, J. R. (1967). A study of social stereotypes of body image in children. *Journal of Personality and Social Psychology*, *7*, 101-104.

Stam, H. (Ed.) (1998). *The Body and Psychology*. London: Sage.

Streeter, S. A., & McBurney, D. (2003). Waist-hip ratio and attractiveness: New evidence and a critique for a 'critical test.' *Evolution and Human Behaviour*, *24*, 88-98.

Sugiyama, L. S. (2004). Is beauty in the context-sensitive adaptations of the beholder? Shiwiar use of waist-to-hip ratio in assessments of female mate value. *Evolution and Human Behaviour*, *25*, 51-62.

Swami, V., & Tovée, M. J. (2005). Female physical attractiveness in Britain and Malaysia: A cross-cultural study. *Body Image*, *2,* 115-128.

Swami, V., & Tovée, M. J. (submitted). Do judgements of food influence preferences for female body weight? *British Journal of Psychology*.

Swami, V. & Tovée, M. J. (submitted). Male physical attractiveness in Britain and Malaysia: A cross-cultural study. *Body Image*.

Swami, V., Caprario, C., Tovée, M. J., & Furnham, A. (in press). A western predicament? Preferences for a slim ideal in Japan and Britain. *European Journal of Personality*.

Swami, V., Furnham, A., Shah, K., Tovée, M. J., & Baguma, P. (submitted). The influence of body weight and shape on female physical attractiveness in Britain and Uganda using biologically valid figures. *Social Sciences & Medicine.*

Swami, V., Knight, D., Tovée, M. J., Davies, P., & Furnham, A. (submitted). Perceptions of female physical attractiveness among Pacific Islanders. *Journal of Cross-Cultural Psychology.*

Swami, V., Tovée, M. J., Furnham, A., & Mangalparsad, R. (submitted). Changing perceptions of attractiveness as observers are exposed to a different culture. *Proceedings of the Royal Society of London B.*

Symons, D. (1995). Beauty is the adaptations of the beholder: The evolutionary psychology of human female sexual attractiveness. In P. R. Abramhamson & S. D. Pinker (Eds.), *Sexual Nature/Sexual Culture* (pp. 80-118). Chicago: Chicago University Press.

Tassinary, L. G., & Hansen, K. A. (1998). A critical test of the waist-to-hip ratio hypothesis of female physical attractiveness. *Psychological Science, 9,* 150-155.

Tovée, M. J., & Cornelissen, P. L. (1999). The mystery of human beauty. *Nature, 399,* 215-216.

Tovée, M. J., & Cornelissen, P. L. (2001). Female and male perceptions of female physical attractiveness in front-view and profile. *British Journal of Psychology, 92,* 391-402.

Tovée, M. J., Brown, J. E., & Jacobs, D. (2001). Maternal waist-hip ratio does not predict child gender. *Proceedings of The Royal Society London B, 268,* 1007-1010.

Tovée, M. J., Emery, J. L., Cohen-Tovée, E. M. (2000). The estimation of body mass index and physical attractiveness is dependent on the observer's own body mass index. *Proceedings of the Royal Society of London B, 267,* 1987-1997.

Tovée, M. J., Hancock, P., Mahmoodi, S., Singleton, B. R. R., & Cornelissen, P. L. (2002). Human female attractiveness: Waveform analysis of body shape. *Proceedings of the Royal Society of London (B), 269,* 2205-2213.

Tovée, M. J., Maisey, D. S., Emery, J. L., & Cornelissen, P. L. (1999). Visual cues to female physical attractiveness. *Proceedings of the Royal Society of London B, 266,* 211-218.

Tovée, M., Mason, S., Emery, J., McCluskey, S., & Cohen-Tovée, E. (1997). Supermodels: Stick insects or hourglasses? *Lancet, 350,* 1474-1475.

Tovée, M. J., Reinhardt, S., Emery, J., & Cornelissen, P. (1998). Optimum body-mass index and maximum sexual attractiveness. *Lancet, 352,* 548.

Wang, J. X., Davies, M., & Norman, R. J. (2000). Body mass and probability of pregnancy during assisted reproduction to treatment: Retrospective study. *Lancet, 321,* 1320-1321.

Wang, Y., Popkin, B., & Thai, F. (1998). The nutritional status and dietary pattern of Chinese adolescents, 1991 and 1993. *European Journal of Clinical Nutrition, 52,* 908-916.

Wass, P., Waldenstrom, U., Rossner, S., & Hellberg, D. (1997). An android body fat distribution in females impairs the pregnancy rate of in-vitro fertilisation-embryo transfer. *Human Reproduction, 12,* 2057-2060.

Wetsman, A. F. (1998). *Within- and between-sex variation in human mate choice: An evolutionary perspective.* Unpublished doctoral dissertation, University of California, Los Angeles.

Wetsman, A. & Marlowe, F. (1999). How universal are preferences for female waist-to-hip ratios? Evidence from the Hadza of Tanzania. *Evolution and Human Behaviour, 20,* 219-228.

White, P. G., & Gillet, J. (1994). Reading the muscular body – A critical decoding of advertisements in Flex magazine. *Sociology of Sport Journal, 11,* 18-39.

Wilkinson, J., Ben-Tovim, D., & Walker, M. (1994). An insight into the personal significance of weight and shape in large Samoan women. *International Journal of Obesity, 18,* 602-606.

Willet, W. C., Manson, J. E., Stampfer, M. J., Colditz, G. A., Rosner, B., Speizer, F. E., & Hennekens, C. H. (1995). Weight, weight change and coronary heart disease in women: Risk within the 'normal' weight range. *Journal of the American Medical Association, 273,* 461-465.

Wiseman, C. V., Gray, J. J., Mosimann, J. E., & Ahrens, A. H. (1992). Cultural expectations of thinness in women: An update. *International Journal of Eating Disorders, 11,* 85-89.

Van Hooff, M. H., Voorhorst, F. J., Kaptein, M. B., Hirasing, R. A., Koppenaal, C., & Schoemaker, J. (2000). Insulin, androgen and gonadotrophin concentration, body mass index, and waist-to-hip ratio in the first years after menarche in girls with regular menstrual cycle, irregular menstrual cycle, or oligomenorrhea. *Journal of Clinical Endocrinology and Metabolism, 85,* 1394-1400.

Yu, D. W., & Shepard, G. H. (1998). Is beauty in the eye of the beholder? *Nature, 396,* 321-322.

Yu, D. W., & Shepard, G. H. (1999). The mystery of female beauty – Reply. *Nature, 399,* 216.

Zaadstra, B. M., Seidell, J. C., van Noord, P. A. H., te Velde, E. R., Habbema, J. D. F., Vrieswijk, B., & Karbaat, J. (1993). Fat and female fecundity: Prospective study of effect of body fat distribution on conception rates. *British Medical Journal, 306,* 484-487.

In: Body Image: New Research
Editor: Marlene V. Kindes, pp. 63-77

ISBN 1-60021-059-7
© 2006 Nova Science Publishers, Inc.

Chapter III

SPORTS ADVERTISING AND BODY IMAGE

Dave Smith, Caroline Wright, Natalie Ross and Sarah Warmington*
University of Chester, Chester CH1 4BJ United Kingdom

ABSTRACT

These studies examined the effects of sport-related advertising on body image. In Study 1, two hundred and twenty four collegiate females were categorised into regular exercisers and non-exercisers. In the pre-test and post-test (i.e., before and after exposure to advertising), each participant completed the Silhouette Measure of Body Image (SMBI; Stunkard, Sorenson & Schlusinger, 1983), the 9-item Social Physique Anxiety Scale (Martin, Rejeski, Leary, McAuley & Bane, 1997) and the Attitudes Towards Sport Advertisements (ATSA; adapted by Sabiston & Monroe, 2001, from Rabak-Wagner, Eickoff-Shemek & Kely-Vance, 1998), and the exercisers completed the 7-subscale Reasons for Exercise Inventory (Silberstein, Striegel-Moore, Timko & Rodin, 1988). They were then assigned to the model or product-related advertising condition. Participants were shown 15 sport-related advertisements either showing models (model condition) or workout shoes (product condition). Participants were given five minutes to view the advertisements, and then completed the questionnaires again. The results showed that the exercisers who were exposed to the model condition scored significantly ($p<.01$) higher on all measures in the post-test compared to the pre-test. The non-exercisers exposed to the model condition increased significantly ($p<.05$) on all measures from pre- to post-test but scored significantly ($p<.05$) lower on all post-test measures than the exerciser group. The product condition groups did not increase significantly on any measure ($p>.05$ in all cases). In Study 2, two hundred and forty nine sedentary undergraduates (126 males, 123 females) completed the SPAS, the SMBI and the ATSA. Following the pre-test, participants were shown 15 sport-related same-sex advertisements. Participants were given five minutes to view the advertisements, before completing the measures again. Group x test ANOVAs revealed that, in both the pre-test and the post-test, females scored significantly ($p<.05$) higher than males on the SMBI

---

* Correspondence concerning this article should be addressed to Dr Dave Smith, University of Chester, Parkgate Road, Chester, CH1 4BJ, UK.

and SPAS. The SMBI, SPAS and ATSA scores of the female participants, and the SPAS and ATSA scores of the males, increased significantly ($p<.05$) from pre- to post-test. Males' SMBI scores were higher in the post-test than the pre-test but the difference was not statistically significant ($p>.05$). These results show that the use of very fit and toned models in the advertisin͡ ͡ort-related products can have a detrimental effect upon body image of both r ͡ ͡ales.

Keywords: bod͡

'veness place a huge emphasis on the ideal of
͡ut impossible for the majority to attain
l for males emphasizes a larger, more
'ope & Gruber, 1997; Pope, Philips &
͡er, this 'ideal' is very different from
r, Henderson and Zivian (1999)
͡ody image and their bodily ideal
ten͡   ͡may engage in unhealthy behaviours,
such   ͡ing patterns in the case of females, or
anaboli͡   ͡comprehensive understanding of the factors
affecting ͡   ͡se attempting to prevent or treat such behaviours.
The aim of ͡   ͡is chapter was to examine the influence of one factor
that may exer͡   ͡luence on individuals' body dissatisfaction, that of sports advertising.

Body image is ͡ ͡eptualised as being malleable (Graham, Eich, Kephart & Peterson, 2000), meaning that it can be shaped or altered by various influences such as; media (Groesz, Levine & Murden, 2001), peers (Stice, Maxfield & Wells, 2003), and culture (Yang, Gray & Pope, 2005). Research has shown that these societal influences are capable of affecting body image perceptions in both males and females. However, Groesz et al. (2001, p.2) claim that the media, including advertisers, are the "loudest and most aggressive purveyors" of body image ideals, using them to sell and promote their products to target audiences.

Evans, Berman and Wellington (1997) describe advertising as something that is designed to inform and persuade potential customers. Advertisements are intended to have an initial impact on a targeted audience and are seen daily in magazines, on billboards, on television and on the Internet. Body image dissatisfaction among males and females is the result of social comparison against unrealistic body ideals, which are continually publicised through advertising and the mass media. Advertisements tend to emphasise extreme subgroups of 'thinness' for females and 'muscularity' for males (McDermott, 1996). These portray unattainable achievements in body weight, shape, and muscularity for the majority of people, which can lead to increased levels of body dissatisfaction (Lindeman, 1999). For example, a study by Hargreaves and Tiggemann (2004) focussed on adolescents who viewed television commercials containing images of 'thin' women, 'muscular' men or non-appearance commercials. They found that exposure to the commercials containing 'ideal' images led to increased body dissatisfaction amongst the female participants.

The commercials used by Hargreaves and Tiggemann (2004) appeared fairly typical examples of the way the media portray the 'ideal' body. For instance, Garner, Garfunkel, Schwartz and Thompson (1980) found that 69% of Playboy centrefolds and 60% of Miss America pageants were 15% or more below the average weight for their height and weight. Yamamiya, Cash, Melnyk, Posavac and Posavac (2005) suggest that the media force the thin ideal on to the consumers by encouraging them that they 'can' and 'should' be thin. They do this through educating them into how to obtain these thin ideals. For example, women's magazines often contain articles that describe methods for losing weight. Wiseman, Gray, Moismann and Aherns (1992) supported this and found from reviewing women's magazines over a 30-year period that there was a total increase in the number of articles relating to exercise and dieting. Stice, Schupak-Nemberg, Shaw and Stein (1994) found that the more a person was exposed to magazines and television during the previous month, the higher the levels of body dissatisfaction he or she reported. Stice et al. concluded from this that the media portray ideals that are unrealistic and cause females to have negative feelings towards their body. The 'thin,' 'muscular', ideals that are portrayed within the media may affect people's attitudes towards their body and lead to increased body dissatisfaction (Hart et al., 1989).

Historically, body dissatisfaction among females has attracted more research interest than that among males, partly because the research has indicated that women report higher levels of body dissatisfaction than men and place a greater value on losing weight. This is thought to contribute to their increased risk of developing an eating disorder (Grover, Keel & Mitchell, 2003; Garner et al., 1980). For example, Grover et al. (2003) found that normal weight women rated themselves heavier than normal weight males, despite there being no actual difference in body size. Furnham and Radley (1989) reported that slightly overweight males were more accepted by both males and females than slightly overweight females. These results suggest that there is a greater pressure for thinness and a narrower acceptability among females than males. Western culture may account for these differences due to the large emphasis they place on thinness as a female ideal of beauty (Garner et al., 1980; Striegel-Moore, Silberstein & Rodin, 1986; Furnham & Radley, 1989; Stice et al., 2003).

However, over the past few decades there has been increasing evidence of body image disorders in males (Holle, 2004; Leit, Gray & Pope, 2002). McCabe and Ricciardelli (2004) reviewed literature on male body image across the lifespan and found that college men were equally divided between wanting to lose weight and wanting to gain weight. They suggested that the discrepancy between the levels of body dissatisfaction among males and females was because studies relied on whether males wanted to lose weight and did not take into account whether males wanted to gain weight. From their review, they proposed that by questioning both dimensions in males, similar levels of body dissatisfaction would be demonstrated between males and females.

According to Holle (2004) there has been an increase in body dissatisfaction in males over recent decades. The results of his study showed that self-perceived overweight and underweight men reported less willingness to volunteer for activities that may involve the body being scrutinised by others than self-perceived normal weight men. A further finding was that an unwillingness to expose the upper torso was significantly associated with a higher fear of negative evaluation and increased social physique anxiety (Holle, 2004). This rise in body dissatisfaction might reflect the increased media attention paid to the muscular male ideal. Pope, Olivardia, Borowiecki and Cohane (2001) analysed advertisements in two American women's magazines from 1958-1998. They counted the number of males and females in each advert and calculated the state to which they were undressed. The findings indicated that from 1958-1998, the level of undressed females in advertisements remained at 20%, but the level of undressed males rose from 3%-35%. Leit et al. (2001) analysed Playgirl centrefolds over a 25-year period (1973-1997) and found that the male body ideal had become increasingly more muscular over the years (especially during the 1990's). Pope, Olivardia, Gruber, and Borowiecki (1999) supported these findings with the level of muscularity in action toys increasing to levels that are impossible to obtain in reality, even for professional bodybuilders consuming large doses of anabolic steroids. The trends that are found within these studies, such as increases in muscularity and increases in male exposure to magazines pose problems when viewed through Festinger's (1954) social comparison theory. This is because men are comparing themselves to unrealistic body images that cannot be achieved through natural methods and could lead to body dissatisfaction (Kimmel & Mahalik, 2004). Leit et al. (2002) supported this, finding that exposure to advertisements containing images of muscular male figures led to an increase in body dissatisfaction. Perceived pressure to adhere to these advertisements has resulted in some males suffering from body image concerns and indulging in pathological behaviours, such as excessive exercising, extreme dieting and steroid use, to achieve this sociocultural ideal (Lantz, Rhea & Mayhew, 2001).

Advertising in general has been shown to affect both males' and females' body image, but does sports advertising affect them in the same way? This is an important question, because the representations of the body used in sports advertising may be perceived by the general public as the standard to which their bodies would be compared in sport or exercise environments. This may affect the activities they choose to participate in and lead to avoidant behaviours, as they are worried about others evaluating their body in a negative way (Crawford & Eklund, 1994; Hart, Leary & Rejeski, 1989). Thus, as some sport psychologists have suggested (Crawford & Eklund, 1994; Hart et al., 1989; Lantz, Hardy & Ainsworth, 1997), individuals with such concerns are more likely to avoid exercise and sports settings where their body can be evaluated by others. Given such potential outcomes, particularly in the context of rising obesity levels and an increasingly sedentary lifestyle in the western world, the possible impact of sports advertising on body image is an important issue for investigation.

Recognising the importance of this issue, Sabiston and Munroe (2001) examined whether sports advertisements were led to increased social physique anxiety in female athletes. Social physique anxiety is a type of body image concern where individuals feel anxious regarding the prospect of others evaluating their physiques (Hart et al., 1989). In their study comparing the effect of exposure to model-only advertising and product-only advertising on social physique anxiety, Sabiston and Munroe found that, after female athletes were exposed to model-only advertising, their social physique anxiety increased, particularly in those who were initially low in social physique anxiety. They suggested that sports advertising could be associated with increased levels of social physique anxiety, but that more research was needed.

The aim of our studies was to build on these findings by examining the effects of sport-related advertising on social physique anxiety and body image disturbance in female and male exercisers and non-exercisers. We hypothesized that the body image disturbance scores of all groups would increase after exposure to model-related advertisments. In Study 1, which focused on comparing female exercisers and non-exercisers, we also hypothesized that increases in body image disturbance would be significantly greater in the exercisers, due to reports of a high incidence of body image disturbances in athletic populations (Petrie, 1993).

In Study 2, which focused on comparing males and females, we hypothesised that males' and females' body image would be disturbed to an equal degree following exposure to the advertising.

STUDY 1 METHOD

Participants

Two hundred and twenty four females between 18 and 25 years were divided into four groups: regular exercisers exposed to model-related advertising, non-exercisers exposed to model-related advertising, regular exercisers exposed to product-related advertising and non-exercisers exposed to product-related advertising. Regular exercisers were defined as those who reported participating in some form of purposeful exercise activity (e.g. running, aerobics, weight training) at least once per week. All participants provided written informed consent prior to participation.

Measures

Silhouette Measure of Body Image (SMBI; Stunkard, Sorenson & Schlusinger, 1983)

The SMBI was used to measure the cognitive modality of body image, an integral thought process in which one evaluates and gains a perception of one's bodily shape and size. It is a 9-point continuum of body figure diagrams, ranging from extremely thin to extremely overweight. Respondents rate their current and ideal body size, and scores are calculated by subtracting the 'ideal' figure rating from the 'current' figure rating. The SMBI has been validated as an anthropometric body size measure, with correlations between body weight and silhouette choice ranging from .65 to .84 for untrained observers and .85 to .92 for trained observers (Mueller, Joos & Schull, 1985). Cohn and Adler (1992) supported the concurrent validity of the scale by finding a strong relationship ($r = .76$) between SMBI scores and self-reported weight dissatisfaction. Also, the internal consistency of the scale is high ($\alpha = .92$; Lavine, Sweeney & Wagner, 1999).

Social Physique Anxiety Scale (SPAS; Martin, Rejeski, Leary, McAuley & Bane, 1997)

The SPAS was used to measure the affective component of body image. It is a 9-item, Likert-scored scale that measures the extent to which participants become anxious about others evaluating their physical appearance. Items include "Unattractive features of my figure make me feel nervous in certain social settings" and "When in a bathing suit, I often feel nervous about the shape of my body". The 9-item SPAS has demonstrated acceptable test-retest reliability (α = .82) and internal consistency (Cronbach's α = .90, Martin et al., 1997). Also, the construct validity of the 9-item scale has been supported by significant correlations between the SPAS and several related scales (Motl & Conroy, 2000).

Reasons for Exercise Inventory (Silberstein, Striegel-Moore, Timko & Rodin, 1988)

This is a 24-item, 7-subscale Likert-scored scale that evaluates motives for exercising. The subscales are weight control, health, fitness, improving body tone, improving physical attractiveness, mood enhancement and enjoyment. Respondents rate the importance of each motive on a scale of 1 (not at all important) to 7 (extremely important). For the purposes of this study we were only interested in the weight control and attractiveness subscales, as these are indicative of the behavioral modality of body image (Sabiston & Munroe, 2001). According to Silberstein et al. (1988), all subscales demonstrate acceptable internal consistency (α > .70 in all cases except the attractiveness subscale, where α = .70).

Attitudes Towards Sport Advertising Scale (ATSA; adapted by Sabiston & Monroe from Rabak-Wagener, Eickoff-Shemek & Kely-Vance, 1998)

The ATSA is an 11-item Likert-scored scale that measures beliefs and behaviours towards sport advertising. It is based upon Rabak-Wagener et al.'s Attitudes Towards Fashion advertising Scale, with the word "fashion" replaced by the word "sport" where appropriate. A total score is calculated from the 11 items to measure overall perception of body image (Rabak-Wagener et al., 1988). The higher the total score, the greater the body image disturbance. Rabak-Wagener et al. found the original scale to have a high test-retest reliability (α = .82).

Procedure

Participants completed all the questionnaires and were then randomly assigned to the model or product-related advertising condition. On a separate occasion, participants were shown 15 exercise-related advertisements either showing female models (model-related condition) or running and workout shoes (product-related condition). The advertisements used were identical to those used by Sabiston and Monroe (2001). They were taken from popular sport and fitness magazines published in the US and Canada, including Shape, Fitness and Self. Each participant was given five minutes to view the advertisements, and then completed the questionnaires again.

STUDY 1 RESULTS

Pre- and post-test means and standard deviations for the SMBI, SPAS, REI weight control, REI attractiveness and ATSA are shown in Figures 1 to 5 respectively. Group x test ANOVAs revealed significant effects for the SMBI for both test, $F(1,220) = 44.41$, $p<.001$, and group x test, $F(3, 220) = 24.28$, $p<.001$. This was also the case for the SPAS, $F(1,220) = 151.73$, $p<.001$ (test), $F(3,220) = 67.11$, $p<.001$ (group x test), REI weight control, $F(1,110) = 22.51$, p<.001 (test), $F(1,110) = 14.11$, $p<.001$ (group x test), REI attractiveness, $F(1,110) = 24.57$, $p<.001$ (test), $F(1,110) = 16.03$, $p<.001$ (group x test), and the ATSA, $F(1,220) = 121.66$, $p<.001$ (test), $F(3,220) = 34.96$, $p<.001$ (group x test). Tukey HSD tests revealed no significant between-group pre-test differences ($p>.05$ in all cases). The exercisers and non-exercisers who were exposed to the model-related condition scored significantly higher on all scales in the post-test compared to the pre-test ($p<.05$ in all cases). However, the non-exercisers scored significantly lower on all scales in the post-test than the exerciser group ($p<.05$ in all cases). The product-condition groups did not increase significantly on any scales in the post-test ($p>.05$ in all cases).

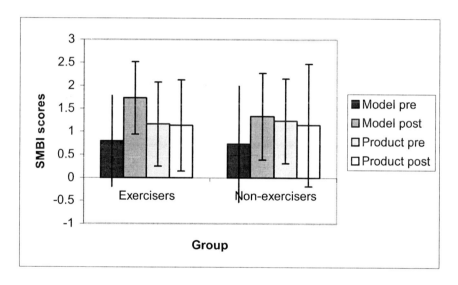

Figure 1. Mean and standard deviation pre- and post-test Silhouette Measure of Body Image scores for model and product conditions.

STUDY 2 METHOD

Participants and Measures

Two hundred and forty nine sedentary undergraduates (126 males, 123 females) between the ages of 18 and 26 were given the SPAS, the SMBI and the ATSA. As in Study 1, all participants provided written informed consent prior to participation.

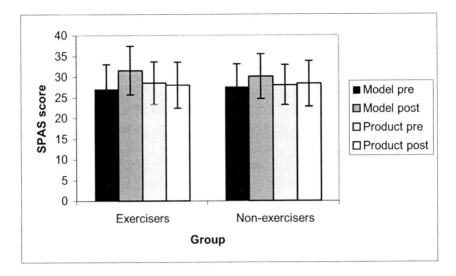

Figure 2. Mean and standard deviation pre- and post-test Social Physique Anxiety Scale scores for model and product conditions.

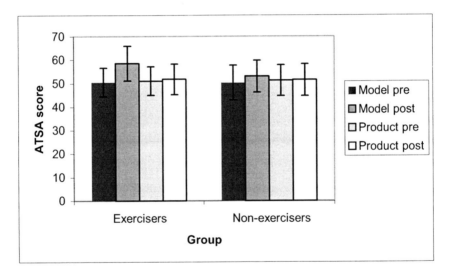

Figure 3. Mean and standard deviation pre- and post-test Attitudes towards Sports Advertising scores for model and product conditions.

Procedure

For the pre-test, participants completed all the questionnaires. On a separate occasion following the pre-test, participants were shown 15 exercise-related advertisements showing either female models (for the female participants) or male models (for the male participants). The female model advertisements were identical to those used in Study 1. The male model advertisements were taken from the following sports and fitness magazines: *Body Fitness, Exercise Protocol, MuscleMag* and *Swimrite*. Each participant was given five minutes to view the advertisements, and then completed the SMBI, SPAS and ATSA again.

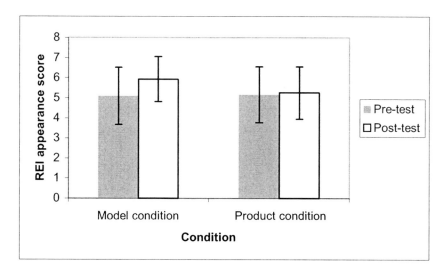

Figure 4. Mean and standard deviation pre- and post-test Reasons for Exercise Inventory appearance subscale scores for model and product conditions.

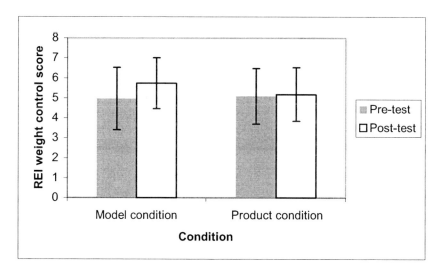

Figure 5. Mean and standard deviation pre- and post-test Reasons for Exercise Inventory weight control subscale scores for model and product conditions.

STUDY 2 RESULTS

Pre- and post-test mean and standard deviation SMBI, SPAS and ATSA scores are shown in Figures 6 to 8 respectively. A group x test ANOVA for the SMBI revealed a significant effect for test, $F(1,247) = 49.99$, $p<.001$ and group x test, $F(1,247) = 13.83$, $p<.001$. In both the pre-test and the post-test, females scored significantly higher than males. The SMBI scores of the female participants increased significantly ($p<.05$) from pre- to post-test. In contrast, though males' SMBI scores were slightly higher in the post-test than the pre-test, the difference was not statistically significant ($p>.05$).

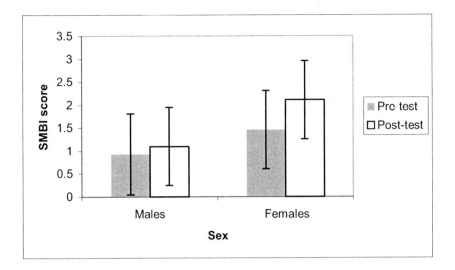

Figure 6. Mean and standard deviation pre- and post-test Silhouette Measure of Body Image scores for males and females.

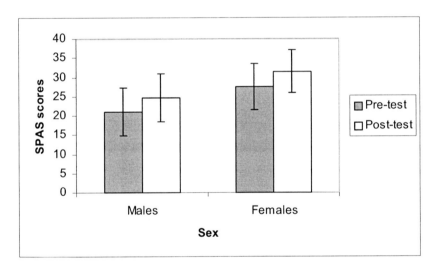

Figure 7. Mean and standard deviation pre- and post-test Social Physique Anxiety Scale scores for males and females.

A group x test ANOVA for the SPAS also revealed a significant for test, $F(1,247) = 410.25$, $p<.001$. However, there was no significant group x test effect, $F(1,247) = 1.06$, $p>.05$, and thus although SPAS scores increased from pre-test to post-test, there was no difference between the groups in the magnitude of the increases. This was also the case with the ATSA, with a significant effect for test. Similar results were found with the ATSA, with a significant effect for test, $F(1,247) = 224.25$, $p<.001$ but no significant group x test interaction, $F(1,247) = 1.23$, $p>.05$.

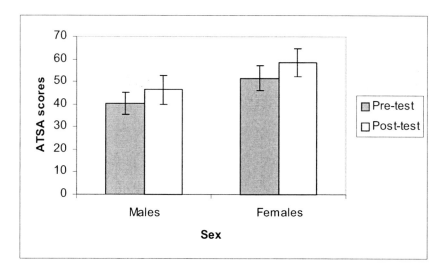

Figure 8. Mean and standard deviation pre- and post-test Attitudes Towards Sports Advertising scores for males and females.

CONCLUSION

The results of these studies concur with the conclusions of Sabiston and Munroe (2001), that the use of very fit and toned models in the advertising of exercise-related products can have a detrimental effect upon body image. All groups of participants exposed to model-related advertising in our two studies showed changes in SPAS and SBMI scores, and in three out of four cases these changes were statistically significant. In contrast, those participants viewing the product-related advertisements did not increase significantly in their SPAS or SBMI scores. Therefore, it is clearly not sports advertising per se, but rather the use of very slim, fit, healthy and attractive models in such advertising that leads to such body image disturbances. These results can be explained by Festinger's (1954) social comparison theory, which emphasises the importance of comparisons with social norms when individuals are evaluating themselves. It appears that the participants compared themselves to the 'ideal', slim, toned or muscular figures shown within the advertisements, which altered how they perceived and evaluated their bodies. The advertisements apparently instilled feelings of inadequacy about the participants' figures and provided an unrealistic standard for comparison. What is particularly noteworthy about this is that these changes in body image occurred after just a few minutes' exposure to the advertisements. Presumably, such increases in body image dissatisfaction will be small compared to the effects of the chronic exposure to such advertisements that individuals experience outside of the experimental setting. This assumption is supported by Stice et al.'s (1994) finding that the more people were exposed to magazines and television, the higher their levels of body dissatisfaction.

In Study 1, the body image of both exercisers and sedentary individuals was detrimentally affected, but the exercisers were affected to a significantly greater degree. As improving the attractiveness of one's body is a major motive for exercise, it appears reasonable to suggest that body attractiveness may be of greater concern to the exercising population. Therefore, they may be more affected by media images such as the ones used in this study, becoming more dissatisfied with their bodies as they begin to compare them with such unrealistic role models. This is very unfortunate, given the links between body dissatisfaction and eating disorders and pathogenic weight control methods.

Although the exercisers in Study 1 were affected more than the sedentary individuals, in one sense the results of the latter group are of even greater concern. That is, as poor body image and high social physique anxiety can make individuals less likely to want to exercise in front of others, the effect of exercise-related advertising on exercise participation and adherence may be very negative. This should be of concern not just to those involved in health and exercise promotion, but also to the advertisers themselves, who may be making a large proportion of their potential market less likely to exercise and, therefore, less likely to buy their products. Of course, the present studies did not actually examine the effect of these body image changes on intention to exercise. Therefore, researchers may wish to examine this by, for example, exposing sedentary individuals in the contemplation stage of exercise behaviour change to advertisements and examining the effect on their intention to exercise. It must be noted that despite the influential power of sport advertising, personality traits may also contribute to the likelihood of developing body image disturbances, and therefore this is also an area worthy of future research, to enable identification of individuals most at risk.

In Study 2, the detrimental effects of exercise-related advertising in sedentary females were again clearly demonstrated. There was also a significant increase for the males on the SPAS and ATSA, showing that the body image disturbance in males can also be increased by exposure to sports advertising. Therefore, our SPAS and ATSA findings show that this is not just a female problem, adding further support to the findings of Leit et al. (2002), who found that exposure to muscular male ideals resulted in males having a large discrepancy between their ideal muscularity and their perceived muscularity. However, our findings on the SMBI appear to contradict this, as the male SMBI scores did not increase significantly after exposure to the advertisements. We argue, however, that this finding may reflect the nature of the measure used (SMBI). This is because the SMBI does not clearly represent different levels of muscularity, just levels of thinness and fatness, and the figure drawings do not clearly show muscular definition. Therefore, future research should use a measure, such as that developed by Hildebrandt, Langenbucher and Schlundt (2004), which shows clear muscular dimensions on the figure drawings. This measure could successfully be used to examine whether males strive towards a more muscular, rather than a slimmer physique.

These findings have some important practical implications. Clearly, sport-related advertising in its typical current form, with very thin female models and very muscular male models, has a detrimental effect on people's body image. To reduce this effect, the use of a mixture of body shapes (of average weight) within advertising, is recommended. Such a change would not only be useful in producing more realistic and psychologically healthy body shape ideals, but may also be useful for the advertisers, allowing more people to relate to the advertisements, hence increasing the target audience. Of particular relevance to sports advertising, more average, realistic body images should also be used in the advertising of sports and fitness facilities and products, as this could encourage sedentary individuals to use such facilities and buy such products. This would produce benefits for both those advertising such facilities and products, and for public health.

REFERENCES

Cohn, L. D., & Alder, N. E. (1992). Female and male perceptions of ideal body shapes. *Psychology of Women Quarterly, 16*, 69-79.

Crawford, S., & Eklund, R. (1994). Social Physique Anxiety, Reasons for exercise and attitudes towards exercise settings. *Journal of Sport and Exercise Psychology, 16*, 70-82.

Evans, J, R., Berman, B., & Wellington, W. J. (1997). *Marketing.* Scarborough, Prentice Hall Canada Inc.

Festinger, L. (1954). A theory of social comparison processes. *Human Relations, 7*, 117-140.

Furnham, A., & Radley, S. (1989). Sex differences in the perception of male and female body shapes. *Personality and Individual Differences, 10*, 653-662.

Garner, D. M., Garfinkel, D., Schwartz, D., & Thompson, M. (1980). Cultural expectations of thinness in women. *Psychology Reports, 47*, 483-491.

Graham, M. A., Eich, C., Kephart, B., & Peterson, D. (2000). Relationship among body image, sex, and popularity of high school students. *Perceptual and Motor Skills, 90*, 1187 1193.

Groesz, L. M., Levine, M. P., & Murnen, S K. (2001). The Effect of Experimental Presentation of Thin Media Images on Body Satisfaction: A Meta-Analytic Review. *International Journal of Eating Disorders, 31 (1)*, 1-16.

Grover, V. P., Keel, P. K., & Mitchell, J. P. (2003). Gender Differences In Implicit Weight Identity. *International Journal of Eating Disorders, 34 (1)*, 125-135.

Hargreaves, D. A., & Tiggemann, M. (2004). Idealized media images and adolescent body image: 'comparing boys and girls'. *Body Image, 1*, 351-361.

Hart, E. A., Leary, M. R., & Rejeski, W. J. (1989) The measurement of social physique anxiety. *Journal of Sport and Exercise Psychology, 11*, 94-104.

Hildebrandt, T., Langenbucher, J., & Schlundt, D.G. (2004). Muscularity concerns among men: development of perceptual and attitudinal measures. *Body Image: An International Journal of Research, 1*, 169–81.

Holle, C. (2004). Male Body Image: Self-Perceived Weight Status and Avoidance of Body Exposure. *Perceptual and Motor Skills, 99 (3)*, 853-860.

Kimmel, S. B., & Mahalik, J. R. (2004). Measuring masculine body ideal distress: development of a measure. *International Journal of Mens Health, 3*, 1-11.

Lantz, C. D., Hardy, C. J., & Ainsworth, B. E. (1997). Social Physique Anxiety and perceived exercise behaviour. *Journal of Sport Behaviour, 20*, 83-93.

Lantz, C. D., Rhea, D. J., & Mayhew, J. L. (2001). The drive for size: a psycho behavioural model of muscle dysmorphia. *International Sports Journal, 5 (1)*, 71-86.

Lavine, H., Sweeney, D., & Wagner, S. H. (1999). Depicting women as sex objects in television advertising: Effects on body dissatisfaction. *Personality and Social Psychology Bulletin, 25*, 1049-1058.

Leit, R. A., Gray, J. J., & Pope, Jr., H. G. (2002). The Media's Representation of the Ideal Male Body: A Cause for Muscle Dysmorphia?. *International Journal of Eating Disorders, 31(3)*, 334-338.

Leit, R. A., Pope, Jr., H. G., & Gray, J. J. (2001). Cultural expectations of muscularity in men: The evolution of Playgirl centerfolds. *International Journal of Eating Disorders, 29,* 90–93.

Lindeman, A. K. (1999). Quest for ideal weight: Costs and consequences. *Medicine Science In Sports & Exercise, 31,* 1135-1140.

Martin, K. A., Rejeski, W. J., Leary, M. R., McAuley, E., & Bane, S. (1997). Is the Social Physique Anxiety Scale Really Multidimensional? Conceptual and Statistical Arguments for a Unidimensional Model. *Journal of Sport and Exercise Psychology, 19,* 359-367.

McCabe, M. P., & Ricciardelli, L. A. (2004). Body image dissatisfaction among males across the lifespan: A review of past literature. *Journal of Psychosomatic Research, 56 (6),* 675-685.

McDermott, L. (1996). Toward a feminist understanding of physicality within the context of women's physically active and sporting lives. *Sociology of Sport Journal, 13, 1,* 1230.

Motl, R., & Conroy, D. E. (2000). Validity and factorial invariance of the Social Physique Anxiety Scale. *Medicine and Science in Sports and Exercise, 32,* 1007-1017.

Mueller, W. H., Joos, S. K., & Schull, W. J. (1985). Alternative measurements of obesity: Accuracy of body silhouettes and reported weights and heights in a Mexican/American sample. *International Journal of Obesity, 9,* 193-200.

Petrie, T. (1993). Disordered eating in female collegiate gymnasts: Prevalence and personality/attitudinal correlates. *Journal of Sport and Exercise Psychology, 15,* 424-436.

Pope, H. G. Jr., & Gruber, A. J. (1997). Muscle dysmorphia: An underrecognised form of body dysmorphic disorder. *Psychosomatics, 38,* 548-557.

Pope, H. G. Jr., Philips, K. A., & Olivardia, R. (2000). *The Adonis complex: The secret crisis of male body obsession.* New York: Free Press.

Rabak-Wagener, J., Eickoff-Shemeck, J., & Kelly-Vance, L. (1998). The effect of media analysis on attitudes and behaviors regarding body image among college students. *Journal of American College Health, 47 (1)* 29-37.

Sabiston, C. M., & Munroe, K.J. (2001). *The Effect of Sport and Fitness Advertising on Social Physique Anxiety among Females.* Proceedings of the annual meeting of the Association for the Advancement of Applied Sport Psychology. Denton, Texas: RonJon Publishing.

Silberstein, L. R., Striegel-Moore, R. H., Timko, C., & Rodin, J. (1988). Behavioural and psychological implications of body attractiveness for women. *Sex Roles, 14,* 519-532.

Spitzer, B. L., Henderson, K. A., & Zivian, M. T. (1999). Gender differences in population versus media body sizes: A comparison over four decades. *Sex Roles, 40,* 545–565.

Stice, E., Maxfield, J., & Wells, T. (2003). Adverse effects of social pressure to be thin on young women: An experimental investigation of the effects of "fat talk". *International Journal of Eating Disorders, 34 (1),* 109-116.

Stice, E., Schupak-Nemberg, E., Shaw, H. E., & Stein, R. I. (1994). Relation of the media exposure to eating disorder symptomatology: An examination of mediating mechanisms. *Journal of Abnormal Psychology, 103,* 836-840.

Striegal-Moore, R., Silberstein, L. & Rodin, J. (1986). Toward an understanding of risk factors for Bulimia. *American Psychologist, 41, 3,* 246-263.

Stunkard, A., Sorensen, T., & Schlsinger, F. (1983). Use of the Danish Adoption Register for the study of obesity and thinness. In S. Kety (Ed.), *The genetics of neurological and psychiatric disorders* (pp.115-120). New York: Raven Press.

Tiggemann, M. (2004). Body image across the adult lifespan: stability and change. *Body Image, 1*, 29-41.

Wiseman, C. V., Gray, J. J., Moismann, J. E., & Aherns, A. H. (1992). Cultural expectations of thinness in women: an update. *International Journal of Eating Disorders, 11*, 85-89.

Yamamiya, Y., Cash, T. F., Melnyk, S. E., Posavac, H. D., & Posavac, S. S. (2005). Women's exposure to thin-and-beautiful media images: Body image effects of media-ideal internalization and impact-reduction interventions. *Body Image, 2*, 74-80.

Yang, C-F. J., Gray, P., & Pope, Jr., H. G. (2005). Male Body Image in Taiwan Versus the West: Yanggang Zhiqi Meets the Adonis Complex. *The American Journal of Psychiatry, 162 (2)*, 263-269.

.

In: Body Image: New Research
Editor: Marlene V. Kindes, pp. 79-108

ISBN 1-60021-059-7
© 2006 Nova Science Publishers, Inc.

Chapter IV

BODY IMAGE AND THE SELF-CONCEPT IN BULIMIA: INFORMATION PROCESSING TO SALIENT FACETS OF THE SELF

Michel Girodo[1],* and Mariette Caner de la Guardia[2]
[1]University of Ottawa, Canada
[2]University of Zurich, Switzerland

ABSTRACT

Body image knowledge and its cognitive organization within the self concept were studied in four partial replicating experiments using young women with bulimic tendencies. We used a choice decision reaction time methodology to establish an empirical foundation for measuring body image schemas and then expanded the paradigm to accommodate the investigation of other facets and dynamics of the self. The classical self-referencing paradigm was first applied to index responses of body image to an actual self, and was adapted to allow for sentence stems to cue the relevant self components of interest such as those of a possible self. The reaction time paradigm was further elaborated to measure encoding to complete sentences by using a letter-word-sentence unfolding method allowing for the study of decisional information processing to self statements of the kind found in psychometrically derived self concept scales.

The first study established baseline data and confirmed the presence of body image schemas when self-referencing to body shape vs. trait words in women preoccupied or not preoccupied with their body shape. In the second study information processing to "dreamed-of" and "feared-of" facets of possible selves revealed that words representing body image concerns are processed as schemas or knowledge structures only if they are referenced to the self, and that actual self and possible self facets can co-exist as constructs within the same person. Body image words in bulimic women activate cognitive schemas only when referenced to an aspect of the self. The third experiment

* Correspondence concerning this article should be addressed to Dr. Michel Girodo, School of Psychology, University of Ottawa, Canada, K1N 6N5. Girodo@uottawa.ca.

replicated the latter findings with women with bulimic behaviors and found that in addition to being schematic for body image words these women tended to be aschematic for attributes that described social and personality traits. The fourth experiment presented items from Physical, Social, and Academic self concept scales and found that negative body image schemas "spill over" and influence social and academic self concepts. Women, distinguished by the presence or absence of bulimic tendencies processed body shape words more quickly when describing themselves, their dreamed of and feared-of body image, and their Physical and Social self concept. The findings that bulimic women aspire more to be thin more than to be socially or academically competent, or to describe themselves positively in terms of personality traits were consistent with the view that self and identity eccentricities in bulimic women originate with socially constructed standards.

Keywords: Self-concept, bulimia, information processing, body image

INTRODUCTION

Writings on the structure of the self have long included the body as a defining feature. Identified as a material self (James, 1890), a somatic substructure (Sarbin, 1952), subjective feelings and attitudes towards one's body (Fisher & Cleveland, 1968), or a physical self (Marsh & O'Neill, 1984), these expressions testify to the acceptance of body image as a universal aspect of personal awareness and psychological development.

Body image began to earned a life of its own mainly after Bruch (1962) drew attention to the clinical significance of body image distortions in anorexia nervosa and other eating disorders (Bruch, 1973). When the notion of "a persistent overconcern with body shape and weight" and the diagnostic criteria for the major eating disorders implicated the self in anorexia nervosa and bulimia nervosa spoke to a "disturbance in the way in which one's body weight and shape is experienced, (and the) undue influence of body weight and shape on self-evaluation" (APA, 1994) body image disturbance acquired a warrant for a wide range of research initiatives. Although the body was allowed as part of the self, much of the early research on the body image construct was conducted outside of a self-concept theoretical framework as many researchers concentrated on the development and validation of techniques for measuring body image perceptions (Thompson, 1990; Williamson, 1990). The diverse findings emerging from these efforts (see Cash & Pruzinski, 1990) generally confirmed the view that eating disordered patients tend to overestimate and be more disparaging of their body shape, but there remained large gaps in our understanding of the fundamental role of body image in disordered psychological functioning and the place of body image within self concept theories. Some believed that, in the absence of an independent validation of the construct "body image disturbance", the concept had been prematurely reified and questioned the need for such a concept for understanding eating disorders (Hsu & Sobriewicz, 1991). Others, were firm about the importance of studying body image in the context of a the self (Fisher, 1970) and claimed that an adequate understanding of a pathological overconcern with body shape and weight could not be obtained without the essential consideration of how body image is implicated in the development and dynamics of the self-concept (Mahoney (1990).

The contributions in this volume reflect the diverse theoretical, methodical, and applied interests the topics of body image and the self concept have evoked over the years. The two topics generally continue to deal with the two topics separately as journals have staked out their own turf for disseminating advances in their defined area. For example, an entire journal is devoted to a social-cognitive approach to self and identity while an international journal on eating disorders no longer serves as a research outlet on body image.

In this chapter we present the findings of a research program aimed at linking ideas related to theories about the self and ideas about how body image are implicated in bulimia. First, we sought to gather evidence about "body image" in terms of basic elements that could be brought to the laboratory with a research paradigm and methodology that could be easily adapted to accommodate new questions as they emerged. Second, we wanted to insert this basic notion of body image into a theoretical framework that fit current notions regarding the structure of the self-concept. Finally, we wanted to use the same methodology for examining the structural and isolated aspects of body image as represented in the "self" to study the dynamic role body image plays socially and developmentally. The chapter begins with an overview of the conceptual and issues underlying the "self" and "body image". It then presents the evolution of ideas that sought to link these two constructs together by describing the findings of four experiments, each of which served as a building block for studying social cognitions of bulimics in the laboratory.

Is "Body Image" a Visual Construction?

In one of the earliest uses of the term "body image" Schilder (1953) wondered whether the concept was represented as an actual mental picture of the body. This is not just a casual curiosity about the term, it is a fundamental question. Everyone can close their eyes and visualize their body in front of them. You can see your body as a visual representation of substance with shape, contour, outline, set off from a background, much like in a photograph. But the fact that we can do this does not mean that it is this type of cognitive representation that impacts psychologically in every day life. And, the fact that most of us are curious about what we look like in a recently taken photograph does not make this the most interesting or fruitful approach for studying how the "concept we have of our body" has a psychological influence.

Researchers have long emphasized the importance of studying body image in the context of the structure of the self, and it was in this connection that Kihlstrom and Cantor (1984) focused on the question of how body image is represented phenomenologically. If it is assumed that an image of the body, in the literal sense, is indeed be represented as an aspect of the self, does it play the same role as other types of self-descriptions? For example, the self is often described with adjectives that are usually trait descriptions of people (e.g., extroverted, emotional) or social attributes (e.g., popular, rich). Compare these with body shape attributes (e.g., tall, plump, skinny, heavy) which are more concrete and capable of evoking a perceptual image. Do these play the same role cognitively as trait adjectives when contributing to the self? Perhaps body shape attributes represent essentially different types of stimuli and are processed differently than trait information. If so, body image attributes may play a fundamentally different role in the self constructions and underlie some of the body image disturbances we see in eating disorders (Altabe & Thompson, 1996).

The history of the self-concept has long included the body as an elemental feature of the construct. William James made an important distinction between two fundamental aspects of the self, the "Me" and the "I" (James, 1890). The "Me" being the self as object, representing an empirical aggregate of things objectively known about the self, and the "I" representing the self as subject, or the knower, the agent responsible for constructing the Me-self by organizing and interpreting one's experiences, thus, viewed as subjective. It is the "Me" that came to be known as the self-concept and defined as "the sum total of all that he [a man] can call his" (James, 1890, p. 291). Moreover, this total can be subdivided into three constituents: the material self, the social self, and the spiritual self. James identified the body or physical self as forming part of the material self and held it to be the innermost part of this aspect of the self-concept (James, 1890). His emphasis on the body as being one of the most fundamental features of the self-concept attests to the importance of body image in shaping this conception. Research on body image, however, although extensive and varied, has generally been conducted outside of a self-concept theoretical framework (Thompson, 1990).

Since body shape attributes evokes a perceptual (nonverbal) image of their referent, in contrast to trait adjectives which are abstract and thus are confined to the verbal domain, (Schilder, 1953), does this make for an important psychological difference? When it comes to the knowledge a person has about him self or herself are these two types of stimuli processed homogeneously as a single cognitive structure or as two separate ones? There are at least two opposing theories concerned with the nature of concepts and the representation of knowledge that are relevant to this question. The first is represented by the classical view of concepts (Smith & Medin, 1981). This view holds that all information, whether verbal or nonverbal, is transformed into a common descriptive format and is then processed homogeneously as a single cognitive structure. The second theory, the dual-coding approach (Paivio, 1986), holds that there are two separate cognitive subsystems, one specializing in the processing of verbal information and another for the processing of non-verbal information. This view implies that the stimulus complex of body image experience would stand as a separate configuration of the self-concept, and therefore, would not be part of the structure defined by verbal representations of the self.

Body Image as a Self Knowledge Schema

James (1890) clearly recognized that one's self-concept is built on knowledge. But, given the sheer variety of information available to us about ourselves at any point in time, and that it generally exceeds that to which most individuals can attend to a given moment, we have to be selective in terms of what information in the environment we should attend to. What appears to have unequaled power in grabbing our attention is self-relevant information (Markus, 1980). Referred to as self-schemata (Markus, 1980), and also known as salient identities (Stryker, 1987) or core conceptions (Russell, Cahill, & Spain, 1992), this provides us with a theoretical framework for studying how the two constructs - - body image and self-concept could be related to one another. As Markus's (1980) claimed, "schemas are the basis of the selectivity that operates in information processing" (p. 109) and they include information about our body, our personality and our social attributes. As we process this information these self-schemas make up knowledge structures or cognitive generalizations about the self. These generalizations are based on past experiences and they develop as a result of the repeated similar categorization of behavior by oneself or others. They serve to organize and interpret incoming information related to the self and form knowledge structures. So, from past social experiences, we might describe ourselves using body shape adjectives such as smart, plump, emotional, and popular and form our self concept on the basis of these self descriptive inferences.

A Research Paradigm for Studying Self Knowledge

The self is not just a passive structure containing information that has been organized around some theme, it is also an active processor of information, capable of influencing the selection and retention of information. Our schemas are only about those aspects of the self that are relevant, important, or distinctive in some way. Because of this, persons with well-articulated self-schemas for a particular trait or dimension of the self-concept can more readily process information (i.e., make faster decisions and judgments) and have relatively better memory for information relevant to that domain (Markus,1980). As such, it can process selectively and shape the content of the self (Markus & Wurf, 1987).

One of the research paradigms for studying knowledge structures and information processing looks at decisional response latencies to stimulus words in the context of a self-referencing instructional set. In other words, we present a word on a computer screen and ask "Does this word describe you?" The time it takes to decide is indexed as the latency to a make a key board response. Information relevant to a person's self-schema has been found to be processed more quickly and to be better recalled than information not central to a person's self-definition (Markus, 1977; Rogers, Kuiper, & Kirker, 1977). Also, the best memory performance is obtained under conditions that encourage meaning-based elaboration or distinctive processing (e.g., Craik & Tulving, 1975). Relative to other information that could be organized around schemas, schemas pertaining to the self organize, discriminate, and process information more quickly, more deeply, and facilitate easier recall (Markus, 1980).

What qualifies as a schema has followed various methodological conventions (e.g. Segal, 1986). Some self-schema studies typically include measures of reaction time to make a judgment, the number of words selected as self descriptive, and an incidental recall of the adjectives presented. Other studies use questionnaires and focus on the descriptive definition of schemas by looking at patterns of attitudes, beliefs and perceptions.

Self-schemas and their facets, as measured by speed of information processing, and memory for schema-consistent information, are constructs in the study of differentiated knowledge structures specifically relevant to the self-concept (Vitousek & Hollon, 1990). Although negative mood and depression may also influence information processing in persons suffering from bulimic symptoms (e. g., Segal, 1988), it is important to examine the ways in which various facets of the self can form self-schemas around body image and how these schemas may impact on information processing in their own right.

BODY IMAGE: ISOLATED OR EMBEDDED IN THE SELF?

In an early application of this paradigm for eating disorders, Markus, Hamill, and Sentis (1987) examined reaction times to body image adjectives in women who were objectively overweight and obese (schematics) compared with normal weight (aschematic) females. Supporting Markus' (1980) model, overweight participants responded affirmatively to a larger number of 'fat' adjectives and silhouettes and did it faster, whereas normal weight participants responded affirmatively to a larger proportion of 'thin' adjectives and silhouettes and did so faster. In a more recent study by Stein and Nyquist (2001) these investigators obtained the same findings among a sample of fifty-three clinically bulimic women. Of equal interest is the question which asks if similar knowledge schemas might be found in persons who think they are fat, but are not so objectively. Elsewhere, the work by Strauman and Glenberg (1994) examining decisional processes for body image information, and by Altabe and Thompson (1996) illustrate different approaches to looking at how body image information may be processed to defining what may be a schema construct.

If body image originates from a process which is independent of the process which underlies trait self knowledge, then body image may not play the same role ascribed to the self-concept. Can information about one's body become organized cognitively in a way that qualifies as a schema? These were the first questions our research had to address before asking other questions about body image and its dynamic role in constructions of self and identity. In all studies informed consent was obtained from all participants following the description of the study and steps were taken to ensure the fulfillment of the ethical standards for conducting research with human participants as set forth by the American Psychological Association.

Experiment 1

The first experiment examined if knowledge related to body image could be represented as cognitive schemas, if they are dependent on their centrality to the self, and if schemas of this kind can differentially influence the memory for such knowledge. We sought to establish an empirical foundation for responding to body image adjectives under self-referencing and non-self-referencing conditions, and to compare responses to body image adjectives versus trait adjectives. The methodology for this first experiment described in detail elsewhere (Girodo, 2003) and which served as the basis for three subsequent experiments is summarized here.

Method

Participants

Among 600 female undergraduates volunteering for an experiment on word perception, 48 participants, aged from 18-25 years, were selected because they had obtained either high or low scores on the Body Shape Questionnaire (BSQ). This 34-item self-report instrument (Cooper & Taylor, 1988; Cooper, Taylor, Cooper, & Fairburn, 1987) assesses excessive concerns, preoccupations and dissatisfaction with body shape in persons with bulimic tendencies. Twenty-four Low scoring (44-63) participants expressing little to no concern with body shape, and 24 High scoring (111-188) participants expressing from moderate to extreme concern with their body shape took part. Participants were asked to indicate their height and weight from which a Body mass Index was calculated from Metropolitan Life Insurance (1983) tables.

Stimulus Materials and Equipment

A set of 40 adjectives, half representing body shape and half personality trait descriptors served as stimulus words. Ten body shape words referred to "thin" attributes (e.g., skinny, lean, slim) and 10 to "fat" attributes (obese, plump, etc.). The list was identical to that used by Markus, Hamill, and Sentis (1977), and was augmented from a thesaurus. Personality trait adjectives were selected from Anderson's (1968) likableness ratings of 55 personality trait words. Ten "positive" words were chosen for their high ratings (e.g., intelligent, generous, brave), and 10 "negative" words for their low ratings (naive, vulgar, unsociable etc.). In the Semantic rating task, 10 non-words (e.g., thol, artnn) were included. Four sets of randomized adjectives with all stimulus words were created. Stimuli were presented and latencies measured on a PC computer A keyboard key was marked "yes" and an adjacent key was marked "no".

Reaction Time Task

Participants rested the fingers of their dominant hand on the two response keys and were instructed to respond "yes" or "no" as quickly as possible to each word presented. Half of the participants were in the Semantic rating condition, where they indicated if the word that appeared on the screen was real or not. The other half were in the Self-referencing condition and were instructed to respond in terms of whether the word described them or not. Words appeared on the screen for 2 s followed by a 4 s interstimulus interval, allowing a 6 s response window. Lists were presented twice.

Measures

Response latency in milliseconds (ms) was measured from the onset of the stimulus to key press. After the response time task two memory measures were obtained: 1. participants provided a free recall measure by writing down over a 5 min period all the words they could recall, and 2. for recognition memory, they were shown a list of the words presented (including 6 additional semantically related foils for each stimulus type), and they checked which words had been shown. Participants then provided self-ratings on each of the 40 adjectives using a 1-7-point scale anchored "very much unlike me" to "very much like me."

Results

High and Low BSQ participants did not differ from each other (126.7 lb and 131.2 lb), or in Body Mass Index (BMI), (21.0 and 21.6. respectively).

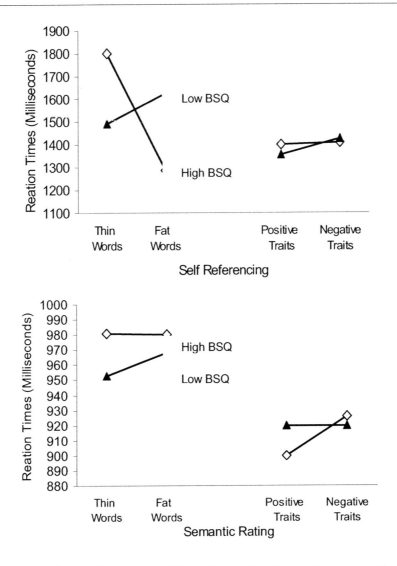

Figure 1. Median reaction time in response to thin and fat words and to positive and negative trait words under Self-referencing (Fig 1a) and Semantic Rating (Fig 1b) conditions by participants scoring high and low on the Body Shape Questionnaire (BSQ).

Self-Ratings

A 4 x 2 x 2 Analysis of Variance (ANOVA) on self ratings showed a main effect for Stimulus Type, $F(3, 41) = 62.94$, $p < .001$, and an interaction with Groups, $F(3, 41) = 24.20$, $p < .001$. Scheffé tests revealed that while Groups did not differ in their ratings of personality trait adjectives, for body adjectives, High BSQ participants rated themselves more as fat ($M = 4.11$) than thin ($M = 2.25$), while the reverse was true for Low BSQ participants (fat $M = 1.60$, thin $M = 5.0$, $p < .01$).

Reaction Times (RT)

The median RT for all "yes" responses averaged over the two trials served as the summary RT statistic. In a 4 x 2 x 2 ANOVA, a Task main effect, $F(1, 33) = 50.88$, $p < .001$, revealed significantly faster RTs under Semantic than Self-referencing conditions. Thus, the same words when contextualized as referring to one's self produced longer latencies than when contextualized semantically.

A significant Group x Stimulus Type interaction, $F(3, 31) = 8.23$, $p < .001$, and a second order interaction with Task, $F(3, 31) = 6.96$, $p < .001$ followed by Scheffé tests confirmed an overall tendency for Low compared with High BSQ participants to endorse thin body words more quickly, and for High BSQ participants to endorse fat body words more quickly ($p < .05$). Figure 1 illustrates these findings.

Memory

An ANOVA on free recall scores showed a significant Task, $F(1, 43) = 74.56$, $p < .001$, Stimulus Type, $F(3, 41) = 9.43$, $p < .001$, and Task x Stimulus Type interaction, $F(3, 41) = 11.25$, $p < .001$. Scheffé tests showed that Self-referencing resulted in better recall for trait words only. Body shape words were equally well recalled under Self-referencing as Semantic conditions. Similar results were obtained for recognition memory: Task, $F(1, 42) = 11.25$, $p < .04$; Task x Stimulus Type, $F(3, 41) = 5.55$, $p < .003$. Scheffé tests showed better recognition memory for Self-referencing trait adjectives only (Girodo, 2003).

While High and Low BSQ females saw themselves in the same way in their trait self-descriptions, they were distinguished by their "fat" and "thin" body self ratings. The faster encoding of fat adjectives by High BSQ females is consistent with the view that body image concerns are organized as a cognitive structure. Four interesting points, which served to launch the next investigations, emerged from these findings.

1. Because the stimulus words e.g., "fat" or "thin" evoke the same response time under Semantic conditions and differential response time under Self referencing condition, this makes it clear that what affects information processing has less to do with the stimuli themselves than with the personal meaning these words have for the participant. It is when the words are contextualized or referred to a self that they acquire their potential. The "self" can indeed act as a processor and organizer of information about body image.
2. When the words are not made to refer to the self, trait words are generally processed faster than body shape words. This baseline difference between abstract and concrete words may suggest that body image information is simply processed differently than information that comes in the form of personality or social adjectives
3. Recall that Markus, et al., (1987) found a cognitive organization of body image stimuli among women who had were objectively overweight, i.e., they had a personal visual or concrete point of reference. In the present study a similar cognitive structure was found in women who did not differ in weight or Body Mass Index but who simply thought they were overweight. Thus, information about body image may not have to be related to an actual physical or visual equivalent. It may suffice that a body image schema can originate out of an imagined body condition. If the condition is imagined, how much of this self is socially constructed, and what role do dynamics of the self play in maintaining the condition?

4. Self-referencing had a clear effect on memory but only for trait adjectives. Body shape words were equally recalled or retrieved following either Semantic or Self-referenced encoding. This is similar to the findings of King, Polivy, and Herman (1991) obtained with females concerned with their weight. They found a good memory for food and weight related information either when self-referenced or when the information was presented as an essay about another person. As a partial answer to the question posed by Kihlstrom and Cantor (1984), an image of the body, at least at the level represented by words, can indeed be represented as an aspect of the self.

Caveats

The fact that Groups and Stimulus Type did not contribute to memory suggests that body image words do not differentially influence retrieval after encoding to the self. Methodological factors may account for this. Self-schema studies (e. g., Markus, 1977) typically allow some time to pass, and/or interpolate a task between stimulus presentation and recall, and this was not the case here. Also, the easy organization of stimulus words and the short list lengths may not have imposed memory demands that might have allowed retrieval differences between groups to emerge. Another source error may be the lack of counterbalancing of the index and middle fingers to signal a "yes" and "no" response.

Another possible limitation of this and the other experiments presented here is that a co-variation with depression might underlie the results. The present results may have been moderated by negative mood activated by the self-referencing task. However, the present study did not find that participants in the High and Low BSQ groups differed in RT or memory for negative body image or trait words. Because a greater salience of negative views of one self from a memory standpoint did not distinguish these females it might be suggested that mood did not play a role in the outcome of the present experiments.

THE ACTUAL SELF AND THE POSSIBLE SELF

The self may be represented by knowledge units other than those defined by "actual" self-descriptions. Various facets of the self-concept such as "possible selves" (Markus & Nurius, 1986), the "ideal self", and more specifically the "Dream-of being" and the "Fear-of becoming" selves (Girodo, 2003) are relevant to establishing if these facets of the self can serve as cognitive constructs. In a reaction-time study of spontaneous generation of ideal personality traits, Deutsch, Kroll, Weible, Letourneau, and Goss (1984) obtained converging evidence for the ideal-self as an integrated knowledge structure. Likewise, Ogilvie (1987) reported on the "undesired self" as a representation of a coherent personality construct. A desired body shape and a fear of weight gain have been studied in connection with physical appearance, perceptual overestimation, and other correlates of body image disturbance (Thompson, Penner, & Altabe, 1990), and a Body-Image Ideals Questionnaire to assess personal investment in body image ideals has been developed (Cash and Czymanski, 1995)

In the next experiment we sought to examine if information processing similar to that found in self schemas for actual body image could be found for a possible body image. Using the same "thin" and "fat" adjectives as in Exp 1 for which reaction time and memory data had been obtained we then re-cast the words into two different facets of the self - - an "I am afraid of" and an "I dream of" self. We sought to examine the extent to which women preoccupied with their body shape and weight could have self-knowledge regarding two types of "possible body image" ("I am afraid of" and an "I dream of" self) organized as more distinct cognitive structures than women who did not share this preoccupation.

Experiment 2

It was predicted that speed of information processing and memory for words that are characteristic of these core schemas would be differentially influenced by the specific facet of the self-schemas into which the words are cast ("I am afraid of" and "I dream of" selves). Thus, in contrast to the faster RTs only to thin words found in Exp 1, it was predicted that faster RTs to fat words also would occur if the self reference was to a "feared-of" self. Importantly, this was a within participant design, and it was expected that both thin and fat words could be encoded quickly by the same participant. This effect it was believed would be amplified in High BSQ participants. Memory for body image words would favor High rather than Low BSQ participants.

The methodology employed the same 40 word list, reaction time equipment, and memory assessment methodology as in Exp. 1. The Self-referencing paradigm was adapted to measure RTs to desired and feared-of body image components. Two sentence stems, "I Dream of Being _____", and "I'm Afraid of Being _____", formed part of two propositional statements. In the experiment, one or the other stem randomly preceded the presentation of either thin, positive trait, or fat, negative trait adjectives, respectively. A yes/no keyboard response indicated whether the word was an exemplar or not of a wished-for/feared-of-self-attribute.

Participants
Thirty-five females aged 17-28 (M= 19.51 years) drawn for the same pre-tested pool of undergraduate females as Exp. 1 were randomly assigned to either a High BSQ (n = 21) or a Low BSQ (n = 14) group.

Instructions
Participants were provided with specific meanings by being told: "We all have special day-dreams and fantasies about the kind a person we would like to be; and we all know of some dreaded or feared of thing that could happen to us. Some words to be shown might represent something you desperately or very much would like to be, and other words could represent things they might be quite afraid of becoming. Now, we want you to distinguish between things that are simply desirable from those that you really dream of being. Likewise, don't make a choice just because it is simply an undesirable thing, choose those things you are really afraid of being.

Procedure

One second (s) prior to showing a pertinent word, the participant was cued with a 2 s "Dream of Being" or "Afraid of Being" phrase that appeared on the screen, the purpose of which was to cue the individual to one or the other "possible self" of interest: the ideal vs. feared or undesired self. This was followed by the appearance of a stimulus word. A 4 s intertrial interval provided a response window. After 10 familiarization trials participants responded to two trials of four randomized word lists. Free recall and recognition memory measures and self-ratings on the 40 adjectives were obtained as in Exp. 1.

Results

As in Exp 1, High and Low BSQ participants did not differ in self reported weight (127.3 lb and 131.1 lb), or BMI (20.9 and 21.2).

Self-Ratings

A 2 x 4 ANOVA of the self-ratings produced similar main and interaction effects as had been obtained with participants in Exp 1: Stimulus Type F (3, 27) = 52.09, $p < .001$; Group x Stimulus Type F (3, 27) = 16.70, $p < .001$. Scheffé tests showed no differences in trait self-ratings between High and Low BSQ participants. As in Exp 1 High BSQ females rated themselves more as fat ($M = 4.55$) than thin ($M = 1.99$) compared with Low BSQ females who showed an opposite pattern of scores (fat $M = 1.60$, and thin $M = 4.98$).

Dream and Fear Endorsements

A 2 x 4 ANOVA on the number of "yes" responses to the various word stimuli produced a significant Stimulus Type $F(3, 27) = 3.40$, $p < .03$, and Groups x Stimulus Type interaction $F(3, 27) = 6.48$, $p < .002$. Scheffé tests showed that High BSQ participants endorsed more thin adjectives ($M = 8.20$) following the "Dream of Being" prompt, and more fat adjectives ($M = 9.01$) following the "Fear of Being" prompt compared with Low BSQ participants ($M = 4.90$, and 4.95, respectively, $p < .01$). In response to Dream of being prompts fewer positive traits were chosen by High than by Low BSQ participants ($M = 5.90$ vs. 8.00, $p < .01$, respectively). No differences in negative trait selections were obtained; High BSQ = 4.55, Low BSQ = 4.75).

Reaction Times

Median RTs showed a significant Stimulus Type $F(3, 27) = 11.58$, $p < .001$, and Stimulus Type x Groups interaction $F(3, 27) = 8.88$, $p < .001$. Scheffé tests confirmed faster RTs for High BSQ participants in response to "Dream of Being" (thin) *and* "Fear of Being" (fat) body words compared with Low BSQ participants. The High BSQ participants, however, were slower in responding to Dream-of-Being (positive trait) attributes compared with Low BSQ participants. These RT findings are illustrated in Figure 2.

Memory

As with the Actual self representations in Exp 1, a 2 x 4 ANOVA on the free recall and recognition memory scores did not reveal any significant main or interaction effects.

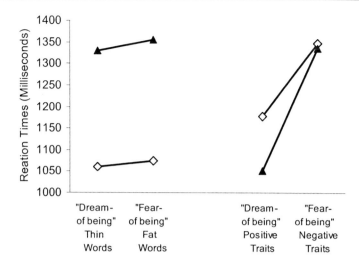

Figure 2. Median reaction time in response to "Dream-of-being" and "Fear-of-being" thin and fat words and to positive and negative trait words by participants scoring High and Low on the Body Shape Questionnaire (BSQ).

Conclusion

The faster encoding of schema-relevant information referenced to "I dream of" and "I am afraid of" body words suggests that, for persons preoccupied with their body shape, these two possible body images may be organized as cognitive structures. Given the comparability of this participant population with that of Exp. 1, and inasmuch as an "I dream of" and an "I am afraid of" body image might be encoded schematically, this would suggest that *possible* body image schemas can exist co-extensively with an *actual* body image schema.

The processing of the same thin and fat words was a function of differences in body shape preoccupation, and whether actual or possible facets of the self were primed. Again, as in Exp 1 we may conclude that it is not so much the semantic meaning of the word "fat" or "thin" that influences information processing for these participants, as it is the facet of the self to which the words are made to refer. The fact that in Exp 1 a faster encoding of the "fat" adjectives was obtained but not to the "thin" adjectives, and that "thin" words were able to produce faster RTs when referenced to a "dreamed-of" self suggests again that it is the organizational capacity of the self rather than en inherent property of the word that gives these stimulus words their capacity to influence processing. The present findings argue in favor of meaning accorded body image stimuli as a function of the facet of the self which gives context and meaning to the stimuli.

Two interesting findings served to launch the next series of investigations.

1.   Exp 1 and 2 taken together showed that both an *actual* body image schema and a *possible* body image schema can coexist in bulimic persons. Such coexistence is a necessary requirement for any theory that would posit that knowledge structures of this kind might be dynamically related within a person. With these actual and possible facets of the self more firmly anchored as cognitive constructs, socio-cognitive research using this same research paradigm can proceed to study such

phenomena as discrepancies between women's actual-body image and their "I dream of" and "I am afraid of" body image.

2. Both High and Low BSQ participants provided similar self ratings in their selection of traits representing dream-of-being. However, High BSQ participants encoded dream-of-being positive trait adjectives more slowly than Low BSQ participants. This is a finding similar to the slower processing of positive trait adjectives when self referenced to an actual aspect of the self in Exp 1. This suggests that females with high scores on the BSQ might have less well developed positive trait cognitive structures (both actual and possible). In the third experiment we were more deliberate in examining RTs and memory for trait adjectives.

DISCREPANCIES BETWEEN ACTUAL AND POSSIBLE SELVES

The discrepancy between actual and ideal self has long been described as a contributor to psychological maladjustment, and efforts through the use of the Q sort technique to index the discrepancy between these two constructs (e.g., Rogers & Dymond, 1954) date back half a century. In a similar vein, the notion of a discrepancy between attainments and standards, has also been the focus of social-cognitive theorists and it also has claimed the status of a psychological construct (e.g., Duval & Wicklund, 1972), and later as a specific cognitive structure with motivational, affective and behavioral consequences (Higgins, 1987; Strauman & Higgins, 1987). Higgins (1989) has made an important distinction between "actual self" and the "ideal self". The actual or real self consisting of the attributes that you or another person believes you actually posses, and the ideal or possible self consisting of the attributes that someone (yourself or another) would ideally like to posses (Higgins, 1989). Today, the self is seen in a broad context (Dunkel & Kerpelan, 2005). The self system contains information not just about one's current characteristics, but one's past and possible future selves (Beike & Niedenthal, 1998).

In a series of studies aimed at finding support for these distinctions Strauman, Vookles, Berenstein, Chaiken, and Higgins, 1991 found evidence for linking actual/ideal discrepancies to bulimic participants, and actual /ought discrepancies to anorexic participants. The cognitive structures were estimated by examining the number of participant generated actual-self descriptive traits and their mismatches with idea-self generated traits. These discrepancies were correlated with measures of body shape dissatisfaction, independent of participants' actual body mass.

Experiment 3

The purpose of the third experiment was to replicate the findings of Exp 2 with young women who showed clear indices of bulimic behaviors rather than only a preoccupation with body shape as measured by the BSQ. Also, we wanted to return to an original question pertaining to visual and semantic body image representation. Here we examined if two types of stimuli associated with body image could produce discrepancies between that would be equally related to their RTs. One type of stimuli in the form of silhouette body shapes, and the other in the form of weight measures in lbs. It was to be from these stimuli that actual/ "dreamed-of" and actual/ "feared-of" self report discrepancies were to be calculated, while RTs to "fat" and "thin" words preceded by a "dreamed-of" or "feared-of" prompt were obtained. Finally, in order to better test predictions of better memory for schema related materials we (a) increased the memory load for all stimuli by adding 20 additional adjectives in the stimulus materials, and (b) introduced a 20 min delay between the RT task and the free recall task.

As in Exp 2 it was hypothesized that more thin body words would be self-referenced to "I dream of being", and more fat body words to "I am afraid of being" by individuals scoring high on the Bulimia test (BULIT) compared to those scoring low; and that both thin and fat words would be encoded more quickly this way by High rather than Low BULIT participants. It was also hypothesized that memory for possible body image words would be better for High rather than Low BULIT participants.

Method

Participants

Thirty-four participants, aged 18-26 years ($M= 20.01$), were randomly selected from 550 female undergraduates who volunteered for an experiment on word perception and who scored at the top or bottom 20% on the Bulimia Test (BULIT). The BULIT (Smith & Thelen, 1984) is a 5-point Likert scale including 32 items, which was validated with bulimic women in the general population. It assesses eating habits, and binging and purging behaviors as described in DSM-III-R (Williamson, 1990). Scores 88 and higher identify individuals with bulimic tendencies. Seventeen females had Low BULIT scores (49 and lower), and 17 females had High BULIT scores (more than 88).

Design and Stimulus Words

Testing in the laboratory involved the 4 (Stimulus Type) X 2 (Groups: High vs. Low BULIT scores) design and reaction time methodology identical to Exp. 2 with some variations. By including the words used as foils in the recognition memory task in the list of words presented in the decisional reaction time task he list length for each Stimulus Type was augmented by 50% for a total of 60 words. Thus, among the 60 adjectives half represented body shape and half personality trait descriptors. Fifteen body shape words referred to "thin" attributes (e.g., skinny, lean, slim) and other 15 referred to "fat" attributes (obese, plump, etc.). These words were obtained from the word-list used by Markus, et al. (1987) and were augmented from a thesaurus. Fifteen "positive" words were chosen for their high ratings (e.g., brave, intelligent, generous) and 15 "negative" words for their low ratings (naïve, vulgar, unsociable, etc.) selected from Anderson's (1968) likeableness ratings of 55 personality trait words. No additional body shape stimulus foils could be generated for adequately assessing recognition memory so only free recall was assessed. The same tasks, instruction, and procedures used in Exp 2 were employed.

Measures

Response latencies in ms were measured from the onset of the stimulus to key press. After having completed the response time task, participants completed a free recall task that consisted of writing down over a 5-min period all the words they could recall. A 20-min task consisting of completing an unrelated questionnaire was interpolated between word presentation and free recall. Participants then provided self-ratings on each of the 60 adjectives by completing a 1-7 point scale anchored "very much unlike me" to "very much like me".

Body Shape and Body Weight Indices

Body Shape Perceptions. Nine silhouettes, 5 cm in height depicting increasingly thin (1) to fat (9) female body shapes, adapted from Williamson (1990), were presented on a single page. Participants were asked three questions: 1: (actual body shape) "Select the silhouette that most closely depicts your current body size, as you see it"; 2: (dreamed-of body shape) "Using the silhouette you chose above as point of departure, which is the *first* figure that represents the body you DREAM of being?"; and 3: (feared-of body shape) "Again, starting from your choice in question 1, which is the *first* figure that represents a body you FEAR of being?"

Body Weight Responses. After having reported on their current (actual) weight, participants were asked, (1) (dreamed-of weight): "What would you consider to be your ideal weight, the weight you dream of being?" and (2) (feared-of weight): "Many women have a fear of being fat or becoming fat. How much would you have to weigh before you reached that point?"

Results

While High BULIT participants did not differ from Low BULIT participants in self reported height (M = 5.53 ft vs 5.58 ft), they did report a greater weight and a correspondingly higher BMI than Low BULIT participants (see below).

Self-Ratings

A 2 x 4 Analysis of Variance (ANOVA) on self-ratings showed a main effect for Stimulus type, F (3, 27) = 52.09, p < .001; and an interaction with Groups, F (3, 27) = 16.70, p < .001. Scheffé tests revealed that High and Low BULIT participants did not differ in their self ratings of positive or negative traits. However, for body adjectives, High BULIT participants rated themselves more as fat (M = 4.55) than thin (M = 1.99) compared with Low BULIT participants (fat M = 1.60, and thin M = 4.98.

Dream and Fear Endorsements

A 2 x 4 ANOVA on the number of "yes" responses produced a significant Stimulus Type F (3, 27) = 3.40, p < .03, and a significant Groups x Stimulus Type interaction F (3, 27) = 6.48, p < .002. Scheffé tests revealed that High BULIT participants endorsed more thin adjectives (M = 8.20) following the "Dream of Being" prompt, and more fat adjectives (M = 9.01) following the "Fear of Being" prompt compared with Low BULIT participants (M = 4.90, and 4.95, respectively, p < .01). As with BSQ participants in Exp 2, following the

"Dream of Being" prompt High BULIT participants responded "yes" to fewer positive personality traits than Low BULIT participants (M = 5.21 vs 7.35, p< .01). No differences were obtained between the two groups terms of negative personality trait responses, (High BULIT = 4.40, Low BULIT = 4.95).

Reaction Time

A 2 x 4 ANOVA on median reaction times revealed a significant Stimulus Type F (3, 26) = 6.18, p <. 001, and a significant Stimulus Type x Group interaction F (33, 26) = 6.06, p < .001. Scheffé tests confirmed faster RTs for High BULIT participants in response to dream of being (thin) and fear of being (fat) body words compared with Low BULIT participants. Again, as with BSQ participants in Exp 2, in comparison to Low BULIT participants, High BULIT participants encoded dreamed-of positive trait attributes more slowly. Figure 3 illustrates these findings.

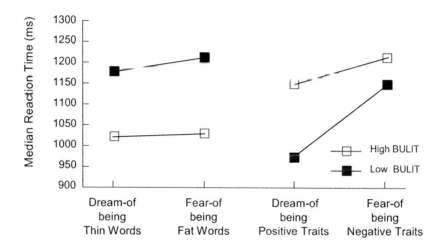

Figure 3. Median reaction time in response to "Dream-of-being" and "Fear-of-being" thin and fat words and to positive and negative trait words by participants scoring High and Low on the Bulimia Test (BULIT).

Memory

A 2 x 4 ANOVA on free recall revealed significant effects for Stimulus Type F (3, 26) = 5.95, p< .01, as well as a Stimulus Type x Group interaction F (3, 26) = 4.87), p< .01. Scheffé tests showed these differences emerged because positive personality trait words were better recalled than any other Stimulus Type by Low BULIT females (M= 6. 75) than High BULIT females (M= 5. 10; p< .01). However, groups did not differ in their recall of thin, fat, or negative trait words.

Weight Responses and Shape perceptions

Table 1 provides a summary of the statistics related to reported weights and silhouette selections between the groups. High BULIT participants chose fatter silhouettes than Low BULIT participants only with respect to self-perceived shape. For both dreamed-of shape and feared-of body shape, both groups selected similar silhouettes. Similarly, while High BULIT participants indicated weighing more than Low BULIT participants, their dreamed-of and feared-of weight reports were identical. The discrepancy measures revealed High BULIT participants to be further away from their dreamed-of body shape and weight, and closer to their feared-of shape and weight compared to the Low BULIT participants' discrepancy measures.

Table 1. Means and t-test Differences Between High and Low BULIT Subjects for Shape and Weight Self-reports.

	Low BULIT	High BULIT	t
Perceived Shape			
1. Actual	3.61	5.14	3.75***
2. Dreamed-of Shape	2.92	2.91	0.00
Discrepancy (1-2)	0.71	2.25	7.32***
3. Feared-of Shape	6.28	6.53	0.02
Discrepancy (3-1)	2.67	1.42	2.77**
Reported Weight			
1. Actual	126.11	137.42	7.76***
2. Dreamed-of Weight	120.84	120.93	0.00
Discrepancy (1-2)	5.15	16.48	8.37***
3. Feared-of Weight	138.05	145.83	1.92
Discrepancy (3-1)	11.94	8.43	2.14*

$* p < .05; ** p < .01; *** p < .001.$

Silhouette/weight selections and RTs to Possible Body Image Words

Correlation coefficients between silhouette selections (actual, "dreamed-of", and "feared-of") and RTs to thin, fat, positive and negative trait words presented after a possible self prompt are presented in Table 2. As is shown, only High BULIT participants produced significant correlations with RTS and almost exclusively only for the silhouette stimulus materials. Significant correlations were obtained between RTs to "dream-of" being thin words and "fear-of" being fat words and the three self-reported silhouette measures. Interestingly, for High BULIT participants their actual silhouette choices and their discrepancies were also correlated with their RTs to negative trait words.

Given Stein and Nyquist's (2001) findings in support of actual body image self-schemas in bulimic individuals and our findings supporting the existence of possible body image schemas among these persons, we can conclude that possible body image schemas can exist co-extensively with actual body image schemas. The fact that both types of schemas can co-exist gives rise to the possibility that they might be dynamically related, and for the discrepancy between the two to be granted a more solid foundation as an intra-psychic processes. The present findings showed that the bigger the distance between actual and ideal body shape, the greater the chances for the dreamed-of body image information to become organized as cognitive schemas, and that the greater the overlap between actual and feared-of shape in bulimic individuals the greater the tendency to process undesirable attributes as a cognitive structure.

Table 2. Correlation Coefficients Between Shape and Weight Self-reports and Speed of Information Processing to Thin and Fat, and Positive and Negative Trait Words.

	Reaction Time "dream of being" thin words		Reaction Time "fear of being" fat words		Reaction Time "dream of being" positive traits		Reaction Time "fear of being" negative traits	
	BULIT		BULIT		BULIT		BULIT	
Perceived Shape	High	Low	High	Low	High	Low	High	Low
1. Actual	-.52 **	-.23	-.51**	+.08	-.29	-.33	-.54**	-.03
2. Dreamed-of Shape	-.08	-.17	-.09	-.31	-.21	-.28	-.02	-.21
Discrepancy (1-2)	-.48*	-.19	-.32	-.27	-.23	-.07	-.55**	-.22
3. Feared-of Shape	-.31	-.01	-.33	-.18	-.18	-.04	-.01	-.13
Discrepancy (3-1)	-.03	-.13	-.04	-.23	-.01	-.11	+.52**	-.19
Reported Weight								
1. Actual	-.29	+.18	-.26	-.14	-.32	-.29	-.14	+.16
2. Dreamed-of Weight	-.09	-.22	-.05	-.32	-.38	-.24	+.06	-.28
Discrepancy (1-2)	-.41	-.21	-.38	-.26	-.27	-.09	-.32	-.27
3. Feared-of Weight	.04	-.38	-.04	-.22	-.21	-.27	+.23	-.15
Discrepancy (3-1)	+.29	+.30	-.17	-.03	-.31	+.21	+.55**	+.15

$* p < .05. ** p < .01.$

Conclusion

1. Results supported the first two hypotheses regarding High BULIT participants' endorsement of more thin and fat body words after the expected prompts, as well as their faster reaction times to "I dream of" thin body words and "I am afraid of" fat body words. This replicates the findings from BSQ participants obtained in Exp 2.

2. If veridical, the greater self-reported weight in High vs. Low BULIT participants counters the commonly held notions of similarity in terms of weight between bulimic and non-bulimics (Thompson & Thompson, 1986). The fact that groups chose similar silhouettes for their dreamed-of and feared-of shape and weight is also at variance with the belief that bulimics have exaggerated ideals (e.g., Zellner, Harner, & Adler, 1989). A study by Thompson and Dolce (1989) found that estimates based on how participants felt about their bodies produced larger indices of overestimation than estimates based on rational judgment of size such as in a silhouette selection. Conceivably, when estimates are anchored and compared using objective stimulus materials as was done with asking for estimates of actual, "dreamed-of" and "feared-of" shapes and weights the subjective element that distorts perceptions may be minimized.

3. In the present study BMI and weight measures or their derived discrepancies were unrelated to any RT measure. This is in contrast to the recent work of Tasca, Balfour, Kurichh, Potvin-Kent, and Bissada (2006). They found higher levels of actual-desired BMI discrepancy (ADBD), lower self concept, and higher body

dissatisfaction among women with a diagnosed bulimia or binge eating disorder. Conceivably, this might be due to their use of a clinically diagnosed eating disorder sample or their method of calculating discrepancies.

4. High BULIT participants showed a consistency in regards measures of schema for certain personality attributes. They: (i) selected fewer positive personality trait words to a "dream-of" being prompt, (ii) produced a slower encoding of positive personality traits to "dreamed-of" attributes, and (iii) had a poorer recall of positive personality trait attributes. Conceivably, this result may have arisen because we were dealing with a more clearly defined bulimic population, and/or because increasing list length and interpolating the RT and memory task with a 20 min delay imposed the additional memory load needed to demonstrate the effects. These results reinforce the serendipitous findings in Exp 2 regarding how positive trait words were processed by persons with bulimic tendencies. A further extension of the choice reaction time paradigm to include comparisons with other traits as the defining stimulus might clarify the role of personality traits in bulimic selves.

5. The bigger discrepancy between actual and dreamed-of shape by individuals with bulimic tendencies is consistent with Strauman et al.'s (1991) findings, who obtained strong correlations between actual/ideal discrepancies and the presence of eating disorders. In the present study the correlations between the discrepancy for feared-of shape and encoding fear-of-being (negative traits) indicate that as the dreamed-of and feared-of discrepancies increase so does the tendency to process undesirable attributes as a cognitive structure. Partial correlations controlling for the Body Mass Index failed to alter the correlations significantly. Why should body image dissatisfaction "spill-over onto other aspects of the self such as negative personality traits? Experiment 4 sought to elucidate this question.

SOCIAL AND ACADEMIC SELF CONCEPT AND BULIMIC BODY IMAGE SCHEMAS

So far we have been focusing on body image and its impact on the particular dimension of the physical self, or one's perceptions and/or estimations of physical appearance. However, body image could also have a powerful impact on other aspects of the self, such as the social and academic self-concepts (Boivin, Vitaro, & Gagnon, 1992; Lerner, Delaney, Hess, Jovanonic, & von Eye, 1990). These other aspects are defined as self perceptions of one's social competence or skill (Blascovich & Tomaka, 1991) and self-perceptions of scholastic competence (Strein, 1993), respectively. The social and academic aspects of a self-concept can be measured reliably.

The Self Descriptive Questionnaire III (SDQ III) developed by Marsh & O'Neill (1984) is clearly the most validated self concept instrument for measuring these aspects of the self. For more than two decades, it has been the object of a long term research strategy to establish its construct validity, as well as its other psychometric properties. The SDQ III is a 136-item instrument designed for university students (aged 18 and older) that measures 13 factors that typically underlie the general self concept in this population. We selected three of the SDQ

III scales: the physical, social, and academic aspects of the self, for study at a methodological and theoretical level. A methodological interest lay in examining if: (1) a psychometrically derived measure of the self would yield the similar results when its stimulus items are presented as a choice reaction time task, i.e., are high scale scores reflecting a strong self concept accompanied by faster reaction times to items that refer to this concept; (2) a linguistic presentation of an SDQ stimulus, in the form of a self descriptive SDQ III declarative statement, might be equivalent to a word stimulus or a pictorial stimulus of body shape in showing the presence of a self schema.

In terms of theory we were interested in testing a compartmentalization model advanced by Showers and Larson (1999). Based on this model, individuals with eating disorders are more likely to display a negatively compartmentalized self-concept overall, that is, it may contain primarily negative attributes, with knowledge about one salient dimension of the self affecting self-beliefs in other domains. Thus, given that in bulimics the physical self is such a salient domain, being mostly characterized by negative self-beliefs around body image (Showers & Larson, 1999), we may ask if such knowledge would also negatively affect the social and academic self-concepts, and whether the physical self-concept, due to its importance for this population, would reflect an even poorer description when compared to the other two self components.

Given Boivin et al. (1992) and Lerner et al.'s (1990) findings concerning the centrality of body image to one's social and academic self-concepts, and based on the compartmentalization model (Showers & Larson, 1999), which holds that individuals with eating disorders are likely to display a self-concept composed of primarily negative attributes, the following predictions were made. It was hypothesized that compared with persons with non-bulimic tendencies, persons with bulimic tendencies would: (1) show a poorer physical, social and academic self-concept overall, and that given the salience of the physical self-concept for this population, they would (2) have less favorable descriptions of their physical self compared with their academic or social self, (3) that their knowledge regarding positive physical self-descriptions would be reflected in h less well organized cognitive structures.

Experiment 4

Method

Participants

Drawing from the same pretested population of 550 university females as in Experiment 3 and based on the same screening criteria, 16 High BULIT and 16 Low BULIT volunteers participated in an experiment on reading and language. The 32 participants were aged from 18-24 years ($M = 19.70$) and were of normal weight.

Stimulus Materials and Procedure

The reaction time methodology of Experiment 3 was adapted for responding to whole propositional sentences. Stimulus materials consisted of 30 items from 3 self concept scales. Ten pertained to a Physical, 10 to a Social, and 10 to an Academic self. Each scale had five positively phrased items (e.g., I have a physically attractive body) and five negatively phrased items (e.g., I dislike the way I look). A 7-point scale anchored *definitely false* to *definitely true* measured certainty of response to each item, with total certainty scores indexing positive self-concepts. The design consisted of a 2 (Groups) x 3 (Self-concept scales).

The sentences were programmed for their structured re-composition on a computer screen. Over a span of about 2 to 5 seconds the letters forming words appeared and remained in view, to form words that unfolded into complete sentences. Word construction at a pace of about 8 characters per second was found during pretesting to simulate a paced reading-rate which generally allowed for sentence comprehension by the time the last word was formed. The end of a sentence and the start of the latency measure for responding "True" or "False" to the statements was signaled by a period punctuation. Immediately following a response, the 7-point scale appeared on the screen and participants indicated the certainty of their previous answer on the keyboard.

Measures

The silhouette and body weight measures related to Actual and Possible Selves (dreamed-of and feared-of shape and weight) described in Experiment 3 were obtained before participating in the SDQ III item reaction time portion of the study. Reactions times were obtained to "True" and "False" keyboard responses for all positively and negatively phrased items. SDQ III scores were from the 7-point certainty responses. The 15 negatively phrased items were reverse scored.

Results

The height and weight and corresponding BMI results from BULIT participants were the same as those obtained in Exp 3.

Scale Scores and Reaction Times to Statements

A 2 (Groups) x 3 (Self-concept Scales) ANOVA on total SDQ III scale scores revealed a significant Groups $F (1, 28) = 17.13, p < .001$, and a significant Groups x Scales interaction $F (2, 28) = 6. 38, p < .005$. High BULIT participants were less positive in their self-evaluations on all three scales: Physical, Social, and Academic, when compared to Low BULIT participants. Scheffé tests revealed that a poor self evaluation by High BULIT participants was significantly accentuated for their Physical self-concept, which for these women also proved to be poorer than their Social and Academic scale scores. $(p< .05)$. Figure 4 illustrates these findings.

A 2 (groups) x 2 (Response Class) x 3 (Scales) ANOVA on median RTs was conducted. The two Response Classes consisted of total scores for "true" (affirming positive statements), and "false" (denying negative statements). This ANOVA revealed a significant Groups $F (1, 52) = 12. 11, p < .001$ effect indicating that High BULIT participants responded slower on all three scales, and a second order interaction with the three factors, $F (2, 52) = 3.22, p < .03$. Scheffé tests revealed that High but not Low BULIT participants produced slower RTs to Physical self-concept statements only, and this, depending on whether they were affirming a positive statement or denying a negative statement $(p < .05)$. Figure 5 illustrates this effect.

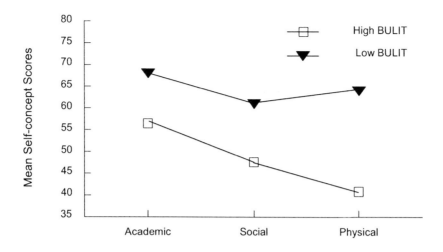

Figure 4. Mean self-concept scores for Academic, Social, and Physical self-concept measures for participants scoring High and Low on the Bulimia Test (BULIT).

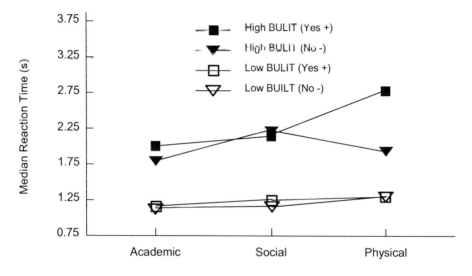

Figure 5. Median reaction time to affirming or denying positive and negative statements for Academic, Social, and Physical self-concept measures for participants scoring High and Low on the Bulimia Test (BULIT).

Actual/Possible Body Image and Discrepancies

Mean actual/dreamed-of/feared-of shape and weight reports and differences between Groups were identical to those found in Experiment 3.

Correlations between Self-concept scales and actual shape perceptions were correlated with Social, Academic, and Physical Self-concept when all participants are included in the sample [r (30) = -.51, -.49, -.60, $p < .001$ respectively]. In terms of the discrepancy between the actual and dreamed-of shape, High BULIT participants discrepancies were correlated with Social ($r = -.55$) and Physical ($r = -.58$, $p < .01$), but not Academic Self-concept ($r = -.15$, ns) scales. As in Exp 3, no significant correlations among any of the measures were found for of Low BULIT participants, and weight data were unrelated to the above measures.

As expected, High BULIT participants showed a poorer self-concept on all three scales, with an even poorer self-concept on the physical self concept dimension. These findings confirm the centrality of body image perceptions for physical (Showers & Larson, 1999), social and academic self-concepts (Boivin et al., 1992; Lerner et al., 1990). They also support the compartmentalization model (Showers & Larson, 1999), showing not only that individuals with bulimic tendencies display a negatively compartmentalized self-concept overall, but also that knowledge about a particularly salient dimension of the self such as the physical domain can have a noteworthy impact on other aspects of the self-concept such as the social and academic.

The degree to which High and Low BULIT participants were certain of their responses to statements paralleled the speed of information processing to the statements. Generally, participants with bulimic tendencies evidenced a less well organized or well developed cognitive structure to all three aspects of the self-concept. The fact that they showed faster RTs when disavowing ("No" keyboard response) an unfavorable Physical self statement, and longer latencies when affirming ("Yes" keyboard response) favorable Physical self statements, is interesting. While High BULIT college women may have a fear of becoming their worst physical self they are rather clear about not having achieved that status yet. It suggests that individuals with bulimic tendencies (perhaps those at a pre-clinical stage) are schematic for a fearful physical state they have *not* yet attained while remaining comparatively less schematic for dreamed-of physical attributes yet to be attained.

CONCLUSION

Implications for Self and Identity

Women with bulimic tendencies in the last three experiments showed a distinct trend in regards their responses to certain personality attributes. In Exp 2, although High BSQ women rated their actual personality traits much the same way as their Low BSQ counterparts, when it came to the RT task where they had to indicate "yes" or "no" if a word corresponded to their "dream-of" being High BSQ women affirmed a fewer number of positive traits as something they aspired to. In addition, these High BSQ participants were slower in encoding Dream-of being positive traits compared with Low BSQ participants. In Exp 3 these results were replicated with High BULIT participants. They encoded dreamed-of positive trait attributes more slowly and endorsed fewer positive trait terms as a dream-of being aspiration than Low BULIT participants. Also, they showed a poorer recall of positive personality trait words while no memory differences were obtained for negative trait words.

The correlations between body shape and reaction times to negative trait words presented in Table 2 is consistent with the compartmentalization model proposed by Showers and Larson, (1999) and its relevance to eating disorders. Aspirations and fears in regard to the physical domain self had a noteworthy impact on other aspects of the self-concept such as the social and academic. Importantly, this body image preoccupation "spilled over" onto how other negative aspects of the self such as fear-of acquiring negative personality or social attributes were cognitively processed. Interestingly, the processing of positive personality trait information was uncorrelated with body shape perceptions and discrepancies.

Taken together the data regarding how positive traits are encoded and retrieved suggest that, compared with other women, persons with bulimic tendencies, are more inclined to be *aschematic* for aspiring to be described as possessing certain positive personality attributes. It should be noted that, consistent with way high and low BSQ women encoded actual trait terms in Exp 1, this tendency to being aschematic for a trait terms does not apply to an actual self but only to a possible self. This is further reinforced by the findings within experiments which showed that trait self ratings referring to an actual self are pretty much the same for all BSQ and BULIT participants, and that they bulimic women were distinguished in their in trait selections, their encoding speed, and their subsequent free recall only when trait terms were self referenced to a "dream-of" self. Conceivable, bulimic women, in addition to having well developed schemas for body image and physical appearance, may also have poorly well organized aspirations for becoming what social and personality attributes represent.

This interpretation is in line with recent work by McElwee and Dunning (2005) where they speculated that notions of what is a "good" or a "bad" (desirable) personality attribute may be determined by what the person thinks are important attributes in others' personalities. Claiming that some normative standard outside of the self concept is what determines what is important to a person may not be new to social-cultural theories of eating disorders. However, finding that social and personality trait attributes in bulimic women are *unimportant* does speak to an absence of certain ego investments with possibly ensuing motivational and achievement-oriented consequences.

Intervention programs that focus on the modification of the pervasive negative schemas that characterize bulimic women may well be playing a role in the maintenance of eating disorder attitudes and behaviors (Stein & Nyquist, 2001) by strengthening this cognitive focus. It may be important for therapy to go beyond the modification of negative knowledge structures and move to promoting the creation of new or strengthened aspirations and possible selves other than the ones configured around the image of the body.

Information Processing Modalities

Our curiosity over whether "body image" is as a verbal or non-verbal representation within the self simply succeeded in provoking new questions. Recall that only perceptions of shape and not weight were associated with aspects of the self-concept. This confirms Markus et al's. (1987) view that objective data pertaining to weight status is a poor indicator of an individual's self-concept or body image, and stresses the importance of one's perception when it comes to the interpretation of information. On the one hand, the differential recall of positive trait words and the lack of differences in terms of the recall of body shape words by the two groups supports the dual-coding approach (Paivio, 1986), suggesting that verbal and nonverbal knowledge units are processed as two separate cognitive structures, with body image information being independent of a self-concept that is composed of trait features. Although body shape (nonverbal) knowledge units may be organized as independent cognitive structures, as conceived in the dual-coding approach (Paivio, 1986), findings from

Experiment 4, on the other hand, which showed that body image information is influenced by other kinds of nonverbal knowledge units suggest that they can be processed homogeneously if these words are arranged to form meaningful sentences. In this latter case, body image words when presented linguistically are not independent of a self-concept contained by trait features, findings that are consistent with the classical view of concepts (Smith & Medin, 1981).

Co-Variation with Depression

A limitation of the four studies was that co-variation of information processing with depression was not examined. Conceivably, the self-referencing task could have activated a negative mood that may have moderated the results. Studies by Kelvin, Goodyer, Teasdale, & Brechin (1999) found that when exposed to a negative mood-induction task, adolescents with a history of depression endorsed significantly more negative personality trait descriptors than when presented with a neutral mood-induction task. Researchers studying a cognitive model of depression focus on the semantic meaning of body image stimuli that constitute particular schemas because these schemas are the basis of information processing mistakes such as selective attention or confirmatory bias and serve to maintain eating disorder symptoms (Hermans, Pieters, & Eelen, 1998). However, the present findings emphasize the importance of meaning accorded body image stimuli as a function of the facet of the self-concept to which the stimulus words are referenced rather than the denotative meaning of the stimulus words themselves. Thus, negative mood inductions could be induced by the stimuli themselves and by the negative self schemas these stimuli activate. However, we only obtained equivocal support for this view here. In the fourth experiment the fact bulimic women recalled fewer positive trait words than negative trait words would imply that positive personality traits evoke a mood that is linked to depression. Recall of negative trait words or negative body words were the same for both groups even though a depressive effect would have been predicted here.

Non Clinical vs Clinical Samples

Another potential limitation of this study concerns the generalizability of the results to the bulimic population given the nature of the two samples that participated. The high BULIT participants that participated in the latter studies more likely resembled a clinical eating disordered population than did the high BSQ samples in the first two studies. Notwithstanding, participants in the four studies were selected from a non-clinically diagnosed sample, and therefore may differ in important ways from clinically diagnosed bulimic individuals. They might differ in aspects such as the severity of the symptomatology as well as the absence of certain co-morbid features that may be present in the already clinically identified population (Hinrichsen, Wright, Waller, & Meyer, 2003). Given that our participants consisted of undergraduate students in their late teens/early twenties, and may not be representative of the overall bulimic population, and future research should be directed at replicating the present findings with clinically diagnosed bulimics of a wider age range.

ACKNOWLEDGEMENTS

This research was supported in part by a grant from the School of Graduate Studies and Research of the University of Ottawa. The assistance of Helen Boyer, Andrée St. Denis and Caroline Ormrod in data collection is gratefully acknowledged.

REFERENCES

Altabe, M., & Thompson, J. K. (1996). Body image: Is there cognitive schema? *Cognitive Therapy and Research, 20*, 171-193.

American Psychiatric Association. (1994). *Diagnostic and statistical manual of mental disorders* (4th ed.). Washington, DC: Author.

Anderson, N. H. (1968). Likeableness ratings of 555 personality-trait words. *Journal of Personality and Social Psychology, 9*, 272-279.

Beike, D. R., & Niedenthal, P. M. (1998). The process of temporal self-comparison in self evaluation and life satisfaction. In P. T. P. Wong & P. S. Fry (Eds.), *The human quest for meaning: A handbook of psychological research and clinical applications.* Mahwah, NJ: Lawrence Erlbaum Associates, Inc.

Blascovich, J., & Tomaka, J. (1991). Measures of self-esteem. In J. P. Robinson, P. R. Shaver, & L. S. Wrightsman (Eds.), *Measures of personality and social psychological attitudes* (pp. 115-160). San Diego, CA: Academic Press.

Boivin, M., Vitaro, F., & Gagnon, C. (1992). A reassessment of the self-perception profile for children: Factor structure, reliability, and the convergent validity of a French version among second through sixth grade children. *International Journal of Behavioral Development, 15*, 275-290.

Bruch, H. (1962). Perceptual and conceptual disturbances in anorexia nervosa. *Psychosomatic Medicine, 24*(2), 187-194.

Bruch, H. (1973). *Eating disorders.* New York: Basic Books.

Cash, T. F., & Pruzinski, T. (1990). *Body images: Development, deviance, and change.* New York: Guilford Press.

Cash, T. F. & Szymanski, M. L. (1995). The development and validation of the Body-Image Ideals Questionnaire. *Journal of Personality Assessment, 64*, 466-477.

Cooper, P. J., & Taylor, M. J. (1988). Body image disturbance in bulimia nervosa. *British Journal of Psychiatry, 153*, 32-36.

Cooper, P. J., & Taylor, M. J., Cooper, Z., & Fairburn, C. G. (1987). The development and validation of the Body Shape Questionnaire. *International Journal of Eating Disorders, 6*, 485-494.

Craik, F. I. M., & Tulving, E. (1975). Depth of processing and the retention of words in episodic memory. *Journal of Experimental Psychology: General, 104*, 268-294.

Deutsch, F. M., Kroll, J. F., Weible, A. W., Letourneau, L. A., & Goss, R. L. (1988). Spontaneous trait generation: A new method for identifying self-schemas. *Journal of Personality, 56,* 327 – 354.

Dunkel, C., & Kerpelan, J. (2005). (Eds.) *Possible selves: Theory, research and applications* Hauppauge, Nova Science Publishers.

Duval, S., & Wicklund, R. A. (1972). *A theory of objective self-awareness.* New York: Academic Press.

Fisher, S. (1986). *Development and structure of body image* (Vol. 1) Hillsdale, NJ: Erlbaum.

Girodo, M. (2003). Actual and possible body-image self-schemas in young women with bulimic tendencies. *Perceptual and Motor Skills, 96,* 1123-1132.

Fischer, S. (1970). *Body experience in fantasy and behavior.* New York: Appleton-Century-Crofts.

Fischer, S. & Cleveland, S. E. (1968). *Body image and personality.* New York: Dover.

Higgins, E. T. (1989). Self-discrepancy theory: What patterns of self-beliefs cause people to suffer? In L. Berkowits (Ed.), *Advances in experimental social psychology, 22.* New York: Academic Press.

Higgins, E. T. (1987). Self-discrepancy: A theory relating self and affect. *Psychological Review, 94,* 319-340.

Hsu, L. K. & Sobriewicz, T. A. (1991). Body image disturbance: Time to abandon the concept for eating disorders? *International Journal of Eating Disorders, 10,* 15-30.

Hermans, D., Pieters, G., & Eelen, P. (1998). Implicit and explicit memory for shape, body weight, and food-related words in patients with anorexia nervosa and nondieting controls. *Journal of Abnormal Psychology, 107,* 193-202.

Higgins, E. T. (1989). Self-discrepancy theory: What patterns of self-beliefs cause people to suffer? In L. Berkowits (Ed.), *Advances in experimental social psychology, 22.* New York: Academic Press.

Hinrichsen, H., Wright, F., Waller, G., & Meyer, C. (2003, August). Social anxiety and coping strategies in the eating disorders. *Eating disorders, 4* (2), 117- 126.

James, W. (1890). *Principles of Psychology.* New York: Holt.

Kelvin, R. G., Goodyer, I. M. Teasdale, J. D, & Brechin, D. (1999). Latent negative self schema and emotionality in well adolescents at risk for psychopathology. *Journal of Child Psychology and Psychiatry,* 40, 959-968.

Kihlstrom, J. F., & Cantor, N. (1984). Mental representations of the self. In L. Berkowitz (Ed.), *Advances in experimental social psychology,* (Vol. 15, pp.1-47). New York: Academic Press.

King. G. A., Polivy, J., & Herman, C. P. (1991). Cognitive aspects of dietary restraint: Effects on person memory. *International Journal of Eating Disorders, 10,* 313-321.

Lerner, R. M., Delaney, M., Hess, L. E., Jovanonic, J., & von Eye, A. (1990). Early adolescent physical attractiveness and academic competence. *Journal of early Adolescence, 10,* 4- 20.

Mahoney, M. J. (1990). Psychotherapy and the body in the mind. In T. F. Cash & T. Pruzinsky (Eds.), *Body images:Development, deviance, and change* (pp. 316-333). New York: Guilford.

Markus, H. (1977). Self-schema and processing information about the self. *Journal of Personality and Social Psychology, 35*, 63-78.

Markus, H. (1980). The self in thought and memory. In D. M. Wegner & R. R. Vallacher (Eds.), *The self in social psychology*. New York: Oxford University Press.

Markus, H., & Wurf, E. (1987). The dynamic self-concept: A social psychological perspective. *Annual Review of Psychology, 38*, 299-337.

Markus, H., Hamill, R., & Sentis, K. P. (1987). Thinking fat: Self schemas for body weight and the processing of weight relevant information. *Journal of Applied Social Psychology, 17*, 50-71.

Markus, H., & Nurius, P. (1986). Possible selves. *American Psychologist, 41*, 954-969.

Marsh, H. W, & O'Neill, R. (1984). Self Descriptive Questionnaire III: The construct validity of multidimensional self-concept ratings by late adolescents. *Journal of Educational Measurement, 21*, 153-174.

McElwee, R., & Dunning, D. (2005). A broader view of "self" in egocentric social judgement: Current and possible selves. *Self and Identity, 4*, 113–130.

Metropolitan Life Insurance Company. (1983). Metropolitan height and weight tables. *Statistical Bulletin, 64*, 3-9.

Ogilvie, D. M. (1987). The undesired self: A neglected variable in personality research *Journal of Personality and Social Psychology, 52*, 379-385.

Paivio, A. (1986). *Mental representations: A dual coding approach*. New York: Oxford University Press.

Rogers, C. R., & Dymond, R. (1954). *Psychotherapy and personality change*. Chicago: University of Chicago Press.

Rogers, T. B., Kuiper, N. A., & Kirker, W. S. (1977). Self-reference and the encoding of personal information. *Journal of Personality and Social Psychology, 35*, 677-688.

Russell, A. M., Cahill, M., & Spain, W. H. (1992). *Occupational identity: The self in context.* (Available from the Center for Educational Research and Development, St. John's, Newfoundland).

Sarbin, T. R. (1952). A preface to a psychological analysis of the self. *Psychological Review, 59*, 11-22.

Schilder, P. (1953). *The image and appearance of the human body*. London: Kegan Paul.

Segal, Z. V. (1988). Appraisal of the self-schema construct in cognitive models of depression. *Psychological Bulletin, 103*, 147-162.

Strauman, T. J., & Higgins, E. T. (1987). Automatic activation of self-discrepancies and emotional syndromes: When cognitive structures influence affect. *Journal of Personality and Social Psychology, 53,* 1004-1014.

Strauman, T. J., & Glenberg, A. M. (1994). Self-concept and body image disturbance: Which self-beliefs predict body size overestimations? *Cognitive Therapy and Research, 18,* 105-125.

Strein, W. (1993). Advances in research on academic self-concept: Implications for school psychology. *School Psychology Review, 22*, 273-284.

Thompson, J. K., Penner, L. A., & Altabe, M. N. (1990). Procedures, problems, and progress in the assessment of body images. In T. F. Cash & T. Pruzinski (Eds.), *Body images: Development, deviance, and change.* (pp. 21-48). New York: Guilford Press.

Vitousek, K, B., & Hollon, S. D. (1990). The investigation of schematic content and processing in eating disorders. *Cognitive Therapy and Research, 14,* 191-214.

Showers, J. C., & Larson, E. B. (1999). Looking at body image: The organization of self-knowledge about physical appearance and its relation to disordered eating. *Journal of Personality, 67* (4), 659-700.

Smith, E. E., & Medin, D. L. (1981). *Categories and concepts.* Cambridge: Harvard University Press.

Smith, M. C., & Thelen, M. H. (1984). Development and validation of a test for bulimia. *Journal of Consulting and Clinical Psychology, 52, 863-872.*

Stein, R. J. (1996). Physical self-concept. In B. A. Bracken (Ed.), *Handbook of self-concept: Developmental, Social and Clinical Considerations* (pp.374-420). New York: John Wiley & Sons, Inc.

Stein, F. K., & Nyquist, L. (2001, January/February). Disturbance in the self: A source of eating disorders. *Eating Disorders Review, 12* (1). Retrieved February, 15, 2004, from http://www.gurze.net/site12_5_00/newsletteredt.htm

Strauman, T. J., Vookles, J., Berenstein, V., Chaiken, S., & Higgins, E. T. (1991). Self-discrepancies and vulnerability to body dissatisfaction and disordered eating. *Journal of Personality and Social Psychology, 61,* 946-956.

Strein, W. (1993). Advances in research on academic self-concept: Implications for school psychology. *School Psychology Review, 22,* 273-284.

Stryker, S. (1987). Identity Theory: Developments and extensions. In K. Yardley & T. Honess (Eds.), *Self and identity.* New York: Wiley.

Tasca, G.A., Balfour, L., Kurichh, K., Potvin-Kent, M., Bissada, H. (2006). Actual-desired BMI discrepancy, body dissatisfaction, and self concept in women with Bulimia Nervosa and Binge Eating Disorder. In P. Swain (Ed.) *Trends in Eating Disorders.* Hauppauge, NY: Nova Science Publishers.

Thompson, J. K. (1990). *Body image disturbance: Assessment and treatment.* New York: Pergamon Press.

Thompson, J. K., & Dolce, J. J. (1989). The discrepancy between emotional vs. rational estimates of body size, actual size, and ideal body ratings: Theoretical and clinical implications. *Journal of Clinical Psychology, 45,* 473-478.

Thompson, J. K., &Thompson, C. M. (1986). Body size distortion and self-esteem in asymptomatic, normal weight males and females. *International Journal of Eating Disorders, 5,* 1061-1068.

Williamson, D. A. (1990). *Assessment of eating disorders: Obesity, anorexia, and bulimia nervosa.* New York: Pergamon Press.

Zellner, D. A., Harner, D. E., & Adler, R. L. (1989). Effects of eating abnormalities and gender on perceptions of desirable body shape. *Journal of Abnormal Psychology, 98,* 93-96.

In: Body Image: New Research
Editor: Marlene V. Kindes, pp. 109-130

ISBN 1-60021-059-7
© 2006 Nova Science Publishers, Inc.

Chapter V

EATING DISORDERS AND ADOLESCENT GIRLS: IMPLICATIONS FROM A DEVELOPMENTAL PERSPECTIVE

April Lynn Lapp* and Craig Winston LeCroy*
Arizona State University School of Social Work
Tucson, AZ

ABSTRACT

The current knowledge base that serves as a foundation for diagnosing and treating eating disorders, disorders grouped due to ill behavior sets with regards to food and nutrition, recognizes EDS as an adolescent or post adolescent phenomenon, with specific overt indicators. As a corollary with eating disorders, also presenting in adolescence (though trending younger) body image and body image distortion (as overt expression) is identified as one of these indicators. However, when researchers and clinicians explore beyond presenting behavioral sets, and beyond the age bracket associated with those behaviors, it becomes clear that these disorders, and bosy image itself, express a much deeper, and more challenging pathology, what is more, exploration may indicate that the eating disorders are related one to another only superficially. Current research on BI is used to illustrate a developmental approach for improved recognition and efficacious treatment aimed at ED prevention.

Keywords: Current vs. Developmental Perspective of Body Image

---

* Correspondence concerning this article should be addressed to: Craig Winston LeCroy, Ph.D., Arizona State University, School of Social Work--Tucson Component, 340 N. Commerce Park Loop, Tucson, AZ 85745

INTRODUCTION

There is a clear, multidimensional dividing line in the treatment literature between Anorexia Nervosa (AN) and Bulimia Nervosa (BN). Not only are the two diagnosis unequal in the amount of literature dedicated to their evaluation, the result is a gulf between the two disorders in knowledge and treatment, and in resources/guidance for clients and practitioners. When the two disorders are compared they show very little similarity in treatment efficacy and outcomes.

One possible explanation for Bulimia Nervosa appearing so much more in the literature base is the fact that the bulimic individual expresses his/her disorders more through maladaptive *external* (i.e. observable, measurable, amenable to scientific study) behaviors *throughout the course of the disorder.* Anorexia, on the other hand, may not be so obvious to the observer until the course of the pathology leads the disordered individual to lose extreme amounts of weight. The criteria for diagnosis in the DSM reflect this. Common outcome measures in AN studies are defined as normal body weight and maintenance (Richards, Baldwin, Frost, Clark-Sly, Berrett, & Hardman, 2000), largely because at the time AN is diagnosed the individual is in such a physically critical condition that they require hospitalization and re-feeding (weight gain) to restore normal body/brain functioning. A recognized element of deception and/or denial on the Anorexic client's part also contributes to late diagnosis. Almost universally the primary outcome measures of treatment itself for AN relate back to the criteria that are purportedly the main features of the pathology according to the DSM manual: again, weight stabilization and resumed menstruation. Attitudinal disturbances, general outcome, and other measures are considered secondary as outcomes of treatment, and therefore as pathology components.

Agreement- what little there is- about success rates with Anorexic clients occur only with regards to the outcome of inpatient (hospitalized) treatment. Weight and menstruation normalize for a time in 50-60%; eating behaviors normalize (in hospital) in 40-50%; 30-40% recover, 30% improve; and mortality rates figures range from 4.4-10%. But each of these studies takes into consideration as positive outcomes only those physical improvements necessary to reverse extreme starvation. Starvation may be a symptom itself, and *there is no data given in these studies on psychological status* (Richards, et al, 2000). Because Anorexia is far less understood, especially those elements not directly related to the biophysical person, much of the criticism in review of evidence based treatment for Eating Disorders (EDs) centers on that diagnosis.

The three most prominent treatments for Anorexia are family therapy, Cognitive-Behavioral Therapy (CBT), and pharmacology (Stein, Saelens, Dounchis, Lewczyk, Swenson, & Wilfley, 2001). No treatment for AN is empirically validated as especially efficacious. Despite desires to expedite treatment (recent trends toward the preponderance of an outpatient setting and brief therapy approaches), the *recommended* length averages one to two years. Combining this with low prevalence rates and the "egosyntonic" nature of the pathology (also effecting motivation to seek treatment), recruitment and retainment becomes difficult for research purposes (Stein, et al, 2001). According to Newton (2001), there is a paucity of controlled empirical studies detailing the treatments availability and their efficacy as percieved by treatment consumers. Only nine controlled studies of outpatient treatment exist; three more were underway at the time of this study. The power of these studies' conclusions is handicapped by low subject participation (small N); they represent initial efforts to study treatment modality trends and, as of yet, stand unreplicated.

Medication may help to stabilize patients to the point where they are capable of doing intrapersonal work, but do not appear efficacious as a substitute for clinical treatment. Pharmacology thus does not address any of the complex etiological and maintaining factors of the disorder, but can be used on an individual basis as a temporary aid to enable the client to address them. Often anorexia is co-diagnosed with personality and mood disorders that could be addressed through medication as well, though the degree to which the pathologies are as separate as multiaxial diagnosis makes them sound is questionable.

Cognitive Behavioral Therapy (CBT) made its way over to the AN treatment field after some documented success with Bulimia Nervosa. CBT aims to modify the fundamental beliefs that theoretically underlie described behavioral and medical symptoms of anorexia nervosa. CBT looks at how the behavioral, including medical, symptoms perpetuate and are caused by illogical belief systems. The specific belief sets targeted in AN individuals are those that construct the sense of self and self worth, in terms of weight and thinness (again, overt presenting concerns). Fear of losing control and of shape change, misinformation about food and how it acts in the body and lack of accurate information about nutrition and body composition are also addressed (Stein, et al, 2001). Maladaptive beliefs and misinformation are targeted for modification and replacement by more adaptive understandings.

However, not all CBT programs have the same target hierarchy. Some models place the need for control as the primary belief target, and the importance of self, and self evaluation by thinness in subsequent position as culture-specific cognitive features (Fairburn, Shafran, & Cooper, 1999). Stein states: "One CBT approach focuses on traditional elements such as interpersonal factors and family relationships". Again, these considerations are secondary in CBT, and are included only as necessary when they present as a block to progress or promote physically defined symptoms (Stein, et al, 2001). Although CBT is very well documented as a fruitful treatment with Bulimia Nervosa, and has filtered into the AN field, very little evidence has been produced to document its efficacy with AN patients (Stein et al, 2001).

One limitation of the CBT approach, and perhaps a partial explanation for the significant portion of Anorexic clients it fails to treat effectively (or who drop out of the program, as opposed to its record with bulimic clients), is its immediate, consistent, and almost exclusive focus on current overt behaviors. However, Anorexia Nervosa, although categorized with BN in the DSM because they both are expressed through food behaviors (though the expression is very different), is less of an externalized pathology. Cognitive over-control of the anorexic's strong ego/mind intrusively dominates her own body, diminishing and starving its voice and role, rather than relinquishing herself to its impulses. The restrictive behavioral elements and bodily presentation of the anorexic are actually part of the anorexic's pathological mindset. The controlled quietness of the Anorexic's dictatorship over herself keeps her from behavioral observation. Anorexic eating behavior is a willful insertion, a controlled expression of the pathology and of the internal self (Woolsey, 2002). As her body is reduced, so is the behavioral expression of herself that others are allowed to observe.

In fact, strong cognitive ability and discipline are known traits of AN individuals well before diagnosis. They are often high achievers, perfectionistic, and present as very successful outside of their disorder (whereas bulimia is often associated with other behavioral and lifestyle dysfunction, like substance abuse). It is typical for an anorexic client to be both a capable, organized, highly functioning adult externally, and also internally be like a child stuck in time- disorganized and incapable of self-soothing. The eating disorder to an anorexic client is a container of the not obvious, internal truth about the non-developed and inhibited self. Though the behavior of a bulimic can contain information from the past (particular food aversions and their link to sexual trauma, for example), it is a behavioral escape. Each behavior of the AN client is a psychotic expression of the unexpressed self- carefully chosen and intentional. To an anorexic, the disorder *is* the self. The truth of this is reflected in the mortality and recovery rate attached to the two diagnosis. AN has a much higher mortality rate, and much poorer recovery rate using current treatment.

Overall the review study by Stein, et al. (2001) tentatively endorses family therapies for early onset cases of AN and cases of and short duration; individual therapies are chosen for later onset. Richards, et al, (2000) agree that family therapy, along with individual therapy, is best post weight restoration. These authors do so under the duress of extremely limited controlled research and literature resources in the treatment field. High drop out rates cloud research data even further. CBT, perhaps the most promising of the modalities used and evaluated thus far, has inconclusive results. There is only "provisional support" for its use (Stein, et al, 2001). Researchers and reviewers agree that more research is required on every single approach used with anorexia, including family therapy, psychodynamic therapy, and CBT (Stein, et al, 2001; Richards, et al, 2000), and on AN etiology itself.

While the startling state of research on anorexia may in itself motivate researchers and clinicians tosome degree; current use of the DSM diagnostic standards for recognition and treatment of eating disorders in general is in reality much more insidious than simple scientific irresponsibility. Both the DSM and CBT fail to recognize the potency and impervious nature of earlier, underlying developmental and psychosocial tasks, and the effects that current tools have on the Anorexic presentation. They consider these matters, as stated above, secondary to the course and presentation of the AN pathology. This is so even though a main tenet of CBT is that belief sets should be targeted for alteration through behavioral means; studies have rarely look at improvement in belief structures such as body image and other self identity structure. Studies that have restrict their perspective to these structures at the time of presentation only.

A specific example of this oversight is Rosen's (1996) review of treatment for body image within eating disorders. He found body image was important in etiology and in recovery, though at the time of his review only 1/3 of cognitive-behavioral treatments addressed it specifically. While body image work is important and salient to the presenting adolescent (as they are very aware of their developing bodies through puberty), it is possible that earlier phonemes of the disorder involve other (or larger) components of the self and self identity/esteem appropriate to those developmental stages. Rosen (1996) himself reports that body image was improved in some treatment situations where the content did not address BI directly; he suggests that this construct could be mediated by broader changes in self esteem and mood.

That the recommended course of treatment for AN is up to 2 years further signifies the need for more effective, earlier, and deeper work for the sake of prevention and reduced recidivism rates. Recidivism is notoriously high with the diagnosis across treatment modalities. While CBT may address dysfunctional beliefs about the physical self and self worth, it does not consider the dynamics that engendered those dysfunctional beliefs in the first place (by supporting and allowing their development). What's more, by focusing so intently and exclusively on eating patterns and their meaning for the self, and by approaching the client through their dysfunctional presentation from the start, CBT may in fact *reinforce* (through negative attention) pathology in the anorexic client, who is attempting to build her identity around the anorexia itself. CBT in particular does has many good qualities; perhaps it should be implemented (especially in extreme cases- arguably every case diagnosable by DSM IV standards), in congruence with methods (or revisions to current methodology) that address contextual and deeper psychological factors (across chronology) contributing to the disorder. The field must explore retrospectively what AN pathology looks like in earlier developmental stages, within earlier developmental tasks, to discover the core of the disorder, especially considering the poor treatment outcomes and high recidivism (not to mention the mortality rate) at the age now considered the age of onset, and the startling number of cases presenting at younger and younger ages. A developmental perspective may be essential to filling in the enormous gaps in our understanding of this disorder, and of those diagnosed, to whom we would offer increased well being and quality of life.

BODY

A developmental perspective catapults the study of eating disorder etiology into a much broader, more complex- but necessary- realm. The resulting implications involve the breadth of treatment, research, and description of eating disorders (specifically Anorexia), as well as our understanding of the process of mental health development on the whole. The current diagnostic system defines the time frame of an eating disorder by how long the *behavior* (overt, food related) has been occurring. However, missed or stunted developmental stages/ tasks can manifest as eating disorders later (Woolsey, 2002). Current behavior, if the disorder is more than a behavioral one, could only be the current expression of underlying illness, as dictated by developmental stage and age-appropriate subjects/themes. Unfortunately, with so little research on ED pathology, these connections must be explored within more general research on childhood mental health and development. At first discouraging, this necessity proves to be unexpectedly fruitful..

Woolsey calls the process of integrating information throughout the developmental stages "building the behavioral highway", and includes detailed description of the biophysical steps the central nervous system takes as it forms what is eventually recognized as behavioral patterns (Woolsey, 2002, p.96). Long term information storage and use produces the culminating behavioral and cognitive representation of the self. Continuing her metaphor, Woolsey identifies behavioral "off ramps", which take an individual away from the ideal destination of whole-person health and wellbeing (Woolsey, 2002, p.97). Roadblocks, insufficient building materials (e.g.,due to poor nutritional intake/status), confusion about proper route and direction, and poor maintenance all contribute to developmental derailing that can be diagnosed as disorder. Such derailing might occur at the time of onset (as described by diagnostics), but more probably was the diathesis that contributed to current presentation under stress. Thus, common ages of onset (adolescence and young adulthood), and manifestations of disordered thought (such as body image disturbance) may not tell the whole biopsychosocial story of the disorder's development in a given client, a story essential to effective treatment. This assertion is well illustrated in one aspect of presenting disturbance, that of body image.

Developmental Stages: Body Image and Eating Disorders

Full manifestation of eating disorders, both Anorexia Nervosa and Bulimia Nervosa, almost exclusively identified in adolescent and post adolescent years, are time and again associated empirically with disturbances in body image. Consequentially, body image formation has also historically been bracketed in the adolescent psychosocial phase, where it is appropriately considered a subcategory of concrete identity formation as a whole (Ashford, LeCroy, & Lortie, 2006).

The idea that eating disorders are, at their deepest level, efforts to achieve social ideals of attraction (e.g. the thin ideal), supports this logical connection with body image formation and adolescence. The emerging pressure and influence of social models (i.e. the thinness ideal) becomes dominant as the young teen or preteen strives to be desirable to the opposite sex (LeCroy & Daley, 2001). Again, following this train of thought, researchers have paid abundant attention to the communicators of socially attractive ideals in ED etiology: specifically to media directed at young women, who make up the vast majority of individuals that present with disordered eating patterns. These investigations have uncovered a great amount of culpability on the part of industries that promote unrealistic image standards, and who fail to safeguard the self esteem and body image of young women.

Given that the pubertal years are marked by obvious and radical changes in biological, psychological, and social functioning, the above assumptions are reasonable. Well- known and documented adolescent developmental themes include conflict with, and desire for, independence from authority (including control), greater emphasis on peer-group relations, preoccupation with the self, abilities to sustain abstract thought (making comparisons to ideals possible), use of metaphorical language, fluctuations in emotions and self esteem, increased self awareness, growth of social awareness and (noted) radical changes in body image (LeCroy & Daley, 2001).

Body image formation is part and parcel of adolescent sexual identity. Accordingly, the biophysical changes that initiate adolescent sexual identity (hormones, onset of menstruation, onset of problems like obesity and acne, and etc), are part of the initiation of body image formation. Emerging adolescent abilities, and the developmental tasks associated with adolescent maturation, are in truth a nice fit with the concept of body image formation. This also allows for the possibility of intra- and interpersonal disturbances being channeled into the body image (BI) construct, into distorted views of the physical self. Not only the adolescent's cognitive characteristics, but the complex building blocks of their social environment, contribute to the appropriateness of theoretical connections between preoccupation with image, social norms and ideals, and body iage formation. Building blocks include: family dynamics, popularity and identification with a peer group, life transitions of greater magnitude than have been experienced prior, and gender role development.

However, an important overstep occurs when BI dissatisfaction is then further *exclusively* linked to adolescence, since BI disturbance is often present in adolescence. Furthermore, since it is often present in the adolescents that enter ED treatment, during the ages when EDs commionly present according to current standards of recognition, eating disorders themselves are also restricted to the adolescent window of development . Body image dissatisfaction has become associated as a companion to the diagnosis of EDs themselves; if A=B and B=C than A=C.

However, there exists a growing body of evidence that suggests that distortions of self concept begin much earlier than adolescence, and in more identity domains than body image alone. Recent studies on identity disturbance have operated from a less two- dimensional take on self concept than was once popular. Oosterwegel and Oppenheimer (2002) studied the self- systems of eight to 18 year olds by including more specific self descriptions (taken through age appropriate measures) from a number of domains (e.g. academic, social, athletic), and across different time frames (past, present, and future). Their theory proposes that identity is the amalgamation of these many different self representations. The goal of their analysis was to explore children's awareness of conflicts within self-descriptors, between real and ideal self-representations, and how these constructs were related to psychological well- being.

According to the authors, the content of self- descriptions is gathered from three sources: reflective knowledge about the self or self-appraisals, appraisals from others, and the child's perception of what trusted others' appraisals are of them. Preadolescents are considered much less capable of self reflective thought than their older counterparts, and as one would expect given the developmental facts, the authors found a sudden jump in conscious awareness of conflicts among internal self-representation between the ages of 12 and 14, when ED pathology is also recognized.

However, there is another interesting finding in the inquiry. Despite this jump in conscious awareness, conflicts between ideal- self and actual- self representations in dynamic self- systems were related to disturbed psychological well being at *every* age studied, even as young as eight. Ill effects of such conflicts on psychological well being include negative affect, depression, neuroticism, and psychosomatic complaints (all present in eating disorders). [Negative emotions, along with internal discrepancies, are causally linked to many other clinical disorders as well (Oosterwegel & Oppenheimer, 2002)]. The authors also record a main effect for *all* age groups and both genders for discrepancies between self appraisals and reflected appraisals of others. When interpreted, these results convey that the negative consequences of disturbances in self- representations exist prior to adolescence, before the integration of distal (domain-specific) self- representations begin to constitute a cohesive identity, and prior even to the young person's conscious awareness of the conflicts present.

Adolescent identity formation, and body image formation should not be a concept discussed only as it is expressed in the adolescent developmental phase. It seems there is some continuity between later conscious adolescent identity confusion and the shadowy precedents of real and ideal representations that are formulated in earlier years. Could there also exist similar shadows and representations of eating disorder pathology in these earlier stages?

BI, the Self, and Younger Age Groups

The idea that earlier developmental phases are significant for identity formation, and body image formation specifically, is not new information. In the recent past, Western academic society has witnessed a maturing description of the occurrence and nature of body image formation and disturbance. Concurrently, there has been a trend toward the study of younger ages. In Western Civilization, body image dissatisfaction, defined as the discrepancy between perceived self and ideal self image, has reportedly been found in girls as young as nine (Sands & Wardle, 2002). Much has been made of the sexualization of girls at younger and younger ages, of the body image ideals and misperceptions of preadolescents, and of the relationship between maternal attitudes and nutritional awareness and dieting behavior in their daughters. The results have been some valuable (if anecdotal) elucidations of the sociocultural environment and expectations imposed upon young women, and on womens' reflection and reaction to that environment.

The examples listed above, however, lay bare a fault in this body of research. Rather than focusing on the core foundational issues of total identity formation- or even on body image as part of total identity- as they are present in younger subjects, these studies have tended to look at such issues solely through the lens of the behaviors, developmental tasks, and sociocultural factors pertaining to adolescence (due to the traditional view of BI). They assume that manifestations of disordered eating patterns in younger ages are necessarily connected to conflicts in physical body image representations, as they seem to be in adolescents, when attractiveness and sexual identity are the focus of energy and biophysical change. However, distinct self- reflection on body image is developmentally less probable in middle childhood, and it has not yet been demonstrated that eating disorders at any age are derived from body image alone, rather than disruptions in other areas of identity that are then channeled into salient, age-appropriate developmental tasks (as they are later channeled into BI in adolescence). These studies, therefore, may generalize inappropriately when they propose to study the origins of eating disorders through the specific domain of body image self- representation, overlooking any relationship between other domain-specific representations in the dynamic self system, or with a more global concept of self.

Incorporating Appropriate Study of Earlier Development

In fact, sound multidimensional assessment tools have not even been developed for young children, who are not yet aware enough or able to verbalize their sense of self in the manner required by adolescent tests, including commonly used eating disorder measures (Van den Bergh & De Rycke, 2003). Despite their incapability, however, self- information may be both *present* and *active*. While the domain of body image may be the domain where self-disturbance is most easily observed in an adolescent (and in some at- risk adolescents in particular by virtue of gender, social influences, exposure to peer teasing, parenting style, etc), it may not be particularly informative about the prepubescent child. Conflict in the middle child's sense of self is experienced more as an immediate and general emotion than self- reflective thought, increasingly so as one retreats from the early teen jump in self-awareness. If this is the case, studies that investigate the antecedents of identity (and sub-domains) disturbance in younger populations using exclusively adolescent constructs may miss the broader negative experiences, and resulting emotional distress which are later channeled into age- specific concerns during adolescence. This precisely may be the reason the research on younger ages has come up with such diffuse and contradictory conclusions, and why ED research with presenting age groups cannot seem to find the bottom of the pathology.

Perhaps eating disorders and disturbance are developed in self- aware adolescents who find conflict only in those domains. However, alternatively, it could be that the most pressing adolescent domain is the first in which a more general disorder and conflict are expressed (when coherent self expression is developmentally possible for the first time), meaning that there *could* be corollary expressions of conflict in earlier developmental tasks. In either case, this preoccupation in research and treatment with the teenage stage, and the biopsychosocial factors that belong to that stage exclusively is shortsighted. What is more, researchers have concluded that Erikson's' stage model is not as consistent with female patterns of development as it is with male (the vast majority of eating disorders as described occur in females, but are on the rise in both genders), and that it labels normality and abnormality using a male standard (Lytle, Bakken, & Romig, 1997). The focus of energy and research, in order to obtain a thorough and useful description of the unhealthy behavior in current ED clients' presentations, needs to focus on taking a creative look at development in the middle childhood ages.

Broad Self Messages

When the characteristics of middle childhood are examined, it seems clear that the self awareness achieved in adolescence is not, after all, a leap atop a sudden cliff, reached from a level plain of prior existence. Rather, it is the clear peak reached through the long and cloudy climb of earlier development. This cloudy climb, the sub- level formation of self concept, is the foundation upon which concrete identity formation, with self- referent thought, later occurs. While "a child at this stage cannot use the logic of formal operations to compare the ideal with the actual", much of the information used in later descriptions and comparisons comes from information gleaned through interaction between the individual and their social environment during middle childhood, with in the context of "child culture" (Ashford, et al., 2006, p.303- 305). Adolescence is thus a process, not a status (Lytle, et al., 1997).

Erikson would actually agree with this; he states that adolescence is a time when past "partial ids" are drawn upon (Lytle, et al., 1997, p.175). His term "industry" itself means "to build" (Ashford, et al., 2006, p.303). Even Freud saw middle childhood as a preparatory stage, a rest between more turbulent seasons that none the less retained an undercurrent of growth. If EDs are essentially communications of disturbances in the self, they too could have developed from much earlier distress. The biophysical, psychological, and social elements of middle childhood, are illustrative of this build-up process, and also of how negative factors in multiple domains can significantly impact future identity development and body image, as it appears in behaviorally-recognized EDs during adolescence.

The slow and steady biophysical growth of this period and the cognitive seeping in of biographic information may result in the ED message. The physical body is in preparation for the later adolescent growth spurt. The changes are not wholly unobservable; girls for the first time outweigh boys and retain fat tissue longer than do boys (Ashford, et al., 2006). Studies have cited that peer teasing during this age contributes to increased body dissatisfaction. Davison and Birch (2002) assessed the relationship among weight status (measured as Body Mass Index), peer weight related teasing, parents' criticism of weight status, and emerging self concept. Their results were largely inconclusive, due in part to poor research design and measurement tools- the same age inappropriate construct problems discussed earlier. What they did find was an association between a history of peer weight related teasing and greater body image problems in late adolescence and into adulthood (Davison & Birch, 2002). Just as striking is the fact that this teasing occurs at all, as it demonstrates the social structure and sensitivity that exists between children of this age, and the presence of referent standards.

Again, this is just one facet of identity information- another example is the athletic domain. Peer-related physical activities are of interest by late middle childhood (Ashford, et al., 2006, p.304). Motor skill development and coordination allow for team play, accompanied by meaningful feedback about ability and inclusion. The increased competitiveness of team sports, which has contributed to a rise in athletic dropout, reveals the extent and effect of comparisons imposed externally. Granted, much of this is normative and does not necessarily constitute risk. However, if the experience of physical growth/ability in general is a negative one, the repercussions can extend long-term. The child is sensitive to these first biographical messages, and their content will later contribute to formation of more stable self descriptors.

The most important expansions of middle childhood, in a constant undercurrent of autobiographical information, are cognitive. Typically, children become less egocentric, and are able to take other view points, as well as consider themselves a part of the larger, more complicated world that does not evolve around them, their thoughts, and their emotions. Their "self concepts begin to change as the result of...increasing ability to understand how people view them", and become more domain specific (Ashford, et al., 2006, p.317). Self representations, for the first time, can include an ideal self and primitive self-consciousness. Logic increases the use of relationships in thought, adding stability and continuity to cognitive processes (conservation, for example) (Ashford, et al., 2006). Children in Middle Childhood gain interpersonal awareness, preparing them for interpersonal relationships, and role- taking generates cooperation with others (Ashford, et al. 2006, pp.302, 319). All of this development is, by definition, foundational to future experiences of the self.

Burton and Mitchell (2003) have noted that between the ages of five and ten, children experience a shift in where they locate authority on knowledge about their 'self', from their parents to themselves. That is, children begin to believe they know best about themselves, or, alternatively expressed, to develop rudimentary self knowledge, in middle childhood. By age 10 nearly every subjects cited themselves as the authority, even when the choice of a parent was available. A subsequent study by the same authors set a lower boundary on awareness of autobiographical knowledge at seven years, whereas former deliberations did not acknowledge the shift until age 11. Not only that, but subjects were able to judge what is known by the self only, and what is available about the self to others, which is fundamental to perspective taking and to social interaction prior to middle childhood, which they define as ages six to 12, where egocentrism is traditionally expected (Burton & Mitchell, 2003). As a result, as children progress through the years, they have increased access to their own thoughts and feelings, as well as others', and to distress or discrepancy in them.

Van den Bergh and De Rycke (2003) concur with Burton and Mitchell's conclusions. Their research attempted to validate an extension of Harter's self-perception profile test to younger ages than were originally intended, in response to the dearth of reliable assessment tools available for ages prior to adolescence. Harter's test explored the domain specific and global (overall) self perceptions of young people using self-report measures. To accomplish their task they altered the questions and response format to match younger styles of expression. In so doing, they log the multidimensionality of responses about the self from 2nd and 3rd graders, who improve on the distinctiveness of domain specific responses with increased age. Their age appropriate measures and observations in multiple arenas reveal a more mature understanding of the self in their subjects than was previously measured (Van den Bergh & De Rycke, 2003).

The authors also assessed global self-worth, or the overall evaluation of the self, through middle childhood. Children as young as six could give a unidimensional sense of global self worth when interviewed directly, which again became more differentiated with age (Van den Bergh & De Rycke, 2003). They cite and support Harter's stress on "the importance of social and cognitive *antecedents* of self representations, [and] socialization experiences [that] provide individual differences in the content of representations, including whether the evaluations of the self are favorable or unfavorable" (emphasis not in original)(Van den Bergh & De Rycke, 2003, p.206). While highlighting these antecedents in their subjects, they also acknowledge that there is no evidence of the middle childhood self being an integrative, higher order sense like that of later stages. Younger ages may have more of a "rudimentary feeling about the self rather than integration of distinct representations" (Van den Bergh & De Rycke, 2003, p.222).

Taken together, the findings of Van den Bergh and De Rycke are significant in their empirical validation of the emergence of a different, yet significant, expression of self worth in middle childhood. From early middle childhood there is some awareness of self concept and self worth, but it is differently experienced and expressed. Throughout the entire process, messages about the self are essential to current wellbeing, and to future identity formation. Developmental research has been short-sighted in its neglect to study, develop reliable measurements, and intervene until the process of healthy identity formation is at its adolescent climax, and the imprint of self-knowledge is already accomplished. Eating Disorders, then, are not alone-the same shortsightedness pervades throughout the mental health field.

Emotional Development and Distress

Woolsey (2002) uses the term distress to describe the unexpressed emotional dimension of the self-disclosure inherent in disordered eating behavior. Emotional development is a subcategory of cognitive development, and is also remarkably pertinent to identity genesis. Pomerantz and Rudolph (2003) link emotional disturbance in middle childhood and youth competence underestimation in a study that incorporated subjects belonging to both age categories. The authors note that while much is known about possible causal pathways for emotional distress, relatively little is known about its effects.

Their findings indicate that emotional distress predicts negative beliefs about the self and the world *over time*. Distress, according to Pomerantz and Rudolph, has developmental implications, which can lead to self- competency underestimation relative to performance (among other future risks). Follow-up pathway analysis supported their causal inference about distress and subsequent negative self evaluation. According to the authors, the process that underlies this relationship is reciprocal. Attribution style for positive or negative performance throughout development, uncertainty about standards, and loss of control are filters for the perception of self, and alter the mood of the child. Mood itself conveys information about a situation, and people with negative moods give their selective attention to negative information about the world and the self in the world (Seligman, 1995). The discouraging evaluative feedback selected in turn lowers estimation of success and ability. Thus the "cycle" begins much earlier. The young person may underestimate competence in isolated, momentary, and domain-specific situations during the elementary years, but these seeming minor incidents could be a reference for stable beliefs about the self in the future, and attendant mood conditions.

The idea proposed by Pomerantz and Rudolph (2003) is also described by Seligman's explanatory style, which highlights the power of the manner in which self- and life-events are described/explained autobiographically to affect self-perception during the constructive transition from diffuse identity (in Erikson's industry versus inferiority stage of middle childhood) to integrative identity in adolescence (Seligman, 1995). The positive or negative quality of interactive experience with the world, and of the self representations in relationship to that world that result, will be determined in large part by the explanatory style of the young person. Once children reach a sufficient level of metacognition for integration, the same explanatory style will determine what information is selected as significant for self identification, and the extent to which adequate or inadequate competency estimation (based on the multitude of single-event self descriptions) is generalized to the global self concept. Explanatory style is therefore a mediator between the identities of the two age brackets. If the young person assumes negative events are pervasive (across contexts), personal (their fault), and stable (with no hope for change), and therefore underestimates their competence to function successfully, their self concept will likewise be depressed (Seligman, 1995).

Aside from poor self esteem and emotional doldrums, competency underestimation is harmful in other ways. For example, chronic under estimators discourage themselves from even attempting difficult tasks, robbing themselves of the opportunity for both mastery and increased skill level (Seligman, 1995). Pomerantz and Rudolph support this reciprocity between depressive symptoms and decreased level of functioning. Negative self perceptions also interfere with defense processes that would normally counter an attack on the ego with affirmative reasoning (Pomerantz & Rudolph, 2003). That the negative interpretation of interaction with the environment can be generalized across areas of competency is further evidence that harmful energy originating outside the body image domain could come to be articulated as body image disturbance and disorder, and other eating disorder pathology/behavior. Explanatory style also explains individual differences in the persistency of emotional distress in some young people and not others, which contributes to unhealthy behaviors and attitudes/ beliefs (Pomerantz & Rudolph, 2003). Pomerantz and Rudolph (2003) characterize the late elementary years as a possible "time of major divergences among children in their competence estimation, with some children setting off on a downward trajectory" (p.332). Could this point of divergence, then, be the ideal time for Eating Disorder intervention, and prevention/intervention of other adolescent disorders?

Just who sets off on the eating disorder trajectory is another matter. Typically, in Pomerantz and Rudolph's (2003) study girls experienced more emotional distress than did boys. Girls used the academic domain to evaluate competency more than boys did, and underestimated their social performance as well. Thus, girls experience stress both due to perceived deficiencies in personal mastery/skill, as well as in their social identity. This extra measure of stress could be as adequate a hypothetical cause as any other for the preponderance of female eating disorder diagnoses. In fact, many of the underlying issues that drive the behavior of a diagnosed individual correlate to the factors that cause general emotional distress in middle childhood: assertion of control, creation of an absolute standard, coping with symptoms of anxiety, uncertainty about meeting the expectations of others, chronic competency underestimation, and delusional attributions for the performance of self and others. It is possible that the social domain becomes the major evaluative measure when girls reach adolescence, and earlier emotional distress, although experienced elsewhere, is generalized and localized in this gender- biased pressure. Consequently, eating disorders and body image distortion are feminized.

Ecological Considerations

The social factors that impact middle childhood development include family systems, parenting style, group formation, school environment, and increased peer influence.

The middle child spends far less time with their parents compared to earlier ages, and parents' opinion decreases in importance (Ashford, et al., 2006). Parenting style is, nevertheless, important, because it can contribute to excessive anxiety (through love withdrawal, for example) and failure to develop certain internal standards (e.g. through lack of induction) (Ashford, et al., 2006). Parents' explanatory style, with its consequences for world view and attributions made in the home environment, will affect the young person's mood, style, and competency beliefs. Mothers' attitudes about image and food specifically influence body image disturbance as well, though not as much as peers' attitudes and beliefs (Sands& Wardle, 2002). Even if eating disorders are not directly translated to the child, then, a pathway is still in place for emotional distress due to many other developmental and contextual factors, such as parental conflict (Park, Woolley, Maurray, & Stein, 2003).

Woolsey identifies four essential dimensions of a healthy family environment; when one is absent or out of balance in the family, disorder may be present in the individual child. These four developmental must- haves are a) unconditional love (most important through all of development), b) freedom letting, and c) limit setting, along with d) open discussion of the reasoning behind given appropriate boundaries. Throughout development unconditional love effects biochemistry and therefore feeding behavior- in fact,the family environment actually contributes to the biochemistry of the developing individual. Unconditional love, secure and consistent, is also the foundation for self esteem and confidence, defined as a sense of worth for who the child *is* (as opposed to what they do or how they look, etc) built through positive mirroring and reflection of the self by parents. Unconditional love is a prior familial factor related both to emotional health and nutritional health. Developing adult self identity, and interacting with the world's realities as an autonomous person (including later tasks like relational intimacy), is a risk requiring a basic sense of worth/ confidence. Again, these are factors that purely behavioral therapy, or even cognitive behavioral therapy dealing only with current problematic patterns, cannot hope to identify.

There also may exist more blatant familial reasons/secrets that motivate the disordered individual to avoid developing further- avoidance of developing sexuality due to past abuse, for example. In this way the disordered behavior carries not only the clients' own message, but also acts as a reliquary for family ills/secrets. Woolsey also asserts that effective treatment oftentimes means recreating the optimal familial relational environment. Whatever the meaning of the emotional message, the safe and accepting environment of the treatment team encourages the client that " knowing the truth is courageous and the authentic way to secure safety" (Woolsey, 2002, p.138).

"Anorexic families" are commonly very close, have strict patriarchal households, in which there is regularly a strong emphasis on achievement and pressure to be successful. Parents of anorexics have often achieved more than their own parents- rising in socioeconomic level. Emotions are frequently ignored or avoided. Parental over-involvement occurs when the parent chooses the activities of the child, enforces their opinions, and is critical of the child's self-assertiveness. This leaves little freedom and time for the developing child to individuate. Conflict results from any act of individuation or new behavior that goes against the grain of familial opinion (or the dominant members opinion), and there are spoken or unspoken family rules about every detail. Parental dictation of emotions thwarts emotional recognition and free expression; problem-solving and communication are suppressed, along with validation of the individual child, in order to maintain control and an image of perfection and familial unity. The child's control over food, expressing their need for control, makes sense as a response to, and reflection of, this type of parental overcontrol.

These are characteristics of the "enmeshed" family. Description of the enmeshed family environment makes evident the unmet basic needs of the anorexic, and provides clues to what is amiss in the four basic parental musts for healthy development. Considering the context, perhaps the core of Anorexia is about autonomous identity, validation of the self (especially the emotional self), and self-valuation, fully arising at the time of individuation (adolescence). There are many developmental pathways formed by this environment that contribute to the anorexic mindset.

Additionally, the primacy of peer influence during the middle childhood period opens the child up to a new range of biographical feedback. For girls, even more so than boys, both intrapersonal and interpersonal information become important (Lytle, et al., 1997). Both aspects, the former concerning individuality and the latter concerning necessary social relationships, are worked on simultaneously in girls. Interpersonal development encompasses the self in relation to others, self and interpersonal control, and the need for substantive relationships rather than superficial ones (Lytle, et al., 1997). Girls in middle childhood feel increased pressure to approximate the expectations of others, and incorporate those expectations as elements of their ideal (Brown & Gilligan, 1993). Peer groups most often occur in school settings, with increased peer contact and stability compared to the past, strengthening the influence of social feedback and group inclusion.

Referents used to determine group inclusion for girls often include physical attributes, and the impact of body image feedback is evidenced, as discussed, by the detrimental consequences of peer teasing. "Peers are critical to the healthy development of a child" and "the absence of peer friendship speaks clearly to how important it is for healthy development" (Ashford, et al., 2006, p.330). Internalized messages of rejection cause considerable emotional distress, anxiety, disengagement, and mental health problems particularly for girls (LeCroy & Daley, 2001). If those messages are based on physical attributes the connection may later be made that the young person is not acceptable for reasons of his/her physical characteristics. If social troubles continue into adolescence, the young person might then assume a common cause even if their body image is normative after the pubertal growth spurt. In this way dysmorphism and overactive regulation might theoretically develop.

Sexual socialization is also retarded when little engagement in peer groups takes place, possibly contributing to the acceptance and internalization of media images of sexual attractiveness to gain access to peer groups. Peer attitudes and the degree of internalization of this "thin ideal" has been closely associated with body image awareness and disturbance, and dieting behaviors in young girls (Sands & Wardle, 2002, p.1). Sociocultural ideals are references for construction of one's own body image (Sands & Wardle, 2002). Both awareness and internalization of the thin body ideal are convergent with body dissatisfaction and eating disturbance (Sands & Wardle, 2002). Additionally, Sands and Wardle did not find that internalization correlated with *change* in dieting behavior over the teen years (16 to 19), suggesting that internalization may take place *exclusively* in the earlier periods, when the behavior is first manifested (Sands & Wardle, 2002). Once again, sublevel messages about the self in middle childhood provide the relevant, *and perhaps the most important,* data. By age nine "some of the psychological processes related to the development of body dissatisfaction may already be in place", before the influx of puberty (Sands & Wardle, 2002, p.201). "Girls in their preadolescent...years are recipients of sociocultural information concerning the importance of thinness" (Sand & Wardle, 2002, p.203)

Yet Sand and Wardles' study did not find that media had the level of influence that significant others did. It is unclear whether others' attitudes toward the sociocultural ideal accounts for their greater influence, or if others' set of expectations in general have the greater power (in which case expectations in other domains would apply as well). In either case, the influence of the macro social environment, with the social expectations of larger society, is mediated by the micro environment of family and peer interpretation of those ideals.

Summarizing the BI Corallary

After all this extensive exploration, it cannot be stated with any certainty whether body image disturbance and disordered eating patterns result from negatively perceived messages in the specific domain of physical appearance, that are consciously realized in adolescence alone and incorporated into the solidifying self; or whether they are caused by latent emotional distress of a broad description that is channeled into the physical domain because it is the primary natural focus during and after puberty. There seems to be some body of evidence for the effects of domain specific influences and events, but the lack of research in other domains fails to rule out their importance, and the current research is often tainted by age inappropriate measures.

It is more obvious in families where there is a history of eating disturbances why young people would express internal conflicts through that behavior, than it is in families with no history of the disorder, especially since immediate influence of significant others seems to outweigh broader sociocultural expectations. That eating disorders and body image disturbance have been documented as endemic to western culture (almost without exception-it can unfortunately be used as an indicator of the infiltration of western ideas into other cultures) does not aid in the determination; one could argue that emphasis on individuality, with de-emphasis on extended family identity and support, could create sufficient emotional distress in adolescents (which is channeled into adolescent issue that have been informed by western ideals) just as easily as one could argue merely for the influence of western media images.

Phenomenological Nature: Back to EDs

According to Woolsey's model there are a million different developmental/behavioral pathways, strung along through years of nature and nurture combined with series of individual choices, which can result in any given behavioral set at time of presentation. Each client has her own personal "off ramps". From an extremely phenomenological viewpoint, there may be as many core reasons for the anorexic mindset and self-representation as there are anorexic clients, and the message each disorder is communicating would likewise be unique. "Each eating disorder is unique, as are situations and emotions that contribute to its development" (Woolsey, 2002, p.103). However, it is the job of the treatment field to put together some description of what risk factors, combined with what certain personality types or traits, can result in this particular expression. Why do clients end up experiencing low tolerance for emotional distress, poor social problem solving, hyper or hypoactive sense of control, reward dependence, harm avoidance, avoidance of emotional intimacy, and overdependence on others ? The answer to these inquiries will aid clinicians in earlier ED recognition, and in treatment that meets clients where thye are emotionally, to better reset these clients on their pathway and equip them to conquer the challenges (including missed developmental tasks) and fears they face on the way to healthy development (Woolsey, 2002)?

A perspective that considers sets of risk factors more broad in scope for ED etiology enlightens the gulf between diagnosis in that category. Differences between anorexic and bulimic expression could have to do with the disorder's nature itself, the personality of the individual presenting, or the particular developmental occurrences and stages/tasks in question- it is a multidimensional dilemma. In any case the eating behaviors themselves are not the root of the pathology, but the strong needs that these behaviors fill, and the broken places they are meant to restructure or mend, are the illness in the client. Eating disorders are actually on the more severe end of derealization. An exclusively biophysical focus may further occludes the repressed trauma, distress, and desires that are present, and structured plans for food intake and weight gain may be counterproductive to healing in as much as they support dissociative pathology.

The nature of an eating disorder dictates that the client will connect unrelated problems to food and body weight. Traditional focus on diet and medical outcomes in identifying, diagnosing, and treating is "inadequate for a combination of reasons" (Woolsey, 2002, p.180). Managed health care, short term and outpatient based treatment leave little room for discovering the hidden secrets of the disorder. Longstanding psychosocial stressors are not as observable or measurable; and are too uncomfortable (or unavailable) to discuss openly (Woolsey, 2002). Clients themselves may not, in some cases, be aware of how medical issues are connected to deeply felt needs, how surface-oriented treatment is, or why they cannot seem to follow through with treatment goals in the long term. The client themselves may hope the medically based treatment plan will solve these deeper developmental issues as well. High rates of failure to respond to treatment and recidivism are not indicative of some fault in the clients, but that the core of the illness was not in the targeted behavior; "the behavior itself was not as important as why the behavior was chosen in the first place" (Woolsey, 2002, p.181).

What Practitioners Understand: the Language of Eating Disorders

As the connection between developmental stress/distress and eating disorders can aid in effective treatment, it can also be observed retrospectively through the lens of effective treatment. Woolsey describes anorexic behavior as an attempt to communicate where other avenues have failed. In her manual for nutritional practice with eating disorders, she insists that excellent treatment of eating disorders must consider the behavior as a means of communication, rather than simply patterns of actions needing change. She shifts the initial treatment focus from diagnosing and categorizing, to empathic questioning of the client and listening to what the client has to say, thus tapping the tip of the broken communication iceberg (which has lead to these maladaptive attempts at self-disclosure) and the many messages lying underneath. Eating pathology and behavior could be an expression of distress over unmet needs or other deeply traumatizing occurrences that had significant meaning for the self; and they may also mask and numb awareness of these true stressors.

Making the primary focus the behaviors in treatment may be related to poor outcome results in the overall field. The practitioner must interpret into words these behavioral expressions, teasing out meaningful behaviors from ED rituals; the question being what the individual is trying to communicate (e.g. important family events, social occurrences, abuse with implications for the self). Thus, food behaviors are a tangible, alternative language that communicate feelings not allowed to be verbally expressed, and an arena for control of emotional affairs and validation. The client's executive self is attempting to manage internal distress and shame. To ignore this message is to reinvent the dynamics tahte ngendered the disorder, and futher solidify the client's belief that her emotions/emotional message (and her self-message) is not considered important or worthwhile.

Eating disordered behaviors and identity give definition, value, control, and substance to clients' with lacking inner sense of worth; they are "an escape and a confidante" to the client (Woolsey, 2002). Woolsey personifies anorexia and bulimia, quoting them as though they were indeed the client speaking themselves, as part of the client's identity: anorexia cries "I can't take it in. I can't take in food, life, or people. I am not good enough"; Bulimia echoes " I dare to take it in, but then I have to get rid of it. I am not entitled to keep it" (Woolsey, 2002, p.312). The client is engaged in an "ongoing process of creating value in one's life (Woolsey, 2002, p.332), of accepting who and what she is. The ultimate goal of eating disorder therapy, according to Woolsey (2002), is to establish a new sense of self, one that replaces the self-identity dependant on the disorder for definition, comfort, protection, intimacy, and salvation.

CONCLUSION

Treatment resources have been, until recently, directed to description of the problem, with the assumption that any relevant variables would be contained in the adolescent stage. It is time for treatment research to delve more deeply into the formation of identity, including physical identity, so that the depth of culpable variables and their effects on the presenting young person can be fully understood. Sociocultural influences aimed at the adolescent who is able to be self aware and self reflective do not fully explain the subconscious and deeply engrained elements of dysmorphism and compulsive ill-nurturing, nor does it give ear to the distressed cry of the individual. It is imperative that the more vulnerable and less guarded middle child, who is constantly and consistently receiving the self impressions that will later inform their very sense of self worth, be examined.

Who can make sense of this illogical way of being? Efforts must continue to examine the clients' self perceptions. Only the client has access to the identity and meaning of her disorder. Although anorexic individuals are caught in the prison of their mental dominance, most clearly understand the details of their behavior, what the goal of their behavior is, and what meaning these goals have for them. Reference the proliferation of pro-anorexic web sites, dubbed the Pro-Ana internet movement, that share in detail the anorexic mind. Certainly this is a difficult nut to crack if the client's basic understanding of the needs that drive the pathology, which they themselves cannot escape, are not what dictates the direction of treatment. To include the voice of the anorexic, which is (dangerously) finding its own forum elsewhere, is our only hope of reaching these clients- and the only way to avoid being drawn into their dysfunctional patterns as a profession.

If our clinical focus for diagnosis and treatment were the client, rather than prescribed overt symptomology, would we find that individuals who present with Bulimia and Anorexia have significant differences that will effect the identity of their pathology and the efficacy of our approach (given the differences in personality of the presenting behavior)? Could two very different pathologies, resulting from different personalities, be expressed through the same medium (food behaviors)? And if this is true for the eating disorders, what implications does this have for other diagnosis in the DSM, for use of it (and the medical model approach) as our primary diagnostic tool ?

If much of the information needed to understand and treat AN, resides in the client him/herself, rather than as it is currently prescribed by a given treatment modality, then the resulting question becomes: can ED clients be highly communicative of their own pathology? As discussed, some in the treatment field consider the eating disorders themselves, and their associated behaviors, as means of communicating core pathology -rather than the substance and content of the pathology.

The treatment research community, as it is represented in literature, cannot continue to prescribe an interpretation of pathology for clients, and then consider improvement based on outcomes measures within that interpretation as success, when there is evidence (from treatment and recidivism data as well as client review) that neither the interpretation (when there is a coherent one) nor the treatment modality itself is particularly helpful. We are essentially trapped in our own models: for example, CBT teaches clients the CBT model of eating pathology, in effect teaching clients what their own disorder is, and then measures outcomes based on the taught model (Stein, et al, 2001). Are clients truly improving in their disorder, or only in what has been proposed by the treatment? What role does the desire for clinical/clinician approval play in their improvement on prescribed measures (an expression of, rather than reduction in, pathology)? Detracting from progress may be self gratification on the part of the treatment/research community, oblivious to the client who walks away still plagued by the unrecognized, undescribed, underlying issues of her pathological behavior. Not only must we recognize the client's need to voice his or her disorder to the depth it occurs on the day of presentation, but also to voice the full message of what has occurred to create such a disturbing and mysterious product.

If the client is allowed to express what is at the core of distress, rather than having that behavior immediately labeled and targeted for change, the clinician may then be able to guide the client through developmental tasks and stages necessary to learn new, healthier behavioral pathways, as their clients themselves come to fully understand what it is they need to decipher. New on ramps are constructed and reinforced in response to stimuli, until the new cognitive and behavioral pathway is preferred (Woolsey, 2002). Anorexia is a reaction to acute stress; however, that stress could be at any point in development, and in any life domain. Though clients at some point develop a mindset that allows for the disorder, the events that trigger the pathology might be different for every client, and the personal story of each client is part of what gives their disorder its very personal identity.

If general developmental stress is at the core of anorexia, treatment must allow for as broad a focus if we hope to capture the realities that maintain the anorexic mindset, if not the anorexia itself, leaving clients so vulnerable to chronicity. It is a biopsychosocial disorder, an excellent example of the relationship among dimensions of human being and living- so that the "answers to these questions are found outside the medical model" (Woolsey, 2002, p.93). One avenue for pinpointing treatment targets broad in scope, and reducing the myriad of contributing factors to an accurate description, is to further examine the client herself.

Getting There

Research, then, should move away from simplistic hypotheses and into a more exploratory paradigm that considers the breadth of possibilities for complex relationships (intrapersonal and interpersonally) between observable manifestations of complex pathologies. After all, by studying manifest variables in diagnosed clients, we not only are confined to the observable tip of the iceberg (and the more conscious tip), but also to attempting to tease out causation through retrospective hypothesizing. The challenge for researchers is to study the etiological and qualitative process, rather than static categories. This requires including more research on sub clinical symptomology (von Ranson, McGue, & Iacono, 2003). Co-morbidity in itself is a testimony to the dynamic and evolving character of disordered thought and behavior. In order to understand the clinical significance of any pathology and its predictive importance to a specific human population, it must be framed in research as what it truly is- a fluid pattern in human behavior and psychology, possibly irreducible from the intricate cocktail of influences that produce, refine, and alter it. The scientific community has not yet built a research foundation solid enough on eating disorders themselves, much less compounded eating disorders and other behaviors.

It is not as impossible as it may seem to combine scientifically responsible practice and research, with an honest view of human behavior within human being and living, once the approach is integrated. The study conducted by Tarter, Sambrano, and Dunn (2002), is a good example that demonstrates the possibility and efficacy of studying the process of pathology, rather than the established product. Their mindset, and the product resulting from their efforts, represents an important new direction. The authors produce a superb example of how to empirically study while using a systems perspective, for the purpose of early intervention and prevention. Rather than being aimed at the disorder per se (e.g., Substance Use Disorder), the authors focused their energy on modifying identified intermediary factors to the development of abuse. Thorough exploration of risk factors associated with the disorder (including social competence, parent involvement, and school bonding, etc...), and early phenotypes particularly at risk, preceded and informed the study of intervention efficacy. The authors conceptualized behavior as the result of individual predisposition toward or away from negative outcomes, the expression of a phenotype produced from a history of successive interactions with the environment. Each new interaction produces a culminating phenotype (a person in process), which moves the individual into more or less risk. By identifying phenotypes that are at risk, interventions can be targeted earlier, rather than deferring treatment until a problem is imminent (diagnosable). The authors studied phenotypes from infancy onward. Their model is dynamic, diathesis-stress related, and takes into account personal volition as well. The authors discuss "vectors", such as personal temperament, each of which have both direction and force as they combine to move the individual toward or away from the targeted outcome.

Multidimensional traits of time, biology, psychology, and environment are included in calculation of overall risk for disorder, a more useful calculation than diagnostic co-occurrence. Their goal is to produce information that would allow for intervention as early as is feasible and efficacious, with those factors most economic and amenable to treatment (Tarter, Sambrano, & Dunn, 2002). Such a model allows for the full range of individual possibilities in pathology development (factors having different weight and interacting uniquely within individual context) while meaningfully applying this information toward a model of intervention. "It is important to conceptualize intervention as an ongoing process throughout the lifespan" (Tarter, Sambrano, & Dunn, 2002). This type of research also encourages funding for general health and wellbeing, where there is skepticism about the value of early interventions that do not produce immediately observable benefits. With new thinking and new research directions progress can be made to prevent and remediate the destructive forces that underlie eating disorders.

REFERENCES

American Psychiatric Association (1994) *Diagnostic and statistical manual of mental disorders: Fourth Edition, text revised.* Washington: American Psychiatric Association.

Ashford, J.B., LeCroy, C.W., & Lortie, K.L. (2006). *Human behavior in the social environment (3rd edition).* Belmont, CA: Wadsworth.

Burton, S.B., & Mitchell, P. (2003). Judging who knows best about yourself: Developmental changes in citing the self across middle childhood. *Child Development, 74,* 426-443.

Davison, K.K., & Birch, L.L. (2002). Processes linked to weight status and self concept among girls from ages 5 to 7. *Developmental Psychology, 38,* 735-748.

Fairburn, C.G., Shafran, R., & Cooper, Z. (1999). A cognitive behavioral theory of Anorexia Nervosa. *Behavior Research and Therapy. 37,* 1-13.

LeCroy, C. W., & Daley, J. (2001). *Empowering Adolescent Girls: Examining the present and building skills for the future.* New York: W. W. Norton.

Lytle, L.J., Bakken, L., & Romig, C. (1997). Female adolescent identity development. *A Journal of Research, 37,* 175-186.

Newton, T. (2001) Consumer involvement in the appraisal of treatments for people with eating disorders: A neglected area of research? *European Eating Disorder Review, 9,* 301-308.

Oosterwegel, A., & Oppenheimer, L. (2002) Jumping to awareness of conflict between self-representations and its relation to psychological wellbeing. *International Journal of Behavior Development, 26,* 548-555.

Park, R.J, Woolley, H., Murray, L., & Stein, A. (2003). Child: *Care, Health, and Development. 29,* 111-120.

Pomerantz, E.M., & Rudolph, K.D. (2003). What ensues from emotional distress? Implications for competence estimation. *Child Development, 74,* 329-345.

Richards, P.S., Baldwin, B.M., Frost, H.A., Clark-Sly, J.B., Berrett, M.E., & Hardman, R.K. (2000). What works for treating eating disorders? Conclusions of 28 outcome reviews. *Eating Disorders 8*, 189-207.

Rosen, J. (1996).Body image assessment and treatment in controlled studies of eating disorders. *International Journal of Eating Disorders. 20*, 331-343.

Sands, E.R., & Wardle, J. (2003). Internalization of the ideal body shapes in nine to 12 year old girls. *International Journal of Eating Disorders, 33*, 193-204.

Seligman, M.E.P. (1995). *The Optimistic Child*. New York: Harper Collins.

Stein, R.L., Saelens, B.E., Dounchis, J.Z., Lewczyk, C.M., Swenson, A.K., & Wilfley, D.E. (2001). Treatment of eating disorders in women. *The Counseling Psychologist, 29*, 695-732.

Tarter, E., Sambrano, S., & Dunn, M. G.(2002). Predictor variables by developmental stages: A center for substance abuse prevention multisite study. *Psychology of Addictive Behaviors 16*, 3-10.

Van den Bergh, B.H., & De Rycke, L. (2003). Measuring the multi-dimensional self-concept and global self-worth of 6- to 8- year-olds. *Journal of Genetic Psychology. 164*, 201-226.

Von Ranson, K. M., McGue, M., & Iacono, W. G. (2003). Disordered eating and substance use in an epidemiological sample: II. Associations within families. *Psychology of Addictive Behaviors 17*,193-202.

Woolsey, M. (2002). *Eating disorders: A clinical guide to counseling and treatment*. Chicago: American Dietetic Association.

In: Body Image: New Research
Editor: Marlene V. Kindes, pp. 131-144

ISBN 1-60021-059-7
© 2006 Nova Science Publishers, Inc.

Chapter VI

BORDERLINE PERSONALITY DISORDER AND BODY IMAGE

Randy A. Sansone[1], and Lori A. Sansone[2]*

[1]Wright State University School of Medicine in Dayton, Ohio
[2]Wright-Patterson Air Force Base 88 MDOS/SGOPC in Dayton, Ohio

ABSTRACT

In this chapter, we describe the manifestations of body image disturbance in individuals with borderline personality disorder as they might appear in psychiatric and medical settings. In psychiatric settings, body image disturbances may be one of several mediators for self-harm behavior, which is commonly observed in patients with borderline personality. In medical settings, body image disturbances may play a meaningful role in ill-defined somatic complaints or somatic preoccupation in patients as well as medically self-harming behavior. In either setting, the body image disturbances encountered in borderline personality disorder are likely to be due to the effects of childhood trauma. If so, then the body image disturbances encountered in borderline personality are not necessarily due to the disorder, itself, but rather to one of the proposed etiological substrates—childhood trauma.

Keywords: body image, borderline personality, self-harm behavior, somatic preoccupation

Borderline personality is an Axis II disorder characterized by a superficially intact social façade, and underlying chronic self-regulation difficulties and self-harm behavior (SHB). Self-regulation difficulties may include eating pathology (e.g., anorexia or bulimia nervosa, obesity), substance abuse (e.g., alcohol, illicit substances, prescription medication),

* Correspondence concerning this article should be addressed to Dr. Randy A. Sansone, M.D., Sycamore Primary Care Center, 2115 Leiter Road, Miamisburg, Ohio, 45342. Telephone: 937-384-6850. FAX: 937-384-6938. E-mail: Randy.sansone@kmcnetwork.org.

promiscuity, an inability to effectively regulate money (e.g., problematic gambling, credit card debt, bankruptcies), and chronic pain syndromes. SHB is generally prolific and ongoing, and ranges from low-lethal behavior such as self-mutilation to high-lethal behavior such as suicide attempts. In the *Diagnostic and Statistical Manual of Mental Disorders, 4th edition* (American Psychiatric Association, 1994), borderline personality disorder (BPD) is classified as a Cluster B personality disorder, which captures the impulsive, erratic, and dramatic characteristics encountered in this type of symptomatology. In this chapter, we discuss the relationships between BPD and body dissatisfaction.

As a preamble to the pages that follow, we will use a variety of terms to capture body dissatisfaction. These include *negative body image* (i.e., the negative perception of one's body), *body dysphoria* (i.e., negative feelings about one's body), *body dissatisfaction* (i.e., discontent or feelings of disappointment about one's body), *body conflict* (i.e., the misperception that one's body is inadequate or defective in some way), and *body image problems* (i.e., a generalized term for the plethora of cognitive, affective, perceptual, and kinesthetic difficulties related to body experience). While these terms are not fully interchangeable, they encompass multiple aspects of negative feelings and attitudes about one's body.

OVERVIEW OF BPD

Epidemiology

Prevalence

According to the DSM-IV (American Psychiatric Association, 1994), the prevalence of borderline personality in the general population is around 2%. According to Stone (1986), however, the community prevalence may be as high as 10%. In inpatient and outpatient psychiatric settings, the prevalence of BPD is fairly high (Quigley, 2005). Widiger and Rogers (1989) found the prevalence of BPD in inpatient and outpatient psychiatric settings to be 15% and 27%, respectively. In addition, Widiger & Weissman (1991) found that up to 50% of inpatients with personality disorders suffer from BPD. In an inpatient psychiatric sample, we determined the prevalence of BPD to be about 50%, either on clinical interview or using a DSM-IV criteria checklist (Sansone, Songer, & Gaither, 2001). In a retrospective review of medical records in a university-based outpatient psychotherapy clinic, we found the prevalence of BPD traits or disorder to be around 20% (Sansone, Rytwinski, & Gaither, 2003). In our studies in primary care settings, the prevalence of borderline personality symptomatology (i.e., not necessarily the full disorder) among outpatients is typically around 20-30% (Sansone, Sansone, & Wiederman, 1995; Sansone, Sansone, & Gaither, 2004).

Gender Distribution

While BPD appears to be diagnosed more in women than men, this may relate to gender differences with regard to presentation. For example, women with BPD tend to demonstrate self-directed SHB (e.g., cutting or burning self), have histrionic features, and manifest high rates of eating disorders and post-traumatic stress disorder (Johnson et al., 2003). In contrast, men with BPD tend to externalize SHB (e.g., bar fights), demonstrate antisocial features with unexpectedly high interpersonal attachment, and have high rates of substance abuse (Johnson et al.). Because of these gender differences, women with BPD tend to surface in mental health settings, while men with BPD tend to wind up in penal institutions.

Ethnic/Racial Distribution

As for ethnic and/or racial distribution, BPD *appears* to be more common in Western cultures (Paris, 1996). In one of the few available US ethnic studies, Chavira and colleagues (2003) found that, compared to Whites and Blacks, Hispanics evidenced higher rates of BPD.

Etiology: A Multi-Determined Disorder

BPD appears to be a multi-determined disorder. However, while genetics (Skodol et al., 2002) and parental psychopathology (Bradley, Jenei, & Westen, 2005; Zanarini et al., 2000; Zanarini et al., 2004) appear to play meaningful roles in the development of BPD, repetitive trauma in early development appears to be a fairly predominant substrate in the majority of afflicted individuals (see Sansone & Sansone, 2000).

According to various studies, early trauma may consist of sexual, physical, or emotional abuse, as well as the witnessing of violence, and various combinations of these childhood adversities (Sansone & Sansone, 2000). Physical neglect, in the sense of insufficient food, inadequate medical care, and/or lack of heat in the home, has not been associated with BPD. While these relationships have been studied primarily in psychiatric or community samples, we also found that traumatic childhood experiences correlated with BPD in a sample of 152 primary care patients (Sansone et al., 1995). *Importantly, we believe that the presence of childhood trauma in BPD accounts for the preponderance of body-image issues encountered in these patients.*

CLINICAL PRESENTATION OF BODY IMAGE ISSUES IN BPD

Body Image Issues in Psychiatric Settings

In addition to a host of other symptoms, SHB is typically encountered in individuals with BPD. While patients with other psychiatric disorders may occasionally manifest SHB (e.g., depression, schizophrenia), such behavior has been described as the "behavioral specialty" (Mack, 1975) of individuals suffering from BPD. Indeed, in our studies of psychiatric and primary care samples, such associations clearly and consistently emerge.

In our experience in psychiatric settings, SHB is frequently acted out on the body. A negative body image, body dysphoria or dissatisfaction, or at the very least, body indifference would seem to facilitate such behavior. Given that SHB is the culmination of internal and interpersonal conflicts, the body is fairly convenient as the recipient of self-destructive acts, as if the body existed apart, or independently, from oneself.

In psychiatric settings, a fairly common form of SHB among patients with BPD is self-mutilation. Nominal self-mutilation may include scratching oneself or excessively rubbing skin surfaces. More dramatic and disfiguring forms of self-mutilation include behaviors such as cutting, burning, or scarring oneself; pulling earrings through one's earlobes; and pulling out head hair and eyelashes. Augmenting the preceding behaviors, other forms of body maltreatment are also fairly common. Examples include hitting oneself, biting the inside of one's mouth, and punching walls (i.e., damage to the hands). More subtle examples of body maltreatment include having multiple "accidents" (e.g., burning oneself with a curling iron, falling down stairs, experiencing repeated grease burns while deep frying foods), avoiding necessary medical care, intentionally starving oneself, purposefully exercising an injury, abusing laxatives and diuretics, and inducing vomiting. The body might also be degraded through promiscuity and/or sadomasochistic relationships with others.

Body Image Issues in Medical Settings

In medical settings, body dysphoria or dissatisfaction among those with BPD may manifest in the preceding traditional ways; however, these dynamics commonly manifest in somatic modes. Oftentimes, this takes the form of multiple somatic complaints or somatic preoccupation (Sansone & Sansone, 2004). These somatic symptoms are typically diffuse (i.e., involve multiple body areas), lack medical confirmation through either physical or laboratory examination, and are ever present. BPD patients may not only develop and maintain multiple somatic symptoms, but may also magnify existing ones. For example, in a study of diabetic outpatients (Sansone, Sansone, & Gaither, 2004), we found that 90% of individuals without BPD accurately identified their medical complications while 50% of those with BPD reported a complication that was not verified in the medical record (i.e., non-existent).

In addition to somatic preoccupation, patients with BPD may actively sabotage their medical care (i.e., intentful propagation of the myth of the medically problematic body?), which has obvious negative consequences for the body and one's health. In support of this, we describe the following two studies. In the first (Sansone, Wiederman, Sansone, & Mehnert-Kay, 1997), we surveyed 411 outpatients in a university-based family practice clinic and found that 7% candidly acknowledged the active sabotage of their medical care. In this study, examples of medical sabotage included exposing oneself to an infected individual with the intent of getting infected; purposefully misusing prescription medications to worsen an illness; not following medical advise to purposefully prolong an illness; and preventing wounds from healing. In this initial study, we confirmed among primary care patients the existence of medically self-sabotaging behavior, with obvious effects on the body; however, we could not conclude that these individuals suffered from BPD. In a second study, we surveyed 118 internal medicine outpatients and found that among medical self-harmers, 80% or more exceeded the cutoff on one of two measures for BPD (Sansone, Wiederman, & Sansone, 2000). This second study confirmed our suspicion that those patients who sabotage their medical care are likely to suffer from BPD. Not surprisingly, we confirmed this relationship in a psychiatric sample (Sansone, Songer, & Gaither, 2000), as well.

In addition to somatic preoccupation and medical self-sabotage, body dysphoria and/or dissatisfaction may also manifest in BPD patients as various chronic pain syndromes (literally, "the body hurts"). In a study of chronic pain patients who were being seen in a family medicine setting, we found that 50% met the criteria for BPD based upon a well-validated semi-structured interview (Sansone, Whitecar, Meier, & Murry, 2001).

Body image conflicts in BPD patients in medical settings may also present as factitious illness, wherein the body is intentionally and illegitimately labeled as defective. In a review of the literature, Sutherland and Rodin (1990) found an association between BPD and factitious disorders. In addition, psychogenic seizures have been associated with BPD (Binzer, Stone, & Sharpe, 2004; Harris, Dinn, & Marcinkiewicz, 2002; Reuber, Pukrop, Bauer, Derfuss, & Elger, 2004). In a dramatic variation of factitious disorder, some patients may manifest Munchausen's syndrome, in which sufferers subject themselves to repeated medical evaluations and potentially painful procedures in a determined effort to maintain their roles as pseudo-patients.

Because of the presence of various body "dysfunctions," patients with BPD in medical settings may wind up on employment disability for medical reasons ("My body's not good enough to work"). In this regard, Ekselius, Eriksson, von Knorring, and Linder (1996) found that the presence of a Cluster B personality disorder predicted an earlier age of longstanding work disability. In addition, in sample of 45 internal medicine outpatients, we found that 72% of the disabled participants met the criteria for BPD on at least one of two measures, as opposed to 26% of nondisabled participants (Sansone, Hruschka, Vasudevan, & Miller, 2003).

EARLY CHILDHOOD TRAUMA AND THE EFFECTS ON BODY IMAGE

We believe that the negative perceptions and feelings about one's body, which are clinically observed in individuals with BPD in both psychiatric and medical settings, are primarily related to trauma dynamics in early development. As mentioned previously, childhood trauma is a known substrate for this Axis II disorder. In the following section, we review the available studies on the relationship between childhood trauma and body image difficulties, both in those with and without BPD.

Borderline Personality and Body Image

Little is written on the topic of borderline personality and body image, per se. Unfortunately, several citations in the literature on the relationship between BPD and body image are written in foreign languages. For example, one is written in German (Haaf, Pohl, Deusinger, & Bohus, 2001) and two in French (Birot, 1993; Nicolopoulou & Kindynis, 1989). However, two studies *are* available in English. In the first, Steiger, Leung, and Houle (1992) examined borderline personality symptomatology and body image issues in a nonclinical sample (high school students) and observed four distinct subsamples: (a) those with high body dissatisfaction and BPD features; (b) those with high body dissatisfaction, alone; (c) those with high BPD features, alone; and (d) those with neither. For our discussion, the most relevant finding was that in a nonclinical sample, these investigators encountered a subsample of participants with BPD features seemingly *without* body dissatisfaction. This might represent the subgroup of BPD patients who do not evidence early-developmental trauma as a contributory substrate.

In the second study, we examined BPD and body image issues in a *clinical* sample (Sansone, Wiederman, & Monteith, 2001) of 48 women in an adult outpatient psychiatric clinic. To examine body image, we asked participants to indicate their response to the following statements using a 7-point Likert-style scale: "Overall, I would rate the attractiveness of my body as..." and "Overall, I would rate the attractiveness of my face as..." We also explored self avoidance due to body image concerns. After controlling for BMI, the preceding body image items all remained statistically correlated to scores on the measure for BPD. These data indicate that, in this outpatient psychiatric sample of women, body image disturbances are associated with BPD. The difference in our findings compared with Steiger and colleagues (1992) may reside in the age of the samples under study, recruitment characteristics (i.e., clinical versus nonclinical samples), and/or the presence or not of trauma factors.

Childhood Sexual Abuse and Body Image

Given that childhood abuse is one of several contributory substrates for BPD, it is relevant to review studies examining body image issues among victims of such abuse. Not surprisingly, the majority of studies examining the effects of childhood abuse on body image relate to *sexual* abuse in *female* subjects. A number of studies indicate a relationship between these two phenomena. Brown (1998) examined 22 women with incest histories and a comparison group of women with no such history; survivors of incest demonstrated greater body image distortion. Truppi (2001) described the effects of sexual abuse in young children, specifically highlighting the findings of distorted body image and low self-concept. Among women who were sexually abused as children, Corbett (1998) described low self-worth and distorted body image. Compared with controls, Wenninger and Heiman (1998) found that victims of childhood sexual abuse ($N = 57$) reported less body esteem and greater perceptions of negative health. Finally, Hunter (1991) compared 52 individuals with histories of childhood abuse to controls and confirmed body image disturbances in female participants with abuse backgrounds.

Several studies have examined particular facets of sexual abuse in childhood and their possible relationship to body image issues. In this regard, O'Neil (1997) found among 489 college women that childhood sexual abuse by a parental figure was associated with less attention to fitness. Whealin and Jackson (2002) examined *unwanted* sexual attention in childhood, rather than overt sexual abuse; the frequency of unwanted sexual attention in childhood was associated with body image difficulties and body anxiety in adulthood. Weiner and Thompson (1997) explored the relationship between covert versus overt sexual abuse, and found that covert abuse was related to the development of body image problems. Finally, among adult males who engage in sadomasochistic relationships, Nordling, Sandnabba, and Santtila (2000) found that childhood sexual abuse correlated with poor body image.

It is important to note that not all studies have found a relationship between childhood sexual abuse and body image problems (Byram, Wagner, & Waller, 1995; Duran, 1998; Haaf et al., 2001; Kolar, 1995; Schaaf & McCanne, 1994). We suspect that the divergent findings of both groups of researchers (i.e., those confirming versus those discounting a correlation between childhood sexual abuse and body image problems) are valid. The differences between these seemingly polar findings are probably in the *context* of abuse as well as the *methodologies* of the various studies.

As for the *context* of childhood sexual abuse, Hyde and Kaufman (1984) described several influential factors that may affect empirical results such as the age at which the molestation began, frequency and duration, relationship of the perpetrator to the victim, the form of abuse, methods used to contain the "secret," the degree of isolation of the "secret," and the manner in which the exposure of the secret is handled. Additional factors may include the number of perpetrators, the availability or not of parental/family support, the presence or not of a threat to one's life or the life of a family member, and the degree of aggression associated with the abuse.

From a *methodological perspective*, studies vary highly in terms of the number of participants, the assessment measures for sexual abuse, sample composition (clinical versus nonclinical), recruitment approach (treatment-seeking versus not, primary versus tertiary care settings), and subject factors. Subject factors include those psychological elements that impair the accurate recollection of abuse. Explicitly, the recollection of events by participants may be compromised by repression, suppression, denial, dissociation, and interpretation. Regarding interpretation, we recall one male subject who adamantly denied any history of abuse, but casually acknowledged that his father routinely beat him on the head with a belt buckle. The subject rationalized this abusive behavior in terms of his own attentional problems—"My dad needed to keep me in line—I suffered from ADHD as a kid." Likewise, subjects may have difficulty interpreting the abuse if they ambivalently enjoyed some aspect of the experience, felt responsible for it, or experienced some level of empowerment from it (i.e., "It's not abuse if I somehow enjoyed it, encouraged it, or benefited from it financially or status-wise.") Finally, there is the statistical dilemma of inquiring about multiple and detailed facets of abuse (e.g., age of onset, relationship of the perpetrator to the victim, type of abuse, duration) and generating large numbers of subsamples that cannot be effectively analyzed due to the small numbers of participants in each study cell.

Other Forms of Childhood Abuse and Body Image

As noted previously, the bulk of studies in this area have concentrated on childhood sexual abuse in females and subsequent body image problems in adulthood. However, there are a handful of additional studies that have examined other forms of childhood abuse and their effects on body image. Treuer, Koperdak, Rozsa, and Furedi (2005) studied 63 patients with eating disorders and found a correlation between childhood *physical abuse* and severe body image distortion in adulthood. Among males, Meston, Heiman, & Trapnell (1999) found a correlation between childhood *emotional abuse* and subsequent poor body image. Finally, O'Toole (2001) examined the effects of parental *verbal abuse* in 168 females and found a correlation with body image disturbance. Excluding those studies relating to childhood sexual abuse, note that *all* other existing studies, albeit few in number, indicate a correlation between various forms of childhood abuse and body image difficulties in adulthood.

THE PSYCHOLOGICAL CONNECTION: CHILDHOOD TRAUMA AND BODY IMAGE PROBLEMS

In the preceding section, we reviewed the available studies exploring the relationship between childhood trauma and body image difficulties. Research has focused primarily on sexual abuse, and secondarily on emotional and physical abuse, but there are various *other* forms of childhood abuse possibilities including the witnessing of violence in the home, variations of emotional abuse such as teasing about appearance (Heinberg, 1996), emotional indifference from caretakers, and caretaking with minimal emotional investment (i.e., "mechanical caretaking"). While the explicit relationships between these various forms of childhood adversity and body image dissatisfaction remain unknown, the pathway is not likely to be a direct one (Cash, 2002). In the following paragraphs, we offer some psychodynamic speculation with regard to that pathway.

Note that each of the preceding forms of maltreatment tend to parallel the absence of personal validation of the child during early development. How can a child assume that he/she has any worth if caretakers do not actively value him/her? Indeed, what if the child is not only under-valued, but actively devalued through repeated emotional, physical, and/or sexual assault? In response, the child victim might easily conclude that he/she lacks personal value or worth (i.e., mirrors the negative environment), and/or is personally faulty, damaged, or inadequate. "Other children are loved—what's wrong with me?" We perceive this lack of parental validation in childhood, which is probably indexed by childhood maltreatment, as the fundamental springboard for a host of self-image problems in both childhood and adulthood.

Feelings of inadequacy and self-deprecation, over time, would likely culminate in a sense of personal shame. In this regard, Kaufman (1989) discusses the experience of shame in children in response to parental anger or parental abandonment (p. 35); imagine more overtly rejecting behavior such as emotional abuse. Because children tend to be fairly concrete, we suspect that shame in children tends to be concretized on a body level. In other words, negative feelings about self are literally relegated to the body. In keeping with this theme, Connors (2001) describes the aftermath of childhood abuse as "self-consciousness about one's body" (p. 151). Literally, the child may interpret these abuse experiences as, "I am bad; I am my body; my body is bad." Body shame seems to persist into adult life (Kearney-Cook & Striegel-Moore, 1996).

The disastrous effects of abusive parenting on the self-image and body image of children may be further complicated by the child's own defenses. To illustrate this, children who are physically and sexually abused are known to dissociate as a means of vacating the traumatizing situation. Given few other internal and external resources, this would seem to be an adaptable and self-preserving psychological maneuver. However, repeated dissociation would seem to foster a sense of separateness between one's inner self (i.e., psychological self) and outer self (i.e., body self). How frequently do we hear in therapy sessions,"I thought to myself, 'you can beat my body, but you'll never get to me.'" Utilized repeatedly, dissociation would seem to consolidate a sense of separateness between psychological self and body self—i.e., an adaptation gone awry.

We also suspect that this sense of separateness between psychological self and body self is augmented by the child's natural psychological tendency for splitting. Split perception (perceiving in the extremes of "good" and "bad") occurs at the beginning of the normal developmental path. Splitting would seem to synergistically accommodate dissociation by reinforcing separateness (i.e., "me" versus "it" or the body). Therefore, it would seem that dissociation, a psychological defense to trauma, and splitting, a natural developmental position, would actively promote the separation of psychological self and body self in the victims of childhood abuse.

Given the ensuing separation of body self and psychological self, it would seem that anxiety about and devaluation of the body would be a natural outgrowth of caretaker maltreatment. The body might be viewed as the damaged barrier facing the outside world—severely wounded by others, without obvious value. Over time, these conclusions about body might then consolidate into an ongoing negative cognitive schema (Gilbert, 2002, p. 20). We believe that this is a critical juncture in the development of body image problems. *A negative cognitive schema of the body would seem to enable the subsequent lowering of the threshold for self-induced body maltreatment.* Essentially, these schemas perpetuate the "bad body" myth. "It doesn't matter if I damage my body...I deserve this...it really doesn't hurt to cut myself..."

In summary, we perceive body dissatisfaction in BPD as a complex evolutionary process beginning with childhood trauma, continuing with defensive and normal functioning (e.g., dissociation and splitting), and culminating in faulty cognitive schemas relating to the body that facilitate body maltreatment. These impressions are bolstered by our clinical observation that people tend to seek out the familiar. If body maltreatment was the experience in childhood, then it tends to be the experience in adulthood. According to Goodwin and Attias (1994, p. 29), body abuse in adulthood may "represent a continuation of childhood abuse with the survivor now incorporating the role of parent-perpetrator." We wish to emphasize that the preceding psychodynamic formulation remains a hypothesis. Figure 1 provides a schematic summary of our hypothesis.

Our proposed sequence of complex events leading to body image difficulties is probably reinforced by a variety of dysfunctional family variables, which have been summarized by Connors (2001). She describes parental unreliability, low maternal warmth, little family support for autonomy, chaotic family environments, parental alcoholism, infrequent parental contact, and high parental expectations—all of which lead to negative attributions about the self.

Whether our preceding psychodynamic speculation is accurate or not is empirically unknown. No studies have examined the relationship of these variables in the evolution of body dissatisfaction in patients with BPD. However, it seems fairly clear that many of these individuals have suffered repetitive childhood trauma, and most, if not all, have very negative self-concepts and pervasive body dissatisfaction in the aftermath.

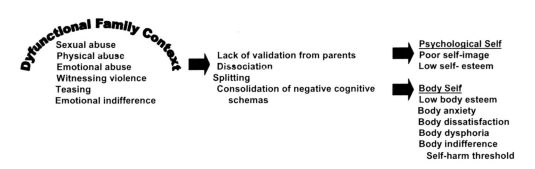

Figure 1. The relationship between childhood trauma and body dissatisfaction: A hypothesis.

CONCLUSION

In this chapter, we have presented a description of individuals who suffer from BPD, highlighting the various manifestations of body dissatisfaction observed among these patients. In psychiatric settings, body dissatisfaction or indifference often manifests as SHB. In medical settings, body dissatisfaction may manifest as somatic preoccupation, the sabotage of one's medical care, chronic pain syndromes, and even factitious illness. Because these medical presentations are associated with impaired functionality, many of these patients may wind up on employment disability.

What is the connection between BPD and body image difficulties? We believe that this relationship is primarily mediated by repetitive trauma in early development. Beyond sexual abuse, childhood trauma may include emotional and verbal abuse as well as physical abuse and the witnessing of violence. While few studies are available, two confirm relationships between BPD and body dissatisfaction. Existing research also confirms relationships between childhood trauma and body image problems. That childhood trauma affects body image suggests that it is the *context* of BPD (i.e., childhood traumatization), rather than BPD, itself, that is the probable etiology of body dissatisfaction in these individuals. While the psychological evolution from childhood trauma to body dissatisfaction is empirically unknown, we have presented a possible hypothesis that is highlighted by dissociation and splitting, the separation of psychological self and body self, and the subsequent lowering of the threshold for body maltreatment. Clearly, these dynamics warrant further investigation in an effort to develop intervention strategies and provide relief to those patients suffering from this debilitating Axis II disorder.

REFERENCES

American Psychiatric Association. (1994). *Diagnostic and statistical manual of mental disorders, 4th edition*. Washington, DC: Author.

Binzer, M., Stone, J., & Sharpe, M. (2004). Recent onset pseudoseizures—clues to aetiology. *Seizure, 13,* 146-155.

Birot, E. (1993). Body image and mental functioning. *Bulletin de la Societe du Rorschach et des Methodes Projectives de Langue Francaise, no. 37,* 57-69.

Bradley, R., Jenei, J., & Westen, D. (2005). Etiology of borderline personality: Disentangling the contributions of intercorrelated antecedents. *Journal of Nervous and Mental Disease, 193,* 24-31.

Brown, L. E. (1998). A comparison of coping styles and body image of abused and non-abused women. *Dissertation Abstracts International, Section B, 59,* 1842.

Byram, V., Wagner, H. L., & Waller, G. (1995). Sexual abuse and body image distortion. *Child Abuse & Neglect, 19,* 507-510.

Cash, T. F. (2002). Women's body images. In G. M. Wingood & R. J. DiClemente (Eds.), *Handbook of women's sexual and reproductive health* (pp. 175-194). New York: Kluwer Academic/Plenum Publishers.

Chavira, D. A., Grilo, C. M., Shea, M. T., Yen, S., Gunderson, J. G., Morey, L. C., et al. (2003). Ethnicity and four personality disorders. *Comprehensive Psychiatry, 44,* 483-491.

Connors, M. E. (2001). Relationship of sexual abuse to body image and eating problems. In J K. Thompson & L. Smolak (Eds.), *Body image, eating disorders, and obesity in youth: Assessment, prevention, and treatment* (pp. 149-167). Washington, DC: American Psychological Association.

Corbett, C. L. (1998). Working representations of self, others and relationships in women who have been sexually abused as children: A qualitative approach. *Dissertation Abstracts International, Section B, 58,* 6841.

Duran, R. R. (1998). Body dissatisfaction in abused versus non-abused college women. *Dissertation Abstracts International, Section B, 59,* 1364.

Ekselius, L., Eriksson, M., von Knorring, L., & Linder, J. (1996). Personality disorders and major depression in patients with somatoform pain disorders and medical illnesses in relation to age at onset of work disability. *European Journal of Psychiatry, 10,* 35-43.

Gilbert, P. (2002). A biopsychosocial conceptualization and overview, with treatment implications. In P. Gilbert & J. Miles (Eds.), *Body shame: Conceptualisation, research and treatment* (pp. 3-54). New York: Brunner-Routledge.

Goodwin, J. M., & Attias, R. (1994). Eating disorders in survivors of multimodal childhood abuse. In M. G. Winkler & L. B. Cole (Eds.), *The good body: Asceticism in contemporary culture* (pp. 23-35). New Haven: Yale University Press.

Haaf, B., Pohl, U., Deusinger, I. M., & Bohus, M. (2001). Examination of body concept in female patients with borderline personality disorder. *Psychotherapie Psychosomatik Medizinische Psychologie, 51,* 246-254.

Harris, C. L., Dinn, W. M., & Marcinkiewicz, J. A. (2002). Partial seizure-like symptoms in borderline personality disorder. *Epilepsy and Behavior, 3,* 433-438.

Heinberg, L. J. (1996). Theories of body image disturbance: Perceptual, developmental, and sociocultural factors. In J. K. Thompson (Ed.), *Body image, eating disorders, and obesity* (pp. 27-47). Washington, DC: American Psychological Association.

Hunter, J. A. (1991). A comparison of the psychosocial maladjustment of adult males and females sexually molested as children. *Journal of Interpersonal Violence, 6*, 205-217.

Hyde, M. L., & Kaufman, P. A. (1984). Women molested as children: Therapeutic and legal issues in civil actions. *American Journal of Forensic Psychiatry, 5*, 147-157.

Johnson, D. M., Shea, M. T., Yen, S., Battle, C. L., Zlotnick, C., Sanislow, C. A., et al. (2003). Gender differences in borderline personality disorder: Findings from the Collaborative Longitudinal Personality Disorders Study. *Comprehensive Psychiatry, 44*, 284-292.

Kaufman, G. (1989). *The psychology of shame*. New York: Springer Publishing Company.

Kearney-Cooke, A., & Striegel-Moore, R. H. (1996). Treatment of childhood sexual abuse in anorexia nervosa and bulimia nervosa: A feminist psychodynamic approach. In M. F. Schwartz & L. Cohn (Eds.), *Sexual abuse and eating disorders* (pp. 155-175). Philadelphia: Brunner/Mazel.

Kolar, B. J. P. (1995). Body image of sexually abused bulimic women. *Dissertation Abstracts International, Section B, 56*, 95.

Mack, J. (1975). *Borderline states: An historical perspective*. New York: Grune & Stratton.

Meston, C. M., Heiman, J. R., & Trapnell, P. D. (1999). The relation between early abuse and adult sexuality. *Journal of Sex Research, 36*, 385-395.

Nicolopoulou, E., & Kindynis, S. (1989). The failure of body image as boundary definition in suicidal patients with borderline personality disorder. *Psychologie Medicale, 21*, 496-498.

Nordling, N., Sandnabba, N. K., & Santtila, P. (2000). The prevalence and effects of self-reported childhood sexual abuse among sadomasochistically oriented males and females. *Journal of Child Sexual Abuse, 9*, 53-63.

O'Neil, D. S. (1997). The relationship of child and adult sexual abuse to body image and dissociation. *Dissertation Abstracts International, Section B, 58*, 2694.

O'Toole, S. K. (2001). The effects of parental verbal abuse: A relational theory perspective. *Dissertation Abstracts International, Section B, 61*, 6143.

Paris, J. (1996). Cultural factors in the emergence of borderline pathology. *Psychiatry, 59*, 185-192.

Quigley, B.D. (2005). Diagnostic relapse in borderline personality: Risk and protective factors. *Dissertation Abstracts International, Section B, 65*, 3721.

Reuber, M., Pukrop, R., Bauer, J., Derfuss, R., & Elger, C. E. (2004). Multidimensional assessment of personality in patients with psychogenic non-epileptic seizures. *Journal of Neurology, Neurosurgery, and Psychiatry, 75*, 743-748.

Sansone, R. A., Hruschka, J., Vasudevan, A., & Miller, S. N. (2003). Disability and borderline personality symptoms. *Psychosomatics, 44*, 442.

Sansone, R. A., Rytwinski, D. R., & Gaither, G. A. (2003). Borderline personality and psychotropic medication prescription in an outpatient psychiatry clinic. *Comprehensive Psychiatry, 44*, 454-458.

Sansone, R. A., & Sansone, L. A. (2000). Borderline personality disorder: The enigma. *Primary Care Reports, 6*, 219-226.

Sansone, R. A., & Sansone, L. A. (2004). Borderline personality: A primary care context. *Psychiatry 2004, 1*, 19-27.

Sansone, R. A., Sansone, L. A., & Gaither, G. A. (2004). Diabetes management and borderline personality symptomatology: A pilot study. *General Hospital Psychiatry, 26,* 164-169.

Sansone, R. A., Sansone, L. A., & Wiederman, M. (1995). The prevalence of trauma and its relationship to borderline personality symptoms and self-destructive behaviors in a primary care setting. *Archives of Family Medicine, 4,* 439-442.

Sansone, R. A., Songer, D. A., & Gaither, G. A. (2000). Medically self-harming behavior and its relationship to borderline personality among psychiatric inpatients. *Journal of Nervous and Mental Disease, 188,* 384-386.

Sansone, R. A., Songer, D. A., & Gaither, G. A. (2001). Diagnostic approaches to borderline personality and their relationship to self-harm behavior. *International Journal of Psychiatry in Clinical Practice, 5,* 273-277.

Sansone, R. A., Whitecar, P., Meier, B. P., & Murry, A. (2001). The prevalence of borderline personality among primary care patients with chronic pain. *General Hospital Psychiatry, 23,* 193-197.

Sansone, R. A., Wiederman, M. W., & Monteith, D. (2001). Obesity, borderline personality symptomatology, and body image among women in a psychiatric outpatient setting. *International Journal of Eating Disorders, 29,* 76-79.

Sansone, R. A., Wiederman, M. W., & Sansone, L. A. (2000). Medically self-harming behavior and its relationship to borderline personality symptoms and somatic preoccupation among internal medicine patients. *Journal of Nervous and Mental Disease, 188,* 45-47.

Sansone, R. A., Wiederman, M. W., Sansone, L. A., & Mehnert-Kay, S. (1997). Sabotaging one's own medical care. *Archives of Family Medicine, 6,* 583-586.

Schaaf, K. K., & McCanne, T. R. (1994). Childhood abuse, body image disturbance, and eating disorders. *Child Abuse & Neglect, 18,* 607-615.

Skodol, A. E., Siever, L. J., Livesley, W. J., Gunderson, J. G., Pfohl, B., & Widiger, T. A. (2002). The borderline diagnosis II: Biology, genetics, and clinical course. *Biological Psychiatry, 51,* 951-963.

Steiger, H., Leung, F. Y., & Houle, L. (1992). Relationships among borderline features, body dissatisfaction and bulimic symptoms in nonclinical females. *Addictive Behaviors, 17,* 397-406.

Stone, M. H. (1986). Borderline personality disorder. In R. Michels & J. O. Cavenar (Eds.), *Psychiatry* (2nd ed.) (pp. 1-15). Philadelphia: Lippincott.

Sutherland, A. J., & Rodin, G. M. (1990). Factitious disorders in a general hospital setting: Clinical features and a review of the literature. *Psychosomatics, 31,* 392-399.

Treuer, T., Koperdak, M., Rozsa, S., & Furedi, J. (2005). The impact of physical and sexual abuse on body image in eating disorders. *European Eating Disorders Review, 13,* 106-111.

Truppi, A. M. (2001). The effects of dance/movement therapy on sexually abused adolescent girls in residential treatment. *Dissertation Abstracts International, Section B, 62,* 2081.

Weiner, K. E., & Thompson, J. K. (1997). Overt and covert sexual abuse: Relationship to body image and eating disturbance. *International Journal of Eating Disorders, 22,* 273-284.

Wenninger, K., & Heiman, J. R. (1998). Relating body image to psychological and sexual functioning in child sexual abuse survivors. *Journal of Traumatic Stress, 11*, 543-562.

Whealin, J. M., & Jackson, J. L. (2002). Childhood unwanted sexual attention and young women's present self-concept. *Journal of Interpersonal Violence, 17*, 854-871.

Widiger, T. A., & Rogers, J. H. (1989). Prevalence and comorbidity of personality disorders. *Psychiatric Annals, 19*, 132-136.

Widiger, T. A., & Weissman, M. M. (1991). Epidemiology of borderline personality disorder. *Hospital & Community Psychiatry, 42*, 1015-1021.

Zanarini, M. C., Frankenburg, F. R., Reich, D. B., Marino, J. F., Lewis, R. E., Williams, A. A., et al. (2000). Biparental failure in the childhood experiences of borderline patients. *Journal of Personality Disorders, 14*, 264-273.

In: Body Image: New Research
Editor: Marlene V. Kindes, pp. 145-197

ISBN 1-60021-059-7
© 2006 Nova Science Publishers, Inc.

Chapter VII

BODY IMAGE DEVIATION IN CHRONIC SCHIZOPHRENIA: NEW RESEARCH

Reiko Koide and Akira Tamaoka*

Institute of Clinical Medicine, University of Tsukuba, Tsukuba-Shi, Ibaraki-Ken, Japan

ABSTRACT

Background

Body image aberration in schizophrenia was earlier conceived as delusional and hallucinatory symptoms. However, perceptions of schizophrenia have changed dramatically, especially with the concept of negative symptoms in the 1980s and in the 1990s, to include the neurocognitive aspects of schizophrenia. Deviations in schizophrenics' body image from the standard underlying various behaviors or allegations concerning the body should be now refocused. In this chapter, using the Body Image Questionnaire (BIQ), comprised of three hypothetical components, anatomical, functional and psychological, attempts were made to resolve some primary questions. They were (1) whether or not there is any related clinical characteristics to schizophrenic body image abberation, (2) whether there are aberrant components of body image specific to schizophrenia, (3) whether or not there is unique link between depression and body image in schizophrenia.

Methods

In study 1, correlations between body image assessed by the BIQ and clinical characteristics as positive and negative symptoms assessed by SAPS and SANS, insight assessed by SAI, and daily dose of conventional antipsychotic drugs were examined. In study 2, three components of body image, that is, anatomical, functional and

---

* Correspondence concerning this article should be addressed to: R. Koide. 1-6-2-905-305, Takezono, Tsukuba-Shi, Ibaraki-Ken, Japan. E-mail: ttn5aks258@mx6.ttcn.ne.jp

psychological, were compared between schizophrenic and non-schizophrenic groups. In study 3, the correlation between depression assessed by SDS and body image assessed by the BIQ was examined. In these studies, 93 chronic schizophrenics, 177 normal adults, and 43 patients with anxiety disorders according to DSM-IV criteria, were examined. In studies 4-5, the additional finding of Rorschach percepts concerning body image in schizophrenia was reported.

Results

Schizophrenics' body image aberration proved to be independent of symptoms and medication. It was also shown that the aberration proved to be limited to functional imageries, and that the anatomical component remained intact. As to depression, a specific link of body image, especially with functional imageries, with the depression characteristic to schizophrenia was found.

Conclusion

All these results showed that body image aberration in schizophrenics is not the result of symptoms or effects of conventional neuroleptic medications, but they are germane to schizophrenia, which is comprised of aberration mainly in functional body imageries. This body image deviation proved to be linked to some serious depressive signs and symptoms in schizophrenia. The subsidiary findings, that is, the Rorschach percepts as a mass of flesh quite often seen in schizophrenia, are congruent with the main findings that schizophrenic patients showed an anticipation of becoming unmovable.

Keywords: Body image, schizophrenia, symptom, insight, depression, perception

PART I. INTRODUCTION

Schizophrenics' Body Image Aberration: An Overview

Since the time of Kraepelin (1919) and Bleuler (1911/1950), schizophrenics' deviant perceptions, feelings, and beliefs concerning their bodies have been described. In this section, the symptoms relevant to body image aberration that have been discussed for over the past half century, as well as psychological measures that were developed to understand these aberrations, are reviewed, to lead to the current status and future prospects for the study of the body image aberration in schizophrenia.

(1) Symptoms Relevant to Body Image Aberration

Disturbances of body experience in schizophrenic patients occur frequently. They have been observed as somatic delusions (McGlichrist & Cutting, 1995), coenaesthesis (Huber, 1957/1971; Rohricht & Priebe, 1997, Schmoll & Koch, 1989; Schmoll, 1994), disturbances of pain perception (Dworkin & Caligor, 1988; Rosenthal et al., 1990; Dworkin, 1994; Guieu et al., 1994; Lautenbacher & Krieg, 1994), out-of-body experiences (Blackmore, 1986;

Twemlow et al., 1982), dysmorphophobia (Connolly & Gipson, 1978; Hay, 1983; Birtchnell, 1988; Snaith, 1992; Philips & McEloroy, 1993; deLeon et al., 1989; Phillips et al., 1994), and self-injury or self mutilation (Feldman, 1988; Burgess, 1991; Martin & Gattaz, 1991; Sonneburn & Vanstraelen, 1992 ; Weiser et al., 1993; Kennedy & Feldmann, 1994). In addition, the effects of body-oriented psychotherapy have been suggested (Darby, 1968; Berman, 1972).

According to Roehricht and Priebe (1997) in a report by Huber and Zerbin-Rueden (1979), although symptoms relevant to body distortion were seen in more than 74% of cases of schizophrenia, little attention has been paid to the evaluation of such symptoms. These symptoms are not included as a prominent component in psychometric approaches to measuring symptoms, such as the Brief Psychiatric Rating Scale, BPRS, (Overall & Gorham, 1962) or the Positive and Negative Symptoms Scale, PANSS (Kay et al., 1987). It is, however, not fair to regard that the issue as being rather neglected. Specifically, bizarre somatopsychic phenomena, e.g., feelings that the body is "being radiated," "being controlled by others," and "being cut up" have been reported in schizophrenia. Some of these abnormal body perceptions have been designated as "Schneiderian first rank symptoms" (Schneider, 1959/1976). Dysmorphophobia was relabeled as "one of the Somatoform Disorders" in 1980. "Body Dysmorphic Disorder," and its counterpart, "Delusional Disorder, Somatic Subtype" in 1987, were included in the *Diagnostic and Statistical Manual of Mental Disorders* (American Psychiatric Association, 1987), which produced considerable concern over delusions regarding appearance of the body (deLeon et al., 1989; Phillips et al., 1994). First, studies of these symptoms relevant to disturbances in body experiences in schizophrenia are reviewed to give an overview of how the problems have been described and treated.

Before Antipsychotics

Even in the era before antipsychotic agents, body image was rather attractive to those who studied the psychopathology of schizophrenia. Since Wernicke foreshadowed the idea of body image in his concept of "somatopsyche," this whole psychological field has been recognized as important in the understanding of psychotic patients, especially in relation to hallucinatory and delusional disturbances (Schilder, 1935; Angyal, 1936; Gerstmann, 1942; Bychowsky,1943).

The initial study of body image was a description of phantom limb. It was succeeded by neurological research from the 1910s to the 1950s (Head, 1911/1926; Pick, 1922; Schilder, 1935), and body image was conceived as the equivalent of "body schema" or "postural schema." This became the traditional definition of the concept. It was introduced to the field of psychiatry by Schilder (1935), and attempts were made to find similar distortions in psychiatric patients (Schilder, 1935; Angyal, 1936).

Bodily Hallucination and Somatic Delusion

Lukianowicz (1967) and McGlichrist and Cutting (1995) classified somatic delusions of psychotic cases including schizophrenia, showing that bodily delusions and hallucinations occur mostly inseparably. Bodily hallucination and somatic delusion have been treated as coenaesthesis in non-English speaking psychiatry, especially in Germany, where it was often reported to herald the onset of schizophrenia (Huber 1957,1971; Rohricht & Priebe, 1997; Schmoll & Koch, 1989; Schmoll, 1994).

Disturbances of Pain Perception

A disorder of proprioception in schizophrenic patients was earlier described by Rado (1959) as a basic element in schizophrenia. He speculated that extensive proprioceptive deficits could lead to distorted awareness of body image and eventually to the thought disorder characteristic of schizophrenia. Rosenbaum et al. (1965) and Ritzler and Rosenbaum (1974) conducted a series of experiments based on his theory with schizophrenic and non-schizophrenic subjects using weight discrimination as a measure of proprioception. They found that schizophrenics performed almost as well as normals do when asked to discriminate heavy weights, but did not discriminate light weights nearly as well as normals. Since light weights do not provide as much proprioceptive feedback as do heavy weights, these results were interpreted as demonstrating a proprioceptive deficit in the schizophrenics. These results, however, were not replicated by other authors (Ritzler, 1977; Leventhal et al., 1982), who showed that a proprioceptive deficit is not unique to schizophrenia.

Since the time of Kraepelin and Bleuler, "pain insensitivity" or "reduced sensitivity to pain" in schizophrenia has been documented. Kraepelin (1919) observed that patients with schizophrenia are often "less sensitive to bodily discomfort; they endure uncomfortable positions, pricks of a needle, injuries...burn themselves with their cigar, hurt themselves." Bleuler (1911/1950) noted that even in well-oriented patients one may often observe the presence of a complete analgesia which includes the deeper parts of the body as well as the skin. The patients "pluck out an eye, sit down on a hot stove and receive severe burns".

Although some authors reported that schizophrenic patients suffer headache (Varsamis & Adamson, 1976; Watson et al., 1981; Philips and Hunter, 1982; Torrey, 1989), the prevalence of pain complaints in schizophrenia appears to be lower than in other psychiatric disorders (Merskey, 1965; Spear, 1967; Delapaine et al., 1978; Watson et al., 1981). There are many descriptions of pain insensitivity in schizophrenia by surgeons and internists (Arieti, 1945; Marchand, 1959; West and Hecker, 1952; Vanderkampt, 1970; Apter, 1981, Fishbain 1982; Bickerstaff et al., 1988, Katz et al., 1990; Rosenthal et al., 1990). Dworkin (1994) reviewed the literature on this issue and argued that the insensitivity, although currently neglected, has important implications for physical health, self-mutilation, homelessness, premorbid development, and affective flattening in schizophrenic patients. Lautenbacher and Krieg (1994) also reviewed the literature and pointed out that pain insensitivity is important in elucidating pathophysiological mechanisms because pain perception is controlled by neurochemical and neurohormonal functions known to be affected by psychiatric disease processes. Guieu et al. (1994), however, assessed the pain thresholds of ten schizophrenic patients and ten controls by measuring the leg flexion nociceptive reflex threshold, and concluded that in most cases the increase in pain threshold is the result of attitude and not alterations in brain function.

Out-of-Body Experiences

A number of studies have pointed out the confusion in the existing psychiatric literature concerning the status of consciousness in which there is an altered perception of the mind/body relationship. They defined out-of-body experience (OBE) as an altered state of consciousness in which one's mind or awareness is experienced as separated from one's physical body. They argued that the increasing numbers of patients who are involved in such phenomena, traditionally classified as psychopathological, should not be treated in the way that a symptom is usually treated (e.g., interpretation or medication) but should be viewed by a physician with "benign neglect" (Twemlow, et al., 1982).

Gabbard et al. developed a questionnaire, Profile of Out-of-Body Experiences, POBE, that included 51 items based on reports of near-death experiences, mystical-religious literature, and philosophical-occult-psychotic literature describing OBE experiences. They tried to clarify this group of phenomena by differentiating OBE from depersonalization, autoscopic phenomena, and schizophrenic body distortions (such as boundary loss). They selected seven points to differentiate OBE from the disturbances in corporal perception found in schizophrenia. That is, the bodily distortions in schizophrenic patients are characterized by loss of reality testing, chronic difficulty with delineation of body boundaries, varied bodily distortions, being uncertain of the location of the body, profound regression in personality, blurred identity, and being experienced as "going crazy," whereas those experiencing OBE show intact reality testing, have episodic and short-lived experiences, basically unvaried distortion, are certain of their location, show no evidence of regression, have an intact identity, and are not experienced as "going crazy."

Blackmore (1986) administered POBE to schizophrenic patients, along with two other questionnaires to assess perception and symptoms, and showed that there is no evidence to consider the typical OBE as pathological or as symptomatic of schizophrenia.

Dysmorphophobia

Extreme concern with aspects of personal appearance was called dysmorphophobia by Morselli in 1886 (Birtchnell, 1988; Phillips, 1991), who defined it as "a subjective feeling of ugliness or physical defect that the patient feels is noticeable to others, although his appearance is within normal limits." Despite its relative neglect in American psychiatry, it is now termed "Somatoform Disorder" in DSM III (1980), "Body Dysmorphic Disorder (BDD)" in DSM III-R with its counterpart, "Delusional Disorder, Somatic Subtype (DDSS)" (1987). It is a distressing and impairing disorder that may lead to occupational and social dysfunction as well as unnecessary and costly cosmetic surgery and dermatologic treatment (Phillips, 1991), and an increase in this disorder has been reported (Phillips et al., 1993; Hollander et al., 1993). It is still described with the term BDD under the heading of Somatoform Disorder in DSM-IV (1994).

In the 19th century, the term "dysmorphophobia" described those patients who present with "a fear of being misshapen" when in fact objectively they have no cause for complaint. However, numerous reports of dysmorphophobia in psychiatric morbidity, including schizophrenia, have been reported (Connolly and Gipson, 1978; Edgerton et al., 1960; Jacobsen et al., 1960; Hay, 1970). In the 1980s, there were continuing debates as to its status as a symptom or discrete psychiatric illness; that is, it is not a phobia because there is no fear of physical abnormality per se—the ugliness of others is tolerated. It was remarked that dysmorphophobia is non-specific as a symptom and can occur in a variety of different psychiatric syndromes, from a sensitive personality development to an attenuated schizophrenic illness (Hay, 1970/1983).

In the 1940s to the 1960s, psychodynamic theories attempted to recognize that a complaint about appearance might be understood in terms of psychological defense mechanisms (Meyer et al., 1960; Jacobsen et al., 1960; Linn and Goldman, 1949; Hill and Silver, 1950). Body parts took on a psychological significance and symbolic function, and a complaint might reflect an underlying conflict. However, reports of excellent results from surgery on the minimally deformed led to criticism to these theories, suggesting neurotic, and even psychotic, patients can benefit from cosmetic surgery (Edgerton et al., 1960; Hay, 1973).

Although the original definition of dysmorphophobia states that the appearance is within normal limits, diagnostic criteria proposed for dysmorphophobia allow for a slight physical anomaly to be present, but with the patient's concern judged disproportionately great (Andreasen and Bardach, 1977). Birtchnell (1988) regarded it as important to maintain a distinction between those patients with minimal deformity (the normal but less than attractive) who might considerably benefit from surgery and those with primary dysmorphophobia distinguished by the vagueness of the complaint, e.g., "the skin under my eyes joins my nose in a funny way," where surgery is contraindicated, rather than, for example, "the tip of my nose is rather bulbous."

The disorder once termed dysmorphophobia was renamed body dysmorphic disorder (BDD) in DSM III-R. As Snaith (1992) reviewed, DSM III-R considered the disorder under two headings: (1) delusional disorder, somatic type, and (2) body dysmorphic disorder. The distinctions between these two categories rests on whether the bodily concern has the characteristics of a true delusion, but a clear distinction cannot always be made. DSM III-R differentiated BDD, a nonpsychotic somatoform disorder in which insight is present, from its delusional counterpart, a psychotic disorder in which insight is absent. The delusional variant of BDD was reported as a more severe form of the disorder (Phillips et al., 1994).

Self-Injury or Self Mutilation

Self-injurious behaviour of various sorts occurs in an appreciable number of individuals with schizophrenia, as well as in those with other disorders (Burgess, 1991). Self-mutilation has been defined as "painful , destructive and injurious acts upon the body without the apparent intent to commit suicide" (Pattison and Kahan, 1983). Reports of self-mutilation in patients with schizophrenia include descriptions of unilateral and bilateral eye enucleation (Feldman, 1988; Kennedy and Feldmann, 1994), self-laceration (Shore et al., 1978; Sweeny and Zamecnik, 1981), and self-amputation of various parts of the body, including the hand (Schweitzer, 1990), breast (Coons et al., 1986), ear (Silva, et al., 1989; Weiser et al., 1993), penis and testicles (Schweitzer, 1990; Martin and Gattaz, 1991), and in what is arguably the most extreme case reported to date, virtually the entire face (Scheftel et al., 1986).

Burgess (1991) studied the relationship of depression and cognitive impairment to self-injury in psychiatric patients including schizophrenics, showing that self-injury was correlated with neurocognitive deficits in borderline and schizophrenic groups.

Body-Oriented Psychotherapy

An early theoretical assumption, currently recognized as invalid, was that the core disturbance in schizophrenia is a breakdown of ego boundaries leading to a dedifferentiation of the self from the non-self (Federn, 1952; Freeman et al., 1958). According to this theory, what is sensed as thought (a process occurring within the mental and physical boundary) is no longer distinguished from what is sensed as lying outside the ego boundary (Berman, 1972). Psychoanalytic theorists have stressed the important role the individual's body plays in bringing about the formation of the ego (e.g., Federn, 1952; Fenichel, 1954; Ferenczi, 1926; Freud, 1962), and the maintenance of the distinction between ego and non-ego was a controversial issue for psychotherapeutic treatment of schizophrenia.

Des Lauriers (1962) theorized that the recovery process in schizophrenia could be conceptualized as a progressive definition and demarcation of the schizophrenic's ego boundaries through a systematically increased awareness of body limits and bodily self. In order to accomplish this, the psychotherapist attempted to stimulate in the schizophrenic patient awareness of, and interest in, the bodily self as the separating boundary from that which is not himself (Darby, 1968; Des Lauriers, 1962). Studies conducted with an inkblot boundary index developed by Fisher and Cleveland (1958), the Barrier and Penetration scores, lend some support to the above conception of schizophrenia and the recovery process, in that schizophrenics were differentiated from neurotics and normals on the basis of their lower Barrier and higher Penetration scores (Fisher and Cleveland, 1958; Reitman and Cleveland, 1964; Holtzman et al., 1961) and that as a schizophrenic improved clinically, his Penetration scores decreased (Cleveland, 1960a). Fisher and Cleveland (1968) suggested that special treatment efforts, aimed at re-identifying and redefining bodily limits, should improve these patients. Because a question arises as to whether directly focusing the schizophrenic patient's awareness and attention on his own body can effect a redefinition of boundaries, attempts were made to demonstrate that focusing on somatic stimuli leads to subsequent changes in inkblot boundary indexes, implying, at least, that it can (Fisher and Renik, 1966; Renik and Fisher, 1968). Attempts were also made to expect alteration of body image change in these indexes by inducing somatic awareness in groups of hospitalized schizophrenics (Darby, 1968). Quinlan and Harrow (1974) examined the boundary in a sample of acute schizophrenics by the use of four types of Rorschach indexes including Barrier and Penetration scores. Their results support the hypothesis that schizophrenics give certain types of responses considered indicative of boundary disturbance, such as contamination responses, although Barrier and Penetration indexes are more benign signs of boundary diffusion.

(2) Psychological Measurement of Body Image Aberration

The above observations have led to an assumption that body image aberration or deviation exists in schizophrenia, and that it is related to the core of schizophrenia. Attempts were made, using the Rorschach test (Quinlan & Harrow 1974; Fisher & Cleveland, 1958/1968; Fisher, 1963), Drawing test (Kokonis, 1972) and inquiries (Fisher & Seidner, 1963; Chapman et al., 1978; Coleman et al., 1996; Koide, 1985; Oosthuizen et al., 1998), to point to characteristic deviations of body image in schizophrenic patients. These are the Body Distortion Questionnaire, BDQ, (Rohricht & Priebe, 1996), the Perceptual Aberration Scale, PAS, (Coleman et al., 1996; Chapman et al., 1978), Dysmorphic Concern Questionnaire,

DCQ (Oosthuizen et al., 1998), and the present Body Image Questionnaire, BIQ (Koide, 1985). However, none of these measures are regarded as well-established (Rohricht & Prieb, 1997).

Projective Method

Early attempts to measeure body image aberrations were made through indirect means, that is, projective techniques. Figure-drawing techniques (Goodenough, 1928; Machover, 1949), have been used often by researchers (Cancro, 1971; Jasker and Reed, 1963; Sugarman and Cancro, 1964); however, most of the differences between schizophrenic and normal subjects appear to reflect nothing more than general inadequacy of drawing skill by schizophrenics (Swensen, 1957/1968). Barrier and penetration percepts on the Rorschach Test were inferred from body image (Fisher and Cleveland, 1958/1968). Barrier percepts are ones that emphasize peripheral-boundary-defining qualities of the percepts (e.g., flower pot or knife in armor). Penetration percepts involve penetration of outer surfaces of things (e.g., squashed bug or x-ray picture). Lowered barrier scores and heightened penetration scores have been reported in schizophrenia (Fisher and Cleveland, 1958/1968; Reitman and Cleveland, 1964; Holtzman et al., 1961/64). A lack of difference has also been reported (Jasker and Reed, 1963). While support for schizophrenic deviancy on the barrier and penetration scores is strong, acceptance of such evidence as support for schizophrenic body-image aberration requires belief in the projective hypothesis (Chapman et al., 1978).

Experimental Measurement

More direct attempts were made to measure body image aberration in the laboratory setting. Traub et al. (1967) performed an experiment in which the subjects adjust a body-distorting mirror until they believe that it reflects them accurately, with the result that schizophrenic patients erred more than the normal control subjects. Controversial results were presented in studies in which the patients were asked to judge the size of their own body. Cleveland (1960) and Cleveland et al. (1962) reported that schizophrenics overestimate the size of their various body parts (hand, foot, stomach, heart) more than control subjects do, although Weckowicz and Sommer (1960) found that schizophrenics underestimate sizes of their hands and feet. Dillon (1962) and Fisher (1966) found no difference between schizophrenic and normal subjects.

Questionnaire Measurement

The first questionnaire that attempted to measure body image aberration in schizophrenia is the Body Experience Questionnaire, BEQ, which is a true-false questionnaire developed by Fisher and Seidner (1963) and Fisher (1964). Their findings showed greater body image aberration in schizophrenics than in non-schizophrenic subjects, but their BEQ focused to a large extent on hypochondriacal concerns and feelings of body inadequacy rather than the more extreme psychosis-like deviancy of perception of the body that is usually attributed to schizophrenia.

Chapman et al. (1978) developed another questionnaire to measure schizophrenic body image aberration, the Perceptual Aberration Scale, PAS, which is composed of 28 items and a four-point rating sale. Items were intended to tap five kinds of deviant experiences that are uncommon in normal people. The experiences dealt with (a) unclear boundaries of the body, (b) feeling of unreality of, or estrangement from, parts of the body, (c) a sense of deterioration of the body, (d) perceptions of change in size, relative proportions, or spatial relationships of body parts, and (e) changes in the appearance of the body. The scale was standardized on normal control groups. Male schizophrenics reported more body image aberration than normal control subjects, but only a portion of the schizophrenics were deviant. In addition, schizophrenic body image aberrations were negatively correlated with time since first hospitalization and had no correlation with the Physical Anhedonia Scale (Chapman et al., 1976) for schizophrenia, suggesting that the two scales, PAS and Physical Anhedonia Scale, may identify alternative manifestations of proneness toward the same schizophrenia, that is, schizophrenia and schizophrenia-proneness. Coleman et al. (1996) administered PAS to a sample of 2000 students to detect a group of schizotypy in a study conducted to examine the empirical links between schizophrenia and schizotypic psychopathology. Through comparisons of thought disorder assessed by the Thought Disorder Index, TDI (Coleman et al., 1993), between high and low PAS groups, the authors supported the hypothesis that psychometrically identified schizotypic individuals tapped by PAS display thought disorder similar to that of schizophrenia.

Oosthuizen et al. (1998) developed a four-point questionnaire, the Dysmorphic Concern Questionnaire, DCQ, to assess dysmorphic concerns, and tried to establish a correlation with clinical variables. The DCQ was loosely based on the General Health Questionnaire, GHQ. A series of seven statements was devised, based on the dysmorphic concern literature, to capture the essence of the problem (e.g., concern about physical appearance, considering oneself misshapen) and past attempts to deal with the problem (e.g., consulting a plastic surgeon, covering up supposed defects). The DCQ was administered to 63 patients including 33 schizophrenics. The results showed dysmorphic concern is often a reflection of cognitive set rather than a diagnosis itself.

The Body Image Questionnaire, BIQ, is a seven-step self-rating questionnaire with 59 body referring items, especially devised to measure schizophrenic body image deviation (Koide, 1985). The BIQ was developed on the basis of the clinical observations made through contact with chronic schizophrenic patients by clinicians and the attempts to grasp their deviations through assessing rather persistent attitudes or feelings toward the patients' own bodies, which are measurable on a graded continuum with those of normals. Thus, what is assessed by the BIQ is not a psychosis-like body distortion experience itself but an underlying readiness for observable aberrant behaviors including distorted body experiences. The patients' deviated concern about their body is revealed by observations. A middle-aged female schizophrenic patient tried to eat her glasses to exemplify the strength of her teeth (image of strong teeth). A young male patient continued to reject walking outside the hospital in the treatment programs because he felt tight like a stone when he tried to go out (image of tightness caused by relaxation). One young female patient talked about her wish to commit suicide because, she said, she wanted to avoid situations in which she imagined herself unable to move her own body by herself (image of becoming immobile). The items of the BIQ were arranged to include three prospectively hypothetical components: namely, anatomical, functional and other psychological elements such as mood and primitive sensation.

Objective of the Study

A wide variety of studies has appeared on body image aberration in schizophrenia; however, the problem inherent in schizophrenic body image aberration remains elusive. Earlier, the body image problems in schizophrenia were regarded as something related to psychotic symptoms, particularly with delusion and hallucination. Our perceptions of the schizophrenia have changed dramatically, particularly over the past two decades. During 1980s, the predominant view of the phenomenology of schizophrenia broadened beyond a narrow focus on psychotic symptoms to include negative symptoms, proprioceptive deficits, and self-injury representing body image problems. In the 1990s, another fundamental change in our perception of the disorder occurred. With this change, we have expanded the phenomenology of schizophrenia even further, beyond symptoms altogether, to include a strong emphasis on neurocognitive aspects of schizophrenia (Green & Neuchterlein, 1999).

Schizophrenia has consequently been investigated using "neuropsychological" procedures in order to uncover evidence of discrete neurological damage or dysfunction that may account for the great impairments in judgment, attention, concentration, planning ability and anticipation. In the late 1970s, a new era of neuropsychological study of schizophrenia began with three different review articles in which the low performance on neuropsychological test in functional patients was compared to organic patients (Goldstein, 1978; Heaton et al., 1978; Malec, 1978), and with the initial publication of in vivo evidence of ventricular enlargement in schizophrenia, as revealed by computerized tomography (CT) (Johonstone et al., 1976; Weinberger et al., 1979).

Focus has been on clarifying the relationships between neurocognitive deficits and psychotic symptoms (Cornblatt et al., 1985; Green & Walker, 1985; Neuchterlein et al., 1986; Green et al., 1992) and negative symptoms (Neuchterlein et al., 1986; Censits et al., 1997; Buchanan et al., 1997), between neurocognitive deficits and functional outcome (Green, 1996), between neurocognitive deficits and insight (Silverstein & Zerwic, 1985; Young et al., 1993; Lysaker & Bell, 1994; Cuesta & Peralta, 1994) and social cognition (Schneider et al., 1995; Bryson et al., 1997). In a current overview, Green and Nuechterlein (1999) searched for meaningful psychopharmacological and cognitive/behavioral interventions for neurocognitive deficits in schiziophrenia. Conventional antipsychotic agents are generally effective for psychotic symptoms, but their effects on neurocognition are relatively weak (Cassens et al., 1990; Strauss, 1993). Novel antipsychotic medications are more encouraging (Hagger et al., 1993; Green et al., 1997; Jeste et al., 1998; Keefe et al., 1999; Kern et al., 1999; Meltzer & McGurk, 1999). Conventional antipsychotic medications involve much coadministration of anticholinergic medications (e.g., benoztropine mesylate) that are known to have a negative effect on neurocognition (Spohn & Strauss, 1989).

To consider body image aberration in the above context, which deficit of body image comes from symptoms and which from medication should be clarified first. The questions are (1) Is body image aberration a result of symptoms seen in attenuated schizophrenic illness? (2) Is body image aberration an effect of medications? (3) What is the schizophrenics' body image's inherently aberrational part? Is there any intact part? (4) Is it remediable by behavioral/cognitive or psychopharmacological intervention? A full investigation of these basic questions is now required. Each section in this chapter is the attempt to clarify these basic problems.

PART II. STUDIES USING BODY IMAGE QUESTIONNAIRE (BIQ)

Study 1. Body Image Aberration and Clinical Characteristics

Introduction

In the era of pre-antipsychotics, disturbance of body experiences in schizophrenia had been documented as pathological experiences, especially in relation to hallucinatory and delusional disturbances. Since the 1970s, several concepts about the course of schizophrenia and recovery from it have been developed in the search for new perspectives (Strauss 1989; Harding et al., 1992). Because there is a growing interest in the recovery phase of schizophrenia, their body image characteristics should be refocused as multi-phased deviation from the normal experiences. In this context, the body image should be redefined rather comprehensively as persistent attitudes and feelings toward one's own body, which would preserve deleterious as well as ameliorative effects in the illness-environment interaction of disorder and recovery. In addition, with the availability of neuroleptics since mid. 1950s, undesirable physical reactions caused by drugs may also contribute to negative body image.

The aim of the study in this section was to reexamine the body image distortion perceived by schizophrenics, using the Body Image Questionnaire, BIQ, (Koide,1982/1985). Special inquiries were made concerning the influence of the clinical variables such as positive and negative symptoms, insight and neuroleptic dosage on body image aberration. The questions addressed in this sections are (1) What are the components of body images? (2) Which phases of body image are aberrant in schizophrenia? (3) Which aberrant body images are related to symptoms? (4) Which aberrant body images are associated with favorable signs of remission? (5) Is body image aberration related to neuroleptic dosage?

Method

Assessment of Body Image Deviation

Body image was assessed using the BIQ, a seven-step self-rating scale (scored as 1 to 7) with three hypothetical components, anatomical, functional and psychological. (See Appendix 1.)

Assessment of Clinical Characteristics

Positive symptoms were assessed using the Scale for Assessment of Positive Symptoms, SAPS, (Andreasen, 1983). Negative symptoms were assessed using the Scale for Assessment of Negative Symptoms, SANS, (Andreasen, 1981). Insight was assessed through Schedule for Assessing Insight, SAI, which comprises three main component scores that include acceptance, recognition of illness, and relabeling of pathological experiences, and one supplemental component, i.e., the hypothetical contradiction, which measures amenability to delusional experiences (David, 1990).

Subjects

The study sample consisted of 93 chronic schizophrenics; 44 were men and 49 were women. The mean (SD) age of the patients was 48.5 (10.1) years. All of them were inpatients at chronic psychiatric wards of a mental hospital in Ibaraki Prefecture in Japan. They were diagnosed as schizophrenic, on the basis of medical records, according to DSM-IV criteria (Subtypes: 24 Paranoid types, 40 Disorganized types, 25 Residual types, 4 Undifferentiated types). The mean (SD) duration of hospitalization was 24.1 (10.6) years, and the mean (SD) age of onset was 24.0 (7.0) years old. Their mean (SD) dose of neuroleptics was 469.8 (397.5) mg/day of chlorpromazine equivalent dose. The mean SAPS scores of the subjects was 26.2. The mean of SANS scores was 67.8. The mean SAI score was 8.4. The normal control group was comprised of 177 normally functioning adults of whom 78 were men and 99 were women. The mean (SD) age was 44.9 (12.6) years old. The normal adults were attending university summer school classes in psychology, and were confirmed to be normal by the General Health Questionnaire, the GHQ (short form, Goldberg, 1972; Goldberg & Williams, 1988). All subjects were informed of the purpose of the study and actively participated with written informed consent. (See Table 1.)

Table 1. Demographic and clinical characteristics of subjects. (Studies 1 and 5.)

	Schizophrenic	Normal
	(N=93)	(N=177)
Demographic characteristics		
Mean Age	48.5	44.9
Gender (% male)	47.3	44.1
Clinical characteristics	Mean (Range)	
Age of Onset	24.0 (14-45)	
Years of Hospitalization	24.1 (3-47)	
Dose of CPZ (mg/day)	469.8 (30-2156)	
SAPS	26.2 (0-94)	
SANS	67.8 (9-152)	
SDS	42.5 (24-64)	
SAI (Insight)	8.4 (0-14)	

Data Analysis

Comparisons of Means of each BIQ Item Scores

The means of the scores of 59 BIQ items were compared between schizophrenic and normal control groups using t-test.

Factor Analysis of the Body Image Questionnaire

On the bases of tentative preliminary analysis, 32 out of the original 59 items that proved to be not relevant to the factor analysis were excluded. However, two exceptional functional items (items 37, 41) from the excluded non-contributing items that proved to be important for discrimination when each item score was compared were re-included. The items of the final version pertain to smallness (items 8, 40, 54, 55), fatness (items 15, 28, 56) and roundness (items 24, 52) for the anatomical body image component; difficulty in manipulating his/her own body into action (items 9, 13, 21), lack of strength (items 1, 3), unusual concern over digestive functions (items 38, 53) and exceptional criterion-oriented standards (items 37, 41) for the functional component; and dissatisfaction and ugliness (items 10, 12, 27, 32), lack of vitality (items 31, 59) and fragility (items 19, 26, 39) for the psychological component.

Table 2. Means of BIQ items differentiating diagnostic groups. (Study 1.)

	Schizophrenic	Normal
01. My body is weak.	3.913	3.175***
03. I often get sick.	3.774	2.943***
06. My body is underdeveloped.	3.612	3.176**
07. My body is clean. ®	3.065	2.604**
09. I move slowly	4.193	3.649**
13. I am good at athletics.®	4.301	3.556**
17. I often lose my balance.	3.591	3.153*
19. I am often injured.	4.010	3.508**
23. My mood is numb.	4.279	3.875*
25. I am clumsy with my hands.	4.064	3.593*
26. I seldom catch a cold. ®	4.173	3.519**
29. My voice is feeble.	4.011	3.491**
31. I am always cheerful. ®	3.752	3.255**
37. I can work well in dark rooms. ®	5.258	4.429***
39. My body is susceptible to infection.	3.892	3.278**
41. I cannot move my body freely.	3.239	2.858*
42. My heart is strong. ®	3.397	2.949*
43. I don't mind being touched by others. ®	4.591	4.000**
44. My body is not meager. ®.	3.709	3.339*
45. I seldom get excited.	4.043	3.653*
47. My teeth are weak.	4.826	4.079***
55. My arms are unusually long. ®	3.989	3.680*
59. I always feel energetic.®	3.957	3.491**

*P<0.05, **P<0.01, ***P<0.001

The combined (schizophrenic and normal) data of the three BIQ hypothetical components, viz., anatomical, functional and psychological, were separately factor-analyzed using varimax rotation as the principal method, and the means of the factor scores were compared between the schizophrenic and normal control groups using t-tests. The factors that proved to be significant in differentiating schizophrenic and normal groups were compared further between the schizophrenic subgroups using t-tests. The schizophrenic subgroups were compared according to high (above or equal to mean) and low (lower than mean) scores on subscales and total scores of SAPS, SANS and SAI. Sub-grouping was also done according to the clinical factors of years of hospitalization and age at onset of disease, as well as daily equivalent dose of chlorpromazine. The SPSS (version 10) was used for statistical analysis.

Results

Group Differences of the BIQ Item Scores

The 23 out of 59 BIQ items proved to be differentiating two diagnostic groups. They were being weak, being prone to sickness, being underdeveloped, being dirty, moving slowly, being poor at athletics, being prone to losing balance, being prone to injury, being numb, being clumsy with hands, being prone to catching colds, speaking with a feeble voice, being always gloomy, being unable to work in dark rooms, being susceptible to infection, being unable to move his/her body freely, having a weak heart, minding being touched by others, being meager, not being prone to becoming excited, having weak teeth, having unusually long arms and being listless. (See Table 2.)

Factor Analysis and Obtained Differential Factors

Factor Analyses

Factor analyses of the three BIQ components, anatomical, functional, and psychological, using varimax rotation as the principal method, identified three factors with eigenvalues greater than 1 for each component. All items except two (items 37 and 41) had substantial loading on each of the factors. Total variances explained were 47.15%, 52.16% and 44.96%, respectively. Each of the three anatomical factors was composed of items indicating the images of smallness, fatness and roundness, respectively. Each of the three functional factors was composed of items indicating the images of dullness in movement, powerlessness and unusually strong gastrointestinal function, respectively. Each of the three psychological factors was composed of items indicating the images of dissatisfaction, lifelessness and fragility, respectively. (See Table 3 & 4.)

Differentiating Factors

Based on the results of the t-test of means of obtained factor scores of schizophrenic and normal control groups, five proved to be factors that differentiated the two groups. These factors are F-1 (dullness in movement, t=3.099, df=159.101, p=0.002), F-2 (powerlessness, t=4.458, df=136.065, p=0.000), F-3 (unusually strong gastrointestinal function, t=2.332, df=263, p=0.020), P-2 (lifelessness, t=3.042,df=260, p=0.003) and P-3 (fragility, t=4.507, df=260, p=0.000). (See Table 4.)

Related Clinical Characteristics

Symptoms

The results of the t-test of differentiating factor scores between schizophrenic subgroups composed of SAPS and SANS scores are shown in Table 5. The high-score (>5.28) group on hallucinations (SAPS-1) showed a statistically significantly higher factor score on F-2 (powerlessness, t=2.567, df=89, p=0.012) and P-2 (lifelessness, t=2.426, df=89, p=0.017) than the low-score group. The high-score (>10.12) group on delusions (SAPS-2) showed a statistically significantly higher factor score on F-2 (powerlessness, t=2.100, df=89, p=0.039) and P-2 (lifelessness, t=3.814, df=89, p=0.000) than the low-score group. The high-score (>8.96) group on positive formal thought disorder (SAPS-4) showed a statistically significantly higher factor score on F-2 (powerlessness, t=2.819, df=89, p=0.006) than the low-score group. The high-score (>26.2) group on total SAPS showed a statistically significantly higher factor score on F-2 (powerlessness, t=2.358, df=89, p=0.021) and P-2 (lifelessness, t=2.175, df=89, p=0.032) than the low-score group.

Table 3. Factor structure of BIQ. (Study 1.)

Items of BIQ components	Factors and Factor Loadings			h^2
Anatomical	*A-1*	*A-2*	*A-3*	
55. My arms are short.	0.716			0.539
08. I am short.	0.65			0.463
54. My legs are short.	0.636			0.418
40. My hands are small.	0.457			0.239
28. I am fat.		0.796		0.673
15. My body is not skinny.		0.792		0.629
56. My neck is short.		0.437		0.348
24. My body is not rough.			0.731	0.536
52. My body is round.			0.413	0.401
Functional	*F-1*	*F-2*	*F-3*	
13. I am poor at athletics.	0.808			0.654
09. I move slowly	0.783			0.644
21. I walk slowly.	0.693			0.492
37. I cannot work well in dark rooms.				0.027
03. I often get sick.		0.881		0.804
01. My body is weak.		0.802		0.693
41. I cannot move my body freely.				0.250
38. My stomach is unusually strong.			0.812	0.666
53. My bowels are unusually strong.			0.673	0.462
Psychological	*P-1*	*P-2*	*P-3*	
32. My body is unattractive.	0.693			0.535
27. I am satisfied with my body.	0.684			0.487
12. My body is ugly.	0.671			0.476
10. My body is defective.	0.568			0.385
59. I always feel listless.		0.933		0.903
31. I am always gloomy.		0.506		0.290
26. I often catch colds.			0.586	0.352
39. My body is susceptible to infection.			0.554	0.339
19. I am often injured.			0.496	0.279

Note: Only items that loaded at >.400 are shown.

Table 4. Means of factor scores in schizophrenic and control groups. (Study 1.)

Anatomical Factors	Schizophrenic	Control
A-1. Smallness	0.092	-0.047
A-2. Fatness	0.114	-0.058
A-3. Roundness	0.057	0.029
Functional Factors		
F-1. Dullness in movement	0.246	-0.128**
F-2. Powerlessness	0.373	-0.195**
F-3. Unusually strong gastrointestinal function	0.168	-0.088*
Psychological Factors		
P-1. Dissatisfaction	0.003	-0.018
P-2. Lifelessness	0.239	-0.127**
P-3. Fragility	0.278	-0.147**

*p<0.05, **p<0.01.

The high-score (>12.2) group on avolition-apathy (SANS-3) showed a statistically significantly higher factor score on F-2 (powerlessness, t=3.852, df=89, p=0.000) than the low-score group. The high-score (>13.7) group on anhedonia-asociality (SANS-4) showed a statistically significantly higher factor score on F-2 (powerlessness, t=2.983, df=89, p=0.004) and P-2 (lifelessness, t=3.272, df=89, p=0.002) than the low-score group.

Insight

The results of the *t*-test of differentiating factor scores between schizophrenic subgroups composed of SAI scores are shown in Table 6. The high-score (>3.29) group on acceptance (SAI-1) showed a statistically significantly lower factor score on F-3 (unusually strong digestive function, t=-2.482, df=89, p=0.015) and higher factor score on P-3 (Fragility, t=2.135, df=89, p=0.036) than the low-score group. The high-score (>1.7) group on hypothetical contradiction (SAI-supplement) showed a statistically significantly lower factor score on F-3 (unusually strong gastrointestinal function, t=-2.348, df=89, p=0.021) than the low-score group.

Other Clinical Characteristics

There was no significant difference between subgroups of body image factor scores in years of hospitalization, age at onset of disease or the daily chlorpromazine-equivalent dose.

Discussion

The factor analysis identified five differentiating factors, which showed that there is body image aberration in schizophrenic patients: dullness in movement, powerlessness, unusually strong digestive function, lifelessness and fragility. These findings, along with those of other investigations (Roehricht & Priebe, 1996; Coleman et al., 1996; Chapman LJ, Chapman & Raulin, 1978), revealed that schizophrenics manifested perceptual and cognitive deficits in body image.

Table 5. Differential BIQ factor scores in high and low score groups of SAPS and SANS. (Study 1).

| Factors | Positive symptoms | | Negative symptoms | |
| | SAPS | | SANS | |
	High	LOW	High	LOW
	SAPS-1		SANS-1	
	Hallucinations		Affective flattening or blunting	
F-1	–	–	–	–
F-2	0.789	0.178*	–	–
F-3	–	–	–	–
P-2	0.608	0.058*	–	–
P-3	–	–	–	–
	SAPS-2		SANS-2	
	Delusions		Alogia	
F-1	–	–		–
F-2	0.708	0.208*	–	–
F-3	–	–	–	–
P-2	0.794	-0.033**	–	–
P-3	–	–	–	–
	SAPS-3		SANS-3	
	Bizarre Behaviour		Avolition Apathy	
F-1	–	–	–	–
F-2	–	–	0.805	-0.013**
F-3	–	–	–	–
P-2	–	–	–	–
P-3	–	–	–	–
	SAPS-4		SANS-4	
	Positive formal Thought Disorder		Anhedonia-associality	
F-1	–	–	–	–
F-2	0.723	0.098**	0.718	0.064**
F-3	–	–	–	–
P-2	–	–	0.599	-0.082**
P-3	–	–	–	–
	SAPS-5		SANS-5	
	Inappropriate affect		Attention	
F-1	–	–	–	–
F-2	–	–		–
F-3	–	–	–	–
P-2	–	–	–	–
P-3	–	–	–	–
	SAPS-Total		SANS-Total	
F-1	–	–	–	–
F-2	.729	0.180*	–	–
F-3	–	–	–	–
P-2	0.556	0.067*	–	–
P-3	–	–	–	–

High =High score group. Low=Low score group. *=p<0.05, **=p<0.01.

Table 6. Differential BIQ factor scores in high and low score groups of SAI. (Study 1.)

BIQ	SAI		SAI	
Factors	High	Low	High	Low
	SAI-1a.		SAI-1b.	
	Treatment compliance (passive)		Treatment compliance (unprompted)	
F-1	–	–	–	–
F-2	–	–	–	–
F-3	0.047	0.546*	–	–
P-2	–	–	–	–
P-3	0.368	-0.059*	–	–
	SAI-2a.		SAI-2b.	
	Awareness of illness		Awareness of illness	
	(mental, physical)		(mental, psychiatric)	
F-1	–	–	–	–
F-2	–	–	–	–
F-3	–	–	–	–
P-2	–	–	–	–
P-3	–	–	–	–
	SAI-2c.			
	Explanation of illness			
F-1	–	–		
F-2	–	–		
F-3	–	–		
P-2	–	–		
P-3	–	–		
	SAI-3a.		SAI-3b.	
	Relabelling		Explanation	
	of psychotic experience		of psychotic experience	
F-1	–	–	–	–
F-2	–	–	–	–
F-3	–	–	–	–
P-2	–	–	–	–
P-3	–	–	–	–
	SAI-total		SAI-supplemental	
			Hypothetical Contradiction	
F-1	–	–	–	–
F-2	–	–	–	–
F-3	–	–	-0.135	0.303*
P-2	–	–	–	–
P-3	–	–	–	–

*=$p < 0.05$

Among the five differential body image factors, only two factors showed correlation with positive symptoms measured by SAPS: powerlessness and lifelessness, and the same factors correlated with negative symptoms. These results highlighted the close relationships between powerless and lifeless body images and severity in symptoms, both positive and negative, implying that the patients with severe symptoms would have powerless and lifeless body images.

Although the current view is that schizophrenics lack insight (Amador et al. 1994, 1991,; Cuesta & Peralta, 1994), the results of the present study showed that there is variation in degree of insight measured by SAI. The results also showed that acceptance of treatment, as one component of insight, as assessed by the SAI, proved to be related negatively with unusual gastrointestinal function and positively with the fragile body image, showing that patients who comply with treatment have fragile body images and have images of digestive organs that are not too strong. It might be well estimated that the fragile body image and the reduction of strength of images of digestive organs enhance the patients' feeling of needing help, which makes them compliant to treatment. Another insight component that showed a relationship with the deviated body image factor was the double-awareness phase, as assessed by the hypothetical contradiction, a supplemental item of the SAI. This was conceived as the degree of the patient's conviction about the delusion, as it appeared in the recovery from delusion (Sacks et al, 1974), and arising "from rapid oscillations between belief and disbelief." The score suggests "the amenability to test still firmly held beliefs against reality" (Sacks et al, 1974). The degree of double awareness was shown to be inversely related with the image of unusual strength of gastrointestinal function, showing that the patients with flexible amenability to delusional ideas have images of digestive organs that are not very strong.

The overall results proved two out of the five factors that differentiated the schizophrenic from the normal group to be related to positive and negative symptoms and two to insight. It is important that one major differentiating factor, dullness in movement, did not show any correlation with symptoms or insight. During the 1990s, observations focused on the fact that while patients' symptoms were improved markedly by antipsychotic agents, the patients still required assisted living arrangements and could not work in highly competitive situations (Goldberg et al, 1993). The fact that the main part of the body image deviancy assessed by BIQ did not relate to positive or negative symptoms is assumed to have some relation to these observations, and suggests the possibility that the main component of body image deviancy, which is independent from severity of symptoms, is closely related to some deficits that are germane to schizophrenia.

Conclusion

The factor analysis of BIQ showed some aberrant phases of schizophrenics' body image. They were: dullness in movement, powerlessness, unusually strong gastrointestinal function, lifelessness and fragility. Powerlessness and lifelessness proved to be related to positive and negative symptoms and unusually strong gastrointestinal functions and fragility, to insight.

Study 2. Schizophrenics' Body Images: What Are They?

Introduction

In Study 1, the attempts with factor analysis to find out the linkage of schizophrenics' aberrant body image with clinical characteristics proved to be exhaustive. However, the results of factor analysis showed that there are some differential body image factors, none of which seemed to relate to an anatomical component of body image of schizophrenia. It was further observed that most of the BIQ differential items were functional and psychological.

Distorted body experiences in schizophrenic patients, especially regarding their images of their body shape or proportions, have been reported since the 1960s. DeLeon et al (1989) denoted dysmorphophobia as a symptom which occurs in a number of different disorders, notably in schizophrenia. Dysmorphophobia as seen in somatoform disorders (1980), body dysmorphic disorder (1987) and delusional disorder, somatic subtype, were included in the Diagnostic and Statistical Manual of Mental Disorders, which produced considerable concern about delusion regarding the appearance of the body. (deLeon et al, 1989; Phillips et al, 1994). There has also been much discussion on distorted body experiences, which are legitimately categorized as psychological derivative imageries, including coenaesthesis (Huber, 1957; Rohricht & Priebe, 1996; Schmoll, 1994). Much concern has been placed on the blurred nature of body boundaries (Quinlan & Harrow, 1974; Fisher S, 1966), and the Rorschach test has been used to examine the vulnerable characteristics of body boundaries such as penetrability. In spite of all these attempts, clinical relevance of body image aberration remains unclear. It is still uncertain whether or not the body images are deviated in the area of visual imagery, or in feelings about their body such as being hard as stone or being fragile.

Thus, the question of which phase of body image links with symptoms and which to recovery? leads to the next question, "What are schizophrenics' body images, or what are their aberrations?" In this section, attempts were made to clarify this question simply by comparing three hypothetical components of BIQ, that is, anatomical, functional, and psychological, between schizophrenic and non-schizophrenic groups.

Method

Assessment of Body Image Deviation

Body images were assessed using the BIQ. The three BIQ component scores, *anatomical, functional,* and *psychological,* were obtained using scoring system with reverse items. (See, Appendix 1-1.) Items included in each component are shown in the Appendix. (See Appendix 1-3, 1-4 and 1-5.)

Subjects

The study sample consisted of 83 chronic schizophrenics; 44 were men and 39 were women. The mean (SD) age of the patients was 48.2 (10.0) years. All of them were inpatients in chronic psychiatric wards of a mental hospital in Ibaraki Prefecture in Japan. They were diagnosed as schizophrenia, according to DSM-IV criteria (Subtypes: 20 Paranoid types, 36 Disorganized types, 23 Residual types, 4 Undifferentiated types). The mean (SD) duration of hospitalization was 23.7 (10.5) years, and the mean (SD) age of onset was 24.2 (7.0) years old. Their mean (SD) dose of neuroleptics was 437.0 (396.9) mg/day of chrolpromazine equivalent dose. The group with anxiety disorders was comprised of 43 patients with anxiety disorders in DSM-IV, including 23 men and 20 women. They were outpatients of a private clinic in Ibaraki Prefecture in Japan. The mean (SD) age was 39.1 (14.1) years old. The normal control group of study 1 was used. All of the study participants were informed of the purpose of the study and actively participated with a written informed consent. (See Table 7.)

Table 7. Demographic and clinical characteristics of subjects. (Study 2.)

	Schizophrenia (N=83)	Anxiety Disorders (N=43)	Normals N=177
Demographic characteristics			
Mean Age	48.2	39.1	44.9
Gender (Male %)	53.0	53.4	44.0
Clinical characteristics of the schizophrenic patients			
	Mean (Range)		
Age of Onset	24.2 (14-45)		
Years of Hospitalization	23.7 (3-47)		
Dose of CPZ (mg/day)	437.0 (30-1256)		

Data Analysis

Means of the three BIQ component scores were compared among groups with schizophrenia, anxiety disorders and normals using ANOVA, followed by multiple comparisons using the Tukey method. The means of each item score of the differential component scores obtained were compared between the schizophrenic and non-schizophrenic groups using ANOVA.

Results

The results of ANOVA are shown in Table 8, and the results of succeeded multiple comparisons are shown in Table 12. Statistically significant group differences in means were found in the BIQ functional component score ($F=12.478$, $df=2/284$, $p=0.000$). Further multiple comparisons of differences of means showed a statistically significant difference between groups with schizophrenia and anxiety disorders ($p =0.021$), and between groups with schizophrenia and normal groups ($p = 0.000$). There was no statistically significant difference among the three diagnostic groups in the BIQ anatomical component score or in the BIQ psychological component score.

The mean scores of BIQ functional items, which composed the differential component, were further compared between schizophrenic and non-schizophrenic groups. Eight out of 17 items showed statistically significant differences, including being weak ($F=7.262$, $df=2$, $p<.001$), being liable to get sick ($F=10.810$, $df=2$, $p<.000$), moving slowly ($F=6.065$, $df=2$, $p<.003$), being poor at athletics ($F=7.743$, $df=2$, $p<.001$),, being liable to lose balance($F=5.092$, $df=2$, $p<.007$), walking slowly($F=3.314$, $df=2$, $p<.038$), being unable to work in dark rooms(F=10.415, df=2, p<.000), and having weak teeth (F=5.614, df=2, p<.004). The means of each functional item are shown in Table 9.

Table 8. Group means of BIQ component Scores. (Study 2.)

	Schizophrenia (N=83)	Anxiety Disorders (N=43)	Normals (N=177)	F
Anatomical	80.6	70.71	79.1	1.818
Functional	78.4	73.07	71.4	12.478***
Psychological	78.4	84.77	72.5	2.800
Total	238.8	228.34	223.1	18.046***

*P<0.05, **P<0.01, ***P<0.001

Table 9. Means of BIQ-Functional items of three diagnostic groups. (Study 2.)

	SC	AD	NO	F
01. My body is weak.	3.853	3.558	3.175	7.264***
03. I often get sick.	3.734	3.558	2.945	10.810***
09. I move slowly.	4.253	3.857	3.649	6.065**
13. I am good at athletics.®	4.465	4.432	3.626	7.743**
17. I often lose my balance.	3.790	3.566	3.153	5.092**
21. I walk slowly.	4.409	3.690	4.101	3.314*
37. I can work well in dark rooms. ®	3.570	3.418	2.783	10.415***
47. My teeth are weak.	4.817	4.209	4.079	5.614**

®=reverse item.
*P<0.05, **P<0.01, ***P<0.001.

Discussion

Results of this study showed aberration restricted to functional imageries, revealing that there are both intact and deficient phases in schizophrenics' body images. Of three hypothesized components, that is, anatomical, functional, and psychological body images, only functional imageries proved to be deviant.

The results of the comparisons of means of the various functional items between groups showed that differences included three categories of ill-functional body imageries. First was vulnerability to illness, including images of being weak and of being liable to get sick. Second was difficulty in manipulating their bodies, including images of being unable to work in dark rooms, being poor at athletics, walking slowly and of moving slowly. The third category was unusual concern over gastrointestinal functions reflected in having weak teeth.

Conclusion

Via the analysis of three hypothetical components of BIQ, the schizophrenic body image deviation proved to be comprised of deviation in functional imageries.

Study 3. Depression and Body Image in Chronic Schizophrenia

Introduction

Although mood disorders are conventionally viewed as nosologically distinct from schizophrenia, depression in schizophrenia has been recognized from the time of Mayer-Gross (1920) and Bleuler (1911/1950). Comorbid depressive signs and symptoms (DSS) in schizophrenia were earlier described as postpsychotic depression (McGlaschan & Carpenter, 1976), resulting from realization of disability once psychosis has abated and insight is recovered. A second view is described as post-treatment depression in which neuroleptic medication causes depression in schizophrenia (Van Puttan & May, 1978 ;Galdi, 1983). The concept has been further elaborated by Van Putten and May (1978), who argued that depression in schizophrenia might be specifically associated with extrapyramidal side effects of neuroleptic medication. A third view relates depression to the schizophrenic process itself. According to this hypothesis, depression forms an integral part of the illness, predicting that depressive symptoms would be most prevalent during the acute phase of illness and subside with treatment (Knights & Hirsch, 1981; Hirsch, 1982).

Recently, DSS have become a target of treatment because novel antipsychotic agents introduce new avenues that may differentially affect schizophrenic signs and symptoms, including depression (Pickar, 1995; Tollefson et al., 1998), and its association with a higher risk of suicide and self-harm (Siris, 1991; Hu et al., 1991; Drake & Cotton, 1986; Caldwell & Gottesman, 1990; Cohen et al., 1990; Roy et al., 1983) has been highlighted. There are studies that reported depressive schizophrenics attempt at unusual self-mutilation (Feldman, 1988; Burgess, 1991; Martin & Gattaz, 1991; Weiser et al., 1993; Kennedy & Feldmann, 1994), which suggest a close relationship between DSS in schizophrenia to body image aberrations.

The report in this section looks at depression in schizophrenia by detecting its unique relationship to patients' body image using BIQ.

Method

Subjects

The subjects in study 1 were used. (See Table 1.)

Assessment of Depression

Depression was assessed by Zung's Self-rating Depression Scale (SDS, Zung, 1965). The SDS scores ranged from 24 to 64, and their mean (SD) was 40.0 (7.9). Based on the distribution, the (schizophrenic and normal) depressive groups were comprised of those who scored 48 or higher, which included 20.3% of all subjects, including schizophrenicc and normal populations. The non-depressive groups were comprised of those who scored 32 or lower, which included 18.9% of all subjects.

Data Analysis

The means of the factor scores obtained in study 1 were compared between the depressive (SDS scores $\geq=48$) and non-depressive (SDS scores $=<32$) groups in schizophrenic and normal control samples, respectively, using *t*-tests. In addition, 59 item scores of BIQ were compared between high and low score groups in these comparative sets using *t*-tests.

Results

Based on the results of the *t*-test of means of obtained factor scores of schizophrenic depressive and non-depressive groups, 5 of these proved to be factors that differentiated the two groups. These factors and their interpretations are factor A-3 (roundness, t=-2.420, df=37, p=0.021), factor F-2 (powerlessness, t=2.407, df=38, p=0.021), factor F-3(Unusually strong gastrointestinal function, t=-2.588, df=38, p=0.014), factor P-1 (Dissatisfuction, t=2.491, df=38, p=0.015) and factor P-2 (Lifelessness, t=2.556, df=38, p=0.015). Among these factors, significant differences were found among normal population in factor P-1 (t= 5.010, df=40, p=0.000), and factor P-2 (t=2.756, df=40, p=0.009), showing that schizophrenic and normal groups had common relationships of depression to body image along with these factors. The other three of the five factors did not differentiate depressive and non-depressive groups in normal samples. Also, there was no factor differentiating depressive and non-depressive group uniquely found in the normal samples. (See Table 10.)

Table 10. BIQ Factors differentiating depressive and non-depressive state. (Study 3.)

Factors	Schizophrenic		Control	
	D	Non-D	D	Non-D
A-1	–	–	–	–
A-2	–	–	–	–
A-3	-2.220	.449*	–	–
F-1	–	–	–	–
F-2	.794	-.030*	–	–
F-3	-.165	.620*	–	–
P-1	.262	-.513*	.764	-.331***
P-2	.751	-.198*	.411	-.356*
P-3	–	–	–	–

D=Depressive group, Non-D=Non-depressive group. *P<.0.05, **P<0.01, ***P<0.001.

There were BIQ items which differentiated depressive and non-depressive groups only in schizophrenic samples. These were; having small eyes, being not meager, being weak, being clumsy with hands, having unusually strong stomach, having strong heart, having strong bowels, being underdeveloped, feeling cold, being dissatisfied, not minding being touched by others, and being getting worse. Schizophrenic and normal control samples shared the most of the differentiating items in the psychological element. (See table 11.)

Table 11. BIQ items differentiating depressive and non-depressive state. (Study 3.)

BIQ items	Schizophrenics		Normals	
	D	Non-D	D	Non-D
Anatomical				
18. I have small eyes.	4.200	3.181*		
44. My body is not meager.®	4.266	3.000**		
Functional				
01. My body is weak.	4.600	3.454*		
03. I often get sick.	4.400	3.000*	3.461	2.655*
17. I often lose my balance.			4.461	2.714***
25. I am clumsy with my hands.	4.833	3.181**		
37. I can work well in dark rooms. ®	5.666	4.181**	3.692	4.655*
38. My stomach is not unusually strong. ®	3.600	5.181**		
42. My heart is strong. ®	3.933	2.272**		
53. My bowels are unusually strong.	3.766	5.000*		
Psychological				
06. My body is underdeveloped.	.3.866	2.636*		
07. My body is clean.®			3.153	2.413**
10. My body is defective.	4.400	3.363*	4.692	3.448**
11. My body feels cold.	4.233	5.363*		
12. My body is beautiful.®	4.333	3.272*	4.769	3.482***
22. I seldom feel tired.®			5.461	4.206**
23. My mood is numb.	3.833	5.090*	2.000	4.724***
27. I am satisfied with my body. ®	3.200	4.727*		
31. I am always cheerful. ®			3.923	2.931**
32. My body is unattractive.			5.153	3.931***
34. I always feel sick.	4.433	3.181*	4.615	3.413***
43. I don't mind being touched by others. ®	4.866	3.636*		
45. I seldom get excited			2.833	4.275**
46. My health is getting better. ®	5.000	3.900*		
49. I am seldom tense.	2.400	3.909**	2.076	3.241**
59. I always feel energetic.®	4.666	3.363**	4.307	3.137**

D=Depressive group, Non-D=Non-depressive group. *P<.0.05, **P<0.01, ***P<0.001.

Discussion

The depression assessed by SDS correlated to 5 factors of body image assessed by BIQ. The findings further demonstrated that 3 among these 5 factors correlated with depression in schizophrenic groups, interpreted as roundness, dullness in movement, and unusually strong gastrointestinal function, none of which differentiated depressive from non-depressive group in normal subjects. It would be reasonable to assume that there is some close link between depression and body image, which is unique and specific to schizophrenia.

Dissatisfied and lifeless body images were found to be related to depression in schizophrenic as well as in normal samples. Dissatisfaction and lifelessness would be a common body image factors they shared regardless of diagnosis. In the schizophrenic sample, three differentiating factors were further observed, one anatomical factor, and two functional factors. It was observed that the more the schizophrenic patients becomes depressed, the less round and the less powerful their imagined body becomes and that the more they depressed, the less powerful their gastrointestinal function becomes in their body images. The results of the comparisons of means of each BIQ item also demonstrated that the variety of functional body image items differentiated depressive from non-depressive patients in the schizophrenic sample. The concern on bodily function proved to be prominent in schizophrenic depressive patients.

These observations may suggest that these depression-related body images in schizophrenia have characteristics, which lead to the anticipation of the serious corporeal deterioration of becoming immovable. This close linkage between depression and undesirable functional body images in schizophrenic patients would be connected with the self-mutilation or higher risk of self-harm observed in schizophrenia.

PART III. STUDIES USING RORSCHACH TEST: SUBSIDIARY FINDINGS

Study 4. A Unique Rorschach Response Observed in Schizophrenic Patients

Introduction

Although recognized as closely linked with psychopathology, distortion of body image has seldom been studied in schizophrenia. The major cause of the neglect of this concept is methodological, i.e., the difficulty in developing assessment techniques. In this section, a new finding concerning body image of schizophrenia, as observed in their Rorschach responses, is reported.

In the attempts to detect body image aberration in the studies using the BIQ, we found that responses that evoke images of a mass of flesh are often seen in schizophrenic Rorschach responses. This was first noticed in the response of a schizophrenic patient (Case A of this study) as "This looks like a mass of flesh of some kind of animal, though I cannot specify which," to Card VI. This response followed to the failure to construct the response "a gorilla" in Card IV, in which she could not identify its legs, arms, or head. According to this Rorschach sequence, a process is assumed to exist in schizophrenic thought that the their bodies are becoming a mere mass of flesh, as if they were being vivisected though still alive, which forms a core of fear of schizophrenic patients. Difficulty in identifying legs, arms, and head of perceived animals or human beings also proved to be a process of perceiving "a mass of flesh."

Starting with these observations, an attempt was made to explore similar responses in schizophrenics' Rorschach responses, and it was found that these responses are quite common in schizophrenic patients. We call the characteristics revealed in these responses as body image "becoming a mass of flesh" and present the hypothesis that this might form a core characteristic of body image of schizophrenia.

Responses such as "mass of flesh", or "muscles in the shoulder of a man," are typical mass of flesh responses because the image of a mass of flesh is clearly verbalized in these responses. Responses such as "a rat without legs" or "a girl, but I cannot see her hands" are also mass-of-flesh responses, because these responses, though indirect, vaguely imagine a mass of flesh through the diminution of head, legs, and arms and emphasis on the trunk.

Four cases are presented. All of them were inpatients of a chronic care ward of a mental hospital in Ibaraki Prefecture and were diagnosed as schizophrenia according to DSM-IV. All patients were informed of the purpose of the study and actively participated with written informed consent. The socio-demographic and clinical characteristics, such as illness type, onset age, years of hospitalization, BPRS scores (Overall & Gorham, 1962), and daily dose of neuroleptics, are shown in Table 12.

Table 12. Demographic and clinical characteristics of subjects. (Study 4.)

	Case A	Case B	Case C	Case D
Age	62	46	33	28
Gender	Female	Female	Male	Female
Years of education	9	7	13	12
Years of employment	2	0	0	4
Illnessl types	Paranoid	Disorganized	Disorganized	Residual
Age at onset	19	16	19	22
Years of hospitalization	37	30	33	5
BPRS	51	49	64	25
Daily dose of neuroleptics (mg)	400	1525	175	350

Case Reports

Case A

Miss A was a 62-year-old woman. She was born to a farmer in Ibaraki Prefecture in Japan as the first of seven children. After she graduated from high school, she went to Tokyo and worked as a housekeeper, but one year later she became restless, sleepless, and went back home. At the age of 22, she was admitted to the hospital with prominent delusional experiences. She left the hospital once, but soon left home, wandered around, stole food from a store and was returned the hospital. Since then, she has been in the hospital for 37 years.

In a semi-structured interview, she said, "A fox is controlling me. He exchanges my body with that of a victim of a traffic accident, so that I feel great pain in my legs, head, and arms. The fox is one of the foxes I keep at home. He changes my body because he gets money through traffic accidents. I am a splendid and super woman. If I had not been ill, I would have made a country. I sculpted on the moon as well as the sun."

In the Rorschach Test, she gave one response per card and gave in seven responses among ten animals with unclear or absent legs, arms, or head, or irregular emphasis on the legs. "Two elephants, but the legs are too short for elephants"(Card II). "A bat, legs are just like those of a bat" (Card V). "An animal I have never seen before. It looks like a gorilla, but this has no head, no legs, and no arms" (Card IV, IX). "A shrimp, with big tails and many small legs"(Card IX).

Case B

Miss B was a 46-year-old woman. She was a third of four children in the family of a public official. She suffered from tuberculosis in the junior high school. One day she was made a fun of by her classmates and refused to go to school. At the age of sixteen, she began to speak in monologues and to spend almost all day in bed. She showed delusions and hallucinations, and entered into the hospital when she was seventeen years old.

In the interview, she said, "I have been suffering from hallucinations everyday for twenty or thirty years. I hear the voice of a middle-aged woman, and she always says bad things about me. It causes severe pain in my shoulder. But I still continue knitting. When I brush my teeth, I feel like I am dying. When I am in bed, and also I am walking, germs move and frighten me, and dogs and cats are lying on me. All animals are transparent so that I cannot see them but they certainly exist."

She presented feelings of "being pressed" in 3 responses among a total of 7. "A calf oppressed by a fixed butterfly" (Card II). "Human beings are pressed down with their hands on the floor" (Card III). "A crab which is compressed, narrow in width" (Card X). She also showed an image of becoming a mass in the response, "A rat, there are no legs" to Card VIII.

Case C

Mr. C was a 55-year-old man. He was born the fourth child of a wealthy family in Tokyo. His father owned a company, and he went to private school. When he was in university, in the first year, he went to a supermarket with the group of his friends to steal some small things. He was expelled from the university. Since then, he complained of anxiety at meeting people, and visited many clinics for medication and psychotherapy, but he gradually came to stay at home almost all day. When he was 22 years old, he entered the hospital with prominent delusions and hallucinations.

In the interview, the patient said, "I suffer from nightmares every night. It is a dream of hell and I feel I cannot survive any more with these ominous ideas. I cannot concentrate. I am slow in thinking. And I have become old-fashioned. Somebody is talking ill of me. I feel suspected as a criminal every time a crime is broadcast on the television. It is because I know the names of the criminals, so that this is my referential delusion."

He showed five human movement responses, none of which identified the agent. "Hitting each other with both hands" (Card I), "Washing" (Card III), "Dancing" (Card VI), "Being astonished (Card VII), and "Talking, with each other" (Card X). He also showed over-clarification of ages in his human percepts, as "old" (Card II), "middle-aged" (Cards III, X), and "young" (Card VII). These estimations of age without evidence suggest the possibility that there might be strong conflict in his subjective inability to experience time, from which he feels excluded.

Case D

Miss D is a 28-year-old woman. She was the second of two children of a family of an artisan in Ibaraki Prefecture. When she was 16 years old, she felt that her classmates are talking ill of her so she refused to go to school. She once consulted with a psychologist. After she graduated from high school, she went to Tokyo and worked for a large company there for five years. When her mother got sick, she came back home to see her mother. Soon after her mother died, she became sleepless, violent especially toward her father, suffered from hallucinations and entered the hospital at the age of 23. After her admission, the hallucinations disappeared, and she returned home to stay several times, although she was not successful in staying home every time because of her violent behaviour toward her father.

In the interview, she said, "I feel miserable because I am under the protection of my father who is so slovenly that he spends a lot of money on bicycle races. My father hit me. But it is because I poured water on him. I am worried that I cannot be independent, though I am old enough to be. To tell the truth, I want to be a child of my elder sister."

She presented the body image as a mass of flesh in the response, "A crab, with torso with a carapace and nippers" (Card III), in which the mass-of-flesh image was covered with the hard shield of a crab and the impression of the whole response was aggressive and defensive, ready for fight. She also showed withdrawal of the body from the outer world in the response, "A piece of clothing, too showy for me." She showed helpless feelings in the response, "A flower, with leaves hanging down and connected with the roots in this way" (Card IX). In this response, the psychological process is presented as a feeling of helplessness that was developed into an attempt to confirm that she was related to her support system.

Discussion

The body image becoming a mass of flesh was seen in four cases as a common characteristics of body image, regardless of their variety of illness type, of degree of severity of symptoms assessed by BPRS, life history and daily dose of neuroleptic medication. Clarification of how this mass-of-flesh image is expressed and is related to the patients' clinical pictures is necessary. Three questions need to be discussed with regard to these patients: (1) Is mass-of-flesh image really related to delusion?: (2) Is it related to hallucinatory behaviour? (3) Is it related to symptoms other than delusional and hallucinatory experiences?

Case A refers to the first question. In this case, body image as a mass of flesh was expressed in a typical form as "a mass of flesh of some animal with a bamboo stick." From this response, it is assumed that she has a catastrophic fear of her body being exposed to the outer world without protection, being penetrated. It is further guessed that this fear is elaborated into a delusional belief to clarify and explain its origin, by thinking that a naughty fox exchanged her body with that of a victim of a traffic accident, and that the fox is one of many foxes she kept at home.

Case B exemplifies to the second question. In this case, the body image of becoming a mass of flesh was expressed as "a rat without arms and legs" and also as "a crab which was compressed" and "a calf that was oppressed by a butterfly." These responses imply that body image as becoming a mass of flesh modified into more sensory form as "being pressed" and developed into a hallucination. She suffered from being oppressed at shoulder presumably caused by a middle-aged woman's voice. She also suffered from being oppressed by germs creeping on her and by transparent animals lying on her.

Case C refers to the third question. In this case, the agents in human Rorschach percepts are frequently not identified. Omission of the head is an indirect expression of body image as a mass of flesh. The lack of identification of the agents of the human percepts implies his avoidance of committing himself to the percepts. With this withdrawal, he tries to maintain distance by regarding the whole situation in which he lives as if it were a fiction, acted on a stage, and regarding himself as an audience. He described his own symptoms as "referential delusion" as if others observe him and felt himself "like a criminal who appears on television". His over-concern about age and many attempts to guess age without enough evidence would be derived phenomenon from this withdrawal from the real world, in which time passes, into a fictional narcissistic world, in which there is no lapse of time. He is worried about "becoming old-fashioned." This concern toward age seems consistent with the age-disorientation of schizophrenia (Crow & Johnstone, 1980; Crow & Stevens, 1978). It was reported that 25% of the schizophrenic patients mistake their own ages by more than 5 years.

In Case D, the mass-of-flesh percepts appeared in the perception, "A crab, with a torso with a carapace and nippers" (Card III). A mass of flesh was seen in the elimination of the legs with armor. This is consistent with her clinical picture, in which her violent acting-out is a prominent problem. As the risk of violence has come to be one of the current issues of schizophrenia (Taylor, 1995; Fottrell,1980; Humphreys et al., 1992) the present finding seems to relate to some illness-specific risk factor to evoke violence in schizophrenic patients. In this case, it is assumed that an "armored mass-of-flesh body image" would be a compromised product of an aggressive premorbid personality and schizophrenic illness.

The body image as becoming a mass of flesh is considered to have four connotations. First, it suggests an image of the body, which is still alive, though exposed to the outer world. Second, it suggests an image of the body that is helplessly threatened and unprotected. Third, it suggests an image of the body that is unmovable. Fourth, it suggests an image of the body that is weakened and helpless. These would constitute an image of potential catastrophe concerning the patients' own body.

The image of becoming a mass of flesh was recognized in two stages. Stage 1 is presented directly with reference to "a mass of muscles" or "mass of flesh," as seen as a typical response one. Stage 2 as presented indirectly as an animal or a human being without legs or arms, or without clarifying them, in which the mass of flesh is vaguely imagined through the diminution of head or legs. In observation of these four cases above, stage 1 presumably works with delusion, especially being closely linked with bizarre delusions and enhancing psychological factors for it. Stage 2 would exist as a rather general, though underlying, disposition in schizophrenic patients. In the case of stage 2, it was further shown that image of becoming a mass of flesh leads to some readiness for age-disorientation as one of the major thought disorders, as well as violent acting-out behaviours, so that one of the future topics to be discussed should be the effect of the image of becoming a mass of flesh on the formation of a variety of schizophrenic symptoms.

Conclusion

Rorschach responses that imply the body images of becoming a mass of flesh were shown in four chronic schizophrenic cases. The body images of becoming a mass of flesh were experienced in two forms: one is experienced by the percept of a mass of muscles. The other is by percepts of an animal or a human being with diminished legs, head, or arms. In studying four cases carefully, these responses were found regardless of the illness type, duration of illness, life history, and neuroleptic doses, but they related not only to delusional and hallucinatory symptoms but also to some other thought disorders such as age-disorientation as well as violence. Because this is just an initial phase of the study, further studies are required to determine whether this finding is a general intrinsic trend of schizophrenia or not.

Study 5. A Mass of Flesh: Schizophrenic Rorschach Percepts

Introduction

The Rorschach test is important in the diagnosis of schizophrenia. Since 1966, 1728 studies using the Rorschach test, among which 126 were concerned with the diagnosis of schizophrenia, have been indexed in Medline. Rorschach protocols have been documented in thought disorders, sometimes in terms of ego impairment, to provide information concerning diagnosis of schizophrenia. Rappaport et al. (1968) are historically credited with systematically identifying deviant aspects of the patient's verbal responses to the inkblot. Attempts have been made to develop specific criteria on the Rorschach designed to make a more accurate assessment of thought disorders, including the Delta Index (Watkins & Stauffacher, 1952), Thought Disorder Index (Johnston & Holzman, 1979), and Schizophrenia Index (Exner, 1974, 1978, 1986a, 1986b, 1991, 1993; Mason et al., 1985). Earlier, methods were developed to assess "primary process" manifestations (Holt, 1977; Meloy, 1984) or boundary disturbance manifestations (Quinlan and Harrow, 1974). During the 1970s to 1980s, methods to assess object relations were developed to differentiate borderline personality disorders from schizophrenia (Urist, 1977; Kwawer, 1980). In the 1990s, Wagner and Frye (Wagner & Frye, 1990) reported the diagnostic implication of the "fragmented" Rorschach W:D (Whole Responses vs. Detail Responses) ratio in schizophrenia, and Perry developed perseveration measures (Perry & Braff, 1998). One of the most widely used of these Rorschach criteria for the evaluation of schizophrenia is the Comprehensive System's Schizophrenia Indices, SCZI (Exner, 1974; Mason et al., 1985). The Comprehensive System began to pay more attention to the importance of systematically measuring unusual verbalizations and identifying reliable test signs that capture a range of aberrations in thought and language. The diagnostic indicators of disordered thinking in Exner's approach pointed to large differences between schizophrenia and control subjects, confirming an impairment of perceptual accuracy, reality testing and reduced emotional control (Di-Nuovo et al., 1988), and the Exner Rorschach was judged to be a valid test for schizophrenia (Vincent & Harman, 1991; Hilsenroth et al., 1998). Another index, the Ego Impairment Index, proved to differentiate among schizophrenics according to the severity of their ego impairment (Perry et al., 1992). Recently, investigators have placed much emphasis on Rorschach indications for thought disorders in regard to sensorimotor gating abnormalities or other information processing in the neurocognitive context (Perry & Braff, 1994; Perry et al., 1999).

In the previous section (study 4), a new finding was reported concerning Rorschach percepts of schizophrenia, that images of a mass of flesh were often seen in schizophrenic Rorschach responses. This was first noticed in the Rorschach response to Card VI of a middle-aged female (Case A) with chronic schizophrenia in the statement, "This looks like a mass of flesh of some kind of animal, although I cannot specify which animal." Before producing this response, the patient had failed to make the response of " a gorilla" to Card IV, in which she could not identify its arms, legs or head. According to these Rorschach sequences, it would be considered that if the patient has failed to see the legs and arms, a gorilla is perceived as a mass of flesh. A similar response was found in another middle-aged male with chronic schizophrenia, who responded to Card IX, "Part of a naked man, the swelling muscles of his shoulder." This patient also responded to Card VIII, "The carcass of an animal. Only bones here, for the flesh is gone." In this response, he imagined a mass of flesh and quickly eliminated it by thinking of it as having been taken away in his fantasy. The third patient, a middle-aged female with chronic schizophrenia, who gave another such response, by responding to Card VIII, saying "Two seals. They are seals, because their legs and arms are quite short. They look like muscles. Only the muscles of seals. With backbones here." In this response, she saw two aquatic animals that have intrinsically diminished (short) legs and arms, and this image soon became muscles with backbones.

Starting with these findings, the attempts were made further to find similar responses in their Rorschach percepts. It was found that the responses in which a mass of flesh or muscles are explicitly verbalized are not often seen in their Rorschach percepts, but that the responses with the same implications in modified and implicit forms, especially in the form of animals or human beings with diminution of head, legs or arms, were quite common in schizophrenic patients.

Although apparently different, these responses share the common characteristic of revealing the perception of a mass of flesh in the Rorschach pattern. The author called the above percept "a mass of flesh" (MF) and considered that the implications of the MFs should be studied further in the diagnosis of schizophrenia. In order to detect MFs reliably, inclusion and exclusion criteria for MFs were developed which describes the details to identify the MFs.

First, this study is an attempt to develop inclusion criteria for detecting these responses based on these observations. Second, to examine whether perception of MFs is characteristic in schizophrenia or not, the presence or absence of the MFs was examined in the Rorschach protocols of patients in the diagnostic groups of acute schizophrenia, anxiety disorders according to DSM-IV criteria, and healthy adults.

Method

Inclusion and Exclusion Criteria for the MF Percept

The idea that schizophrenics produce percepts of a mass of flesh evolved through our earlier observations in the evaluation of 7 chronic schizophrenia patients. Thereafter, particular attention was given to the responses of 69 consecutive chronic schizophrenic patients (76 in total) to confirm whether or not they produced any response which had a connotation of a mass of flesh or its implicit representation, mainly reflected in diminution of head, arms or legs, of any living thing. After it was confirmed that 75 out of 76 (98%) chronic schizophrenic patients produced some MFs, a list of criteria for MFs was made to detect them reliably.

MFs are, in their explicit and typical form, responses in which a mass of flesh or muscle is explicitly verbalized. The MFs, in their implicit forms, include responses in which diminution of arm, leg, and head is mentioned. In these responses, absence, unusual shortness or vagueness of arms, legs or head is verbalized. The things or living things with a mass-like shape, or perceived as folded or unfolded, are also included because these responses reflect the image of a mass of flesh or the process of becoming a mass of flesh or its denial. Exclusion criteria were made as a guide to exclude misleading responses. Inclusion and exclusion criteria are summarized in Appendix 2.

Test Administration and Scoring

All Rorschach tests were administered by the present authors. The presence or absence of any response that fit the criteria was examined in each case. The cases were divided into two groups, that is, one with MFs and one without.

Inter-Rater Reliability

Inter-rater agreement was determined by evaluating the MFs according to the protocols of 20 chronic schizophrenics. Independent ratings was made by two raters. Nineteen among 20 protocols were scored as showing MF (MF +) by two independent scorers, and 95% inter-rater agreement was obtained.

Subjects

The socio-demographic data of the subjects used for evaluation of the MFs are shown in Table 13. The chronic schizophrenic patients were those of Study 2, who agreed to participate to the study using the Rorschach test. There were 41 men and 35 women. The mean (SD) age of the patients was 49.4 (9.4) years. The mean (SD) chlorpromazine-equivalent dose was 474.8 (406.3) mg. Twenty-two acute schizophrenic patients, 10 male and 12 female, are inpatients of a hospital in a Tokyo suburb. The Rorschach test was administered within one month after their first admission. Their mean (SD) age was 21.8 (3.3) years. All of them were medicated, and the mean (SD) chlorpromazine-equivalent dose was 1082.3 (536.8) mg. All of them had been diagnosed with schizophrenia, according to DSM-IV criteria. Thirty patients with anxiety disorders according to DSM-IV, 16 male and 14 female, were outpatients of a private clinic in Tokyo. Their mean (SD) age was 35.9 (13.4) years. Twenty-eight healthy adults, 14 men and 14 women, were graduate students, hospital staff members, businessmen, office employees, and housewives. The mean (SD) age was 34.1 (12.8) years old. All normal adults were demonstrated to be healthy by administering General Health Questionnaire (Goldberg, 1972; Goldberg & Williams, 1988). Written informed consent was also obtained. (See Table 13.)

Table 13. Demographic characteristics of subjects. (Study 5.)

	Schizophrenia		Anxiety Disorders	Nprmals
	Chronic	Acute		
	(N=76)	(N=22)	(N=30)	(N=22)
Mean Age	49.4	21.8	35.9	34.1
Gender (% male)	53.9	45.5	53.3	50.0

Statistics

The number of subjects perceiving MFs and those not perceiving MF was calculated in each diagnostic group.

Results

Seventy-five out of 76 chronic schizophrenic patients (98%) saw MFs. All 22 acute schizophrenic patients saw MFs. Twenty-eight out of 30 patients with anxiety disorders did not perceive MF. None of the healthy adults saw the MF. It would be reasonable to regard the MFs as characteristic of schizophrenia. The number of subjects perceiving MFs (MF+) and those not perceiving MF (MF-) in schizophrenic and non-schizophrenic groups are shown in Table 14 (x^2 = 11.308, df=1, p=0.001).

Both of two patients with anxiety disorders who perceived MFs were young adolescent males and had brief psychotic episodes in their life histories. One patient with chronic schizophrenia who did not perceive MF was a middle-aged male patient who scored the least total response to the inkblots. (His total response was less than ten.)

Table 14. MFs in schizophrenic and non-schizophrenic groups. (Study 5.)

	Schizophrenic		Non-schizophrenic	
	Acute	Chronic	Anxiety Disorders	Normal
	(N=22)	(N=76)	(N=30)	(N=28)
MF+	22	75	2	0
MF-	0	1	28	28

Discussion

The primary contribution of this investigation is to find that Rorschach percepts of a mass of flesh are characteristic of schizophrenia. It was found that although there are some differences in their responses, the perception of a mass of flesh in Rorschach inkblot stimuli was broadly seen as living things with diminished arms, legs or head. By developing inclusion and exclusion criteria for MFs, detection of MFs would become easier and more reliable. To test whether the perception of MFs in inkblots is unique to schizophrenia or not, we examined the Rorschach Test data of 22 acute schizophrenia, 30 anxiety disorders and 28 healthy adults. Ninety-seven out of 98 schizophrenic patients saw MFs, although only two out of 30 patients with anxiety disorders saw MFs. Further, healthy adults did not see any MF. Thus, MFs proved to be characteristic of schizophrenia.

An index for detecting such responses is particularly important because it provides a tool for detecting schizophrenia in its early phase. Ninety-eight percent of chronic schizophrenics, as well as 100% of acute schizophrenic patients, perceived MFs. The perception of MFs might exist from the time of onset and therefore be able to detect a very early phase of schizophrenia, suggesting the diagnostic predictive value of MF perception. As a greater understanding of the nature of schizophrenia has refocused attention on the early course of psychosis in the from of early detection and intervention around the onset (McGlashan & Johannessen, 1996) the inclusion and exclusion criteria would have more value if MFs are found in the prodrome of schizophrenia.

The findings that schizophrenic patients produce MF percepts may lead to improvement of our understanding of thought disorder of schizophrenia. The use of the Rorschach test in the study of thought disorder is well established. However, using the Rorschach test for the purpose of eliciting perceptual deficits, manifested in global and affective percepts such as MFs, might provide a new opportunity to understand the cognitive dysfunction of schizophrenia patients.

Conclusion

The Rorschach test was given to schizophrenic and non-schizophrenic subjects to determine whether schizophrenic patients more frequently produced the "mass of flesh" percept than the non-schizophrenic groups did.

PART IV. DISCUSSION AND CONCLUSION

Discussion

The major findings of the studies on schizophrenics' body image aberration in this chapter are: (1) There is some aberration in schizophrenics' body image. (2) There are aberrant as well as intact phases in their body images. (3) Aberration was found in functional imageries, while anatomical imageries are intact. (4) Aberration is independent of symptoms and conventional neuroleptic medication.

The main questions raised in the introduction were whether aberration comes from symptoms or is an effect of neuroleptics, and whether it is remediable or not. What the components of body image are and which phase of body image is aberrant in schizophrenia was the first question we tried to answer by attempts at classification of body image items by factor analysis. Nine body image factors were obtained, and some factors proved to differentiate schizophrenics from normal controls. Although these factors were variously named, after rather exhaustive attempts, the only discrete common feature among factor-analytic studies was that functional imageries may contribute substantially to the factors that meaningfully differentiated groups or were related to depression. In addition, almost no significant correlation was found between aberrant body image factors and clinical characteristics such as symptoms, insight, or neuroleptic dosage. The results of Study 1 showed that when each component of symptoms and insight was cross-validated to the BIQ factors, there were some symptoms and some insight components related to body image factors; however, the overall results showed their relationship was quite weak. The only strong evidence gained through these studies was the fact that there are some differential body image factors, most of which seemed to relate to functional body imageries, but none of which seemed to relate to the anatomical component of body image of schizophrenia.

Thus the question of which phase of body image links with symptoms and which to recovery? leads to the next question, "What are the body images of schizophrenics and what is aberrant for them?" In Study 2, attempts were made to clarify this question simply by comparing three hypothetical components of body image, that is, anatomical, functional, and psychological, between schizophrenic and non-schizophrenic groups. The results showed clearly that anatomical, that is, the visual or the spatial, component is intact in schizophrenia and limited their aberration mainly to functional component.

The fact that schizophrenics have aberrant body images in function, i.e., they have unmovable body images, is controversial with regard to the possibility that it reflects perseverance in motor activity. Schizophrenic patients might have difficulty in the shifting the response set in motor activity in light of the feedback that a previous response was incorrect and consequently "persevere" in making the same response, creating difficulty in movement cognition. Perseveration is a cardinal feature of frontal lobe disease (Bilder & Goldberg, 1987). It is one of the presenting basic neurocognitive deficits, observed since the time of Bleuler (1911/1950), who wrote that schizophrenic patients "remain fixed to the same circle of ideas, the same words, the same sentence structure or at any rate, return to them again and again without any logical need."

The degree of perseverance of schizophrenic patients is similar to that of patients with known frontal pathology (Levin, 1984). Since Weinberger et al. (1986) reported a negative correlation between the percentage perseveration as measured by the Wisconsin Card Sorting Test, WCST, (Milner, 1963) and prefrontal blood flow, these associations have supported the hypothesis that schizophrenic patients have an impairment of the frontal or prefrontal cortex.

Because the clinical interpretation of test data can often point to multiple studies that converge on a set of frequent severe and selective deficits, patients with schizophrenia typically demonstrate abnormalities in attention, memory, and executive function that stand out against a background of diffuse impairment (Pantelis et al., 1996). However, some areas of function appear to be relatively more intact than others, i.e., some aspects of language (Gold et al., 1994; Saykin et al., 1991; Daniels et al., 1988; Barr et al., 1989; Frith, 1993) and some types of visual spatial processing (Kolb & Whishaw, 1983; Goldberg et al., 1990; Goldberg et al., 1993a). These neuropsychological profiles implicate specific brain regions, i.e., frontal-medial dysfunction (Kolb & Whishaw, 1983; Taylor and Abrams, 1984). The finding that the aberration referred to functional body imageries would imply body image deficits that have some relation to dorsolateral deficits, and the fact that the anatomical, that is, visual and spatial, imageries remain intact is consistent with the previous finding that some types of visual spatial processing is intact in the neuropsychological profile of schizophrenics.

In Study 3, body image aberration was considered through an attempt to detect specific body image characteristics related to depression in schizophrenia by comparing the BIQ factor scores between depressive and non-depressive groups comprised by Zung's Self-rating Depression Scale (SDS) in normal and schizophrenic groups respectively. The results showed some body image factors related uniquely to depression in schizophrenia, which, again, referred to functional body images. The result of this part of the study might cast light on future prospects of the study of body image aberration using a device such as the BIQ because of its link with DSS which has become a target for treatment of schizophrenia, with the novel antipsychotic medications. The studies performed for this chapter all revealed that neuroleptics did not relate to body image aberration; however, novel antipsychotic agents were not discussed or studied. This would be relevant to the final question as to whether or not the body image aberration is remediable.

Study 4 and Study 5 are reports of subsidiary findings of our main studies using the BIQ, in which schizophrenic patients produced Rorschach responses implying or referring to "mass of flesh." Study 4 is composed of the initial observations. In Study 5, the Rorschach test was given to schizophrenic and non-schizophrenic subjects to determine whether schizophrenic patients more frequently produced the "mass of flesh" percept than the non-schizophrenic groups did. These findings suggest that there might be a fear of immobility in schizophrenia that is congruent with our main findings.

Conclusion

Schizophrenic body image aberration was considered in the current context. The schizophrenic body image aberration was unrelated to symptoms, insight, or conventional neuroleptic medication, but proved to be germane to schizophrenia. The schizophrenic body image aberration also proved to be limited to functional imagery while anatomical imageries remained intact.

ACKNOWLEDGEMENTS

We would like to express our appreciation to Dr. Chin-Piao Chien, professor emeritus of UCLA, and Dr. Shoji Shin'ichi and Dr. Susumu Oda, professors emeriti of Tsukuba University. We also thank Dr. Toshihiko Maeda of tne Institute of Statistical Mathematics for the statistical consultation.

Part of the text was re-edited from *Psychiatry and Clinical Neurosciences*, Vol. 56, pp9-15, "Body image, symptoms and insight in chronic schizophrenia" by Koide et al (2002), with permission from Blackwell Publishing, and from *Comprehensive Psychiatry*, Vol.43, pp474-477, "A mass of flesh: Schizophrenic Rorschach Percepts" by Koide R., et al (2002), with permission from Elsevier.

REFERENCES

Amador, X. F., Flaum, M,, Andreasen, N.C., Strauss, D. H., Yale, S. A., Clark, S. C. & Gorman, J. M. (1994). Awareness of illness in schizophrenia and schizoaffective and Mood disorders. *Archives of General Psychiatry, 51*, 826-836.

Amador, X. F., Strauss, D.H., Yale, S.A., & Gorman JM. (1991). Awareness of illness in schizophrenia. *Schizophrenia Bulletin, 17*,113-132.

American Psychiatric Association. (1980). *Diagnostic and statistical manual of mental disorders (3rd edition)*. Washington, DC: American Psychiatric Association.

American Psychiatric Association. (1987). *Diagnostic and statistical manual of mental disorders (3rd edition revised)*. Washington, DC: American Psychiatric Association.

American Psychiatric Association. (1994). *Diagnostic and statistical manual of mental disorders (4th edition)*. Washington, DC: American Psychiatric Association.

Andreasen, N. C. (1981). *Scale for the assessment of negative symptoms*. Iowa City, IA: The University of Iowa Press.

Andreasen, N. C. (1983). *Scale for the assessment of positive symptoms*. Iowa City, IA: The University of Iowa Press.

Andreasen, N. C., Arndt, S., Alliger, R., Miller, D., & Flaum, M. (1995). Symptoms of schizophrenia: methods, meanings, and mechanisms. *Archives of General Psychiatry, 52*, 341-351.

Andreasen, N, & Bardach, J. (1977). Dysmorphophobia:Symptom or disease? *American Journal of Psychiatry, 134*, 673-676.

Angyal, A. (1936). Experiences of body self in schizophrenia. *Archives of Neurology and Psychiatry, 35*, 1629-1634.

Apter, J.T. (1981). The "silent" acute abdomen in schizophrenia. *Journal of the Medical Society of New Jersey, 78*, 679-680.

Arieti, S. (1945). Primitive habits and perceptual alterations in the terminal stage of schizophrenia. *Archives of Neurology and Psychiatry, 53*, 378-384.

Barr, W. B., Bilder, R. M., Goldberg, E. H., Caplan, E., & Mukherjee, S. (1989). The neuropsychology of schizophrenic speech. *Journal of Communication Disorders, 22*, 327-349.

Berman, A. L. (1972). Videotape self-confrontation of schizophrenic ego and thought processes. *Journal of Consulting and Clinical Psychology, 39,* 78-85.

Bickerstaff, L. K., Harris, S. C, Leggett R S, & Cheah K. C. (1988). Pain insensitivity in schizophrenic patients: A surgical dilemma. *Archives of Surgery, 123*, 49-50.

Bilder, R. M., & Goldberg, R. E. (1987) Motor perseverations in schizoiphrenia. *Archives of Clinical Neuropsychology, 2*, 195-214.

Birtchnell, S. A. (1988). Dysmorphophobia - a centenary discussion. *British Journal of Psychiatry, 153 (suppl 2)*, 41-43.

Blackmore, S. (1986). Out-of-body experiences in schizophrenia. A questionnaire survey. *Journal of Nervous and Mental Disease, 174*, 615-619.

Bleuler, E. (1911) *Dementia Praecox, or the Group of Schizophrenias*. Translated by J Zinkin. New York: International Universities Press (1950).

Braff, D. L., Heaton, R., Kuck, J., Cullum, M., Moranville, J., Grant, I., & Zisook, S. (1991). The generalized pattern of neuropsychological deficits in outpatients with chronic schizophrenia with heterogeneous Wisconsin Card Sorting Test results. *Archives of General Psychiatry, 158*, 340-345.

Brebion, G., Smith, M. J., Amador, X., Malaspina, D., & Gorman, J.M. (1997). Clinical correlates of memory in schizophrenia: differential links between depression, positive and negative symptoms, and two types of memory impairment. *American Journal of Psychiatry, 154*, 1538-1543.

Bryson, G., Bell, M., Lysaker, P. (1997). Affect recognition in schizophrenia: A function of global impairment or a specific cognitive deficit. *Psychiatry Research, 71*, 105-113.

Buchanan, R. W., Strauss, M. E., Breier, A., Kirkpatrick, B., & Carpenter, W.T. (1997). Attentional impairements in deficit and nondeficit forms of schizophrenia. *American Journal of Psychiatry, 154*, 363-370.

Burgess, J. W. (1991). Relationship of depression and cognitive impairment to self-injury in borderline personality disorder, major depression, and schizophrenia. *Psychiatry Research, 38*, 77-87.

Bychowsky, G. (1943). Disorders of the body image in the clinical picture of psychoses. *Journal of Nerveous and Mental Disease, 97*, 310-334.

Caldwell, C. B., & Gottesman, I.I. (1990). Schizophrenics kill themselves too: a review of risk factors for suicide. *Schizophrenia Bulletin, 16*, 571-589.

Cancro, R. (1971). Sophistication of body concept in process-reactive schizophrenia. *Perceptual and Motor Skills, 32*, 567-570.

Cassens, G., Inglis, A. K., Appelbaum, P. S., & Guthcil, T. G. (1990). Neuroleptics: Effects on neuropsychological function in chronic schizophrenic patients. *Schizophrenia Bulletin, 16*, 477-499.

Censits, D. M., Ragland, J. D., Gur, R. C., & Gur, R. E. (1997). Neuropsychological evidence supporting a neurodevelopmental model of schizophrenia: A longitudinal study. *Schizophrenia Research, 24*, 289-298.

Chapman, L. J., Chapman, J.P., & Raulin, M. L. (1976). Scales for physical and social anhedonia. *Journal of Abnormal Psychology, 85*, 374-382.

Chapman, L. J., Chapman, J. P., & Raulin, M. L. (1978). Body-image aberration in schizophrenia. *Journal of Abnormal Psychology, 87*, 399-407.

Cleveland, S. E. (1960a). Body image changes associated with personality reorganization. *Journal of Consulting Psychology, 24*, 256-261.

Cleveland, S. E. (1960b). Judgements of body size in a schizophrenic and a control group. *Psychological Reports, 7*, 304.

Cleveland, S. E., Fisher, S., Reitman, E. E., & Rothaus, P. (1962). Perception of body size in schizophrenia. *Archives of General Psychiatry, 7*, 277-285.

Cohen, L. J., Test, M. A. & Brocon, R. L. (1990). Suicide and schizophrenia: data from a prospective community treatment study. *American Journal of Psychiatry, 147*, 602-607. Correction, 147, 1110.

Coleman, M. J., Carpenter, J. T., Waterneaux, C., Levy, D. L., Shenton, M. E., Perry, J., Medoff, D., Wong, H., Manoach, D., Meyer, P., O'Brien, C., Valentino, C., Robinson, D., Smith, M., Makowski, D. & Holzman, P. S. (1993) The Thought Disorder Index: A reliability study. *Psychological Assessment, 5*, 336-342.

Coleman, M. J., Levy, D. L., Lenzenweger, M. F. & Holzman, P. S. (1996) Thought disorder, perceptual aberrations, and schizotypy. *Journal of Abnormal Psychology, 105*, 469-473.

Connolly, F. & Gipson, M. (1978). Dysmorphophobia. A long term study. *British Journal of Psychiatry, 132*, 458-470.

Coons, P. M., Ascher-Svanum, H, & Bellis, K. (1986). Self-amputation of the female breast. *Psychosomatics, 27*, 667-668.

Cornblatt, B. A., Lenzenweger, M. F., Dworkin, R. H. & Erlenmeyer-Kimling, L. (1985). Positive and negative schizophrenic symptoms, attention, and information processing. *Schizophrenia Bulletin, 11*, 397-408.

Crider, A. (1997). Perseverations in schiziophrenia. *Schizophrenia Bulletin, 23*, 63-74.

Crow, T. J. & Johnstone, E. C. (1980). Dementia praecox and schizophrenia: was Bleuler wrong? *Journal of the Royal College of Physicians, 14*, 238-240.

Crow, T. J. & Stevens, M. (1978). Age disorientation in chronic schizophrenia: the nature of the cognitive deficit. *British Journal of Psychiatry, 133*, 137-142.

Cuesta, M. J. & Peralta, V. (1994). Lack of insight in schizophrenia. *Schizophrenia Bulletin, 20*, 359-366.

Cuesta, M. S., Peralta, V., Caro, F, & de Leon, J. (1995). Schizophrenia syndrome and Wisconsin Card Sorting Test dimensions. *Psychiatry Research, 58*, 45-51.

Daniels, E. K., Shenton, M. E., Holzman, P. S., Benowitz, L. I., Coleman, M. ,Levin, S. & Levine, D. (1988). Patterns of thought disorder associated with right cortical damage, schizophrenia, and mania. *American Journal of Psychiatry, 145*, 944-949.

Darby, J. A. (1968). Pychotheraputic treatment of schizophrenia: Theory and case study. *Psychotherapy: Theory, Research, and Practice, 5*, 234-239.

David, S. A. (1990). Insight and psychosis. *British Journal of Psychiatry, 156*, 798-808.

Delaplaine, R., Ifabumuyi, O. I., Merskey, H. & Zarfas, J. (1978). Significance of pain in psychiatirc hospital patients. *Pain, 4*, 361-366.

deLeon, J., Bott, A. & Simpson, G. H. (1989). Dysmorphophobia: body dysmorphic disorder or delusional disorder, somatic type? *Comprehensive Psychiatry, 30*, 457-472.

Des Lauriers, A. M. (1962). *The experience of reality in childhood schizophrenia*. New York: International Universities Press.

Dillon, D. J. (1962) Measurement of perceived body size. *Perceptual and Motor Skills,14*, 191-196.

Dingman, C. W. & McGlashan, T. H. (1986). Discriminating characteristics of suicides: Chestnut Lodge follow-up sample including patients with affective disorder, schizophrenia and schizoaffective disorder. *Acta Psychiatrica Scandinavica, 74*, 91-97.

Dingman, C. W. & McGlaschan, T. H. (1988). Characteristics of patients with serious suicidal inpatients who ultimately commit suicide. *Hospital and Community Psychiatry, 39*, 295-299.

Di-Nuovo, S., Laicardi, C. & Tobino, C. (1988). Rorschach indices for discriminating between two schizophrenic syndromes. *Perceptual and Motor Skills, 67*, 399-406.

Drake, R. E. & Cotton, P. G. (1986). Depression, hopelessness and suicide in chronic schizophrenia. *British Journal of Psychiatry, 148*, 554-559.

Dworkin, R. H. (1994). Pain insensitivity in schizophrenia: A neglected phenomenon and some implications. *Schizophrenia Bulletin, 20*, 235-248.

Dworkin, R. H. & Caligor, E. (1988). Psychiatric diagnosis and chronic pain: DSM III-R and beyond. *Journal of Pain and Symptom Management, 3*, 87-98.

Edgerton, M., Jacobsen, W. & Meyer, E. (1960) Surgical/ psychiatric study of patients seeking plastic (cosmetic) surgery: 98 consecutive patients with minimal deformity. *British Journal of Plastic Surgery, 13*, 136-145.

Exner, E. J. Jr. (1974). *The Rorschach: A Comprehensive System: Vol.1.* Basic Foundations. New York: Wiley.

Exner, E. J. Jr. (1978). *The Rorschach: A Comprehensive System: Vol.2.* Current Research and Advanced Interpretation. New York: Wiley.

Exner, E. J. Jr. (1986a). *The Rorschach: A Comprehensive System: Vol.1.* Basic Foundations. 2nd ed. New York: Wiley.

Exner, E. J. Jr. (1986b). Some Rorschach data comparing schizophrenics with borderline and schizotypal personality disorders. *Journal of Personality Assessment, 50*, 455-471.

Exner, E. J. Jr. (1991). *The Rorschach: A Comprehensive System: Vol.2.* Current Research and Advanced Interpretation. 2nd ed. New York: Wiley.

Exner EJ Jr. (1993). *The Rorschach. A Comprehensive System: Vol.1.* Basic Foundations (3rd edition). New York: Wiley.

Federn P. (1952). *Ego Psychology and the psychosis.* New York: Basic Books.

Feldman MD. 1988 The challenge of self-mutilation: a review. *Comprehensive Psychiatry, 29*, 252-269.

Ferenczi, S. (1926). The problem of acceptance of unpleasant ideas: Advances in knowledge of the sense of reality. *International Journal of Psychoanalysis, 7*, 312-323.

Fishbain, D. A. (1982) Pain insensitivity in psychosis. *Annals of Emergency Medicine, 11*, 630-632.

Fisher, S. (1963). A further appraisal of the body boundary concept. *Journal of Consulting Psychology, 27*, 62-74.

Fisher, S. (1964). Body image and psychopathology. *Archives of General Psychiatry, 10*, 519-529.

Fisher, S. (1966). Body image in neurotic and schizophrenic patients. *Archives of General Psychiatry, 15*, 90-101.

Fisher, S. & Cleveland, S. E. (1958). *Body image and personality.* Princeton, NJ; Van Nostrand.

Fisher, S. & Cleveland S. E. (1968). *Body image and personality 2nd edition).* New York: Dover Publications.

Fisher, S. & Renik, O.D. (1966). Induction of body image boundary changes. *Journal of Projective Techniques and Personality Assessment, 30*, 429-434.

Fisher, S. & Seidner, R. (1963). Body experiences of schizophrenic, neurotic and normal women. *Journal of Nervous and Mental Disease, 137*, 252-257.

Fottrell, E. (1980). A study of violent behaviour among patients in psychiatric hospitals. *British Journal of Psychiatry, 136*, 216-221.

Freeman, T., Cameron, J. L. & McGhie, A. (1958). *Chronic Schizophrenia.* New York: International Universities Press.

Freeman, T. & Gathercole, L. E. (1966). Perseveration in chronic schizophrenia and organic dementia. *British Journal of Psychiatry, 112*, 27-32.

Freud, S. (1962). *The ego and the id.* New York: Norton.

Frith, C. (1993). *The Cognitive Neuropsychology of Schizophrenia.* Erlbaum, Hove.

Galdi, J. (1983). The causality of depression in schizophrenia. *British Journal of Psychiatry, 142*, 621-624.

George, L. & Neufeld, R. W. (1985). Cognition and symptomatology in schizophrenia. *Schizophrenia Bulletin, 11*, 264-285.

Gerstmann, J. (1942). Problem of imperception of disease and of impaired body territories with organic lesions. Relation to body schema and its disorders. *Archives of Neurology and Psychiatry, 48*, 890-913.

Gold, J. M., Hermann, B.P., Wyler, A., Randolph, C., Goldberg, T.E. & Weinberger, D. R. (1994). Schizophrenia and temporal lobe epilepsy: a neuropsychological study. *Archives of General Psychiatry, 51*, 265-272.

Goldberg, D. P. (1972). *The detection of psychiatric illness by questionnaire.* Maudsley Monograph 21. London: Oxford University Press.

Goldberg, D. & Williams, P. (1988). *A user's guide to the General Health Questionnaire.* Windsor, Berkshire: Neer-Nelson.

Goldberg, T. E., Gold, J. M., Greenberg, R., Griffin, S., Schulz, S. C., Picker, D., Kleinman, J. E., & Weinberger, D. R. (1993a). Contrasts between patients with affective disorder and patients with schizophrenia on a neuropsychological screening test battery. *American Journal of Psychiatry, 150*, 1355-1362.

Goldberg, T. E., Greenberg, R. & Griffin, S. (1993b). The impact of clozapine on cognition and psychiatric symptoms in patients with schizophrenia. *British Journal of Psychiatry, 162*, 43-48.

Goldberg, T.E., Ragland, D.R., Gold, J., Bigelow, L.B., Torrey, E.F. & Weinberger, D. R. (1990). Neuropsychological assessment of monozygotic twins discordant for schizophrenia. *Archives of General Psychiatry 47*, 1066-1072.

Goldstein, G. (1978). Cognitive and perceptual differences between schizophrenics and organics. *Schizophrenia Bulletin, 4*, 160-185.

Goodenough, F. L. (1928). Studies in the psychology of children's drawings. *Psychological Bulletin, 25*, 272-279.

Green, M. F. (1996). What are the functional consequences of neurocognitive deficit in schizophrenia? *American Journal of Psychiatry, 153*, 321-330.

Green, M. F., Marshall, B. D., Wirshing, W. C., Ames, D., Marder, S. R., McGurk, S., Kern, R. S. & Mintz, J. (1997). Does risperidone improve verbal working mempry in treatment–resistant schizophrenia? *American Journal of Psychiatry, 154*, 799-804.

Green, M. F. & Nuechterlein, K. H. (1999). Should schizophrenia be treated as a neurocognitive disorder? *Schizophrenia Bulletin, 25*, 309-318.

Green, M. F., Nuechterlein, K. H. & Geier, D.J. (1992). Sustained and selective attention in schizophrenia. *Progress in Experimental Personaity and Psychopathology Research, 15*, 290-313.

Green, M. F. & Walker, E. (1985). Neuropsychological performance and positive and negative symptoms in schizophrenia. *Journal of Abnormal Psychology, 94*, 460-469.

Guieu, R., Samuelian, J. C. & Coulouvrat, H. (1994). Objective evaluation of pain perception in patients with schizophrenia. *British Journal of Psychiatry, 164*, 253-255.

Hagger, C., Buckley, P., Kenny, J. T., Friedman, L., Ubogy, D. & Meltzer, H. Y. (1993). Improvement in cognitive functions and psychiatric symptoms in treatment –refractory schizopherenic patients receiving clozapine. *Bioliogical Psychiatry, 34*, 702-712.

Harding, C. M., Zubin, J. & Strauss, S. (1992). Chronicity in schizophrenia. *British Journal of Psychiatry, 161 (Suppl 18)*, 27-37.

Hay, G. (1970). Dysmorphophobia. *British Journal of Psychiatry, 116*, 399-406.

Hay, G. (1973). Changes in psychometric test results following cosmetic nasal operations. *British Journal of Psychiatry, 122*, 89-90.

Hay, G. (1983). Paranoia and dysmorphophobia. *British Journal of Psychiatry, 142*, 309-310.

Head, H. (1911). Sensory disturbunce from cerebral lesions. *Brain, 34*, 187-189.

Head, H. (1926). *Aphasia and Kindred Disorders of Speech*. London: Cambridge University Press.

Heaton, R. K., Baade, L. E. & Johnson, K. L. (1978). Neuropsychological test results associated with psychiatric disorders in adults. *Psychological Bulletin, 85*, 141-162.

Hill, G. & Silver, G. (1950). Psychodynamics and esthetic motivations for plastic surgery. *Psychosomatic Medicine, 12*, 345-355.

Hilsenroth, M. J., Fowler, J. C. & Padawer, J. R. (1998). The Rorschach Schizophrenia Index (SCZI): an examination of reliability, validity, and diagnostic efficacy. *Journal of Personality Assessment, 70*, 514-534.

Himelhoch, S., Taylor, S. F., Goldman, R. S. & Tandon, R. (1996). Frontal lobes, antipsychotic medication, and schizophrenic symptoms. *Biological Psychiatry, 39*, 227-229.

Hirsch, S. R. (1982). Depression "revealed" in schizophrenia. *British Journal of Psychiatry, 140*, 421-424.

Hollander, E., Cohen, L. T. & Simeon, D. (1993). Body dysmorphic disorder. *Psychiatric Annals, 23*, 359-364.

Holt, R. (1977). A method for assessing primary process manifestations and their controls in Rorschach responses. In M. Rickers-Ovsiankina (Eds), *Rorschach Psychology (2nd edition, pp375-420)*. Huntington, NY: Krieger.

Holtzman, W. H., Gorham, D. R. & Moran, L. J. (1964). A factor-analytic study of schizophrenic thought processes. *Journal of Abnormal and Social Psychology, 69*, 355-364.

Holtzman, W. H., Thorpe, J. S., Swartz, J. D. & Herron, E.W. (1961*). Inkblot perception and personality: Holtzman inkblot technique*. Austin: University of Texas Press.

Hu, W. H., Sun, C. M., Lee, C. T., Peng, S. L., Lin, S. K. & Shen, W. W. (1991). A clinical study of schizophrenic suicides: 42 cases in Taiwan. *Schizophrenia Research, 5*, 43-50.

Huber, G. (1957). Die coenaesthetische Schizophrenie. *Fortschritte der Neurologie und Psychiatrie, 25*, 491-520.

Huber, G. (1971). Die coenaesthetische Schizophrenie als Praegnanztyp schizophrener Erkrankungen. *Acta Psychiatrica Scandinavica, 47*, 349-362.

Humphreys, M. S., Johnstone, E. C., MacMillan, J. F. & Taylor, P. J. (1992). Dangerous behaviour preceding first admission s for schizophrenia. *British Journal of Psychiatry, 161*, 501-505.

Jacobsen, W., Edgerton, M., Meyer, E., Canter, A. & Slaughter, R. (1960). Psychiatric evaluation of male patients seeking cosmetic surgery. *Plastic and Reconstructive Surgery, 16*, 356-372.

Jasker, R. O. & Reed, M. R. (1963). Assessment of body image organization of hospitalizd and non-hopspitalized subjects. *Journal of Projective Techniques, 27*, 185-190.

Jeste, D. V., Lohr, J. B., Eastman, J. H., Rockwell, E. & Caligiuri, M. P. (1998). Adverse neurobiological effects of long term use of neuroleptics: Human and animal studies. *Journal of Psychiatric Research, 32*, 201-214.

Johnston, M, & Holzman, P. (1979). *Assessing Schizophrenic Thinking*. San Francisco: Jossey-Bass.

Johnstone, E. C., Crow, T. J., Frith, C. D., Husband, J. & kreel, L. (1976). Cerebral ventricular size and cognitive impairment in chronic schizophrenia. *Lancet II*, 924-926.

Katz, E., Kluger, Y., Rabinovici, R., Stein, D. & Gimmon, Z. (1990). Acute surgical abdominal disease in chronic svhizohrenic patients: A unique clinical problem. *Israel Journal of Medical Sciences, 26*, 275-277.

Kay, S. R., Fiszbein, A. & Opler, L.A. (1987). The positive and negative syndrome scale (PANSS) for schizophrenia. *Schizophrenia Bulletin, 13*, 261-276.

Keefe, R. S. E., Silva, S. G., Perkins, D. O. & Lieberman, J. A. (1999). The effects of atypical antipsychotic drugs on neurocognitive impairmaent in schizophrenia: A review and meta-analysis. *Schizophrenia Bulletin, 25*, 201-222.

Kennedy, B. L. & Feldmann, T. B. (1994). Self-inflicted eye injuries: case presentation s and a literature review. *Hospital Community Psychiatry, 45*, 470-474.

Kern, R. S., Green, M. F., Marshall, B. D., Wirshing, W. C., McGurk, S. R., Marder, S. R. & Mintz, J. (1999). Risperidone vs haloperidol on secondary memory: Can newer antipsychotic medications aid learning? *Schizophrenia Bulletin, 25*, 223-233.

Knights, A. & Hirsch, S. R. (1981). "Revealed" depression and drug treatment for schizophrenia. *Archives of General Psychiatry, 38*, 806-811.

Koide, R. (1985). Body image differences between schizophrenic and normal female adults. International *Review of Applied Psychology, 34*, 335-347.

Kokonis, N. D. (1972). Body image disturbance in schizophrenia. A study of arms and feet. *Journal of Personality Assessment, 36*, 573-575.

Kolb, B. & Whishaw, .IQ. (1983). Performance of schizophrenic patients on tests sensitive to left or right frontal temporal, and parietal function in neurologic patients. *Journal of Nervous and Mental Disease, 171*, 435-443.

Kraepelin, E. (1919). *Dementia Praecox and Paraphrenia*. Edinburgh, Scotland: E. and S. Livingstone.

Kuechenhoff, J. (1984).Dysmorphophobie. *Nervenarzt, 55*, 122-126.

Kwawer, J. (1980). Primitive interpersonal modes, borderline phenomena and Rorschach content. In J. Kwawer, H. Lerner, P. Lerner & A. Sugarman (Eds). *Borderline Phenomena and Rorschach Test* (pp. 257-274). New York: International University Press.

Lautenbacher, S. & Krieg, J. C. (1994). Pain perception in psychiatric disorders: a review of the literature. *Journal of Psychiatry Research, 28*, 109-122.

Leventhal, D. B., Schuck, J. R., Clemons, J. T. & Cox, M. (1982). Proprioception in schizophrenia. *Journal of Nervous and Mental Disease, 170*, 21-26.

Levin, S. (1984). Frontal lobe dysfunction in schizophrenia II. Impairments of psychological and brain functions. *Journal of Psychiatric Research, 18*, 27-55.

Liddle, P. F. & Morris, D.L. (1991). Schizophrenic syndromes and frontal lobe performance. *British Journal of Psychiatry, 158*, 340-345.

Linn, L. & Goldman, I. (1949). Psyciatric observations concerning rhinoplasty. *Psychosomatic Medicine, 11*, 307-309.

Lukianowicz, N. (1967). Body image disturbances in psychiatric disorders. *British Journal of Psychiatry, 113*, 31-47.

Lysaker, P. & Bell, M. (1994). Insight and cognitive impairment in schizophrenia: Performance on repeated administrations of the Wisconsin Card Sorting Test. *Journal of Nervous and Mental Disease, 182*, 656-660.

Machover, K. (1949). *Personality projection in the drawing of the human figure. Springfield, III.*: Chalcs C Thomas.

Malec, J (1978). Neuropsychological assessment of schizophrenia versus brain damage: a review. *Journal of Nervous and Mental Disease, 166*, 507-516

Manschreck, T. C., Maher, B. A., Hoover, T. M. & Ames D. (1985). Repetition in schizophrenic speech. *Language and Speech, 28*, 327-349.

Marchand, W. E. (1959). Practice of surgery in a neuropsychiatric hospital. *Archives of General Psychiatry, 1*, 123-131.

Martin, R. L., Cloninger, C. R. & Guze, S. B. (1985). Frequency and differetial diagnosis of depressive syndromes in schizophrenia. *Journal of Clinical Psychiatry, 46*, 9-13.

Martin, T. & Gattaz, W. F. (1991). Psychiatric aspects of male genital self-mutilation. *Psychopathology, 24*, 170-178.

Mason, B., Cohen, J. & Exner, J. E. Jr. (1985). Schizophrenic, depressive, and nonpatient personality organizations described by Rorschach factor structures. *Journal of Personality Assessment, 49*, 295-305.

Mayer-Gross, W. (1920). Uber die Stellungsnahme auf abgelaufenen akuten psychose. *Zeitschrift fuer die Gesamte Neurologie Psychiatrie, 60*, 160-212.

McGlaschan, T. H. & Carpenter, W. T. Jr. (1976). An investigation of the post psychotic depressive syndrome. *American Journal of Psychiatry, 133*, 14-19.

McGlashan, T. H. & Johannessen, J. O. (1996). Early detection and intervention with schizophrenia: Rationale. *Schizophrenia Bulletin, 22*, 201-222.

McGlichrist, I. & Cutting, J. (1995). Somatic delusions in schizophrenia and the affective psychoses. *British Journal of Psychiatry, 167*, 350-361.

Meloy, J. (1984). Thought organization and primary process in the patients of schizophrenics. *British Journal of Medical Psychology, 57*, 279-281.

Meltzer, H. Y. & McGurk, S. R. (1999). The effects of clozapine, risperidone, and olanzapine on cognitive function in schizophrenia. *Schizophrenia Bulletin, 25*, 233-255.

Merriam, A. E., Kay, S., Opler, L. A., Kushner, S. F. & van Praag, H. M. (1990). Neurological signs and the positive-negative dimension in schizophrenia. *Biological Psychiatry, 28*, 181-192.

Merskey, H. (1965). The characteristics of persistent pain in psychological illness. *Journal of Psychosomatic Research, 9*, 291-298.

Meyer, E., Jacobsen, W., Edgerton, M. & Canter, A. (1960). Motivational patterns in patients seeking elective plastic surgery (women who seek rhinoplasty). *Psychosomatic Medicine, 22*, 193-199.

Milner, B. (1963). Effect of different brain lesions in card sorting. The role of the frontal lobes. *Archives of Neurology, 9*, 100-110.

Nuechterlein, K. H., Edell, W. S., Norris, M. & Dawson, M. E. (1986). Attentional vulnerability indicators, thought disorder, and negative symptoms. *Schizophrenia Bulletin, 12*, 408-426.

Oosthuizen, P., Lambert, T. & Castle, D. J. (1998). Dysmorphic concern: prevalence and associations with clinical variables. *Australia and New Zealand Journal of Psychiatry, 32*, 129-132.

Overall, J. E. & Gorham, D. R. (1962). Brief Psychiatric Rating Scale (BPRS). *Psychological Reports, 10*, 799-812.

Pantelis, C., Nelson, H. E. & Barnes, T. R. E. (1996). *Schizophrenia: A neuropsychological perspective.* Chichester, West Sussex: John Wiley & Sons.

Pattison, E. M. & Kahan, T. (1983). The deliberate self-harm syndrome. *American Journal of Psychiatry, 140*, 867-872.

Perry, W. & Braff, D. L. (1994). Information processing and thought disorder in schizophrenia. *American Journal of Psychiatry, 151*, 363-367.

Perry, W. & Braff, D. L. (1998). A multimethod approach to assessing perseveration in schizophrenia patients. *Schizophrenia Research, 33*, 69-77.

Perry, W., Geyer, M. A. & Braff, D. L. (1999). Sensorimotor gating and thought disturbance measured in close temporal proximity in schizophrenic patients. *Archives of General Psychiatry, 56*, 277-281.

Perry, W., Viglione, D. & Braff, D. L. (1992). The Ego Impairment Index and schizophrenia: a validation study. *Journal of Personality Assessment, 59*, 165-175.

Phillips, K. A. (1991). Body dysmorphic disorder: The distress of imagined ugliness. American *Journal of Psychiatry, 148*, 1138-1149.

Phillips, K. A. & McElroy, S. L. (1993). Insight, overvalued ideation, and delusional thinking in body dysmorphic disorder: Theoretical and treatment implications. *Journal of Nervous and Mental Disease, 181*, 699-702.

Phillips, K. A. & McElroy, S. L., Keck, P. E., Hudson, J. I. & Pope, H. G. Jr. (1994). A comparison of delusional and nondelusional body dysmorphic disorder in 100 cases. *Psychopharmacology Bulletin, 30*, 179-186.

Philips, C. & Hunter, M. (1982). Headache in a psychiatric population. *Journal of Nervous and Mental Disease, 170*, 34-40.

Pick, A. (1922). Stoerung der Orientierung am eigenen Koerper. *Psychologische Forschung, 1*, 303-315

Pickar, D. (1995). Prospects for pharmacotherapy of schizophrenia. *Lancet, 345(8949)*, 557-562.

Quinlan, D. M. & Harrow, M. (1974). Boundary disturbance in schizophrenia. *Journal of Abnormal Psychology, 83*, 533-541.

Rado, S. (1959). Dynamics and classification of disorder behavior. *American Journal of Psychiatry, 1*, 651-656.

Reitman, E. E. & Cleveland, S. E. (1964). Changes in body image following sensory deprivation in schizophrenic and control groups. *Journal of Abnormal and Social Psychology, 68*, 168-176.

Renik, O. D. & Fisher, S. (1968). Induction of body image boundary changes in male subjects. *Journal of Projective Techniques and Personality Assessment, 32*, 45-49.

Ritzler, B. & Rosenbaum, G. (1974). Proprioception in schizophrenics and normals: Effects of stimulus intensity and interstimulus interval. *Journal of Abnormal Psychology, 83*, 106-111.

Ritzler, B. (1977). Proprioception and schizophrenia: A replication study with nonschizophrenic patient controls. *Journal of Abnormal Psychology, 86*, 501-504.

Roehricht, F. & Priebe, S. (1996). Body image of patients with acute paranoid schizophrenia: A follow-up study. (Das Koerpererleben von Patienten mit einer akuten paranoiden Schizophrenie. Eine Verlaufsstudie.) *Nervenarzt, 67*, 602-607.

Roehricht, F. & Priebe, S. (1997). Disturbances of body experience in schizophrenic patients.(Stoerungen des Koerpererlebens bei schizophronen Patienten.) *Fortschritte der Neurologie-Psychiatrie, 65*, 323-336.

Rosenbaum, G., Flenning, F. & Rosen, H. (1965). Effects of weight intensity on discrimination thresholds of normals and schizophrenics. *Journal of Abnormal Psychology, 70*, 446-450.

Rosenthal, S. H., Porter, K. A. & Coffey, B. (1990). Pain insensitivity in schizophrenia: Case report and review of the literature. *General Hospital Psychiatry, 12*, 319-322.

Roy, A., Thompson, R. & Kennedy, S. (1983). Depression in chronic schizophrenia. *British Journal of Psychiatry, 142*, 465-470.

Sacks, M. H., Carpenter, W. T. & Strauss, J. S. (1974). Recovery from delusions. *Archives of General Psychiatry, 30*, 117-120.

Saykin, J. A., Gur, R. C., Gur, R. E., Mozley, P. D., Mozley, L. H., Resnick, S. M, Kester, D. B. & Stafiniak, P. (1991). Neuropsychological function in schizophrenia: selective impairment in memory and learning. *Archives of General Psychiatry, 48*, 618-624.

Schafer, R. (1960). Bodies in Schizophrenic Rorschach Responses. *Journal of Projective Techniques, 24*, 267-281.

Schafer, R. (1986). *Projective Testing and Psychoanalysis. Selected Papers.* International Universities Press, INC.

Scheftel, S., Nathan, A. S., Razin, A. M. & Mezan, P. (1986). A case of radical facial self-mutilation: An unprecedented event and its impact. *Bulletin of the Menninger Clinic, 50*, 525-540.

Schilder, P. (1935). *The image and appearance of the human body.* London: Kegan Paul, Trench, Trubner & Co.

Schmoll, D. (1994). Coenaesthetische Schizophrenie. *Fortschritte der Neurologie Psychiatrie, 62*, 372-378.

Schmoll, D. & Koch, T. (1989). Leibgefuehlsstoerungen in der schizophrenen Psychose. Eine Kasuistik. *Nervenarzt, 60*, 619-627.

Schneider, F., Gur, R. C., Gur, R. E., Shtasel, D. L. (1995). Emotional processing in schizophrenia: Neurobehavioral probes in relation to psychopathology. *Schizophrenia Research, 17*, 67-75.

Schneider, K. (1959). *Klinische Psychopathologie, 12th ed.* Stuttgart: Georg Thieme Verlag, (5th eds. Translated by M. W. Hamilton. Clinical Psychopathology. New York: Grune and Stratton, 1976.)

Shore, D., Andreasen, D. J. & Cutler, N. R. (1978). Prediction of self-mutilation in hospitalized schizophrenics. *American Journal of Psychiatry 135*:1406-1407.

Schweitzer I. 1990 Genital self-amputation and the Klingsor Syndrome. *Australian and New Zealand Journal of Psychiatry, 24*, 566-569.

Silva, J. A., Leong, G. B. & Weinstock, R. (1989). A case of skin and ear self-mutilation. *Psychosomatics, 30*, 228-230.

Silverstein, M. L. & Zerwic, M. J. (1985). Clinical psychopathologic symptoms in neuropsychologically impaired and intact schizophrenics. *Journal of Consulting and Clinical Psychology, 53*, 267-268.

Siris, S. G. (1991). Diagnosis of secondary depression in schizophrenia: Implications for DSM-IV. *Schizophrenia Bulletin, 17*, 75-98.

Snaith, P. (1992). Body image disorders. *Psychotherapy and Psychosomatics, 58*, 119-124.

Sonneburn, C. K. & Vanstraelen, P. M. (1992). A retsospective study on self-inflicted burns. *General Hospital Psychiatry, 14*, 404-407.

Spear, F. G. (1967). Pain in psychiatric patients. *Journal of Psychosomatic Research, 11*,187-193.

SPSS. (1997). *SPSS Base 7.5 Application Guide.* Chicago, Illinois: SPSS.

Spohn, H. E. & Strauss, M. E. (1989). Relation of neuroleptic and anticholinergic medication to cognitive functions in schizophrenia. *Journal of Abnormal Psychology, 98*, 367-380.

Strauss, M. E. (1993). Relations of symptoms to cognitive deficits in schizophrenia. *Schizophrenia Bulletin, 19*, 215-231.

Strauss, S. (1989). Subjective experiences of schizophrenia: Toward a new dynamic psychiatry – II. *Schizophrenia Bulletin, 15*, 179-187.

Sugarman, A. A. & Cancro, R. (1964). Field dependence and sophistication of body concept in schizophrenics. *Journal of Nervous and Mental Disease, 138*, 119-123.

Sweeny, S. & Zamecnik, K. (1981). Predictors of self-mutilation in patients with schizophrenia. *American Journal of Psychiatry, 138*, 1086-1089.

Swensen, C. H. (1957). Empirical evaluations of human figure drawings. *Psychological Bulletin, 54*, 431-466.

Swensen, C. H. (1968). Empirical evaluations of human figure drawings: 1957-1966. *Psychological Bulletin, 70*, 20-44.

Taylor, M. A. & Abrams, R. (1984). Cognitive dysfunction in schizophrenia. *American Journal of Psychiatry, 141*, 196-201.

Taylor, P. J. (1995). Schizophrenia and the risk of violence. In S. R. Hirsh & D. R. Weinberger (Eds). *Schizophrenia*. Oxford: Blackwell Science Ltd.

Tollefson, G. D., Sanger, T. M., Lu, Y. & Thieme, M.E. (1998). Depressive signs and symptoms in schizophrenia: a prospective blinded trial of olanzapine and haloperidol. *Archives of General Psychiatry, 55*, 250-258.

Torrey, E. F. (1989). Headache in schizophrenia and seasonality of births. *Biological Psychiatry, 26*, 847-858.

Traub, A. C., Olson, R., Orbach, J. & Cardone, S. C. (1967). Psychophysical studies of body image: III. Initial studies of disturbance in a chronic schizophrenic group. *Archives of General Psychiatry, 17*, 664-670.

Twemlow, S. W., Gabbard, G.O. & Jones, F. C. (1982). The out-of-body experience: a phenomenological typology based on questionnaire responses. *American Journal of Psychiatry, 139*, 450-455.

Urist, J. (1977). The Rorschach test and the assessment of object relations. *Journal of Personality Assessment, 41*, 3-9.

Vanderkampt, H. (1970). Clinical anomalies in patients with schizophrenia. *Experimental Medicine and Surgery, 28*, 291-293.

Van Puttan, T. & May, P. R. A. (1978). 'Akinetic depression' in schizophrenia. *Archives of General Psychiatry, 35*, 1101-1107.

Varsamis, J., Adamson, J. D. (1976). Somatic symptoms in schizophrenia. *Canadian Psychiatric Association Journal, 21*, 1-6.

Vincent, K. R. & Harman, M. J. (1991). The Exner Rorschach: an analysis of its clinical validity. *Journal of Clinical Psychology, 47*, 596-599.

Wagner, E. E. & Frye, D. (1990). Diagnostic and intellectual implications of the fragmented Rorschach W:D ratio. *Perceptual and Motor Skills, 71*, 887-890.

Watkins, J. & Stauffacher, J. (1952). An index of pathological thinking in the Rorschach. *Journal of Projective Techniques, 16*, 276-286.

Watson, G. D., Chandarana, P. C. & Merskey, H. (1981). Relationships between pain and schizophrenia. *British Journal of Psychiatry, 138*, 33-36.

Weckowicz, T. E. & Sommer, R. (1960). Body image and self-concept in schizophrenia, an experimental study. *Journal of Mental Science, 106*, 17-39.

Weinberger, D. R., Berman, K. F. & Zec, R. F. (1986). Physiologic dysfunction of dorsolateral prefrontal cortex in schizophrenia: I. Regional cerebral blood flow evidence. *Archives of General Psychiatry, 4*, 114-124.

Weinberger, D. R., Torrey, E. F., Neophytides, A. N. & Wyatt, R.J. (1979). Lateral cerebral ventricular enlargement in chronic schizophrenia. *Archives of General Psychiatry, 36*, 735-739.

Weiser, M., Levy, A. & Neuman, M. (1993). Ear Stuffing: An unusual form of self-mutilation. *Journal of Nervous and Mental Disease, 181*, 587-588.

West, B. M. & Hecker, A.O. (1952). Peptic ulcer: Incidence and diagnosis in psychotic patients. *American Journal of Psychiatry, 109*, 35-37.

Young, D. A., Davila, R. & Scher, H. (1993). Unawareness of illness and neuropsychological performance in chronic schizophrenia. *Schizophrenia Research, 10*, 117-124.

Zung, W. W. K. (1965). A self-rating depression scale. *Archives of General Psychiatry, 12*, 63-70.

APPENDIX

Appendix 1. Manual for Scoring the Body Image Questionnaire

Appendix 1-1. Overview of the questionnaire and the scoring system

Reverse items The BIQ is composed of 59 items, including 28 reverse questions. Reverse items are Nos. 2, 4, 7, 12, 13, 14, 15, 22, 26, 27, 28, 30, 31, 33, 35, 36, 37, 38, 42, 43, 44, 46, 48, 50, 52, 55, 57 and 59.

Scoring system In *Regular items*, answers are scored as 7 when one "strongly agrees" with the statements, and scored as 1 when one "strongly disagrees" to the statements. In the *Reverse items*, answers are scored as 1 when one "strongly agrees" with the statements, and scored as 7 when one "strongly disagrees" with the statements. Answers as "neither agree nor disagree" are scored as 4.

BIQ component BIQ has three Components, Anatomical, Functional and Psychological. *Anatomical items* are Nos. 4, 8, 15, 16, 18, 20, 24, 28, 36, 40, 44, 48, 52, 54, 55, 56, 57 and 58. (See Apendix 1-3.) *Functional items* are: Nos. 1, 2, 3 , 5, 9, 13, 17, 21, 25, 33, 37, 38, 41, 42, 47 and 53. (See Appendix 1-4.) *Psychological items* are Nos. 6, 7, 10, 11, 12, 14, 19, 22, 23, 26, 27, 29, 30, 31, 32, 34, 35, 39, 43, 45, 46, 49, 50, 51 and 59. (See Appendix 1-5.)

Appendix 1-2. Body Image Questionnaire (BIQ)

	Strongly disagree					
		Moderately disagree				
			Slightly agree			
				Neither agree nor disagree		
					Slightly agree	
						Moderately agree
						Strongly agree
01. My body is weak.						
02. My eyesight is good. ®						
03. I often get sick.						
04. My complexion is pale. ®						
05. My body is limber.						
06. My body is underdeveloped.						
07. My body is clean.®						
08. I am short.						
09. I move slowly						
10. My body is defective.						
11. My body feels cold.						
12. My body is beautiful.®						
13. I am good at athletics.®						
14. I am becoming stronger. ®						

Appendix 1-2. Body Image Questionnaire (BIQ) (Continued)

15. My body is skinny. ®							
16. My body is small.							
17. I often lose my balance.							
18. I have small eyes.							
19. I am often injured.							
20. I am poorly proportioned.							
21. I walk slowly.							
22. I seldom feel tired.®							
23. My mood is numb.							
24. My body is rough.							
25. I am clumsy with my hands.							
26. I seldom catch a cold.®							
27. I am satisfied with my body. ®							
28. I am thin.®							
29. My voice is feeble.							
30. My skin is not easily poisoned. ®							
31. I am always cheerful. ®							
32. My body is unattractive.							
33. My posture is good. ®							
34. I always feel sick.							
35. I am not allergic to many things. ®							
36. My skin is smooth.®							
37. I can work well in dark rooms. ®							
38. My stomach is not unusually strong. ®							
39. My body is susceptible to infection.							
40. My hands are not unusually large.							
4I. I cannot move my body freely.							
42. My heart is strong. ®							
43. I don't mind being touched by others. ®							
44. My body is not meager.®							
45. I seldom get excited.							
46. My health is getting better. ®							
47. My teeth are weak.							
48. My body is symmetrical.®							
49. I am seldom tense.							
50. I am not prone to bump into others. ®							
51. My body is not consistent with my sex.							
52. My body is rectangular. ®							
53. My bowels are unusually strong.							
54. My legs are unusually short.							
55. My arms are unusually long. ®							
56. My neck is unusually long.							
57. My head is large. ®							
58. My hair is unusually short.							
59. I always feel energetic.®							

®=reverse item.

Appendix 1-3. BIQ-Anatomical items.

04. My complexion is pale. ®
08. I am short.
15. My body is skinny. ®
16. My body is small.
18. I have small eyes.
20. I am poorly proportioned.
24. My body is rough.
28. I am thin. ®
36. My skin is smooth. ®
40. My hands are not unusually large.
44. My body is not meager. ®.
48. My body is symmetrical. ®.
52. My body is rectangular. ®
54. My legs are unusually short.
55. My arms are unusually long. ®
56. My neck is unusually long.
57. My head is large. ®
58. My hair is unusually short.

®=reverse item.

Appendix 1-4. BIQ-Functional items

01. My body is weak.
02. My eyesight is good. ®
03. I often get sick.
05. My body is limber.
09. I move slowly
13. I am good at athletics.®
17. I often lose my balance.
21. I walk slowly.
25. I am clumsy with my hands.
33. My posture is good. ®
37. I can work well in dark rooms. ®
38. My stomach is not unusually strong. ®
41. I cannot move my body freely.
42. My heart is strong. ®
47. My teeth are weak.
53. My bowels are unusually strong.

®=reverse item.

Appendix 1-5. BIQ Psychological items

06. My body is underdeveloped.
07. My body is clean. ®
10. My body is defective.
11. My body feels cold.
12. My body is beautiful. ®
14. I am becoming stronger. ®
19. I am often injured.
22. I seldom feel tired. ®
23. My mood is numb.
26. I seldom catch a cold. ®
27. I am satisfied with my body. ®
29. My voice is feeble.
30. My skin is not easily poisoned. ®
31. I am always cheerful. ®
32. My body is unattractive.
34. I always feel sick.
35. I am not allergic to many things. ®
39. My body is susceptible to infection.
43. I don't mind being touched by others. ®
45. I seldom get excited.
46. My health is getting better. ®
49. I am seldom tense.
50. I am not prone to bump into others. ®
51. My body is not consistent with my sex.
59. I always feel energetic.®

Appendix 2. Inclusion and exclusion criteria for perception of flesh masses

Inclusion
1. Explicit verbalization of a mass of flesh or muscles.
2. The remains of a mass of flesh.
3. Diminution of head, arm or leg.
4. Elongation of neck, arm or leg.
5. Plants or vehicles described as "without arms or legs.[1]"
6. A creature with the shape of a mass[2].
7. A single organ vaguely detected with no further explanation.
8. "Being cut and opened," "being folded," "being unfolded," or "being stuck together".
Exclusion
1. Underdeveloped animals or human beings, or animals that have intrinsically short arms or legs, without further explanation concerning diminution of arms or legs.
2. Omission of legs in the response to Card VII.

Note: 1. Examples are: "A tropical flower. I cannot find its arms or legs." "An airplane. It doesn't have any arms or legs." 2. Example is: "A prawn. It is in this globular shape, with his back hunching up in this way."

In: Body Image: New Research
Editor: Marlene V. Kindes, pp. 199-213

ISBN 1-60021-059-7
© 2006 Nova Science Publishers, Inc.

Chapter VIII

THE PSYCHOPATHOLOGY OF A BRAZILIAN TREATMENT-SEEKING SAMPLE OF PATIENTS WITH BODY DYSMORPHIC DISORDER

*Leonardo L. Telles[1], Ygor A. Ferrão[2], Gabriela Bezerra de Menezes[1],
Antonio Leandro do Nascimento[1], Bruno P. Nazar[1],
Mauro V. Mendlowicz[3] and Leonardo F. Fontenelle[1, 3]**

[1]Anxiety and Depression Research Program, Institute of Psychiatry, Universidade
Federal do Rio de Janeiro (IPUB/UFRJ), Rio de Janeiro-RJ, Brazil;
[2]Psychiatric Service, Presidente Vargas Hospital, Porto Alegre-RS, Brazil
[3]Department of Psychiatry and Mental Health, Universidade Federal Fluminense
(MSM/UFF), Niterói-RJ, Brazil.

ABSTRACT

Objective

The main characteristic of body dysmorphic disorder (BDD) is a preoccupation with an imagined defect in appearance in a normally appearing person or an excessive preoccupation with appearance in a person with a small physical defect. In this study, our objective was to describe the socio-demographic and phenomenological characteristics of a Brazilian sample of 28 patients with BDD from two university clinics.

Methods

Chart-review.

---

* Correspondence concerning this article should be addressed to Leonardo F. Fontenelle Rua Otávio Carneiro 93 apt 601, Icaraí, Niterói Rio de Janeiro CEP: 24230190, Brazil. lfontenelle@gmail.com.

Results

Our combined sample was characterized by a predominance of female (n=15; 53.6%), single or divorced (n=23; 82.1%), and economically unproductive patients (n=23; 82.1%). We found an average of 2.4 current imagined defects per patient. The most frequently reported body parts of excessive current concern were the overall appearance, size or shape of the face (n=10; 35.7%), the hair (n=8; 28.7%); the nose (n=8; 28.7%); skin (n=7; 25%), and the body build and the weight (n=7; 25%). Most individuals exhibited a chronic condition (n=20; 71.4%) and had the same concerns during the course of the disorder (n=20; 71.4%). All patients displayed compulsive behaviors, including recurrent mirror checking (n=18; 64.3%), camouflaging (n=16; 57.1%), reassurance seeking by means of repetitive questioning of others (n=16; 57.1%) and excessive use of cosmetics (n=7; 25%). Two patients reported "do-it-yourself" surgeries. Ten patients had current suicidal ideation (37.5%). Eight patients (28.6%) showed no insight over their dysmorphic beliefs. Twenty-five patients (89.3%) exhibited psychiatric comorbidities, mostly obsessive-compulsive disorder (OCD) [n=14, 50%] and major depressive disorder (n=15; 53.6%).

Conclusions

Our results are consistent with the characterization of BDD as a true trans-cultural disorder.

Keywords: body dysmorphic disorder, psychopathology, cross-cultural studies.

INTRODUCTION

The importance of physical attractiveness across different cultures was the subject of interest of several studies, as recently reviewed by Bohne et al. (2002a). Physical attractiveness has been valued over time and across different ethnic backgrounds (Buss et al., 1990; Jones et al., 1996). Although the perception of beauty is essentially subjective, there are some common culture-specific notions of physical attractiveness (Strzalko and Kaszycka, 1992). Across different cultures, however, striking peculiarities have been reported in the concept of physical attractiveness (Cogan et al., 1996; Hodes et al., 1996) and in the importance placed on it. North Americans, for example, rely more heavily on appearance and attractiveness in their perception of human differences than do their Japanese and Chinese counterparts (Crystal et al., 1998). They also seem to place greater value on physical attractiveness in a potential mate (Buss and Angleitner, 1989) and to display higher rates of body image concerns than do Germans (Bohne et al., 2002a).

Some have argued that Brazil, a South American sun-soaked tropical country, is a fertile ground for vanity (Finger, 2003). In fact, in the feverish pursuit of an ideal body, many Brazilians may have become deeply "obsessed" by physical beauty. Economic stabilization during the past 10 years has made it possible for middle-class Brazilians (with an average income of US$350 a month) to satisfy their innermost cosmetic dreams. For example, Brazil is already the second largest market for botulinum toxin in the world, with more than US$30 million being spent on the drug each year (Finger, 2003). Paradoxical as it may seem, while the health system remains in disarray, Brazil's plastic surgery industry is thriving. Once restricted to the wealthy, cosmetic plastic surgery has become so popular that many women do not hesitate to pay costly monthly installments in exchange for a more attractive pair of breasts. Brazil now ranks second behind the USA in terms of number of cosmetic plastic-surgery procedures (Finger, 2003).

When physical attractiveness affects the value attributed to an individual, the importance of an aesthetically pleasing appearance increases and body image concerns become more likely (Bohne et al., 2002a). Therefore, one may expect that the cultures that place greater value on physical attractiveness have a higher prevalence rate of people experiencing increased levels of body image concerns (Bohne et al., 2002a). While it has been demonstrated that Western idealization of thinness may affect the prevalence and be an etiological factor for some forms of eating disorders (especially bulimia nervosa) [Keel and Klump, 2003], the importance of cultural factors and their etiological role in the origins of body dysmorphic disorder (BDD) are unclear.

Unfortunately, despite the importance of physical attractiveness in modern Brazilian society, there are almost no systematic investigations on BDD in Brazil (Fontenelle et al., in press). More specifically, the extent to which Brazilian culture affects the phenomenology of body image concerns in patients with BDD is an important, yet relatively unexplored topic of research. In this article, our objective was to describe the socio-demographic and phenomenological features of an expanded Brazilian sample of 28 patients with BDD.

METHODS

We performed a retrospective chart review of the 296 consecutive patients who sought treatment at the Obsessions, Compulsions, and Impulsions Subprogram (OCSP) of the Anxiety and Depression Research Program, a teaching and research unit of the Institute of Psychiatry of the Universidade Federal do Rio de Janeiro (IPUB/UFRJ), the largest academic psychiatric hospital of the state of Rio de Janeiro, Brazil (n=166); and the Obsessive-Compulsive Spectrum Disorders Clinic of the Presidente Vargas Hospital, located in the city of Porto Alegre, state of Rio Grande do Sul (n=130). The chart-review covered the period between July 1998 and July 2005. Both units are dedicated to the diagnosis and treatment of patients presenting obsessions and compulsions across different psychiatric disorders (the so-called obsessive-compulsive spectrum disorders). Patients attending these clinics sought treatment spontaneously or were recruited through referrals from clinicians, word of mouth, and advertisements in newspapers.

The first author filled out a structured questionnaire using the information contained on the charts of the 296 patients. This questionnaire, which was elaborated by us, assessed the presence of BDD according to the Structured Clinical Interview for DSM-IV Axis I Disorders (SCID-I, First et al., 1995) and collected several other socio-demographic, phenomenological and clinical data deemed relevant: age at presentation for treatment; gender; marital status; educational level; employment status; age at onset of BDD; number and types of different imagined physical defects, their persistence across time, and the level of insight into them [according to the Insight question of the Yale-Brown Obsessive-Compulsive Scale (Y-BOCS)]; global severity of symptoms of BDD [according to the BDD-Clinical Global Impression (BDD-CGI)]; course of symptoms [chronic or episodic (i.e. a history of spontaneous symptomatic remission which persisted for at least two months]; comorbid psychiatric disorders (according to the SCID-I); the presence of BDD-related compulsive and avoidant behaviors; suicidal ideation and behavior; and the history of psychiatric hospitalizations.

RESULTS

Twenty-eight patients with BDD were identified (9.45% of the sample). The mean age at presentation was 28.04 (±8.4) years, with a discrete predominance of female patients (n=13; 53.6%). The disorder had a relatively early age at onset (17.2±7.2 years), with most patients exhibiting a chronic course (n=20; 71.4%). The mean number of current imagined defects per patient was 2.4 (±1.2). The most frequently reported body parts of excessive current concern were the appearance, size or shape of the face (n=10; 35.7%), the hair (n=8; 28.7%), the nose (n=8; 28.7%), the skin (n=7; 25%), the overall body build and weight (n=7; 25%), the mouth or the teeth (n=5; 17.8%), the breasts (n=5; 17.8%), the stomach (n=3; 10.7%), the penis (n=3; 10.7%), and the eyes (n=2; 7.1%) [see Table 1]. The mean score on the Body Dysmorphic Disorder-Clinical Global Impression (BDD-CGI) at the first assessment was 5.1 (±1.0).

The body area with the imagined defect changed or new beliefs were added to the first imagined defects in a significant proportion of cases, but in the majority of patients, the beliefs regarding the imagined defects remained the same during all the duration of the illness (n=20; 71.4%). All patients exhibited compulsive behaviors, including repetitive mirror checking, (n=18; 64.3%), camouflaging (n=16; 57.1%), excessive use of cosmetics (n=8; 28.6%) and reassurance seeking (n=16; 57.1%). Two patients performed *"do-it-yourself"* (DIY) surgeries.

The great majority of patients with BDD were non-married (single, separated or divorced) [n=25; 89.3%] and economically unproductive (n=23; 82.1%), thus suggesting that BDD is associated with an important social and economic disability. Two patients (7.1%) had a history of psychiatric hospitalization, one because of severe BDD symptoms and the other because of a manic switch during treatment with paroxetine. Three patients (10.7%) had a history of suicidal behavior and ten (35.7%) displayed significant suicidal ideation.

A lack of insight according to the Y-BOCS was found among eight patients (28.6%). Only 5 patients (17.9%) had full insight regarding the absurdity of their dysmorphic beliefs. Twenty-five patients (89.3%) displayed at least one additional DSM-IV axis I diagnosis. The most common comorbid disorders were obsessive-compulsive disorder (OCD) [n=14, 50%] and major depressive disorder (n=15, 53.6%).

Other comorbid mental disorders included eating disorders (25%), panic disorder (17.9%), social phobia (14.3%), dysthymia (10.7%), bipolar disorder (7.1%), generalized anxiety disorder (7.1%), Tourette syndrome (7.1%), and agoraphobia (7.1%). All cases of bulimia and anorexia nervosa in our BDD sample were found among the female patients (n=5; 17.9%). Up to one third of the female patients with BDD in our sample exhibited an eating disorder.

Table 1: The description of some phenomenological features (Imagined defects and patterns of comorbidity) of BDD patients.

Patient #	Age (in years), gender	Imagined defects	Comorbidities
1	20, female	"I have a big stomach", "I have crispy hair", "I have a huge nose", "My skin is too dark", "My breast is extremely big".	OCD, BN
2	20, male	"I have too much zits on my face", "I am too thin and weak", "My hair is dry and rebel".	OCD
3	21, female	"I have small breasts", "I am too much underweight", "My hair is dry and not straight enough".	Social phobia
4	21, male	"I am ugly".	BP
5	21, male	"I have old and thin arms", "I don't like these flecks on my face", "My skin is wrinkled".	Social phobia
6	23, male	"My penis is too small".	OCD, MDD, PD, AG, BED
7	24, female	"I have a huge nose".	OCD
8	24, male	"It seems that I have one leg and one shoulder bigger than the others". "It seems that my eyes are unleveled".	OCD, TS, PD, MDD
9	25, male	"I feel too thin", "I have dark circles under my eyes", "I have protruding ears".	OCD, MDD
10	26, female	"I feel disfigured", "I feel too thin but heavy", "My nose is grotesque".	AN
11	28, male	"I feel like a foul odor emanates continuously from my body*"	MDD
12	29, male	"I have crooked teeth", "The hair coming out of my nostrils is disgusting".	Absent
13	29, male	"I feel underweight", "My face, body, and teeth seem asymmetric".	OCD, PD
14	31, female	"I am afraid to have vitiligo".	OCD, TS, BP, AN
15	39, male	"I have a small penis".	Social Phobia
16	41, female	"I have a rounded face", "I have crooked and dark teeth", "I have huge stomach" "My breasts are enormous" "My thighs are so big they touch each other".	MDD, AN
17	43, female	"I feel ugly and horrible", "I have a wrinkled face", "I have small buttocks", "I have a big nose".	OCD, PD
18	47, female	"I have a limp and fly-away hair".	OCD, GAD, Dysthymia, Specific Phobia
19	30, male	"I have a prominent facial bone structure", "My whole face is disharmonic", "My hair is extremely crispy".	MDD, Social Phobia

Table 1: Continued.

Patient #	Age (in years), gender	Imagined defects	Comorbidities
20	40, female	"I have too much scars and varicose veins in my skin", "I have twig-like arms and legs", "My hair is rebel".	OCD
21	16, female	"My hair looks like a steel sponge" "My breasts are ugly and asymmetric"	MDD
22	20, female	"My face is ugly and disproportionate" "My mouth is oversized"	MDD
23	22, male	"My teeth are ugly and rotten"	MDD
24	22, female	"My face is ugly" "I have big fat buttocks" "My hair is opaque and ugly"	BN
25	24, male	"My skin is wrinkled" "My penis is wry" "My face is ugly" "I have several stains on my face"	BP
26	26, female	"I am masculinized" "I have big breasts" "I have an ugly stomach"	AN, BN
27	30, female	"My nose is ugly and wry".	Absent
28	41, female	"I have an internal defect inside my nose"	Delusional disorder

Legend: AG: agoraphobia; AN: anorexia nervosa; BD: bipolar disorder; BED: binge eating disorder; BN: bulimia nervosa; MDD: major depressive disorder; OCD: obsessive-compulsive disorder; PD: panic disorder; TS: Tourette syndrome.
* According to Lochner and Stein (2003), the closest DSM-IV diagnosis of patients with olfactory reference syndrome is BDD.

DISCUSSION

BDD is characterized by the preoccupation with an imagined defect in the appearance in a normal appearing person or a markedly excessive concern about a slightly imperfection (Allen and Hollander, 2000). To meet diagnostic criteria, the preoccupation must cause clinically significant distress or impairment in functioning, and the symptoms cannot be better accounted for by another mental disorder, such as preoccupation with being fat in anorexia nervosa or distress about physical sexual characteristics in gender identity disorder. BDD is a relatively common psychiatric disorder in clinical practice, affecting 0.7 to 2.2% of the general population (Faravelli et al., 1997; Otto et al., 2001) and 4.0 to 5.3% of university students (Bohne et al., 2002a; Bohne et al., 2002b; Cansever et al., 2003). Despite having been described more than a century ago (Morselli, 1891), only recently has BDD become the subject of systematic clinical and scientific scrutiny.

Patients with BDD may describe themselves as looking unattractive, deformed, hideous, or monstrous. BDD is frequently found among outpatients with anxiety disorders [e.g., 11% of the individuals with social phobia (Brawman-Mintzer et al, 1995) and 8 to 37% of the individuals with OCD (Brawman-Mintzer et al, 1995; Simeon et al., 1995; Hollander et al., 1993)], with mood disorders [e.g., 14.4% of the patients with atypical depression and 5.1% of the patients with non-atypical depression (Nierenberg et al., 2002)], and with impulse control disorders [32% of the individuals with *skin-picking* (Wilhelm et al., 1999)]. Moreover, increased rates of major depression, social phobia, OCD, and substance abuse disorders are found among outpatients with BDD (Gunstad and Philips, 2003).

In this study, an expanded socio-demographic and phenomenological description of a South-American treatment-seeking sample of individuals with BDD previously described (Fontenelle et al., in press), the majority of our findings are consistent with the previous reports of BDD patients available in the international literature. In other words, although there is an increasing importance of physical attractiveness in modern Brazilian society, it seems that the clinical characteristics of our patients are quite similar to those reported in developed countries, such as England (Veale et al., 1996), Italy (Perugi et al., 1997b), and North America (Phillips et al., 2005b). These results are consistent with the existence of BDD as a true trans-cultural disorder.

The prevalence of clinically significant BDD in patients attending the OCSP (in the city of Rio de Janeiro) and the Obsessive-Compulsive Spectrum Disorder Clinic (in the city of Porto Alegre) was 9.45%. This rate is much higher than the prevalence of BDD, diagnosed according to the SCID, in general psychiatric outpatients (3.2%) [Zimmerman and Mattia, 1998]. In fact, as mentioned above, previous studies showed increased lifetime rates of BDD in clinical samples of patients with OCD, ranging from 8% (Brawn-Mintzer et al., 1995) to 37% (Hollander et al., 1993). However, since our clinics are dedicated to the diagnosis and clinical care of patients with several disorders belonging to the obsessive-compulsive spectrum (including, but not restricted to, OCD), it must be stressed that we are not reporting here the prevalence of BDD in patients with OCD *per se*.

Our sample was characterized by a discreet predominance of female patients, a finding that dovetails with the majority of previous reports of treatment-seeking individuals with BDD (Phillips et al., 2005b; Perugi et al., 1997b; Rosen et al., 1995). For example, in the largest series to date published on the socio-demographic features of patients with BDD (n=200), 68.5% of the subjects were women. Only Hollander et al. (1993) found a preponderance of men in their North American sample. In fact, as a number of studies provide significant empirical support for the conceptualization of BDD as an affective spectrum disorder (Phillips, 1999), it is not surprising to find that patients with BDD share some typical socio-demographic and clinical features with those with MDD (such as female sex predominance). It is conceivable that differences arising from referral bias, inclusion/exclusion criteria and severity of illness may account for the discrepancies reported in sex ratios among clinical samples of BDD (Perugi and Frare, 2005).

Unfortunately, due to the small number of individuals identified in our sample, we were unable to compare the phenomenological features of male and female patients with BDD. However, at least two studies have investigated clinical differences between genders (Phillips et al., 1997; Perugi et al., 1997a). A North American study (Phillips et al., 1997) found that females were more likely than males to focus on their hips and weight, to be concerned about defects on their skin, to camouflage these imagined defects with makeup, and to have bulimia nervosa. On the other hand, men were more likely to be unmarried, to be preoccupied with body-building and with the size of their genitals, to be concerned about hair loss, to use a hat for camouflaging, and to have alcohol-related disorders. An Italian study (Perugi et al., 1997a) found that women were more likely to focus on their breasts and legs, to check their appearance in mirrors, to camouflage their perceived defects, and to have concomitant bulimia nervosa, generalized anxiety disorder and panic disorder. Conversely, men were more likely to focus on their genitals, height, and excessive body hair and to suffer from lifetime co-morbid bipolar disorder.

We found a significant preponderance of single, separated or divorced (89.3%) and economically unproductive (82.1%) individuals in our sample of patients with BDD, a finding that highlights the important social and economic disability associated with this disorder. Similar findings have been already described in several samples (Phillips, 1991; Phillips and Diaz, 1997; Perugi et al., 1997b). For example, according to a case series, 89.6% of patients with BDD avoided usual social activities and 51.7% showed a significant impairment in their academic or job performance because of their symptoms [Perugi et al., 1997b]. Another study found similar rates of social dysfunction and an even greater prevalence (80%) of job/academic impairment [Phillips and Diaz, 1997].

Functional disability is a major problem in patients with BDD because they experience severe distress and anxiety in situations which may expose their perceived defect, leading them to avoid several social activities, such as shopping, dining in a restaurant, or going to the gym or to the beach (Perugi and Frare, 2005). Some patients may particularly avoid non-structured social interactions (such as going to a party, to a club, or dating) and sexual relationships or they may leave home only at night in order not to meet people. In many cases, avoidance of social interactions may worsen and generalize and patients may become housebound for long periods (Perugi and Frare, 2005). The social impact of BDD may be even more devastating in a country placing greater emphasis on physical attractiveness such as Brazil.

A current preoccupation with an average of 2.4 imagined defects were found in our BDD clinical sample. They were more commonly located on the face, skin, hair, and nose. In fact, it has been suggested that BDD subjects worry about a greater number of affected body areas over the course of their illness, e.g. an average of 5 to 7 [Phillips, 1993, Perugi et al., 1997b, Phillips et al., 2005b]. Previous studies suggested that body dysmorphic concerns generally shift from one body part to another over time or that additional areas may become involved. However, in our study, most patients with BDD exhibited a chronic condition and kept the same concerns during the whole course of the disorder. It is possible that the retrospective design of our chart-review may have led to an overestimation of the topographic stability of the concerns in BDD.

All individuals of our sample of subjects with BDD exhibited compulsive behaviors, including repetitive mirror checking, camouflaging, excessive use of cosmetics, and reassurance seeking. These findings dovetail with those of previous studies showing that nearly all patients with BDD show repetitive, time-consuming and compulsive behaviours related to their body concerns (Perugi et al., 1997b; Phillips et al., 2005b). The intent of these behaviours is generally to examine, hide, improve, correct or seek reassurance about their perceived physical defect(s).

For example, patients with BDD may spend several hours a day checking the reflection of the affected parts of their bodies in the mirror. BDD patients usually worry very much about being watched by strangers or of addressing people outside their circle of family and close friends for fear that their defect will be noticed (Perugi and Frare, 2005).

As a result, another very common compulsive behaviour is camouflaging their perceived flaw with several, sometimes bizarre, methods (Perugi and Frare, 2005; Fontenelle et al., 2003). Patients may employ specific hairstyles or wigs, large amounts of make-up or gentian violet, articles of clothing or accessories such as a hat, a scarf, or sunglasses, masks or hoods, or simply use their hands or adopt a certain body position in order to try to conceal their imagined defect. Some patients with BDD spend large amounts of money buying cosmetic articles. A few less-endowed individuals may engage in shoplifting or petty crime to support this particular behaviour. Reassurance-seeking compulsive behaviours are particularly annoying for both patients and their close relatives, since positive verbal feedback about appearance seems to have at best a temporary calming effect (Perugi and Frare, 2005).

Many BDD patients may also experience suicidal ideation or undertake suicidal attempts. The fact that 35.7% of our patients experienced suicidal ideation underlines the importance of assessing suicidality in patients with BDD, as suggested by several authors (Perugi et al. 1997; Grant et al., 2002; Phillips et al., 2005a). For example, in a study that systematically collected data on the suicidality associated with BDD, Phillips et al. (2005) found that 55% of their sample had experienced suicidal ideation attributed primarily to BDD. We found that 10.7% of our subjects had a history of attempted suicide, a figure that is somewhat inferior to those previously reported in North American subjects by Phillips and Diaz (1997) [22%] and Phillips et al. (2005) [28%] and in British patients by Veale et al [24%]. It is much lower, though, than the rate of 63 % described by Grant et al (2002) in inpatients with anorexia and BDD.

Although still significant, our lower rates of suicidal ideation and of previous suicide attempts may reflect the fact that BDD was not the primary diagnosis in some of our subjects. In fact, as pointed out in the study by Phillips et al. (2005), the lifetime suicide rates of 15-28% in subjects with BDD are lower than those described for schizophrenia (23-55%) or bipolar disorder (31-35%), within the range reported for depressed outpatients (7-35%), and much higher than those found for generalized anxiety disorder (15-17%), panic disorder (8-9%) or agoraphobia (6%) (Warshaw et al., 2000; Warshaw et al., 1995; Asnis et al., 1993; McHolm et al., 2003; Leverich et al., 2003; Beck et al., 1991; Goisman et al., 1994; Radomsky et al., 1999).

Eight patients (28.6%) had no insight over their imagined defect, according to the Y-BOCS insight item. Our rate of delusional BDD is quite similar to those reported (36-39%) in studies employing continuous measures of delusionality, such as the Brown Assessment of Beliefs Scale (BABS) [Eisen et al., 2004; Phillips et al., in press-a]. There is an ongoing heated debate, however, about whether patients with this "delusional ugliness" should be best described as suffering from BDD or from delusional disorder, somatic type (DDST) (Fontenelle et al., in press). Actually, the DSM-IV-TR current criteria allow patients to be diagnosed with both disorders.

At least three studies have compared delusional and non-delusional patients with BDD (McElroy et al., 1993; Phillips et al., 1994, Phillips et al., in press-a). They have generally agreed that there are more similarities than difference between the two subtypes and that the delusional variant of BDD (or DDST) may be a more severe form of the non-delusional BDD. In these studies, delusional and non-delusional BDD patients were similar with regard to demographic features, BDD characteristics, measures of functional impairment and quality of life, comorbidity, and family history. They also had a comparable probability of remitting from BDD over a one-year prospective follow-up period. However, delusional subjects had significantly lower educational attainments, were more likely to have attempted suicide, had poorer social functioning on several measures, were more likely to have drug abuse or dependence, were less likely to be currently receiving mental health treatment, and had more severe BDD symptoms. However, after controlling for the severity of the symptoms of BDD, the two groups differed only in terms of educational attainment.

A substantial proportion of our patients exhibited psychiatric comorbidities, the most frequent ones being OCD (50%), MDD (53.6%), and eating disorders (25%). In the largest study reporting the rates of comorbid psychiatric disorders in patients with BDD under treatment (n=118), Gunstad and Phillips (2003) found the prevalence of OCD and MDD to be 35% and 78%, respectively. While the increased prevalence of OCD in our sample could be interpreted as reflecting a recruitment bias (given that we are reporting the characteristics of a sample of BDD ascertained in an obsessive-compulsive spectrum disorders clinic), it has been extensively demonstrated that the association between these disorders is not a mere artifact. For example, both OCD and BDD are characterized by obsessions and compulsions (Frare et al., 2004, Phillips et al., 1998) and seem to respond to treatment with high-doses of serotonin-reuptake inhibitors (Hollander et al., 1999; Phillips et al., 2002). As previously noted, the lifetime rates for BDD in patients with OCD also appear to be high, ranging from 8% (Brawn-Mintzer et al., 1995) to 37% (Hollander et al., 1993). There are also significantly increased rates of BDD among first-degree relatives of patients with OCD (Bienvenu et al., 2000).

More recently, important outcome data clarifying the relationship between OCD and BDD has emerged from a follow-up study by Phillips et al. (in press - b). These authors found that, when both disorders co-occur, the improvement in OCD significantly increased the likelihood of subsequent remission from BDD, suggesting that BDD and OCD may be linked - or that BDD may be secondary to OCD – at least for some of their subjects. However, they also found that only 10% of the patients with BDD had a full remission after OCD has remitted, suggesting that BDD may not simply be a symptom of OCD. If it were, BDD symptoms would be expected to remit completely in all subjects for whom OCD had remitted.

The prevalence of MDD in our patients of patients with BDD is consistent with the rates previously reported in several samples, which ranged from 36% (Veale et al., 1996) to 76% of subjects (Gunstad and Phillips, 2003). Conversely, studies have found a high prevalence of BDD among patients with MDD, especially the atypical subtype, with prevalence rates ranging from 14 to 42% (Nierenberg et al., 2002, Phillips et al., 1996; Perugi et al., 1998). Based on the well-known high levels of comorbidity between BDD and depression, and their positive response to antidepressants (particularly SRIs), Phillips (1999) have hypothesized that BDD is related to affective disorders, i.e. that it belongs to the so-called "affective spectrum disorder".

Although BDD may be related to MDD, the available data suggest that it is not simply a symptom of depression. For example, BDD is characterized by prominent obsessions and compulsive behaviors, and available data suggest that, while SRIs and cognitive-behavioral therapy (CBT) may be effective for BDD, other useful modalities of treatment for depression (e.g. non-SRI antidepressants, ECT, and other types of psychotherapy) are often ineffective in BDD (Phillips, 1999). In addition, clinical observations suggest that depressive symptoms in BDD patients often appear to be "secondary" to the distress and demoralization that BDD often causes (Phillips, 1999).

One additional aspect of the patterns of comorbidity in our sample of patients with BDD deserves attention. The prevalence rate for eating disorders found in our study (21.44%) was quite higher than those reported in previous ones describing the socio-demographic and phenomenological features of outpatients with OCD in Brazil (Fontenelle et al., 2004). More specifically, three female patients had anorexia nervosa (10.7%), four female patients had bulimia nervosa (14.3%), and one male patient had binge eating disorder (3.6%). In fact, previous studies have already reported similar rates, suggesting that the association between BDD and eating disorders is a true trans-cultural phenomenon (Zimmerman and Mattia, 1998; Gunstad and Phillips, 2003; Rufollo et al., in press).

The lifetime prevalence of anorexia and /or bulimia nervosa found in the current study (21.4%) is consistent with that reported by Zimmerman and Mattia (1998) in 16 subjects with BDD (19%) and somewhat higher than that reported in the Gunstad and Phillips (2003) sample of 293 subjects (10%). More recently, Rufollo et al. (in press) found that 32.5% of their BDD subjects had a comorbid lifetime eating disorder: 9.0% had anorexia nervosa, 6.5% had bulimia nervosa, and 17.5% had an eating disorder not otherwise specified.

In this latter study, the comorbid group was more likely to be female, less likely to be African American, had more comorbidities, and had significantly greater body image disturbance and dissatisfaction. Moreover, a higher proportion of the subgroup with comorbid eating disorder had been hospitalized for psychiatric problems. This group had also received a greater number of psychotherapy sessions and of psychotropic medications.

It is beyond question that BDD and eating disorders share some phenomenological similarities. Both disorders involve excessive concerns regarding physical appearance, body image dissatisfaction, and body image disturbance (Grant and Phillips, 2004, Phillips et al., 1995). Some authors have suggested that a disturbance in body image may be the core pathology of both BDD and eating disorders (Cororve and Gleaves, 2001; Rosen et al., 1998).

CONCLUSION

Our Brazilian patients with BDD were found to display increased levels of social and economic disability. They exhibited more than two body concerns at presentation, which tended to persist unchanged during the course of the disorder. All patients had compulsive behaviors, including repetitive mirror checking, camouflaging, reassurance seeking, and excessive use of cosmetics. Our Brazilian patients with BDD also reported frequently suicidal ideation and behaviors. Some of them undertook life-threatening "do-it-yourself" surgeries. Several of our Brazilian patients with BDD had no insight over their dysmorphic beliefs and were found to frequently exhibit comorbid OCD, MDD and eating disorders. Despite the increasing importance of physical attractiveness in modern Brazilian society, it seems that the phenomenological features of Brazilian patients with BDD are quite similar to those reported in developed countries, such as England (Veale et al., 1996), Italy (Perugi et al., 1997b), and North America (Phillips et al., 2005b). These findings are consistent with the existence of BDD as a true transcultural disorder.

REFERENCES

Allen A, Hollander E. Body dysmorphic disorder. *Psychiatr Clin North Am* 2000; 23: 617-28.

Asnis GM, Friedman TA, Sanderson WC, Kaplan ML, van Praag HM, Harkavy-Friedman JM. Suicidal behaviors in adult psychiatric outpatients, I: Description and prevalence. *Am J Psychiatry* 1993; 150: 108-12.

Beck AT, Steer RA, Sanderson WC, Skeie TM. Panic disorder and suicidal ideation and behavior: discrepant findings in psychiatric outpatients. *Am J Psychiatry* 1991; 148: 1195-9.

Bienvenu OJ, Samuels JF, Riddle MA, Hoehn-Saric R, Liang KY, Cullen BA et al. The relationship of obsessive-compulsive disorder to possible spectrum disorders: results from a family study. *Biol Psychiatry* 2000; 48: 287-93.

Bohne A, Keuthen NJ, Wilhelm S, Deckersbach T, Jenike MA. Prevalence of symptoms of body dysmorphic disorder and its correlates: a cross-cultural comparison. *Psychosomatics* 2002a; 43: 486-90.

Bohne A, Wilhelm S, Keuthen NJ, Florin I, Baer L, Jenike MA. Prevalence of body dysmorphic disorder in a German college study sample. *Psychiatry Res* 2002b; 109: 101-4.

Brawman-Mintzer O, Lydiard RB, Phillips KA, Morton A, Czepowicz V, Emmanuel N, Villreal G, Johnson M, Ballenger JC. Body dysmorphic disorder in patients with anxiety disorders and major depression: a co-morbidity study. *Am J Psychiatry* 1995; 152: 1665-7.

Buss DM, Abbott M, Angleitner A, Asherian A: International preferences in selecting mates: a study of 37 cultures. *J Cross-Cultural Psychol* 1990; 21:5-47.

Buss DM, Angleitner A: Mate selection preferences in Germany and the United States. *Pers Individ Dif* 1989; 10:1269-1280

Cansever A, Uzun O, Donmez E, Ozsahin A. The prevalence and clinical features of body dysmorphic disorder in college students: a study in a Turkish sample. *Compr Psychiatry* 2003; 44: 60-4.

Cogan JC, Bhalla SK, Sefa-Dedeh A, Rothblum ED: A comparison study of United States and African students on perceptions of obesity and thinness. *J Cross-Cultural Psychol* 1996; 27:98-113

Cororve MB, Gleaves DH. Body dysmorphic disorder: a review of conceptualizations, assessment, and treatment strategies. *Clin Psychol Rev* 2001; 21: 949-70.

Crystal DS, Watanabe H, Weinfurt K, Wu C. Concepts of human differences: a comparison of American, Japanese, and Chinese children and adolescents. *Dev Psychol* 1998; 34: 714-22.

Eisen JL, Phillips KA, Coles ME, Rasmussen SA. Insight in obsessive compulsive disorder and body dysmorphic disorder. *Compr Psychiatry* 2004; 45: 10-5.

Faravelli C, Salvatori S, Galassi F, Aiazzi L, Drei C, Cabras P. Epidemiology of somatoform disorders: a community survey in Florence. *Soc Psychiatry Psychiatr Epidemiol* 1997; 32: 24-29.

Finger C. Brazilian Beauty. *Lancet* 2003; 9395: 1560.

First MB, Spitzer RL, Gibbon M, Williams, JBW. *Structured clinical interview for DSM-IV Axis I Disorders - patient edition (SCID-I/P, Version 2.0)*. New York: Biometrics Research Department, New York State Psychiatric Institute, 1995.

Fontenelle LF, Mendlowicz MV, Kalaf J, Versiani M. The problem of delusional ugliness: is it really body dysmorphic disorder? *World J Biological Psychiatry* (in press).

Fontenelle LF, Mendlowicz MV, Marques C, Versiani M. Trans-cultural aspects of obsessive-compulsive disorder: a description of a Brazilian sample and a systematic review of international clinical studies. *J Psychiatr Res* 2004; 38:403-11.

Fontenelle LF, Mendlowicz MV, Mussi TC, Marques C, Versiani M. The man with the purple nostrils: a case of rhinotrichotillomania secondary to body dysmorphic disorder. *Acta Psychiatr Scand* 2002; 106: 464-6.

Fontenelle LF, Telles LL, Nazar BP, Bezerra de Menezes G, do Nascimento AL, Mendlowicz MV, Versiani M. A Sociodemographic, phenomenological, and long-term study of Brazilian patients with body dysmorphic disorder. *Int J Psychiatry Med* (in press).

Frare F, Perugi G, Ruffolo G, Toni C. Obsessive-compulsive disorder and body dysmorphic disorder: a comparison of clinical features. *Eur Psychiatry;* 19: 292-8, 2004.

Goisman RM, Warshaw MG, Peterson LG, Rogers MP, Cuneo P, Hunt MF et al. Panic, agoraphobia, and panic disorder with agoraphobia - data from a multicenter anxiety disorders study. *J Nerv Ment Dis* 1994;182: 72-9.

Grant JE, Phillips KA. Is anorexia nervosa a subtype of body dysmorphic disorder? Probably not, but read on... *Harv Rev Psychiatry* 2004; 12:123-6.

Grant JE, Kim SW, Eckert ED. Body dysmorphic disorder in patients with anorexia nervosa: prevalence, clinical features, and delusionality of body image. *Int J Eat Disord* 2002; 32: 291-300.

Gunstad J, Phillips KA. Axis I comorbidity in body dysmorphic disorder. *Compr Psychiatry* 2003; 44: 270-6.

Hodes M, Jones C, Davies H: Cross-cultural differences in maternal evaluation of children's body shapes. *Int J Eat Disord* 1996; 19:257-263

Hollander E. Obsessive-compulsive related disorders. Washington (DC): *American Psychiatric* Press: 1993.

Hollander E, Cohen LJ, Simeon D. Body dysmorphic disorder. *Psychiatry Ann* 1993; 23: 359-364.

Jones D: *Physical Attractiveness and the Theory of Sexual Selection: Results From Five Populations: Anthropological Papers 90*. Ann Arbor, Mich, Museum of Anthropology Publications, 1996.

Keel PK, Klump KL. Are eating disorders culture-bound syndromes? Implications for conceptualizing their etiology. *Psychol Bull* 2003; 129: 747-69.

Leverich GS, Altshuler LL, Frye MA, Suppes T, Keck PE Jr, McElroy SL et al. Factors associated with suicide attempts in 648 patients with bipolar disorder in the Stanley Foundation Bipolar Network. *J Clin Psychiatry* 2003; 64: 506-15.

Lochner C, Stein DJ. Olfactory reference syndrome: diagnostic criteria and differential diagnosis. *J Postgrad Med* 2003; 49: 328-31.

McElroy SL, Phillips KA, Keck Jr. PE, Hudson JI, Pope HG Jr. Body dysmorphic disorder: does it have a psychotic subtype? *J Clin Psychiatry* 1993; 54: 589-95.

McHolm AE, MacMillan HL, Jamieson E. The relationship between childhood physical abuse and suicidality among depressed women: results from a community sample. *Am J Psychiatry* 2003; 160: 933-8.

Morselli E. Sulla dismorfofobia e sulla tafefobia. *Bolletinno della R accademia di Genova* 1891; 6:110-9.

Nierenberg AA, Phillips KA, Petersen TJ, Kelly KE, Alpert JE, Worthington JJ et al. Body dysmorphic disorder in outpatients with major depression. *J Affect Disord* 2002; 69: 141-8.

Otto MW, Wilhelm S, Cohen LS, Harlow BL. Prevalence of body dysmorphic disorder in a community sample of women. *Am J Psychiatry* 2001; 158: 2061-3.

Perugi G, Akiskal HS, Giannotti D, Frare F, Di Vaio S, Cassano GB. Gender-related differences in body dysmorphic disorder (dysmorphophobia). *J Nerv Ment Dis* 1997a; 185: 578-82.

Perugi G, Akiskal HS, Lattanzi L, Cecconi D, Mastrocinque C, Patronelli A et al. The high prevalence of "soft" bipolar (II) features in atypical depresion. *Compr Psychiatry* 1998; 39: 63-71.

Perugi G, Frare F. *Body Dysmorphic Disorder: A Review.* Maj M, Akiskal H, Mezzich JE, Okasha A (eds.). Somatoform Disorders (WPA series Evidence and Experience in Psychiatry). Chichester: John and Wiley & Sons, 2005, p 191-221.

Perugi G, Giannotti D, Di Vaio S, Valori E, Maggi L, Frare F et al. Prevalence, phenomenology and co-morbidity of dysmorphophobia (body dysmorphic disorder) in a clinical population. *Intern J Psych Clin Practice* 1997b; 1: 77-82.

Phillips KA. Body dysmorphic disorder and depression: theoretical considerations and treatment strategies. *Psychiatr Q* 1999; 70: 313-31.

Phillips KA. Body dysmorphic disorder: the distress of imagined ugliness. *Am J Psychiatry* 1991; 148: 1138-49.

Phillips KA, Coles ME, Menard W, Yen S, Fay C, Weisberg RB. Suicidal ideation and suicide attempts in body dysmorphic disorder. *J Clin Psychiatry* 2005a; 66: 717-25.

Phillips KA, Diaz SF. Gender differences in body dusmorphic disorder. *J Nerv Ment Dis* 1997; 185: 570-7.

Phillips KA, Gunderson GG, Mallya G, McElroy SL, Caster W. A comparison study of body dysmorphic disorder and obsessive-compulsive disorder. *J Clin Psychiatry* 1998; 59: 568-75.

Phillips KA, McElroy SL, Keck PE Jr., Hudson JI, Pope HG Jr. A comparison of delusional and nondelusional body dysmorphic disorder in 100 cases. *Psychopharmacol Bull* 1994; 30: 179-86.

Phillips KA, McElroy SL, Keck PE, Pope HG Jr., Hudson JI. Body dysmorphic disorder: 30 cases of imagined ugliness. *Am J Psychiatry* 1993; 150: 302-8.

Phillips KA, Menard W, Fay C, Weisberg RB. Demographic characteristics, phenomenology, comorbidity, and family history in 200 individuals with body dysmorphic disorder. *Psychosomatics* 2005b; 46: 317-25.

Phillips KA, Menard W, Pagano ME, Fay C, Stout RL. Delusional versus nondelusional body dysmorphic disorder: Clinical features and course of illness. *J Psychiatr Res* (in press-a).

Phillips KA, Nierenberg AA, Brendel G, Fava M. Prevalence and clinical features of body dysmorphic disorder in atypical major depression. *J Nerv Ment Dis* 1996; 186: 125-9.

Phillips KA, Stout RL. Associations in the longitudinal course of body dysmorphic disorder with major depression, obsessive-compulsive disorder, and social phobia. *J Psychiatr Res* (in press-b).

Radomsky ED, Haas GL, Mann JJ, Sweeney JA. Suicidal behavior in patients with schizophrenia and other psychotic disorders. *Am J Psychiatry* 1999; 156: 1590-5.

Rosen JC, Reiter J, Orosan P. Cognitive-behavioural body image therapy for body dysmorphic disorder. *J Consult Clin Psychol* 1995; 63: 263-9.

Rosen JC, Ramirez E. A comparison of eating disorders and body dysmorphic disorder on body image and psychological adjustment. *J Psychosom Res* 1998; 44: 441-9.

Ruffolo J, Phillips KA, Menard W, Fay C, Weisberg RB. Comorbidity of body dysmorphic disorder and eating disorders: Severity of psychopathology and body image disturbance. *Int J Eat Disord* (in press).

Strzalko J, Kaszycka KA. Physical attractiveness: interpersonal and intrapersonal variability of assessments. *Soc Biol* 1992; 39: 170-6.

Simeon D, Hollander E, Stein DJ, Cohen L, Aronowitz B. Body dysmorphic disorder in the DSM-IV field trial for obsessive-compulsive disorder. *Am J Psychiatry* 1995; 152: 1207-9.

Veale D, Boocock A, Gournay K, Dryden W, Shah F, Willson R et al. Body dysmorphic disorder. A survey of fifty cases. *Br J Psychiatry* 1996; 169: 196-201.

Warshaw MG, Dolan RT, Keller MB. Suicidal behavior in patients with current or past panic disorder: five years of prospective data from the Harvard/Brown Anxiety Research Program. *Am J Psychiatry* 2000; 157: 1876-8.

Warshaw MG, Massion AO, Peterson LG, Pratt LA, Keller MB. Suicidal behavior in patients with panic disorder: retrospective and prospective data. *J Affect Disord* 1995; 34: 235-47.

Wilhelm S, Keuthen NJ, Deckersbach T, Engelhard IM, Forker AE, Baer L et al. Self-injurious skin-picking: clinical characteristics and comorbidity. *J Clin Psychiatry* 1999; 60: 454-9

Zimmerman M, Mattia JJ. Body dysmorphic disorder in psychiatric outpatients: recognition, prevalence, co-morbidity, demographic, and clinical correlates. *Compr Psychiatry* 1998; 39: 265-270.

In: Body Image: New Research
Editor: Marlene V. Kindes, pp. 215-227

ISBN 1-60021-059-7
© 2006 Nova Science Publishers, Inc.

Chapter IX

BODY IMAGE IN MORBID OBESITY

Carlos Delgado[1],, Mª José Morales[2], Purificación Parada[3],
Isabel Otero[3], Ignacio Maruri[3] and Victor del Campo[4]*
Services of [1]Psychiatry, [2]Endocrinology, [3]Surgery and [4]Preventive Medicine, Hospital
Meixoeiro, Vigo (Pontevedra), Spain.

ABSTRACT

Obesity has been considered by WHO as the epidemic of XXI century, affecting a considerable amount of persons in developed countries, being associated to an increase in cardiovascular risk. Morbid obesity, defined by a BMI > 40 Kg/m^2 is the extreme type of obesity associated with a great number of diseases: mellitus diabetes type 2, arterial hypertension, cardiovascular disease, arthropathy and sleep apnoea syndrome. It's a fact that western society emphasizes thinness and denigrates excess weight, stigmatising obese people, and determining a poor body image in obese individuals.

The objective of this chapter is to establish the degree of body image dissatisfaction in morbid obese individuals and how it's modified by bariatric surgery with a result of significant weight loss. In the first part we will make a review of current literature on the relationship between obesity and body image, the body image dissatisfaction and distortion that experience obese individuals and apparent risk factors (degree of overweight, being female, binge eating, early age of onset of obesity and race). In the second part we will show the results of our group, using the Body Dissatisfaction and Drive for Thinness subscales of EDI (Eating Disorder Inventory) in 100 morbid obese candidates for bariatric surgery, appreciating a high body image dissatisfaction and a significant drive for thinness, finding as the only indicator associated to a higher body image dissatisfaction, an age greater than 40 years; and in 31 operated morbid obese persons (evaluated at a mean postoperative period of 16 months) with a statistically significant reduction in body dissatisfaction. Finally we present a discussion of our results and tentative conclusions.

---

* Correspondence concerning this article should be addressed to Carlos Delgado Calvete. Servicio de Psiquiatría. Hospital do Meixoeiro. Meixoeiro s/n. 36214 Vigo (Pontevedra). Spain. E- mail: cdelcal@yahoo.es

Keywords: Body image, Morbid obesity, Bariatric surgery

INTRODUCTION

Obesity constitutes the most frequent form of malnutrition in developed countries, conditioning a health status in the individual that negatively influences his body. Different measures have been used to assess the degree of nutrition, varying according to them the definition of a subject as obese. The most widely used indicator at present is the Quetelet index or Body Mass Index (BMI) that is defined as BMI = weight (in Kg.)/height^2 (in m.). According to this index, all subjects with a BMI>30 Kg/m^2 are considered obese. Morbid obesity (MO) is an extreme degree of obesity that directly and negatively influences the health of an individual and mainly increases all the medical problems related with excess body fat and even with a demonstrated increase in mortality; it is considered that a subject has MO when the BMI is >40 Kg/m^2. The prevalence of obesity in the United States has grown from 15% in 1980 to 30% in 2000 [1]. In Spain the SEEDO 2000 study [2] shows a prevalence of 14.5%. Other developed nations have also seen dramatic increases in the rates of this disorder, which has prompted the World Health Organization to label obesity a global epidemic.[3]

Obesity is absent of psychiatric classifications, however the increase in its frequency and the seriousness of the problems associated to it, conditions its multidisciplinary approach, relevantly including its psychological and psychiatric aspects.

Obese individuals live in a society in which thinness prevails as an ideal of beauty, as is reflected in an anecdotic way in a recent article of the BMJ [4] in which authors observed that bust and hip size decreased as waist size increased over time in Playboy centrefold models over 49 years. In occidental western society obese individuals suffer social rejection and negative valuation from the general population and even from health professionals. Obese people are associated with negative stereotypes as indolent, weak willed, lazy, excessive eaters, social and sexually unattractive and bad workers. In this anti-fat atmosphere an obese individual is locked in a body that finds unpleasant (starting from the rejection that generates in others). An extreme example of that degree of discomfort is reflected in a study of Rand & Mcgregor [5] in that a group of morbid obese persons, 100% preferred to be of normal weight with a bigger handicap (deaf, dyslexic, diabetic, blind, with bad acne, with a heart disease) than to be morbid obese. All of the patients said that they preferred to have a normal weight than to be morbid obese multimillionaires.

The first part of this article consists of a revision of previous studies about the valuation that obese individuals make of their corporal image, the dissatisfaction and distortion that present on it, risk factors for these alterations and changes that have been observed in studies made before and after significant losses of weight (as those observed in morbid obese patients after bariatric surgery).

BODY IMAGE DISSATISFACTION AND DISTORTION IN OBESE PERSONS

It can be distinguished as two aspects in the alterations of body image in obese persons:

Body Image Dissatisfaction

It implies the degree in which individuals value or reject their own body. Wadden et al [6] studied corporal dissatisfaction in a group of 393 obese and not obese adolescent girls, detecting a significantly greater dissatisfaction with regard to their weight and figure in obese girls. Klesges et al [7] found in a sample of 132 children that physical self-competence was inversely related to body fat. Brodie & Slade [8] determined body-fat, estimate of body size and body dissatisfaction in a sample of voluntary women, finding a significant relationship between the increase of body fat and body dissatisfaction. In a previous study of our group [9], we confirmed the existence of a high degree of body dissatisfaction in morbid obese individuals through the Body Dissatisfaction scale of EDI. It is interesting the fact that the parts of the body with which are most unsatisfied both men and women are the waist and the abdomen [10] In conclusion of the meta-analysis that was carried out on this topic, Friedman and Brownell [11] affirm that "although body image disparagement may be in fact very high in obese individuals, the effect of obesity on body image disparagement appears to vary across populations."

Body Image Distortion

It supposes the imprecision in the determination of body size. Diverse methods have been used for the measure of it, what implies difficulty to establish comparisons among results obtained in the different studies. In the above mentioned study of Brodie & Slade [8] the 'accuracy' measures were found to be unrelated to measures of adiposity. Garner et al [12] compared individuals with anorexia nervosa (AN) or obesity with control subjects using the distorting photograph technique, finding that obese and anorexia nervosa patients presented a normal distribution of the degree of distortion, with half underestimating and half overestimating their body widths, while most of the control subjects underestimated their body widths. Collins et al [13], in a new investigation comparing the variability of body perceptions of subjects with AN, bulimia nervosa, obesity, and control subjects, found that control subjects were accurate, while the three clinical groups were significantly less accurate, overestimating body size. In another study of Bell et al [14] also with anorexics, obese and normal weight control subjects using a silhouette chart to assess accuracy in body size estimation, obese patients underestimated, anorexics overestimated and control subjects were accurate in their estimation of body size. In short, an important discrepancy is observed among the results of the diverse studies, discrepancies that can be due to the different methods used for evaluation and the different populations included in the studies (obese in weight loss programs or general population).

RISK FACTORS ASSOCIATED TO BODY IMAGE DISSATISFACTION IN OBESE INDIVIDUALS

Beyond the verification of the existence of dissatisfaction and distortion of body image, recent studies have been focused on the determination of risk factors for the appearance of them. The main studied risk factors are the following ones (Table I):

Table I. Main risk factors associated to body image dissatisfaction in obese individuals.

Main risk factors associated to body image dissatisfaction in obese individuals
Current weight
Gender
Race
Binge eating disorder
Age of obesity onset and appearance teasing
Low self-esteem and depression

Current Weight

It seems logical to suppose that body dissatisfaction is bigger as weight increases. In fact, Hill & Williams [15] in a non-clinical sample of obese women divided in 3 groups according to their BMI (30-34, 35-39 and > 40 Kg/m^2) found that body dissatisfaction increased from the lowest to the highest BMI groups. However this relationship doesn't appear so clear in other studies in that subgroups are analysed. Eldredge & Agras [16] studied a fundamentally feminine sample from a commercial weight loss program and found that those with a binge eating disorder (BED) showed a greater weight and shape concern than did individuals without eating disorders, but concerns were not linked to weight category. Sarwer et al [10] and Matz et al [17] didn't find a significant correlation between BMI and body dissatisfaction studying in both cases obese women in treatment for reduction of weight.

Gender

Most of the studies on obesity and body image have been with primarily or exclusively feminine samples, both for the bigger frequency of obesity in women and their greater participation in weight loss programs; however some studies have analysed the difference between men and women in this aspect. In general there have been observed evidence of a bigger body dissatisfaction in women. Cash & Hicks [18] comparing groups of men and women with normal weight and overweight, and asking their own valuation like normal weight or overweight, found that among women that labelled themselves as overweight there was bigger dissatisfaction in those that in fact presented it, while in the case of the men, dissatisfaction was lower among those that in fact presented it; their explanation is a certain valuation of men like "big and strong" more than as fat. In a similar way Wardle & Johnson

[19] in a wide sample of British adults, found a bigger tendency among overweight women to recognize themselves as such (28%) than in men (22%). Nevertheless in another study of Sorbara & Geliebter [20] men overestimated in more degree its body weight that women, without showing a bigger degree of body dissatisfaction.

Race

Most of studies are carried out on individuals of white race, however in some case differences have been analysed in connection with race. A lower degree of body dissatisfaction has been appreciated among obese (men and women) of black race with regard to those of white race [21], what can be related with different cultural patterns with respect to body attractiveness.

Binge Eating Disorder

Several studies insist on considering obese individuals with Binge Eating Disorder (BED) as a subgroup in which has been registered a bigger frequency of psychopathology [22-24] (depression, anxiety, substance abuse and personality disorders) comparing with those without BED. Besides some studies have shown a bigger body dissatisfaction in obese persons with BED. Wilfley et al [25] found that obese persons with BED presented bigger levels of concern for its figure and weight than obese persons without BED, results that agree with those of Eldredge & Agras [16]. Sorbara & Geliebter [20] communicate a bigger degree of discrepancy and dissatisfaction in obese individuals with BED. Finally two recent studies confirm the correlation between the presence of binge eating and body dissatisfaction in adults [26] and adolescents [27].

Age of Obesity Onset and Appearance Teasing

It has been considered the early beginning of obesity and suffering teasing in childhood like a risk factor to present body dissatisfaction in obese adults. Grilo et al [28] finds that women with childhood-onset obesity reported greater body dissatisfaction, and that the frequency of being teased about weight as a child correlated with body dissatisfaction. Sorbara & Geliebter [20] study body image disturbance as a composite of three aspects (distortion, discrepancy and dissatisfaction) and finds that early-onset of obesity subjects show more discrepancy than adult-onset subjects, and that following weight loss early-onset subjects still show more discrepancy and dissatisfaction than adult-onset subjects. Matz et al [17], however, found that only adult teasing (and not childhood teasing) correlated with current poor body image. Adami et al [29] studied a group of morbid obese persons before and after reduction of weight by bariatric surgery, not finding differences in the valuation pre-surgery in function of the age of onset of the obesity, but after surgery those with childhood-onset obesity had poorer body image than adult-onset ones, concluding these authors that age of onset of obesity does not affect body dissatisfaction in obese individuals, but onset of obesity at an early age increases the durability of poor body image following weight loss.

Low Self-Esteem and Depression

Some authors have also studied the relationship of the level of self-esteem and the presence of depression with body dissatisfaction, being the results in general contradictory. In this section it is curious that the contributions are centred in the group of Pennsylvania University, with several articles in that the same authors participate (Wadden & Foster) with diverse results. Following a chronological order Wadden et al [6] didn't find high levels of depression in obese adolescents in spite of verifying their high body dissatisfaction. Foster et al [30] detect a relationship between the positive valuation of body image and high levels of self-esteem and lower levels of dysphoria. Sarwer et al. [10] found that body image dissatisfaction correlated significantly with reports of depressive symptoms and lower self-esteem. Finally Matz et al [17] also communicates that levels of self-esteem predicted body image dissatisfaction. As conclusion it seems to exist relationship among body image dissatisfaction and low self-esteem and not so clearly with depressive symptoms, without it can be necessary a cause-effect relationship in one or another sense.

Variation with the Reduction of Weight

It is important to analyse the variation that takes place in body image dissatisfaction (BID) observed in obese individuals when a significant reduction of weight takes place, like it happens in the case of morbid obese persons that are intervened by bariatric surgery. Numerous works exist in that sense, and in all them an improvement of BID is verified. The author that has published most on this aspect is Adami et al [29,31-33]. In all their works he verifies the improvement of BID with the reduction of weight, getting levels similar to normal weight persons, although he reflects the persistence of a certain degree of dissatisfaction in subject over-worried about weight [31], with childhood onset of obesity [29] and with previous binge eating disorder [32]. Finally in his most recent article [33] he reflects that certain aspects, like distressing preoccupation with weight and shape, persist beyond the reduction of weight. In a similar way other authors [34-35] verify the improvement of the body image with the loss of weight.

MATERIALS AND METHODS

Subjects

The present investigation was carried out with a group of morbid obese (MO) individuals candidates (and already intervened) to bariatric surgery, including two samples. Sample 1 consists of 100 MO persons candidates to be operated on by bariatric surgery as treatment for their morbid obesity. All of them underwent a clinical interview and a questionnaire was administered that included demographic variables (age, gender, civil status, educational level, profession), anthropometric data (weight, height, BMI), family composition, personal and family antecedents, data on the evolution of obesity and on eating habits (food eaten, intake of sweets, bulimic behaviour). Sample 2 consists of a group of 31 MO patients who underwent bariatric surgery and where evaluated again at a mean time of 15,65 months following bariatric surgery. Demographic and anthropometric data of both samples are included in Tables II and III.

Table II. Demographic data.

		Sample 1	Sample 2	
		Number	Number	%
Gender	Women	88	27	87,10
	Men	12	4	12,90
Civil Status	Married	70	19	61,29
	Single	25	11	35,48
	Widow(er)	3	1	3,23
	Separated	1		
	Divorced	1		
Studies	Basic Education	50	14	45,16
	Secondary education	19	5	16,13
	Vocational education	15	8	25,81
	Read and write	6		
	Middle University	7	3	9,68
	Upper University	3	1	3,23
Profession	Skilled worker	28	8	25,81
	Unskilled worker	29	10	32,26
	Housewife	26	4	12,90
	Own Business	9	3	9,68
	Student	5	3	9,68
	State worker	3	3	9,68

Table III. Anthropometric data.

	Sample 1		Sample 2	
	Mean	Stand. Dev.	Mean	Stand. Dev.
Age (Years)	38,51	10,56	36,68	10,67
Weight (kg.)	132,04	21,30	132,9	23,15
Height (m.)	1,62	9,14	1,63	0,10
BMI (kg/m^2)	50,32	5,86	49,88	6,75
Months from Surgery			15,65	8,98
Post Weight (kg.)			88,66	15,72
Post BMI (kg/m^2)			33,46	5,84

Psychometric Evaluation

In addition, the following test was administered before and after surgery:

Eating Disorder Inventory (EDI) [36]: This is a self report questionnaire of 64 items, designed for the assessment of psychological and behavioural traits among eating-disordered individuals. The EDI consists of 8 subscales measuring: 1) Drive for Thinness, (DT), 2) Bulimia (B), 3) Body Dissatisfaction (BD), 4) Ineffectiveness (I), 5) Perfectionism (P), 6) Interpersonal Distrust (ID), 7) Interoceptive Awareness (IA) and 8) Maturity Fears (MF). For the purposes of this study we used the Body Dissatisfaction Subscale to quantify the body image disparagement and the Drive for Thinness subscale as an indicator of excessive concern with dieting and weight, in the search of risk factors for body image disparagement.

Statistics

The differences between subgroups in Sample 1 were evaluated by the Independent Student's t-Test or the U Mann-Whitney test for unpaired comparisons depending of the number of cases of each subgroup and by the Paired Student's t-Test in Sample 2 to see differences between evaluation pre and post surgery.

RESULTS

Sample 1

The results of the different EDI subscales are presented in Table IV, indicating the maximum possible score in each subscale. As is evident in it, exists a great Body Dissatisfaction in our group of MO individuals (Mean Score 21,03/27) with a significant Drive for Thinness (Mean Score 10,45/21), while the scores in the other subscales are very low.

Table IV: EDI Results for 100 MO individuals.

EDI Subscales N=100	Mean	Stand. Dev.
Drive for Thinness/ 21	10,45	5,42
Bulimia /21	2,79	4,04
Body Dissatisfaction /27	21,03	6,47
Ineffectiveness /30	6,27	6,50
Perfectionism /18	5,02	3,70
Interpersonal Distrust /21	5,01	3,04
Interoceptive Awareness /30	6,68	5,69
Maturity Fears /24	4,84	4,58

In order to identify risk factors for Body Dissatisfaction we made comparisons between several subgroups in relation to the scores in the Body Dissatisfaction (BD) and Drive for Thinness (DT) subscales attending to: Gender, Age (< or >40 yrs.), Civil State (Married or not), Studies (Basic or no Education, or higher), Profession (Skilled or Unskilled), Psychiatric past history, BMI (< or >50), Child obesity, Age of beginning of obesity (< or > 16 yrs), Binge eating. The differences statistically significant detected between subgroups in relation to BD and DT subscales are shown in Table V.

Table V: Significant differences in BD and DT subscales.

	BD/DT	Mean	Mean	p
>40 vs <40	BD	22,49	19,63	0,03
Married vs Not Married	DT	11,08	8,65	0,05
No Child obesity vs yes	DT	11,55	9,21	0,03
>16 vs <16 onset obesity	DT	11,92	8,98	0,006

Sample 2

The results of the different EDI subscales before and after bariatric surgery and the level of significance of the differences are shown in Table VI.

It is evident from this results that there is a significant reduction in the scores of both subscales after bariatric surgery and the important reduction of weight obtained with it.

Table VI: EDI Results for 31 MO before and after bariatric surgery.

N=31	Before Surgery		After Surgery		
EDI Subscales	Mean	Stand. Dev.	Mean	Stand. Dev.	p
Drive for Thinness/ 21	9,90	5,39	6,55	5,31	0,002
Bulimia /21	2,03	2,83	0,45	0,85	0,005
Body Dissatisfaction /27	20,68	6,65	11,03	7,89	0,000
Ineffectiveness /30	6,68	6,73	5,26	7,53	n.s.
Perfectionism /18	4,74	3,79	4,84	3,93	n.s
Interpersonal Distrust /21	4,97	2,93	5,06	4,46	n.s
Interoceptive Awareness /30	6,19	5,30	5,68	6,91	n.s
Maturity Fears /24	3,87	4,40	4,35	4,74	n.s

DISCUSSION

The sociodemographic characteristics of the samples show a clear predominance of women (88%, 87,1%), which is according to all the epidemiological studies on obesity that reflect its greater frequency in women than in men, and to the studies made in clinical settings that show a greater predominance than in epidemiological ones. For civil status, there is a larger number of married subjects (70%, 61,29%) which is according with a mean age of

38,51 and 36,68 years. The predominant level of studies is basic (50%, 45,16%), and the most common professional level is unskilled worker, what points to middle-low socio-economic level. The BMI in both samples is around 50 Kg/m^2, which corresponds to superobesity more that to morbid obesity. An elevated proportion of obesity in relatives (83%) and significant childhood onset of obesity (47%) are reported. Patients were asked about having experienced a negative influence of obesity in their life in three different areas (professional, social and sexual) recognizing negative repercussions in social sphere in 55%, with lower figures in sexual and professional areas (49 and 43% respectively); these values are not especially high, in relations to a physical state that presents a high degree of rejection in the general population.

Looking at the results in the EDI subscales in Sample 1 (100 morbid obese individuals), we can see a high degree of Body Dissatisfaction ((Mean Score 21,03 over a maximum possible score of 27) with a significant value in the Drive for Thinness suscale (Mean Score 10,45/21), while the scores in the other subscales are very low. The values obtained in the different EDI subscales are very similar to those reported by Sanchez Planell et al.[37] and Adami et al.[31], that use the same questionnaire, although in our sample body dissatisfaction is greater and the scores in bulimia are lower than those in both studies.

When we try to find risk factors for body dissatisfaction, in our sample, the only factor that offers differences statistically significant is age, being greater in persons older than forty. If we look to the drive for thinness subscale we find significant differences regarding to the civil state (bigger in married persons) and the age of the beginning of obesity (bigger in persons with an onset later than 16 years and with no obesity in childhood). The main conclusion we can extract is that our sample is very homogeneous with respect to the degree of body dissatisfaction, which can be explained by the high degree of obesity. Another tentative conclusion is that body dissatisfaction increases with age, an aspect we have not found reflected in previous literature, and that concern with weight is bigger in persons married and with late onset of obesity, what could be attributed to a less discomfort with his body in persons who have lived obesity in early years and are single. We could not confirm in our sample other risk factors that have been detected in another studies as gender [18-20], current weight (BMI) [15], binge eating [16,20,25-27], and age of onset of obesity [20,28]. The relation between body image dissatisfaction and BMI has been detected in the study of Hill & Williams [15], although without differentiating groups above a BMI of 40 kg/m^2, but other studies have failed detecting these correlation [10,16-17], as we can see in our sample.

The results in Sample 2 show clearly a reduction in the scores of all subscales of EDI, being statistically significant in drive for thinness, bulimia and body dissatisfaction. This results agree with those of other studies that evaluate body dissatisfaction before and after bariatric surgery [20,29,31-33], and offer an indirect evidence of the improvement of the quality of life in these persons beyond the weight loss.

CONCLUSION

Obese persons live in a society in which thinness prevails as ideal of beauty and a clear negative prejudice exists against them. In this situation obese individuals feel locked in an unpleasant body. Body image dissatisfaction and distortion are evident in the different studies revised. The main risk factors associated with these facts (according to the revised literature) are current weight, gender, race, binge eating disorder, age of obesity onset, appearance teasing, low self-esteem and depression. Morbid obesity constitutes the extreme form of obesity, and body image dissatisfaction appears in a marked way, as do all the unpleasant consequences of obesity. In our sample of 100 morbid obese individual candidates to bariatric surgery, we find a high body image dissatisfaction and a significant drive for thinness, but we failed to confirm the risk factors detected in other studies; the only indicator associated to a higher body image dissatisfaction was an age greater than 40 years.

Bariatric surgery constitutes a suitable therapeutic option for these persons. It allows them to obtain significant weight reductions and to study the possible variations in the perception of their body. In our study of 31 morbid obese individuals that had undergone bariatric surgery, a drastic reduction in body image dissatisfaction and drive for thinness was confirmed at a mean postoperative period of 16 months.

REFERENCES

[1]   Flegal, KM; Carroll MD; Ogden CL; Johnson CL. Prevalence and trends in obesity among US adults, 1999-2000. *JAMA*, 2002, 288, 1723–1727.

[2]   Aranceta, J; Perez Rodrigo, C; Serra Majem, L; Ribas Barba, L; Quiles Izquierdo, J; Vioque, J; Tur Mari, J; Mataix Verdu, J; Llopis Gonzalez, J; Tojo, R; Foz Sala, M; Grupo colaborativo para el Estudio de la Obesidad en España. Prevalencia de la obesidad en España: resultados del estudio SEEDO 2000. *Med Clin (Barc)*, 2003 May 3, 120(16), 608-12.

[3]   World Health Organization. *Obesity: Preventing and Managing the Global Epidemic.* Geneva: World Health Organization; 1998.

[4]   Voracek, M & Fisher, ML. Shapely centrefolds? Temporal change in body measures: trend analysis. *BMJ*, 2002 Dec 21 ,325 (7378), 1447-8.

[5]   Rand, CS & Macgregor, AM. Successful weight loss following obesity surgery and the perceived liability of morbid obesity. *Int J Obes*, 1991 Sep, 15(9), 577-9.

[6]   Wadden, TA; Foster, GD; Stunkard, AJ; Linowitz, JR. Dissatisfaction with weight and figure in obese girls: discontent but not depression. *Int J Obes*, 1989, 13(1), 89-97.

[7]   Klesges, RC; Haddock, CK; Stein, RJ; Klesges, LM; Eck, LH; Hanson, CL. Relationship between psychosocial functioning and body fat in preschool children: a longitudinal investigation. *J Consult Clin Psychol*, 1992, 60(5),793-6.

[8]   Brodie, DA & Slade, PD. The relationship between body-image and body-fat in adult women. *Psychol Med*, 1988, 18(3), 623-31.

[9]   Delgado Calvete, C; Morales Gorría, MJ; Maruri Chimeno, I; Rodríguez Del Toro, C; Benavente Martín, JL; Núñez Bahamonde S. Conductas alimentarias, actitudes hacia el cuerpo y psicopatología en obesidad mórbida. *Actas Esp Psiquiatr*, 2002, 30(6), 376-81.

[10]   Sarwer, DB; Wadden, TA; Foster, GD. Assessment of body image dissatisfaction in obese women: Specificity, severity, and clinical significance. *J Consult Clin Psychol*, 1998, 66, 651–4.

[11]   Friedman, MA; Brownell, KD. Psychological correlates of obesity: Moving to the next research generation. *Psychol Bull*, 1995, 117(1), 3-20.

[12]   Garner, DM; Garfinkel, PE; Stancer, HC; Moldofsky, H. Body image disturbance in anorexia nervosa and obesity. *Psychosom Med*, 1976, 38, 327–36.

[13]   Collins, JK; Beaumont, PJV; Touyz, SW; Krass, J; Thompson, P; Philips, T. Variability in body shape perception in anorexic, bulimic, obese, and control subjects. *Int J Eat Disord*, 1987, 6: 633–8.

[14]   Bell, C; Kirkpatrick, SW; Rinn, RC. Body image of anorexic, obese, and normal females. *J Clin Psychol*, 1986, 42, 431–9.

[15]   Hill, AJ & Williams, J. Psychological health in a non-clinical sample of obese women. Int *J Obes Relat Metab Disord*, 1998, 22, 578–83.

[16]   Eldredge, KL & Agras, WS. Weight and shape overconcern and emotional eating in binge eating disorder. *Int J Eat Disord*, 2002, 19, 73–82.

[17]   Matz, PE; Foster, GD; Faith, MS; Wadden, TA. Correlates of body image dissatisfaction among overweight women seeking weight loss. *J Consult Clin Psychol*, 2002, 70(4), 1040-4.

[18]   Cash, TF & Hicks, KF. Being fat versus thinking fat: Relationships with body image, eating behaviors, and well-being. *Cognitive Therapy and Research*, 1990, 14, 327–41.

[19]   Wardle, J & Johnson, F. Weight and dieting: Examining levels of weight concern in British adults. *Int J Obes Relat Metab Disord*, 2002, 26(8),1144-9.

[20]   Sorbara, M & Geliebter, A. Body image disturbance in obese outpatients before and after weight loss in relation to race, gender, binge eating, and age of onset of obesity. *Int J Eat Disord*, 2002, 31(4),416-23.

[21]   Smith, DE; Thompson, JK; Raczynski, JM; Hilner, JE. Body image among men and women in a biracial cohort: the CARDIA Study. *Int J Eat Disord*, 1999, 25(1), 71-82.

[22]   Yanovski, SZ; Nelson, JE; Dubbert, BK; Spitzer RL. Association of binge eating disorder and psychiatric comorbidity in obese subjects. *Am J Psychiatry*, 1993 Oct, 150(10), 1472-9.

[23]   Marcus, MD; Wing, RR; Ewing, L; Kern, E; Gooding, W; McDermott, M. Psychiatric disorders among obese binge eaters. *Int J Eat Disord*, 1996, 9, 69-77.

[24]   Specker, S; De Zwaan, M; Raymond, N; Mitchell, J. Psychopathology in subgroups of obese women with and without binge eating disorder. *Compr Psychiatry*, 1994, 35, 185-190.

[25]   Wilfley, DE; Schwartz, MH; Spurrell, EB; Fairburn, CG. Using the eating disorder examination to identify specific psychopathology of binge eating disorder. *Int J Eat Disord*, 2000, 27, 259-69.

[26]   Cena, H; Toselli, A; Tedeschi, S. Body uneasiness in overweight and obese Italian women seeking weight-loss treatment. *Eat Weight Disord*, 2003, 8(4), 321-5.

[27]   Isnard, P; Michel, G; Frelut, ML; Vila, G; Falissard, B; Naja, W; Navarro, J; Mouren-Simeoni, MC. Binge eating and psychopathology in severely obese adolescents. *Int J Eat Disord*, 2003, 34(2), 235-43.

[28] Grilo, CM; Wilfley, DE; Brownell, K D; Rodin, J. Teasing, body image, and self-esteem in a clinical sample of obese women. *Addictive Behaviors*, 1994, 19, 443–50.

[29] Adami, GF; Gandolfo, P; Campostano, A; Meneghelli, A; Ravera, G; Scopinaro, N. Body image and body weight in obese patients. *Int J Eat Disord*, 1998, 24(3), 299–306.

[30] Foster, GD; Wadden, TA; Vogt, RA. Body image in obese women before, during, and after weight loss treatment. *Health Psicol.*, 1997, 16(3), 226-9.

[31] Adami, GF; Gandolfo, P; Campostano, A; Bauer, B; Cocchi, F; Scopinaro, N. Eating disorder inventory in the assessment of psychosocial status in the obese patients prior to and at long-term following biliopancreatic diversion for obesity. *Int J Eat Disord*, 1994 Apr, 15(3), 265-74.

[32] Adami, GF; Marinari, GM; Bressani, A; Testa, S; Scopinaro, N. Body image in binge eating disorder. *Obes Surg*, 1998 Oct, 8(5), 517-9.

[33] Adami, GF; Meneghelli, A; Bressani, A; Scopinaro, N. Body image in obese patients before and after stable weight reduction following bariatric surgery. *J Psychosom Res*, 1999, 46(3), 275-81.

[34] Dixon, JB; Dixon, ME; O'Brien, PE. Body image: appearance orientation and evaluation in the severely obese. Changes with weight loss. *Obes Surg.* 2002, 12(1), 65 71.

[35] Camps, MA; Zervos, E; Goode, S; Rosemurgy, AS. Impact of Bariatric Surgery on Body Image Perception and Sexuality in Morbidly Obese Patients and their Partners. *Obes Surg*, 1996, 6(4), 356-60.

[36] Garner, DM; Olmstead, MP; Polivy, J. Development and validation of a multidimensional eating disorder inventory for anorexia nervosa and bulimia. *Int J Eating Disorders*, 1983, 2, 15-34.

[37] Sánchez Planell, L; Díez, C; Martínez, B. Alteraciones psicopatológicas en la obesidad mórbida. *Endocrinologia (Barc)*, 1992, 38(8), 360-364.

In: Body Image: New Research
Editor: Marlene V. Kindes, pp. 229-242

ISBN 1-60021-059-7
© 2006 Nova Science Publishers, Inc.

Chapter X

THE ASSOCIATION BETWEEN ACTUAL FATNESS, BODY RATINGS AND APPEARANCE PERCEPTION IN CHILDREN

Patrick W. C. Lau[*]

Hong Kong Baptist University
Kowloon Tong, Kowloon, Hong Kong

ABSTRACT

Due to the trendy emphasis on the slimmer body in which not only women or adults are suffering with different weight-related sickness, our young Chinese children in this generation is also facing a huge challenge in their weight and appearance concern. In last decades, clinical eating disorders have been documented in Hong Kong and commercial body slimming products are very common in the Chinese society. Little is known in the literature if the western lifestyle (physical inactivity and diet) has already influenced the Chinese children regarding the psychological and sociological perspectives. This paper intended to examine the associations between Chinese children's body rating, actual fatness, gender and age impact, and the cultural issue regarding the weight and body weight issue.

Keywords: Childhood obesity, physical perception, body weight, appearance

Western culture has increasingly valued physical appearance and in particular slenderness (Nardini, 1998; Sparkes, 1997). Unrealistic targets of thinness and excessive weight loss have been resulted due to the traditional ideal female body shape/appearance in the last twenty years (Katzmarzyk & Davis, 2001). Not only women were suffered from this

---

[*] Correspondence address: Dr. Patrick W.C. Lau, Associate Profesor, Department of Physical Education, Hong Kong Baptist University, Kowloon Tong, Kowloon, Hong Kong. Email: wclau@hkbu.edu.hk

social pressure of the cultural ideal body, but men were also gradually exposed to the similar kind of body preference (Philips & Drummond, 2001). Drive for thinness and body dissatisfaction were alarmingly recorded in certain studies with women and these two factors were identified as the most important contributors for eating disorders, obligatory exercise and certain mental health (Hill & Williams, 1998; Nardini, 1998). And unfortunately this trend has extended and permeated among children of younger and younger ages – first reported in the America, Canada, and now in countries in Europe (Ball, Marshall, Roberts, & McCargar, 2001; Berg, 1997; Crocker, Snyder, Kowalski, & Hoar, 2000; International Obesity Taskforce, 2003; Kraig & Keel, 2001).

Looking thin as a valued commodity was also positioned against increasing levels of overweight and obesity in the developed world. In the U.K. for example trebled in 20 years and in the United States of America, 64% of adult population was estimated either overweight or obese in the survey of the 1999-2000 National Health and Nutrition Examination Survey (NHANES) (International Obesity Taskforce, 2003). The adult figures were also reflected in young children aged from 2 to 9 years old in the way that children treated fat figures in a more negative attitude and prejudice manner (Kraig & Keel, 2001; Turnbull, Heaslip, & McLeod, 2000). Children have therefore faced with increasing social and psychological pressures to look slender at a time when the environment through lack of activity and increased availability of high-energy dense foods has been increasing fatness. These pressures posed considerable challenges to the self-esteem and mental well being of children and there was evidence that this was deteriorating (Phillips & Hill, 1998).

Little is known about these influences on Hong Kong Chinese children. Uniquely placed at the cultural boundary between Western and Eastern philosophies, developments provide particular insight into the spread of cultural norms and pressures. Western influences have been evident in a recent increase in childhood obesity and eating disorders in Hong Kong. The obesity rate of children has increased from 11.2% in 1995 to 16.1% in 2004 (Department of Health, 2005) and clinical cases have been documented (Lee, Chan, Kwok & Hsu, 2005). The causes were not fully known but it has been conceived to the impact of western ideal body figure (Forbes, Doroszewicz, Card, & Adams-Curtis, 2004). Studies have not been conducted on how the Chinese children perceived their body appearance and it might reflect western body tensions on them. This study therefore investigated the following issues:

1. The associations between body ratings (actual and ideal) and children's actual fatness (BMI).
2. The predictive ability of actual fatness (BMI), and actual-ideal body rating discrepancy to children's appearance self-perception.
3. The gender and age impact on the measured variables.

METHOD

Participants

Three hundred and twenty Chinese children (45% girls, 55% boys) aged 7-12 were recruited as participants in the present study. They came from a standard primary school selected from primary grade 3 to 6. They represented a typical children population in Hong Kong Chinese and their families were low to middle social class from an urban area of the city. Participants and their parents were given consent letters, which explained to them about the aims and procedure, before the start of the study. They were also reminded that their participation in the study was voluntary and they could withdraw at any time of the study without any prejudice. No participants and their parents refused to take part. School approval was also sought. A total of 291 completed questionnaires were received. The response rate was 91%.

Measures and Procedures

Global self-esteem and physical self-concept were measured using the Physical Self-Descriptive Questionnaire (PSDQ) (Marsh, Richards, Jonhnson, Roche, & Tremayne, 1994). The theoretical framework and design of the PSDQ were based on the well-established multidimensional Self-Description Questionnaire and its psychometric properties have been validated in very diversified cultures (e.g., Marsh, Marco, & Abcy, 2002; Marsh et al., 1994). The PSDQ consists of 70 items designed to measure nine specific components of physical self-concept (health, coordination, physical activity, body fat, sports competence, appearance, strength, flexibility, endurance), global physical self-concept and global esteem. Each of the 70 PSDQ items was a simple declarative statement to be responded with a 6-point scale. Only the subscales of body fat and appearance were used in this study since these were the two subscales employed by Marsh and Roche (1996) in the study of body appearance.

In the measurement of body image, the children's version of silhouette matching task (SMT) was adopted from Marsh and Roche (1996) and conducted. Children were presented with a set of silhouette pictures of 9 girls and 9 boys varying from very thin to very obese. Respondents were asked to choose the silhouette that was most like them. The instruments were administered in classes after school.

The PSDQ subscale scores were computed by averaging the responses to items designed to measure each component with negatively worded items being reversed scored. The SMT were scored by the number of the silhouette chosen by each child, which could range from 1 (very thin) to 9 (very obese). The body image disparity was represented by the actual-ideal body discrepancy, which was derived from subtracting the actual body rating from the ideal body rating. A zero score meant no body image difference whereas a positive score indicated actual body thinner than ideal and a negative score indicated actual body fatter than ideal.

The questionnaires were conducted during the intact physical education classes. The researcher distributed the questionnaires and explained the objective of the study, with the assistance of the class teachers. Children were told that the questionnaires were not tests and there were no right or wrong answers. All data collected would be destroyed after the study and could be reached by the researcher only. Children were informed to work on the answers individually without discussing with other classmates. The assessments were completed in 35 minutes. Their height and weight were measured before the questionnaires administered by the researcher and their teachers.

Statistical Analysis

Several statistical analyses were conducted. Cronbach's alpha was used to estimate the internal consistency of the body fat and the appearance. Correlational analysis was used to study the bivariate linear relationship among the variables. Two hierarchical regression analyses were conducted to test the research hypotheses. The first hierarchical regression was regression BMI on age and gender as Block 1 and on actual body rating and ideal body rating as Block 2. This analysis compares whether actual body rating and ideal body rating have additional contribution over age and gender in predicting BMI. In the second hierarchical regression, appearance was regressed on age, gender in Block 1 while BMI and the discrepancy between the actual body rating and the ideal body rating were entered in Block 2. The actual-ideal body rating discrepancy score is employed to represent the level of individuals' body satisfaction. The body size discrepancy score was calculated by subtracting the *actual* score from the *ideal* score. When the actual score was higher than the ideal score, the child would like to reduce the body weight. When the actual score was lower than the ideal score, the child wants to increase weight. When there were no differences between the actual body size score and the ideal body size score, those children were satisfied with their current body shape. This analysis may help us to understand the uniqueness of BMI and the discrepancy between the actual body rating and the ideal body rating over age and gender in predicting children's appearance perception. It is believed that the smaller the discrepancy is, the higher the body satisfaction of the children will be.

RESULTS

The Cronbach's alphas for the body fat and appearance subscales were .89 and .78, respectively. This indicates that the reliability of these two subscales is acceptable. The descriptive statistics are shown in Table 1. Several observations are noted. First, BMI is strongly positively correlated with body fat and actual body rating while it is weakly negatively correlated with appearance. These suggest that children's perception is highly related to the actual body weight. Second, ideal body rating is not significantly correlated with BMI, body fat and appearance subscales at all while it is weakly correlated with actual body rating. These suggest that children's ideal body shape is not related to their true weight or body image at this age.

By running a hierarchical regression on BMI, the results show that all predictors are significant in predicting BMI (see Table 2). Age and gender are moderate in predicting BMI ($R^2 = .08$, $p < .01$) while actual body rating and ideal body rating are strongly predictive (ΔR^2

= .36, $p < .01$). Actual body rating is positively correlated with BMI while ideal body rating is negatively correlated with BMI. By checking the regression coefficients, it seems that the actual body rating (1.08) is stronger than the absolute regression coefficient of the ideal body rating (.43). To test this hypothesis, these regression coefficients were compared statistically (see Faraway, 2005). The result shows that the actual body rating is much stronger than the ideal body rating in predicting BMI ($F (1, 275) = 35.56, p < .001$).

Table 1. Correlations and Descriptive Statistics of the Variables

	(1)	(2)	(3)	(4)	(5)	(6)	(7)
(1) BMI	1.00						
(2) Body fat	.69**	1.00					
(3) Appearance	-.16**	-.24**	1.00				
(4) Actual body rating	.58**	.57**	-.07	1.00			
(5) Ideal body rating	-.05	-.09	-.06	.25**	1.00		
(6) Age	.26**	.12*	-.24**	.10	.02	1.00	
(7) Gender	.13*	.09	.07	-.06	-.05	-.02	1.00
Means	17.79	2.49	3.34	6.59	6.64	9.75	.57
Standard deviations	3.17	1.46	1.19	1.78	1.52	1.54	.50

$*p < .05. **p < .01.$

Table 2. Hierarchical Regression on BMI.

	Variables	Unstandardized coefficients	Standard errors	Standardized coefficients
Step 1	Intercept	12.31	1.17	
	Age	.51	.12	.25
	Gender	.85	.36	.14
Step 2	Intercept	9.01	1.14	
	Age	.40	.09	.20
	Gender	1.04	.28	.17
	Actual body rating	1.08	.08	.62
	Ideal body rating	-.43	.09	-.21

Note. $R^2 = .08$ for Step 1; $\Delta R^2 = .36$ for Step 2 ($p < .01$). All unstandardized coefficients are significant at alpha = .01, except Gender in Step 1 which $p = .02$.

In the next analysis, hierarchical regression on predicting appearance was conducted. Results show that age and gender as a whole were significant in predicting appearance ($R^2 = .06, p < .01$). When checking the significance of individual predictors, only age was significant while gender did not. In the second block, BMI and the actual-ideal discrepancy score were entered into the model. The R^2 change was non-significant with $F (2, 275) = 2.06, p = .13$. The regression coefficients were shown in Table 3.

Table 3. Hierarchical Regression on Appearance.

	Variables	Unstandardized coefficients	Standard errors	Standardized coefficients
Step 1	Intercept	4.95		
	Age	-.18***	.04	-.23
	Gender	.16	.14	.07
Step 2	Intercept	5.68		
	Age	-.15**	.05	-.20
	Gender	.21	.14	.09
	BMI	-.06*	.03	-.15
	Discrepancy	-.04	.04	-.07

Note. $R^2 = .06$ for Step 1 ($p < .01$); $\Delta R^2 = .01$ for Step 2 ($p = .13$). * $p < .05$. ** $p < .01$. *** $p < .001$.

DISCUSSION

To answer the first research question, the associations between actual body ratings, body fat subscale and children's actual fatness (BMI) is found positively correlated. This finding demonstrates that the Chinese children have an accurate assessment and perception on their body weight. This finding is consistent with a recent study conducted to Korean adolescents that they have accurate perception between actual BMI and perception of body weight (Kim & Kim, 2003). It also reflects the different phenomenon to the western society in which distortion of individuals' body weight and image is relatively popular (Paquette & Raine, 2004; Thompson & Smolak, 2001). Western women and young girls, who are already at a healthy weight, have been preoccupied with tremendous weight concern. And non-realistic judgment of body shape characterized by perfectionism, body obsession and narcissism leads into pursuit of ultra-thinness (Lindeman, 1999).

With regards to the ideal body rating, BMI, body fat subscale and appearance subscale have no associations with children's ideal body shape. It may reflect to the fact that Chinese children dream or expect an ideal body without considering how fat or slim they actually are, but just depends upon factors other than their current body size. To illustrate this issue, Thompson and Smolak (2001) stipulated that youngsters including boys and girls, are heavily influenced by the mass media's projection on the appearance standard. Super model body shape in which has been obsessed by adults only, right now, it applies to children too. Both researchers also suggested that the influencing factors to children's body shape or body satisfaction are extensive besides media. They are parents' weight practice or attitudes, peers' body ideal, teasing pressure on their body, unrealistic images of attractiveness, early pubertal maturation, sexual abuse or harassment. Based upon the present finding, the above-mentioned social factors should be monitored proactively and carefully in order to prevent the body dissatisfaction syndromes including excessive body weight concern, eating disorder, dysmorphic disorder. As a result, Chinese children can immune from all of these unhealthy body weight related sicknesses which are getting popular in western societies.

The first hierarchical regression analysis indicated that actual body rating has stronger predictive ability to predict children's actual fatness (BMI). This finding implies that Chinese children are quite precise and realistic to their body shape. The discrepancy between their perception of body size or weight is very small. Although ideal body rating is not as strong as actual body rating being a predictor variable, the result suggested that all children would like to reduce their body weight to achieve their ideal figure. This finding demonstrated that the western influence that slimmer body is a more beautiful body has been conquering the Chinese belief regarding the standard of human body aesthetic.

To answer the second research question, another hierarchical regression analysis was conducted to find out which constructs are predictive to the appearance scale in Chinese children. It is expected that the actual-ideal body rating discrepancy could explain the appearance perception of Chinese children because the discrepancy score refers to the body dissatisfaction level either the individual is underweight or overweight. Results demonstrated that only age was found significant in predicting appearance while all other constructs did not. This finding suggested that the perception of children being attractive or ugly is totally independent from their actual fatness (BMI) and the discrepancy of their body ratings. The hypothesis which expected bigger discrepancy would induce larger dissatisfaction of children's perception of body attractiveness or ugliness is irrelevant, and therefore rejected. This finding is consistent with previous studies conducted by Raudsepp (2000) and Markey, Markey and Birch (2004) that body attractiveness or satisfaction is not related to individual's actual body fatness although these studies only examined adult females. Other cross-cultural studies conducted in Arabian country (Musaiger, Shahbeek, & Al-Mannai, 2004) and Poland (Forbes, Doroszewicz, Card, & Adams-Curtis, 2004) indicated that body shape preference of Arab women and body ideal of Polish women are found irrelevant with their actual body fatness. This study suggested that the finding can be universal and beyond cultural boundaries.

Then, what kind of factors influence Chinese children's perception of attractiveness is a very interesting issue to explore, if actual body fatness and actual-ideal body discrepancy are not underneath components. According to the recent western literature, there are two categories which might explain how people view their body appearance. First are the physical components that include general physical self-worth, exercise behavior, physical competence, and skill performance (Hayes, Crocker, & Kowalski, 1999; Raudsepp, Viira, & Liblik, 1999; Reel, 2001; Smith, Hale, & Collins, 1998). Social elements like gender role, parental weight practice, exercise environment and atmosphere, mass media belongs to the second category (Cameron & Ferraro, 2004; Leit, Gray, & Pope-Jr, 2002; Miller & Heinrich, 2001; Ogle & Damhorst, 2003; Yin, 2001). The first category contentions may need to be reconsidered since more and more recent findings demonstrated a similar message with the present study that physical components and actual body fatness did not contribute much to the perception of body attractiveness. This can be an implication that the second category i.e. socio-cultural are more influential than body elements like body fatness, perception or fitness, etc to individual's body attractiveness. Unfortunately, all these are adult studies and more children study is needed for follow up and further clarification.

Cultural ideal body shape in western societies has been an interesting issue in past 40 years and it may be able to provide some hints for reference. Garner and Garfinkel, Schwartz and Thompson (1980) and Wallace (2001) had documented the shift and a longitudinal trend toward a slimmer ideal shape for females. They found that the magazines and TV media demonstrated a thinner standard particular in the last decade and the slimmer body symbolized individuals' social status and self-satisfaction. Socio-cultural epidemic has been labeled to this sociological pressure to be thinner. Weigh control is equal to self-control and deemed a successful element in society (Grogan & Richard, 2002). Likewise, social comparison is another element raised to explain this phenomenon (Thomsen, Bower, & Barnes, 2004). Thomsen and his colleagues found that physical prowess was found lesser and lesser influential on this issue in adolescents. Instead, socio-cultural context of body appearance is more emphasized. Paquette and Raine (2004) further revealed that body appearance is not a static construct in females, but is dynamic and fluctuates with new environments and experiences. This ever-changing construct depends on the updated interpretation of individuals through their digestion and absorption of surrounding media. It can result in either positive or negative outcomes, i.e. self-confident or self-critical. But most cases are negative self-judgment among females (Thomsen et al., 2004). They suggested that it is a self-reflective process that the re-interpretation of body appearance will constantly occur consciously or unconsciously (Paquette & Raine, 2004).

A body of recent literature has suggested that internalization of social stereotypes of slimmer body for women and muscular for men is an important contributor in individuals' body perception (Druxman, 2003; Halliwell & Dittmar, 2004; Jones, Vigfusdottir, & Lee, 2004; Tiggemann & McGill, 2004). It is believed that certain body norm and conformity, reactions to this norm have been established and internalized in western (Taub, Fanfilk, & McLorg, 2003). The stereotypical gender expectation on body appearance is considered very static or rigid in females especially (Jagger, 2001). This western stereotype even extends to special population including pregnant or physically disabled individuals (Earle, 2003; Taub et al., 2003) and permeates into different ethnicity like Arabian, Brazilian, Chinese, Israeli, Turkish, through TV, fashion magazine and other medias (Almeida Junior, 2001; Davidson, Thill, & Lash, 2002; Musaiger et al., 2004). Among these people from different countries, consistent misconception of "ideal body appearance" is frequently demonstrated in both women and men's judgment and the cultural boundary seems to be attenuated and fading out recently. Instead, a uniformed idea of "ideal body" is creeping in and goes beyond physical and cultural boundaries of diverse cultures (Demarest & Allen, 2000; Safir, Flaisher-Kellner, & Rosenmann, 2005).

All these findings lead to the direction that body appearance is no longer a physical attribute and the present finding provided support to it. Likewise, cultural differences become to play a lesser role in shaping body norm due to the fact that ideal body becomes a social learning perspective (Markey, Tinsley, Ericksen, Ozer, & Markey, 2002; Safir et al., 2005). Consequently, sociological issue or presentation is the only one left for a meaningful explanation. Different sociological constructs including consumerism, gender role identity, age, social comparison, peer pressure, media, have shown that sociological consideration should be paid more attention to prevent and monitor misconception on body perception (Agliata & Tantleff-Dunn, 2004; Almeida Junior, 2001; Grogan & Richard, 2002; Jagger, 2001; Ortiz & Houvouras, 2003; Tiggemann & McGill, 2004).

Regarding the gender and age impact on the children's body appearance, age is found as the only significant but negative predictor in the present study. It means that the older the children's are, the more body dissatisfaction they experienced. This finding is partially consistent with the recent findings although the variance explained is not strong. Kanter, Agliata and Tantleff-Dunn (2001) discovered that both genders have significant negative perception of aging effect on their physical appearance and females are found more vulnerable and willing to consider all artificial strategies including cosmetic surgery. They suggested that age and gender have very important impact on determining both males' and females' body satisfaction and attractiveness. Another study conducted by Ortiz and Houvouras (2003) also confirmed Kanter et al. finding that age is rated as one of the sociological factors in differentiating students' interpretations on ideal body appearance. Again, gender and age are deemed equally important in the self-assessment of body appearance in the most recent study of Safir et al. (2005). To conclude, the unique finding of the present study is that gender effect on body appearance is excluded and age is the sole factor imposes body appearance concern in Chinese children.

To explain the age influence, recent studies in the literature have investigated exclusively to college students and young adults. This age group is self-evident that they are very alert to their body characteristics among peers since socially determined appearance is clearer and more important than pre-adolescent children (Lau, Lee, Ransdell, Yu, & Sung, 2004). Older students in college had more concern about their body appearance and this could have a greater impact on their body satisfaction or dissatisfaction than the pre-adolescents (Moode & Wiggins, 1999). Age factor, therefore, is expected to play a critical role in body concern between older and younger student. Moode and Wiggins (1999) suggested that the maturation process due to aging can be a major factor accounting for the body appearance concern. Furthermore, recent studies indicated that the discrepancy of body concern or obsession between genders is getting closer although not equally serious (Agliata & Tantleff-Dunn, 2004; Grogan & Richard, 2002; Phares, Steinberg, & Thompson, 2004). Grogan and Richard (2002) stated that males are also suffering from body dissatisfaction although their desirable body shape is muscular instead of slimness for females. But the perfectionism or narcissism is still the origin which leads to heavier anxiety on their body appearance (Druxman, 2003).

CONCLUSION

In the present study, the sociological importance has been singled out for further investigation. According to the sociological studies, mass media, body accessories, parents' weight practice or attitudes, peers' body ideal, teasing pressure on their body, unrealistic images of attractiveness, early pubertal maturation, sexual abuse or harassment have contributed to the body stereotype overwhelmingly especially for young generations (Jagger, 2001; Ortiz & Houvouras, 2003; Reaves, Hitchon, Park, & Yun, 2004; Thompson & Smolak, 2001; Tiggemann & McGill, 2004). Consequently, it is imperative to examine the extent of sociological impacts on body perception solely in the future study.

Cultural difference is considered by the researcher that it is still very influential but the globalization effect has pervaded into different regions in the world. A uniformed body appearance norm is growing and it seems that it is irresistible. On the contrary, regional or unique body culture to appreciate or accept different body shapes or sizes as a desirable body image such as Samoa, in which fatness is desirable body culture, is fading out. Instead, cultural body norm is replaced by western super model figure. This phenomenon is supported by the findings of different Asian, Arabian, and South American studies that body norm becomes more westernized (Almeida Junior, 2001; Davidson et al., 2002; Kim & Kim, 2003; Musaiger et al., 2004).

In order to ensure broader range and acceptance of different body shapes and avoid stereotyped body obsession, it is imperative to implement certain measures to counter-balance the slim-beauty logic and the unlimited drive to thinness. The following are certain measures which may be able to help enhance body satisfaction without too critical of their body appearance:

1.   Care and value your body at all times.
2.   Dress the way you feel good.
3.   Participate enjoyable physical activity to boost your self-esteem.
4.   Learn to trust your body.
5.   View yourself as a whole body instead of focusing on certain body parts.
6.   Set goals on physical and emotional health instead of physical appearance
                                                                          (Druxman, 2003).

To conclude, the dynamic relationship of sociological, cultural factors and globalization or westernization effect on the body appearance norm deserves in-depth investigation across different populations. The researcher in the present study believes that the body norm will be getting more uniformed in terms of the aesthetic standard and the drive to thinness will continue to dominate if no appropriate measures to alert the negative affect to the public. As a result, the above proposed measure should be implemented as soon as possible to alleviate this problem.

REFERENCES

Agliata, D., & Tantleff-Dunn, S. (2004). The impact of media exposure on males' body image. *Journal of Social and Clinical Psychology, 23(1)*, 7-22.

Almeida Junior, A. R. (2001). The electronic mirror. *Cadernos do IFAN, 28*, 49-72.

Ball, G. D. C., Marshall, J. D., Roberts, M., & McCargar, L. J. (2001). Adiposity- and sex-related differences in physical activity, aerobic fitness, and self-esteem among 6-10 year old children. *Avante Gloucester, 7(2)*, 14-26.

Berg, F. M. (1997). *Afraid to eat: Children and teens in weight crisis (2nd ed.)*: Healthy Weight Publishing Network.

Cameron, E. M., & Ferraro, F. R. (2004). Body satisfaction in college women after brief exposure to magazine images. *Perceptual & Motor Skills, 98(3)*, 1093-1099.

Crocker, P. R. E., Snyder, J., Kowalski, K. C., & Hoar, S. (2000). Don't let me be fat or physically incompetent! The relationship between physical self-concept and social physique anxiety in canadian high performance female adolescent athletes. *Avante, 6(3)*, 16-23.

Davidson, D., Thill, A. D. W., & Lash, D. (2002). Male and female body shape preferences of young children in the united states,mainland china and turkey. *Child Study Journal, 32(3)*, 131-143.

Demarest, J., & Allen, R. (2000). Body image: Gender, ethnic, and age differences. *Journal of Social Psychology, 140(4)*, 465-472.

Department of Health. (2005). Http://www.Info.Gov.Hk/dh/.

Druxman, L. (2003). The body image. *IDEA Health & Fitness Source, Nov*, 40-48.

Earle, S. (2003). "bumps and boobs": Fatness and women's experiences of pregnancy. *Women's Studies International Forum, 26(3)*, 245-252.

Faraway, J. J. (2005). *Linear model with r*. Fla.: Chapman & Hall.

Forbes, G. B., Doroszewicz, K., Card, K., & Adams-Curtis, L. (2004). Association of the thin body label, ambivalent sexism, and self-esteem with body acceptance and the preferred body size of college women in poland and the united states. *Sex Roles: A Journal of Research, 50*, 331-345.

Garner, D. M., Garfinkel, P. E., Schwartz, D., & Thompson, M. (1980). Cultural expectations of thinness in women. *Psychological Reports, 47*, 483-491.

Grogan, S., & Richard, H. (2002). Body image: Focus groups with boys and men. *Men and Masculinities, 4(3)*, 219-232.

Halliwell, E., & Dittmar, H. (2004). Does size matter? The impact of model's body size on women's body-focused anxiety and advertising effectiveness. *Journal of Social and Clinical Psychology, 23(1)*, 104-122.

Hayes, S. D., Crocker, P. R. E., & Kowalski, K. C. (1999). Gender differences in physical self-perceptions, global self-esteem and physical activity: Evaluation of the physical self-perception profile model. *Journal of Sport Behavior, 22(1)*, 1-4.

Hill, A. J., & Williams, J. (1998). Psychological health in a non-clinical sample of obese women. *International Journal of Obesity, 22(6)*, 578-583.

International Obesity Taskforce. (2003). *Waiting for a green light for health? Europe at the crossroads for diet and disease. IOTF position paper*. London: IOTF.

Jagger, E. (2001). Marketing molly and melville: Dating in a postmodern, consumer society. *Sociology, 35(1)*, 39-57.

Jones, D. C., Vigfusdottir, T. H., & Lee, Y. (2004). Body image and the appearance culture among adolescent girls and boys. *Journal of Adolescent Research, 19(3)*, 323-339.

Kanter, A., Agliata, D., & Tantleff-Dunn, S. (2001). *College students' attitudes towards age-related changes in physical appearance*. Paper presented at the Annual Conference of the American Psychological Association, San Francisco, CA.

Katzmarzyk, P. T., & Davis, C. (2001). Thinness and body shape of playboy centerfolds from 1978 to 1998. *International Journal of Obesity, 25*, 590-592.

Kim, O., & Kim, K. (2003). Comparisons of body mass index, perception of body weight, body shape satisfaction, and self-esteem among korean adolescents. *Perceptual & Motor Skills, 97(3)*, 1339-1346.

Kraig, K. A., & Keel, P. K. (2001). Weight-based stigmatization in children. *International Journal of Obesity, 25(11),* 1661-1666.

Lau, P. W. C., Lee, A., Ransdell, L., Yu, C. W., & Sung, R. Y. T. (2004). The association between global self-esteem, physical self-concept and actual versus ideal body size rating in chinese primary school children. *International Journal of Obesity, 28(2)*, 314-319.

Lee, Chan, Kwok & Hsu (2005). Relationship between control and the intermediate term outcome of anorexia nervosa in Hong Kong. *The Australian and New Zealand journal of psychiatry, 39(3),* 141-145.

Leit, R. A., Gray, J. J., & Pope-Jr, H. G. (2002). The media's representation of the ideal male body: A cause for muscle dysmorphia? *International Journal of Eating Disorders, 31(3),* 334-338.

Lindeman, A. K. (1999). Quest for ideal weight: Costs and consequences. *Medicine & Science in Sports & Exercise, 31(8),* 1135-1140.

Markey, C. N., Markey, P. M., & Birch, L. L. (2004). Understanding women's body satisfaction: The role of husbands. *Sex Roles: A Journal of Research, 51*, 209-216.

Markey, C. N., Tinsley, B. J., Ericksen, A. J., Ozer, D. J., & Markey, P. M. (2002). Preadolescents' perceptions of females' body size and shape: Evolutionary and social learning perspectives. *Journal of Youth and Adolescence, 31(2),* 137-146.

Marsh, H. W., Marco, I. T., & Abcy, F. H. (2002). Cross-cultural validity of the physical self-description quesitonnaire: Comparison of factor structures in australia, spain, and turkey. *Research Quarterly for Exercise and Sport, 73*, 257-270.

Marsh, H. W., Richards, G. E., Jonhnson, S., Roche, L., & Tremayne, P. (1994). Physical self-description quesionnaire: Psychometric properties and a multitrait-multimethod analysis of relations to existing instruments. *Journal of Sport and Exercise Psychology, 16*, 270-305.

Marsh, H. W., & Roche, L. (1996). Predicting self-esteem from perceptions of actual and ideal ratings of body fatness: Is there only one ideal "supermodel"? *Research Quarterly for Exercise and Sport, 67(1),* 13-26.

Miller, J. L., & Heinrich, M. (2001). Gender role conflict in middle school and college female athletes and non-athletes. *Physical Educator, 58(3),* 124-133.

Moode, F. M., & Wiggins, M. S. (1999). An analysis of the body esteem of female high school and college athletes. *K.A.H.P.E.R.D. Journal, 35(1),* 19-21.

Musaiger, A. O., Shahbeek, N. E., & Al-Mannai, M. (2004). The role of social factors and weight status in ideal body-shape preferences as perceived by arab women. *Journal of Biosocial Science, 36(6),* 699-707.

Nardini, M. (1998). *Body image, disordered eating, and obligatory exercise among women fitness instructors. Eugene, Or.:* Microform Publications, University of Oregon.

Ogle, J. P., & Damhorst, M. L. (2003). Mothers and dauhters: Interpersonal approaches to body and dieting. *Journal of Family Issues, 24(4),* 448-487.

Ortiz, M. M., & Houvouras, S. K. (2003). *Ideal female and male bodies: An analysis of college students' drawing.* Paper presented at the Southern Sociological Society.

Paquette, M., & Raine, K. (2004). Sociocultural context of women's body image. *Social Science & Medicine, 59(5),* 1047-1058.

Phares, V., Steinberg, A. R., & Thompson, J. K. (2004). Gender differences in peer and parental influences: Body image disturbance, self-worth, and psychological functioning in preadolescent children. *Journal of Youth and Adolescence, 33(5)*, 421.

Philips, J. M., & Drummond, M. J. N. (2001). An investigation into the body image perception, body satisfaction and exercise expectations of male fitness leaders: Implications for professional practice. *Leisure Studies, 20(2)*, 95-105.

Phillips, R. G., & Hill, A. J. (1998). Fat, plain, but not friendless: Self-esteem and peer acceptance of obese pre-adolescent girls. *International Journal of Obesity, 22*, 287-293.

Raudsepp, L. (2000). Perceived and actual physical competence and body attractiveness in young females. *Anthropology*, 171-177.

Raudsepp, L., Viira, R., & Liblik, R. (1999). Perceived physical competence and achievement goal orientations as related with physical activity of adolescents. *Acta Kinesiologiae, 41999*, 186-198.

Reaves, S., Hitchon, J. B., Park, S., & Yun, G. W. (2004). "you can never be too thin"-or can you? A pilot study on the effects of digital manipulation of fashion models' body size, leg length and skin color. *Race, Gender & Class, 11(2)*, 140-155.

Reel, J. J. (2001) Slim enough to swim? Weight pressures for competitive swimmers and coaching implications. *The Sport Journal, 4(2)*.

Safir, M. P., Flaisher-Kellner, S., & Rosenmann, A. (2005). When gender differences surpass cultural differences in personal satisfaction with body shape in israeli college students. *Sex Roles: A Journal of Research, 52*, 369-378.

Smith, D. K., Hale, B. D., & Collins, D. (1998). Measurement of exercise dependence in bodybuilders. *Journal of Sport Medicine and Physical Fitness, 38(1)*, 66-74.

Sparkes, A. C. (1997). Reflections on the socially constructed physical self. In K. R. Fox (Ed.), *The physical self: From motivation to well-being* (pp. 83-110). Champaign: Human Kinetics.

Taub, D. E., Fanfilk, P. L., & McLorg, P. A. (2003). Body image among women with physical disabilities: Internalization of norms and reactions to nonconformity. *Sociological Focus, 36(2)*, 159-176.

Thompson, J. K., & Smolak, L. (2001). Body image, eating disorders, and obesity in youth --- the future is now. In J. K. S. hompson, L. (Ed.), *Body image, eating disorders, and obesity in youth: Assessment, prevention and treatment*. Washington, DC: American Psychological Association.

Thomsen, S. R., Bower, D. W., & Barnes, M. D. (2004). Photographic images in women's health, fitness, and sports magazines and the physical self-concept of a group of adolescent female volleyball players. *Journal of Sport and Social Issues, 28(3)*, 266-283.

Tiggemann, M., & McGill, B. (2004). The role of social comparison in the effect of magazine advertisements on women's mood and body dissatisfaction. *Journal of Social and Clinical Psychology, 23(1)*, 23-44.

Turnbull, J. D., Heaslip, S., & McLeod, H. A. (2000). Pre-school children's attitudes to fat and normal male and female stimulus figures. *International Journal of Obesity, 24(12)*, 1705-1706.

Wallace, D. B. (2001*). The female ideal of undernutrition: An anthropometric analysis of playboy playmates and miss americas.* Paper presented at the Society for the Study of Social Problems.

Yin, Z. (2001). Setting for exercise and concerns about body appearance of women who exercise. *Perceptual & Motor Skills, 93(3)*, 851-855.

In: Body Image: New Research
Editor: Marlene V. Kindes, pp. 243-262

ISBN 1-60021-059-7
© 2006 Nova Science Publishers, Inc.

Chapter XI

BODY IMAGE IN CHILDREN AND MOTOR ABILITY – THE RELATIONSHIP BETWEEN HUMAN FIGURE DRAWINGS AND MOTOR ABILITY

Chie Tanaka

Kobe Shinwa Women's University
51-1111 Kobe City North Ku bell Orchid Taipei Cho 7-13-1, Japan

ABSTRACT

In this research, in order to figure out how normal healthy children actually regard their own bodies, the Human Figure Drawing test: Goodenough-Harris Drawing test (also called Draw-A-Man test, or DAM test) was used as one resource tool, and body image in children was scored from the development process of human figure drawings quantitatively. Since the body is the key to both motor ability and sports activities, they have an intimate relationship with body image, thus suggesting that physical exercise changes body image. For this reason, a survey of motor ability was performed to reveal its mutual relationships with the DAM test, which is thought to hold a relationship with body image. For the human figure drawing scoring, based on Goodenough's handbook of human intelligence testing, one point was awarded for each of 15 body parts that met achievement criteria for that drawing component (for a maximum of 15 points). In our study, the total score is the body image score, and the higher the score, the greater the child's awareness of body parts, and that child can be considered to have a more developed body image. Since previous research has shown that motor ability in children from 4.0 to 6.5 years of age is comprised of the lower range of power, flexibility, muscle strength, balance, and endurance, the four categories of 25-meter dash, standing jump, softball throw, and body support time were surveyed. With regards to the relationship between DAM test and motor ability, in 4-year olds, while a significant correlation could not be determined between body image score as a score of 15 body parts that could be drawn correctly in the human figure drawing, and the total score of the four motor ability tests (using T scores), a significant positive correlation was observed for 5-year olds (r = .284). These results showed that the higher the child's motor ability, the greater the change in body image, the higher the awareness of body parts, and the more firmly established body image held by the child. Also, that individual differences for human figure drawing and motor ability were smaller and more stable for 5-year olds than 4-year olds was indicated as one factor affecting the correlation between body image and motor ability.

Keywords: young children, body image, motor ability.

PURPOSE

Body image, as a component element of self-concept, has been a topic of interest for years, and to this day remains a multidimensional phenomenon defined in a variety of ways (Cash, 1990). Schilder (1935) said this body image reflects the self-concept of one's own body. Gorman (1969) asserted that body image is a fundamental concept of our own bodies. Furthermore, Fisher (1990) recently defined body image as the "psychological experience of one's own body." Cash (1990) stated that body image is "a view from within." McCrea, Summerfield, and Rosen (1982) regarded body image as "the subjective evaluation of one's own body and the feelings and attitudes attached to this evaluation." Taking these comments into consideration, in this study body image was defined as the perception or awareness of body through life experiences.

Body image research has mainly been conducted in the psychiatry and psychology fields. However, very little attention has been directed to body image in the field of education (Naruse, 1977). The goal of the field of education is not limited to handing down culture through instructors and lesson materials and the development of thinking ability, but education also aids children and students to develop well adjusted personalities and self-realization skills. Formation of appropriate body image is thought to be the basis for a healthy adaptive personality in children and students. The same can be said for the field of child care, and there is value in performing research specifically targeting children in that changes in body image can be thought of as relatively early traits.

Childhood is generally considered to be the period from approximately two years old to approximately six years old, and according to the Scammon (1930) development curve, 80% of the neural system is completed by around age four. The changes in motor ability and neural functions during this period are dramatic, and this is the main physical period of development for physical development as well. Even though these changes in structure and outward appearance are occurring, in body image research targeting children, Nagy (1953) and Gellert (1962) found that children only held an extremely basic concept of their own bodies. Also, Kasuga (1990) stated that from infancy, the development of body image is largely dependent on the interpersonal synchronous mechanisms also tied to later development, and furthermore Wallon (1965) regarded the formation of body image and personality as being closely linked.

Most previous research targeting children also involved illnesses or was clinical in nature, conducted to discover "distorted (peculiar or abnormal)" body image, and was conducted with the objective of returning the subject to health or correcting an illness. When considering body image from a human development perspective, most research cites that the development of body image of a single individual, together with changes in the body of that person who is continuing to develop, body image dominates both of these as the conceptualization of the body that is integrated into the individual as that individual matures. Most researchers agree that this image is formed by seven years of age.

From previous studies that were performed in an attempt to understand body as a powerful element in personality, it is suggested that all physical exercise and activity have a relationship with body image because they are conducted through the body as the medium, and that these motor activities contribute to changes in body image (Fisher and Cleveland, 1958; McCrea et al., 1982). In a study that targeted university age men and women, Adame et al. (1990) found a positive correlation between forward looking positive outlook on physical exercise and body image. However, there are no similar previous studies that take children as the research subjects.

Many activities are inseparable from development and unification of body image, and for children, it is thought that the various senses and muscular sensations that are acquired through actively engaging in the environment play a role in developing body image. On the other hand, this suggests that less physically active children should have less of this kind of opportunity. Thus, for this research, from a developmental perspective, in order to investigate body image, an important keystone in self concept and awareness of the physical world, a method was adopted based on the human figure drawing method to visualize body image that children hold inside themselves. Thus, for body image, we set as the objective of our study to disclose the relationship between human figure drawing and motor ability. Beginning from body image, with traditional methods alone it is not possible to regard these intrinsic body-related images. However, self-figure drawing is cited as one way internal body image can be externally represented. Swensen (1968) successfully defined a person's drawing of a human figure as an indication of his "body image," and validated other purported measures against the drawing of the human figure.

With male and female high school student as subjects, Delatte and Hendrickson (1982) utilized Human Figure Drawing to examine the relationship between self-drawing size and self-esteem. When considering the correlation between self-drawing size and self-esteem as measured by using the Rosenberg Self-Esteem Scale, they results confirmed that, for males only, there were significant positive correlations between vertical height of self-drawings and self-esteem, and self-drawing surface areas and self-esteem.

Accordingly, the Human Figure Drawing is considered a useful tool to visualize body image. Also, since Human Figure Drawing is not dependent on language, it is presumed to be effective in body image research on young children where limited language facilities would make this evaluation difficult. An estimate of a child's intellectual maturity may be obtained from the Draw-A-Person test using the scoring criteria and normative data supplied by the Harris revision (1963) of the Goodenough Draw-A-Man test (Goodenough, 1926). The Human Figure Drawing, of which the Draw-A-Man test is an example, has been widely used as a psychological assessment procedure (Harris and Pinder, 1977).

Regarding body image in children, research by Gellert (1962) on the initial development of body image demonstrated that young children have a vague self-image of their own bodies. Additionally, research by Fisher (1986) suggests that children and adults maintain fundamentally different body images.

Reports show that motor ability of school age children in Japan is worsening year by year. According to the statistical reports from 1997 (Kondo et al., 1998), significant reductions occurred in all categories regardless of sex and age group compared to the results from 11 years earlier, making us again aware of the downward trend in motor ability in children. In research investigating the development of motor ability and motor skills in children, there are studies that investigated the quantitative measurement of motor ability (Matsuda and Kondo, 1978), the various factors contributing to or affecting motor ability and skills structure (Aoyagi and Matsuura, 1982), research investigating the correlation between quantitative development and qualitative development (Kim and Matsuura, 1988). However, there is no previous research looking at the relation between motor ability and body image, so if it is possible to reveal the conceptual characteristics behind body image, this should forward language based educational improvements including ways to verbally communicate with children and types of physical play that positively impact motor development.

With 8- to 12-yr.-old primary school children as subjects, from the perspective of the Collins (1991) picture scale and actual height, weight, and body fat measurements, Rolland, et al. (1996) investigated what children consider to be the most ideal physique. In all groups, girls were more likely than boys to choose pictures depicting figures physically slimmer than themselves. Much of the recent research – including those studies cited so far in this paper has concerned itself with eating disorders, with the goal of explaining the relationship between ideal body image and eating disorders such as anorexia in adolescent men and women. Our intention is to develop norms for body image in children that take into account their special development circumstances. With such norms, it would be possible to detect abnormal body images to facilitate the prevention of environmental adaptation disorders.

Also, for instances of abnormal body image, it will be easier to develop physical activity programs to improve body image or prevent abnormal body image that could be used at the place of childcare or at the home. Thus, with regarding motor ability as physical achievement in physical exercise or sports activities, we perform motor ability tests to reveal its relationship with body image. If a relationship between motor ability and body image in children is found to exist, this should serve as an aid to the development of exercise programs to improve body image. Also, it is expected to aid in resolving problems of adaptability in social skills and developmental disorders, two issues that are problems in childcare and the home. Concurrent with our look at developmental changes of body image in children, we shall also consider these characteristics from the perspectives of age and sex difference.

METHOD

1. Subjects

A total of 120 children (60 boys, 60 girls) attending public kindergarten in Nara City were the target of this research. 62 children were 4-year olds (age range; 4 years, 3 months – 5 years, 3 months) and 58 children were 5-year olds (age range; 5 years, 3 months – 6 years,

3 months). Since Year 4 and Year 5 curricula in kindergartens in Japan is markedly different from a developmental perspective, and the number of years a child has attended in school is different, it was felt that one "school year" difference would have a large relationship with age and sex. Accordingly, we set two age groups for Year 4 and Year 5 students, arranged with children between 4:3 yr. and 5:3 yr. in the 4-yr.-old group and listed as 4-yr.-olds. Children between 5:3 yr. and 6:3 yr. were in the 5-yr.-old group.

2. Measurement

1) DAM Method

In this study, as a method of revealing in what way children are actually cognizant of their bodies, the human figure drawing method is used. According to Ayres (1961), the most commonly used method to measure body image is the human figure drawing, and the human figure drawing is a direct reflection of the way individuals recognize their own bodies. Considering the objective to quantitatively measure human figure drawings, and the fact that it is difficult to standardize measurement of drawing tests that include language instruction or scoring, of the many human figure drawing methods, in this research we focus on the Goodenough-Harris Drawing Test (also called the Draw-A-Man Test, or DAM) as a human figure drawing evaluation method. A psychological quantitative approach of Goodenough (1926) and Harris (1963), The DAM method quantifies human figure drawings in order to reveal the intellectual level of children. The test is also standardized in Japan (Kobayashi, 1977). Due to the non-linguistic properties of the DAM evaluation method, it is especially suited for young children for evaluation of traits that are difficult to express through language. In our study, the methodology and scoring of the human figure drawing experiment was performed based on the methods outlined by Kobayashi (1977). Since the DAM method is based on a developmental scale extracted from human figure drawings, it can be applied to children from approximately three years of age. This is the age at which the human body image begins to take shape. Furthermore, the drawing ratio of drawing items as proposed by Goodenough increases for the period between ages three and nine together with the developmental stages, and has high statistical significance as a method of evaluating level of development (Kobayashi, 1977). Thus, from the perspective of understanding developmental tendencies in young children as well the DAM method, it is most appropriate.

For the items to be scored, the scoring categories that shall be used in this study are 1) human figure body parts, 2) size ratio of human figure body parts, and 3) level of detail of the human figure and the body parts. The results are evaluated for developmental level using a comprehensive score based on 1) agreement between senses—motor system, 2) body image, 3) orientation—space awareness, and 4) amount of body-related awareness, and they form a portion of the scored items used for scoring body image. Also, for the theories of children's drawings of Schilder (1935) and Goodenough (1926) who state that "there is a special relationship between expression of the sense of sight and body image," this suggests the existence of a relationship between body image and the DAM method. From the human figures drawn by children, together with understanding the traits formed by body image for each of the body parts and revealing the age and sex differences, body image score is evaluated in children from the human figure drawing developmental process. Then, when taking body image score as the total score for the human figure drawing, the objective of this study was to analyze body image traits of children from the perspective that children with higher scores will have greater awareness of the body parts, and therefore also possess a formed body image.

a) Procedure

From the results of a preliminary survey, we selected Number 2B pencils, erasers, and 380mm x 270mm size construction paper (used in the vertical orientation). As the result of discussions with childcare providers who preferred that a drawing board be used for the entire class if possible, and that drawing activities occur in the place where children normally do their drawings, from the group method and individual methods (Kobayashi, 1977), in this research the group method was selected. For the DAM method, the subjects were asked to draw a single person, being told, "Please draw one person. Draw the whole person from head to toe." In Kobayashi (1977), the childcare provider was instructed to verify the gender of the first human figure drawing completed, and then ask the child to draw a member of the opposite sex on a sheet of drawing paper folded in half. That same method was used in this experiment.

b) DAM Measurement

Of drawings collected from the children, only the male human figure images were used for scoring (Kobayashi, 1977) in this study. Commenting on expression of self through drawing clothing, Machover (1953) states that since male images wear pants unlike female images, who may wear skirts, scoring of males allows scoring for especially the area where the legs connect to the body. It is for this reason that only male images were used for scoring in this study. Also, with consideration to the anatomical categorization of body parts of Gorman (1969), general age shift of drawing components (Hibi, 1994), and body part awareness of Matsunaga (1996), drawings were categorized into the 15 categories of head (head outline), trunk, neck, arms, hands (palms), legs, feet, fingers, hair, eyebrows, eyes, nose, mouth, ears and clothing. For scoring, based on Goodenough's handbook of human intelligence testing (Kobayashi, 1977), one point was awarded for each of 15 body parts that met achievement criteria for that drawing component (for a maximum of 15 points). In our study, the total score is the body image score, and the higher the score, the greater the child's awareness of body parts, and the more that child may be considered to have a developed body image. Also, for age, our study considered the developmental changes between 4-year olds (second year preschool students) and 5-year olds (third year preschool students).

2) Motor Ability Test

From the 1950s, there are several studies that used factor analysis methods to investigate the structure of motor ability in children. According to Larson and Yocom (1951), motor ability is a hierarchical structure comprised of physique and basic motor skills (running, jumping, throwing). The basic motor skills here include flexibility, balance, and agility. Also, from previous research by Murase and Idemura (1990), motor ability of children aged 4.0 – 6.5 years is reported to be comprised of the subordinate realms domains of power, flexibility, muscle strength, balance and muscle stamina, and are further understood to be comprised of the basic actions of "standing," "running," "jumping" and "throwing." Based on the observations of these previous studies, in our study, four categories—25-meter dash, standing jump, softball throw, and body support time (Suzuki et al., 1980; Matsuura et al., 1990; Matsunaga, 1992/1996) —were employed.

a) Measurement of Each Item

25-meter dash (sec): A two member team was directed separate to each end of a line 25 meters long, and at the blow of the whistle to run to the flag (the flag was placed beyond the actual 25 meter goal point). The time to run to the goal line itself, which preceded the actual location of the flag, was manually measured with a stopwatch.

Standing jump (cm): Subjects performed standing jumps on a mat, and the jumping distance from toe to heal was measured. Each subject was measured two times and the best score of the two trials was taken as the result.

Softball throw (m): Using a softball (Child Size 1), subjects performed a single hand overhand throw, and were directed to throw the ball as far as possible from a limit line, without taking a running start. The distance from the limit line to the point where the ball hit the ground was measured in meters. Each subject was measured two times and the best score of the two trials was taken as the result.

Body support time (sec): With two desks placed at approximately the height the elbows of the subject when standing with arms lowered to the body, the elapsed time in seconds was measured for how long subjects could raise themselves up with their two arms (with feet not touching the ground).

RESULTS

1. Quantitative Development of Body Image as Seen in 15 Body Parts

The total number of times each body part could be drawn was taken as the body image score (see Table 1). In order to observe the sex difference and developmental difference tendencies, a t-test was employed. The results of the t-test showed a significantly higher body part awareness for 5-year olds than 4-year olds (t=7.62, p<.001), but a significant difference was not found for sex difference for both 4-year olds or 5-year olds.

2. 15 Body Image Traits for Body Parts According to Age

The body image traits for the 15 body parts for 4-year olds and 5-year olds are shown in Table 2 (figures in parentheses are the drawing ratios). The body parts for which 100% of 4-year olds and 5-year olds were able to draw were the head and eyes. In order to observe the developmental difference tendencies, a χ^2 test was employed. The results of the χ^2 test showed that the body parts for which 5-year olds had significantly higher drawing ratios than 4-year olds were the 10 items of: neck, trunk, arms, legs, feet, fingers, hair, nose, ears, and clothing. Furthermore, 5-year olds had higher drawing ratios which were more than twice as high as those of 4-year olds for the 4 body parts of: neck, feet, fingers, and ears.

Table 1. Body image scores as seen in 15 body parts.

Age		N	M	±	SD	Score Range
4-year olds	Total	62	8.19	±	1.96	4-13
	boys	31	7.81	±	2.12	4-13
	girls	31	8.58	±	1.73	4-12
5-year olds	Total	58	10.67	±	1.57***	8-14
	boys	29	10.38	±	1.40	8-14
	girls	29	10.97	±	1.70	9-14

***$p < .001$

Table 2. Human figure drawing frequency and drawing ratio for each body part.

Body Parts	Age			
	4-year olds		5-year olds	
Head (head outline)	62	(100)	58	(100)	
Neck	15	(24.2)	36	(62.1)	***
Torso	54	(87.1)	58	(100)	**
Arms	57	(91.9)	58	(100)	*
Hands (palms)	0		4	(6.9)	*
Legs	57	(91.9)	58	(100)	*
Feet	5	(8.1)	13	(22.4)	*
Finger	26	(41.9)	53	(91.4)	***
Hair	46	(74.2)	58	(100)	***
Eyebrows	12	(19.4)	14	(24.1)	
Eyes	62	(100)	58	(100)	
Nose	21	(33.9)	31	(53.4)	*
Mouth	60	(96.8)	58	(100)	
Ears	11	(17.7)	27	(46.6)	***
Clothing	21	(33.9)	35	(60.3)	**

Note; ( ) = figures in parentheses are drawing ratios.
*$p < .05$, **$p < .01$, ***$p < .001$

Looking at attributes of drawings of each body part, the drawing ratio was especially high for head and chest, main body trunk parts including the head (head outline), neck, and chest area. Then, the majority of both 4-year olds and 5-year olds were able to draw the four appendages including the arms, hands, legs and feet. However, drawing ratios for hands and feet were especially low for 4-year olds. For facial features, 100% of both 4-year olds and 5-year olds were able to draw the eyes and mouth, but both ages had low drawing ratios for the eyebrows, nose and ears. Also, 5-year olds could draw hair and clothing with 100% drawing ratios.

Figure 1. Human figure drawing developmental example

Next, to investigate the process related to the formation of body image, Figure 1 shows development examples of human figure drawings according to each sex and each age group. These drawings illustrate the trend of developmental changes for human figure drawings drawn by children. One characteristic observed is that of 4-year olds drawing larger heads overall. They use straight lines to represent the four body appendages. Especially human figure drawings drawn by younger[21] 4-year olds, both girls and boys characteristically drew bodies with large heads. They were also unable to draw the fingers and toes of the four appendages. For the older 4-year old boys, a change is evident in that they have used lines to draw fingers and toes. Older 4-year old girls drew the four appendages in three dimensions, and these drawings stand out as looking more human compared to drawings of boys. 5-year olds are more able to draw heads with sizes with better balance to the overall drawing. Younger 5-year old boys are able to draw the four appendages and fingers, but there is no overall balance. A sex difference was observed with younger 5-year old girls, however, being able to draw the four appendages with balanced proportions. Older 5-year old boys showed a change in development compared to younger 5-year old boys, and were able to more accurately draw the location of the four appendages with more balanced proportions. Older 5-year old girls produced drawings with a better overall balance, including the four appendages, and they were also able to draw in detail eyebrows, clothing, and parts of fingers - details which are difficult to draw. Approximately 5-year olds and up begin to add many body-related parts, and a tendency appears in which separate sections with border lines is growing. We can see that the 6-year olds are able to draw with accurate location, size and balance. As evident from the emergence of the neck in drawings of younger 5-year olds compared to earlier ages, the head and body parts share a common boundary at the neck. The ability to draw fingers is present from the older 4-year olds, but it is not until the older 5-year olds before the correct number can be drawn. In this way, from the development shown in human figure drawings, we can see that drawing ability improves with age, as well as the number of body parts that can be drawn. Also, this indicates a trend of development to move from the center to the extremities, and to move from the head to the legs. These developments mirror the same tendency of human development.

3. Drawing Characteristics of Each Body Part

1) Body Trunk

Drawing ratios were especially high for the main body parts including head, neck and chest, showing the same results as Matsunaga and Matsunaga (1997). Both 4-year olds and 5-year olds displayed head drawing ratios of 100%. Also from the fact that especially 4-year olds had only 25% drawing ratios for drawing the neck, indicating that awareness of this body part is low and body image formation is low. However, since the majority of children were able to draw the chest, this indicates high body awareness similar to the head and high body image formation. As seen from trunk body parts, it is thought that awareness comes easily for large body parts such as head and chest, but body parts like the neck are surmised

---

[21] When dividing one year into 12 months, children belonging to the first six months are referred to as 'younger'

to be either difficult to draw even though they can be visually observed and there is awareness, or cannot be drawn consciously. For clothing, an age difference was observed.

2) Four Appendages

The majority of 4-year olds and 5-year olds were able to the arms and legs of the four appendages including the arms, hands, legs and feet, and these results are consistent with the research results of Matsunaga and Matsunaga (1997). Especially because also 100% of 5-year olds were able to draw the arms and legs, this indicates that body part awareness is high and the formation of body image is high. However, for the hands and feet, both 4-year olds and 5-year olds had drawing ratios of less than 25%. It is difficult for children to draw the extremities, and this revealed the low body part awareness and low body image formation. While based on scoring of human figure drawing research conducted Kobayashi (1977) to standardize for DAM, for hands, scoring was performed separately for fingers and wrists. Also, since a ratio is specified whether leg and feet have separate outlines, and height from the sole to the top of the foot, it was surmised that scoring was especially difficult. An age difference was observed for the fingers. It is thought that perhaps even though 4-year olds were visually aware of fingers, they were unable to draw them because their drawing skills were too immature, or because they thought that fingers are included in drawings of arms and hands.

3) Facial Area

The body parts related to the face are mainly the hair, eyes, eyebrows, mouth, ears and nose, and 5-year olds showed higher drawing ratios for hair. Both 4-year olds and 5-year olds had high 100% drawing ratios for the eyes. Based on observations of the order the drawings were completed, this is thought to be related to the fact that most children first drew the head and then the eyes. Also, the eyes and the head were the only body parts that all subject children successfully drew, indicating that body part awareness is high and that it has high body image formation. From the fact that both boys and girls had drawing ratios of less than 25% for the eyebrows, this revealed that awareness of this body part was low as well as low body image formation. This shows that interestingly, the eyebrows are a body part that is difficult to remember to draw, unless we pay attention to them. While no age difference was seen for the mouth, 5-year olds had higher drawing ratios than 4-year olds for both the nose and ears.

4. Motor Ability Traits Attributable to Age and Sex

Table 3 shows the development trend results for each item for each sex of girls and boy, and for each age group. In order to observe the sex difference and developmental difference tendencies, a t-test was employed. Those results showed that 5-year olds had significantly higher motor abilities than 4-year olds for the four categories of 25-meter dash (t=4.57,

children, while those belonging to the second six months are referred to as 'older' children.

p<.001), standing jump (t=3.61, p<.001), softball throw (t=4.08, p<.001), and body support
time (t=3.70, p<.001).

Table 3. Motor ability traits attributable to age and sex.

Items	Age	Sex						
		boys			girls			
25m dash (sec)	4-year olds	6.6	±	0.5	6.7	±	0.5	
	5-year olds	6.1	±	0.7	6.2	±	0.6	
Standing jump (cm)	4-year olds	112.2	±	1.0***	104.3	±	8.2	
	5-year olds	119.4	±	9.1†	112.8	±	14.4	
Softball throw (m)	4-year olds	5.6	±	1.4***	4.2	±	1.0	
	5-year olds	7.4	±	2.4***	5.1	±	1.1	
Body support time (sec)	4-year olds	38.1	±	22.1	39.4	±	31.0	
	5-year olds	54.6	±	31.2	75.9	±	60.7†	

Note; the numerical value = M±SD.
†p < 1.0, ***p < .001

Next, in order to observe sex tendencies for each age, a t-test was performed. For softball
throwing for 5-year olds, boys achieved significantly higher motor ability results than girls
(t=4.53, p<.001). For standing jump boys had a significantly higher tendency than girls
(t=1.69, p<1.0), but for body support time, girls had a significantly higher tendency than boys
(t=1.71, p<1.0). Contrasting with those results, no significant difference was observed for
only the 25-meter dash. Next, for standing jump and softball throwing for 4-year olds, boys
achieved significantly higher motor ability results than girls (t=3.46, p<.001; t=4.31, p<.001).
For body support time and 25-meter dash, significant differences were not observed (t=0.19,
p<1.0; t=1.53, p<1.0). These results revealed that overall, boys tended to excel more than
girls in the categories. For only body support time, in each age group, girls achieved better
scores than boys.

5. Relation of Body Image in Children and Motor Ability

In calculating the correlation between motor ability of children and body image score
(hereafter referred to as BI score), a correlation coefficient was calculated for each year (see
Table 4). Also, in order to investigate the total scores of each category, a T-score was
calculated to standardize the score for each category. From those results, for both 4-year olds
and 5-year olds, a correlation was found between BI score and the total score for each of the
four motor ability tests (hereafter referred to as 4T-score), and in each category a significant
correlation was observed (see Table 4). For the correlation between BI score and 4T score,
while a significant relation was not found for 4-year olds, since a significant positive
correlation was observed for 5-year olds (r=.284) (see Table 4), a subordinate test was
performed to reveal the relationship between motor ability and body image score.

Table 4. Correlation between motor ability of children and body image score for each age.

	BI score	4T score	Standing jump	Body support time	Softball throw	25-m dash
BI score		.284*	.194	.301*	-.057	.026
4T score	-.075		.697**	.519**	.580**	-.168
Standing jump	-.132	.632**		.224	.470**	-.575**
Body support time	.002	.641**	.234		-.126	-.260*
Softball throw	-.061	.716**	.493**	.289*		-.409**
25-m dash	.053	-.180	-.560**	-.353**	-.465**	

Note;Lower left value is data for 4-year olds: upper left value is data for 5-year olds.
The numerical value = correlation coefficient.
*p < .05, **p < .01

Shown in Figure 2 is a distribution diagram which depicts the correlation between BI score and 4T score, and shown in Figure 3 is a distribution diagram which depicts the correlation between BI score and body support time. In Figure 3, for BI score and body support time, the lines are different for boys and girls and there is dispersion, but for BI score and 4T score in Figure 2, the lines for boys and girls are similar, and although girls are situated to the left and boys are situated to the right, the dispersion and line shape are similar.

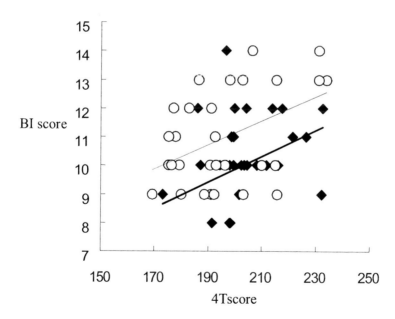

Figure 2. Correlation between BI score and 4T score. Note; ◆=boys: o=girls:=Line shape(boys): = Line shape(girls)

As a subordinate test, in order to observe the sex difference in 5-year olds, a t-test was performed. A significant sex difference was observed for 4T scores, where boys (4T score=203.9) had significantly higher (t=1.97, p<.05) scores than girls (4T score=195.8). Significant sex differences were not indicated for either BI score or body support time.

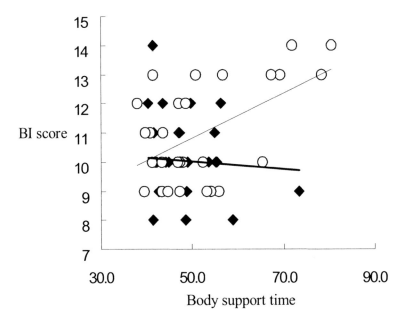

Figure 3. Correlation between BI score and body support time. Note; ◆=boys: o=girls: =Line shape(boys): = Line shape(girls).

DISCUSSION

1. Development of Body Image in Children

From the t-test for BI score which was conducted to observe sex and developmental tendencies, it was revealed that 5-year olds had significantly higher body part awareness than 4-year olds, and a developmental difference tendency revealed an increase of body image formation concordant with increases in age. Since a trunk can be seen in nearly all of the human figure drawings of 5-year olds, this strongly suggests these children have moved from the head-feet drawing developmental stage to the next higher stage. For the period of four years of age, even during Piaget's (1947) pre-operational phase, the symbolic thought stage and intuitive thought phase are located here. For human figure drawings, according to Lowenfeld (1963) and Kellog (1971) who performed research on many pictures drawn by children, in the developmental stage of moving from the symbolic stage to the schematic stage, their results showed that compared to 5-year olds, the drawing completion ratio for 4-year olds for detailed body parts was lower, and the same trend was observed in our the results of our research.

For 5-year olds, the results of our research showed that the basic body parts of the human figure – the face, trunk, and four major appendages - were all clearly drawn. The period between five and six years of age aligns with Piaget's (1947) intuitive thought phase. For human figure drawings, our research results indicated that it is possible to have a comprehensive understanding of placement of each of the parts to be drawn and their interrelations, and especially for detailed parts, the drawing ratios were comparatively high. Overall, the results agree with the findings of Matsunaga and Matsunaga (1997) which indicate that children are able to draw a relatively complex human figure drawing except for the neck, and the awareness of body parts before school age exceeds 80%, the same finding as reported by Kondo (1971).

2. Development of Motor Ability in Children

When comparing the development tendencies for each category for boys and girls for each age, 5-year olds showed significantly higher motor abilities than 4-year olds for each of the four categories of 25-meter dash, standing jump, softball throw, and body support time. In addition to revealing a development difference consistent with increase in age (Nakamura and Matsuura, 1979), these results also indicated that overall, boys tended to excel more than girls. In only the category of body support time did girls performed better than boys for each age group, and in order to further observe the sex difference trend due to age, a t-test was performed. For both 4-year olds and 5-year olds for softball throwing, boys showed significantly higher motor ability than girls, but for the 25-meter dash only, no significant difference was observed. Boys showed significantly higher motor ability than girls for the standing jump, especially for 4-year olds.

As was evident from the standing jump and softball throwing results, there was a tendency for boys to excel in categories that depended upon muscle strength (Ishii et al., 1980; Kobayashi et al., 1990). Our results mirrored the observations of Kondo et al. (1998), which revealed that in childhood, quickness and speed develop earlier in boys than in girls, and that this sex difference increases with age. As was especially evident from the softball throwing results, boys did well in those categories that required finesse and power (Kobayashi et al, 1990). Girls achieved higher average scores than boys for the body support time category, and this tendency increased with increase of age. Even though the body support time activity required muscular endurance, girls excelled in this category for every age group. Especially for muscular endurance, unlike the tendency observed by Kondo et al. (1998), who found sex difference did not tend to be a factor in childhood, our results suggest that girls excel in activities requiring muscular endurance (Gallahue and Ozmun, 1995).

3. Relation of Body Image in Children and Motor Ability

While no significant relation was found between BI scores and 4T scores for 4-year olds, for 5-year olds a significant positive correlation was found between BI scores and 4T scores. These results showed that BI score and 4T score develop with age, and that the higher the child's motor ability, the greater the body image score, and that together with a high awareness of body parts, the child has a firmly established body image of his or her own body. Previous research focusing on the relation between motor ability and intelligence in children had shown a positive correlation between motor ability and intelligence (Shimada, 1984), and the same trend was observed in this study. Supporting Schilder's (1935) assertion that body image in children is cultivated through various senses and physical experiences, we may surmise that body image develops in parallel with the development of senses and motor abilities in children.

From the fact that especially for 5-year olds, the dispersion and line for BI score and 4T score are similar for both boys and girls, the fact that 5-year olds have less variability than 4-year olds in human figure drawing and motor ability, is thought to be one factor involved in the correlation between BI score and 4T score. From these results, according to the approach that BI score and 4T score are necessary in formation of basic body image in children, the following three points can be raised.

1) The Support of each Developmental Stage

In support of each developmental stage, in order to reduce the individual score difference for 4-year olds, it is surmised that individual support is required for the human figure drawings and basic motor skills tasks. This is because it is thought that a clear understanding of the development needs facing each child will lead to developmental results for each child. It is important to foster development of basic motor abilities such as walking, running, jumping, pushing, pulling, throwing, picking up, and kicking, based on "running, jumping and throwing" in everyday life through natural means, and it is thought that because it occurs in the course of daily living, traditional exercise should lead to smooth development of motor activities that lead to acquisition of growth over time. On the other hand, for 5-year olds, more than individual support, it is thought that a certain level of basic ability is formed for motor ability tests are human figure drawings (Piaget, 1947). For example, by engaging in group activities that make use of a ball, such as dodgeball or soccer, it is thought that various practice effects are obtained through this play, and by using these efficiently, this leads to the formation of body image and improved motor abilities. In considering the reason why sex difference was seen in the different types of activities, for body support time, it is suggestive of a correlation with body image, especially in 5-year old girls. Body support time can be cited as unique in that girls had higher scores than boys, but the relation with muscle endurance and sense of balance is thought to be strong.

2) The Perspective of Personality Support

For the perspective of personality support, it is important to develop the stance that children take when interacting with their environment in such a way that they are able to face a single problem without giving up easily. Especially for basic motor skills, this tendency was strongly observed in body support time. However, from the perspective of childcare support, it is important for the caregiver to not be the only individual who is posing challenges to the child, but it is also important that the child is protected. Because it is thought that the degree of enjoyment of exercise and consideration for differences in developmental level are important (Kondo, 1994), the experience of enjoyment in drawing is also thought to be important, and as seen in problem resolution study methods such as the small step method, it is important to present individuals with challenges matching their developmental levels.

3) The Support for Sex Difference

For support for sex difference, from the fact that boys had higher total scores for motor ability than for human figure drawings, it is suggested that boys excel more at motor activities than at human figure drawings. It is possible to think of sex differences in child play as being a factor in these cases. When engaging in active play outdoors, boys naturally are exposed to the experience of using motor skills such as "running" and "throwing." Since it is asserted this difference in experience allows boys to develop motor abilities more quickly than girls (Iwasaki et al., 1999), it surmised that support from motor perspective, including traits of body support time that require support or muscular endurance such as increasing body part awareness (Gallahue and Ozmun, 1995), are necessary in the development of body image.

Unlike boys, it is suggested that girls, on the other hand, excel at human figure drawings more than motor abilities due to the fact that they had higher total scores for human figure drawing than for motor abilities. From previous studies that revealed that boys excelled over girls in development of equilibrium and showed increasing ability with age (Kawakami et al., 1982), except for activities such as body support time which are involved with muscular endurance, an exercise-based approach is needed to foster development of body image. Childhood abilities related to agility and speed are stronger in boys than in girls from an early age, and there is a tendency for this difference grow with age (Kondo et al., 1998), and considering that girls have less outside play experience than boys, this suggests that efforts to increase the amount of active play for girls, including outdoor play through regular play, would have a positive effect. This suggests that these results could be applied in providing active verbal encouragement to children and in developing active play, both of which would positively effect motor ability.

CONCLUSION

In this study, the human figure drawings of children were analyzed from 15 body parts, and a consideration of the traits of childhood body image was conducted, based on the DAM method and relation with motor ability. From those results, for both body image score and motor ability, age-dependent developmental changes were observed. Especially for 5-year olds, a significant positive correlation was found between the body image score and motor ability, thus revealing that the more active the child, the higher the body score, and the higher the awareness of the body parts, and the greater the establishment of the child's own body image. The smaller sizes of the individual differences for human figure drawing and physical development for 4-year olds than 5-year olds was indicated as one factor affecting the correlation between body image and physical development.

Previous research investigating the relation between motor ability and intelligence in children has shown a positive correlation between motor ability and intelligence (Shimada, 1984), and the same tendency was observed in this study, suggesting that the age differences were affected by intellectual differences. From Schilder's (1935) assertion that body image in children is cultivated through various senses and motor experiences, we can surmise that body image in children develops in parallel with the development of their senses and motor development, and this also suggests that it one factor in why 5-year olds who have comparatively greater physical experiences than 4-year olds also have greater awareness of body parts.

As evident in the kindergarten featured in this study, in which an environment has been provided in which standing jumps and other activities can be done naturally in the course of normal play, it is possible to surmise that improvement of motor ability in children is related to the childcare environment. We would like to conduct future research to further investigate the abovementioned approach and to also reveal the type of environment necessary and physical activities that would aid in developing motor ability. The researchers would also like to continue investigating the relationship between the benefit of physical exercise and body image.

ACKNOWLEDGEMENT

The researchers would like to thank the kindergarten teachers and all of the children who participated in this study.

REFERENCES

Adame, D. D., Johnson, T. C., Cole, S. P., Matthiasson, H.& Abbas, M. A. (1990) Physical fitness in relation to amount of physical exercise, body image, and locus of control among college men and women. *Perceptual and Motor Skills, 70*, 1347-1350.

Ayres, A. J (1961) Development of the body scheme in children. *American Journal of Occupational Therapy, 15(3)*, 99-128.

Aoyagi, O., & Matsuura, Y (1982) On the structure of motor ability in childhood. *Japan Journal of Physical Education, Health and Sport Sciences, 26(4)*, 291-303.

Cash, T. F. (1990) The psychology of physical appearance: aesthetics, attributes, and images. In T. F. Cash & T. Pruzinsky (Eds.), *Body images: development, deviance and change*. New York: Guilford. Pp. 52-59.

Collins, M. E. (1991) Body figure perceptions and preferences among preadolescent children. *International Journal of Eating Disorders, 10*, 199-208.

Dalatte, J. & Hendrickson, N. (1982) Human figure drawing size as a measure of self-esteem. *Journal of Personality Assessment, 46(6)*, 603-606.

Fisher, S., & Cleveland, E. S. (1958) *Body image and personality*. New York: Dover Publication.

Fisher, S. (1986) *Development and structure of the body image*. Hillsdale, NJ: Erlbaum

Fisher, S. (1990) The evolution of psychological concepts about the body. In T. F. Cash & T. Pruzinsky (Eds.), *Body images: development, deviance and change*. New York: Guilford. Pp. 3-20.

Goodenough, F. L. (1926) *The measurement of intelligence by drawings*. New York: World Books.

Gellert, E. (1962) Children's conception's of the content and functions of the human body. *Genetic Psychology Monographs, 65*, 293-405.

Gorman, W. (1969) *Body image and the image of the brain.* St. Louis, MO: Warren H. Green.

Gallahue, D. L., & Ozmun, J. C. (1995) *Understanding motor development: Infants, children, adolescents, adults(3rded).* Madison, WI: Brown & Benchmark, Pp.215-223.

Harris, D. B. (1963) *Children's drawings as measures of intellectual maturity: a revision and extension of the Goodenough Draw-A-Man test.* New York: Harcourt, Brace & World.

Harris, D. B., & Pinder, G. D. (1977) Goodenough-Harris Test estimates of intellectual maturity of youths 12-17 years: demographic and socioeconomic factors. *Vital and Health Statistics, Series, 11(159)*, 1-11.

Hibi, H (1994) *Human figure drawing method (DAM): Intelligence and character which are expressed by the picture.* Kyoto: Nakanishiya publication.

Ishi, M., Seki, M., Tokida, N., & Nikaido, K. (1980) Research regarding the motor abilities of preschool children (I): The relation between physical growth and the motor abilities. *Japan Women's College of Physical Education bulletin, 10*, 84-93.

Iwasaki, Y., et al. (1999) *A child's physical activity and mental development.* Tokyo: Konpakusya publication.

Kellogg, R. (1971) *Development process of children's drawings: From Scribbles to Pictures.* Translation by Fukada, N. Nagoya: Reimei publication.

Kawakami, M., Matsubara, K., & Ota, M. (1982) Synthetic analysis of infantile (4-7 yr.-old) physical strength: Relation between coordination and balance development, and intelligence. *Okayama University of Science bulletin, 18(A)*, 109-120.

Kasuga, K. (1990) Development and body awareness and barriers. *Journal of Health, Physical and Recreation, 40*, 261-268.

Kim, Y., & Matsuura, Y. (1988) Research on the quantitative qualitative changes of fundamental athletic skills in infants and children: Focus on running, jumping and throwing motor abilities. *Japan Journal of Physical Education, Health and Sport Sciences, 33(1)*, 27-38.

Kobayashi, S. (1977) *DAM: Goodenough human figure drawing intelligence test handbook.* Kyoto: Sankyobou publication.

Kobayashi, K., et al (1990) *Early childhood development kinematics.* Kyoto: Minelva publication. Pp.76-77, 85-87.

Kondo, M. (1971) Regarding exercise and language instruction of young children (I). *Collection of research papers by the Japan Society of Research on Early Childhood Care and Education*, Pp.413.

Kondo, M. (1994) *Infantile physical activity and mental development.* Tokyo: Sekaibunkasha publication.

Kondo, M., Sugahara, T., Mori, S., &Yoshida, I. (1998) Recent motor abilities of young children. *Journal of Health, Physical and Recreation, 48(10)*, 851-859.

Larson, L.A., & Yocom. (1951) *Measurement and education in physical, health and recreation education.* St.Louis, The C. V. Mosby Company.

Lowenfeld, V. (1963) *Human growth through the fine arts.* Translation by Takeuchi,K. Nagoya: Reimei publication.

Machover, K. (1953) Human figure drawings of children. *Journal of Projective Techniques, 17(1)*, 85-91.

McCrea, C. W., Summerfield, A. D., & Rosen, B. (1982) Body image: a selected review of existing measurement techniques. *British Journal of Medical Psychology, 55*, 225-233.

Matsuda, I., & Kondo, M. (1978) Research regarding motor abilities of pre-school children: Creating motor ability development criteria for pre-school children. *Physical Education Bulletin of the Tokyo University of Education, 7*, 33-47.

Matsuda, N., et al. (1990) On the relation between manual dexterity and athletic ability in young children. *Kyoto Journal of Physical Education, 5(19)*, 25-34.

Matsunaga, K. (1992) Body awareness in young children: Comparison of a nursery and a kindergarten. *Bulletin of Nagasaki Prefectual Women's Junior College, 40*, 124-135.

Matsunaga, K. (1996) Effects of nurture environments on body awareness in children. *Bulletin of Nagasaki Prefectual Women's Junior College, 44*, 84-85.

Matsunaga, K., & Matsunaga, J. (1997) A study on the development of body awareness in preschool children (II). *Journal of Growth Development Research, 25*, 1-12.

Murase, T., & Idemura, S. (1990) Consideration of an infantile athletic ability evaluation method: The presumed relation between "athletic ability test" and "yes-no decision test". *Japan Journal of Physical Education, Health and Sport Sciences, 35*, 207-217.

Nagy, M. H. (1953) Children's conception's of some bodily functions. *Journal of Genetic Psychology, 83*, 199-216.

Naruse, G. (1977) Looking back on my clinical psychology research. Kyushu University Department of Education, Mental Educational Counseling Room, *Journal of Clinical Psychology Research, 3*, 154-160.

Nakamura, E., & Matsuura, Y. (1979) Development of fundamental motor ability of boys and girls aged four to eight. *Japan Journal of Physical Education, Health and Sport Sciences, 24(2)*, 127-135.

Piaget, J. (1947) *La psychologie de l' intelligence*. Librairie Arman Colin.

Rolland, K ., Farnill, D., & Griffiths, R. A. (1996) Children's perceptions of their current and ideal body sizes and body mass index. *Perceptual and Motor Skills, 82*, 651-656.

Scammon, R. E. (1930) The measurement of the body in children. In J. A. Harris, C. M. Jackson, D. G. Patterson, & R. E. Scammon (Eds.), *The measurement of man*. University of Minnesota Press.

Schilder, P. (1935) *The image and appearance of the human body*. New York: International University Press.

Swensen, C. H. (1968) Empirical evaluations of human figure drawings. *Psychological Bulletin , 70(1)*, 23.

Shimada, M. (1984) Research on intellectual development in infancy (I): Relation between athletic ability, and intelligence and vocabulary. *Bulletin of Seiwa University, 12*, 185-201.

Suzuki, M., Takeshima, N., & Hirata, T. (1980) Consiedering an appraisal method for physical strength and fitness tests for boys. *Journal of Educational Medicine, 26(2)*, 49-51.

Wallon, H. (1965) *The origin of the personality in children*. Translation by Kubota,M. Tokyo: Meijitosyo publication, Pp.157-181.

In: Body Image: New Research
Editor: Marlene V. Kindes, pp. 263-289

ISBN 1-60021-059-7
© 2006 Nova Science Publishers, Inc.

Chapter XII

CLINICAL TREATMENT FOR BODY IMAGE DISTURBANCES: VARIATIONS ON A THEME INTERACTIVE GUIDED IMAGERY, EMPTY CHAIR WORK, AND THERAPEUTIC LETTER-WRITING[*]

Patrice Rancour[*]
Ohio State University, Columbus, Ohio

ABSTRACT

As medical and surgical treatments become ever more invasive and complicated, people today are living with treated illnesses, which would have resulted in death only a matter of years ago. Increasingly intense use of technology can often complicate the rehabilitation of such patients who must adapt to radical changes in body appearance and/or function. If the patient survives the illness and treatment, but his/her quality of life is never restored, how can one call the treatment successful?

The author has used three specific intervention strategies to assist patients who are recovering from such experiences: interactive guided imagery, empty chair work, and therapeutic letter-writing. All three can be effective methods to assist patients to adjust mentally, emotionally and spiritually to perceived attacks on their physical bodies.

Interactive guided imagery is conceptually described as a tool from the school of Psychosynthesis. This form of guided imagery is verbally interactive, and used to assist patients to employ their visualization skills to "dis-identify from" and therefore "relate to" changing body parts and functions. The purpose of this technique is help them to grieve their losses and reintegrate the altered parts/functions back into a cohesive whole once again.

---

[*] For the purposes of this work, all case illustration names have been changed to protect the privacy of the individuals involved.

[*] Correspondence to: Patrice Rancour, MS,RN,CS, 1978 Glenn Avenue, Columbus, Ohio 43212 Email: rancour.1@osu.edu

Empty chair work is derived from the Gestalt school and takes the imagery work a bit farther as the therapist invites the patient to "put the affected body part in the chair" and proceed with a dialogue, again to work through attendant grief issues and to work towards re-integration.

The literature recommends the use of journaling as an adjunct to treatment. More specifically, therapeutic letter-writing moves the locus of attention from "writing about" to "writing to/from" the affected body part, always the more evocative, more powerful form of therapy.

This chapter describes the conceptual frameworks and techniques of each of the above intervention strategies. Case illustrations are offered to describe their use with patients who experience medical and/or surgical alterations to their bodies as a result of illness and/or its treatment.

Keywords: Body image, guided imagery, empty chair technique, therapeutic letter-writing.

INTRODUCTION

Although the world is full of suffering, it is full also of the overcoming of it.
                                                                                  - Helen Keller-

In his classic work, Stigma, Erving Goffman graphically described the world of people whose physical appearance or function force them to lead marginal lives in society. [Goffman] Certainly the Americans with Disabilities Act and other human rights movements in this country have continued to move the society as a whole toward ever-increasing levels of tolerance with regards to countenancing variety in form and function among its citizenry.

However, living in a society obsessed with "extreme makeovers" as we do, the media-hype promoting voluntary alteration of our selves in order to become physically acceptable in this competitive culture is a living testament to the need for equally extreme counter-measures. Despite the overt religiosity which continues to prevail in this country, materialism and consumerism commodify people according to physical appearance. This may pose challenges to the individual's psychospiritual development when confronted by the very real threat of illness and/or injury to the physical body. The operational word here is spiritual (personal meaning) as opposed to religious (liturgical or dogmatic organization). This is especially so as body image is strongly associated with self-esteem and the individual's eventual ability to self-actualize [Maslow].

As medical and surgical treatments become ever more invasive and complicated, people today are living with treated illnesses which would have resulted in death only a short number of years ago. Increasingly intense use of technology can often complicate the rehabilitation of such patients who must adapt to radical changes in body appearance and/or function. If the patient survives the illness and treatment, but his/her quality of life is never restored, how can one call the treatment successful?

The need for focused work with such individuals remains paramount. One-to-one therapy with them can be aided with the use of specific interventions designed to help them remember that:

1. while they have a body, they are not their bodies.
2. while not everything is fixed, not everything is broken.
3. as a whole, they are greater than the sum of their parts.
4. the experiences one faces, as unpleasant as they are, can be used as opportunities to learn. (Although one patient insisted she "learned just as well from joy as I do from pain, thank you very much!"), and more specifically,
5. this experience is an opportunity to learn to hold themselves larger.

Some practitioners may be uncomfortable with the inherent spiritual nature of some of the above assumptions. However, it is difficult to conceive of how to help someone confront the existential issues inherent in radical body alterations without incorporating psychospiritual approaches into the recovery work.

For further reference as to how this translates into the psychospiritual experience of patients undergoing such identity transitions, the reader is directed to a description of that process in *Close to the Bone: Life-Threatening Illness and the Search for Meaning*, a work derived from a Jungian sensibility. [Bolen] The author harkens back to archetypes such as the crossing of the River Styx (crossing the treatment threshold), descents into Hades (active treatment), the stripping away of individual identity markers (clothing, body parts, wrist bands with numbers, etc.), and meetings with guides (presumably health care professionals.) on the treatment journey.

This imagery is suggestive of Viktor Frankl's descriptions of concentration camp survivors who also had to reinvent new versions of the self in order to survive (clothing, lost body parts, tattooed identification numbers, etc). [Frankl] As he indicated, the person can be stripped of external identifiers, but the one thing that cannot be removed unless it is given away is how one chooses to perceive one's self. Certainly many modern treatments can simulate the sense of being in a combat zone. Patients are told they must cultivate a "fighting spirit," procedures and drugs are described as being part of a "treatment armamentarium," and even the professional caregivers are understood to suffer from a kind of "combat fatigue."

Once the patient emerges from the trial by fire, the return passage across the River Styx (re-entry into mainstream society) back into the land of the living is accomplished albeit under a newly-revised identity; one that incorporates a new vision of one's self and ultimately, one's life purpose. Frequently, these revisions of the self, including the affected body image, take on a redemptive quality, as people may use their own suffering in the service of healing others, another archetype redolent of the wounded healer. LeShan writes that no amount of therapy can replace answering the following existential questions: "What does it mean to live under my name on this planet? What gives my life meaning? What makes me laugh?" [LeShan] Great suffering is ultimately bearable if it is found to be meaningful.

The process is reminiscent of the vision quest familiar to indigenous tribal communities, wherein the individual embarks on a transformational journey, encounters guides along the way, and returns to community with a new identity, role and purpose. [Doore, Campbell] The new identity may come replete with a change in name, status, and even new physical markings, such as tattoos, circumcisions, body piercing and other permanent adornments to distinguish the successful completion of a rite of passage. These physical trappings make it possible for others in the community to recognize the life experience, changed role or status of the member; much as the young woman with the bald head at the mall is immediately recognized as a chemotherapy patient today. (For example, a couple of young cancer patients, again recognizable by their bald heads, both having survived hemipelvectomies, were having lunch at a restaurant and were surprised to learn that another customer had paid their bill for them. When queried, the waiter informed them that their patron had already left and had merely added that he too had once been a member of that "elite club and understood only too well what they were going through.")

CLINICAL CONSIDERATIONS

All growth takes place initially in the dark.
                                        -Matthew Fox-

Today's patients facing serious medical/surgical passages (or quests) can be greatly aided by the assistance of a multidisciplinary team of people (or guides) who can provide them with, not only technical assistance to treat the disease, but also with opportunities to grieve the loss of threatened body parts or functions. This is accomplished as a prelude to accommodating a newly integrated concept of self as a whole individual.

For some patients, the prospect of having to face such radical procedures may preclude them from proceeding with treatment which could ultimately prove life-saving. Certainly it is within the realm of reason for people to refuse treatment; hopefully, however, this is done once all options have been exhausted, including psychotherapeutic efforts to help them to cope and adapt. [Schneider] Patients should also be evaluated for depression and suicidal ideation to ensure their basic safety, as well as to make sure that their ultimate decision with regards to treatment is based on a careful assessment of mental capacity and competence. Antidepressant medication may be indicated as an adjunct to therapy in some instances.

Ideally, the process should start pre-treatment, but this is not always possible; for example, in the case of unanticipated injury sustained as a result of an accident. However, when a recommended treatment is known to radically alter a person's body, attention to body image should begin as soon as possible.

A number of intervention strategies can be most helpful in this endeavor. Art therapy can be a highly evocative modality. [Malchiodi] When the patient draws an image of self before, during and after treatment, the pictures can be used as springboards to investigate how the patient sees him throughout the process of becoming. Some of these pictures are particularly striking if the patient lies down on a large roll of paper and the outline of the body is traced to be filled in with emerging images. These canvases are dense with information about how patients see themselves as they draw in features, organ systems and other aspects of their physical or allegorical selves which may not be so apparent merely from talk therapy. This adjunct enriches the therapy by culling information from non-linear, non-logical (as opposed to illogical) ways of knowing.

Work with children is especially fruitful using not only art therapy, but also play therapy. [James] Puppets, dolls, sand trays with miniature collections of figurines used for narrative purposes all can help children express feelings which may be hard for them to abstractly understand. Storytelling is another useful modality whereby a book about a related experience can be read to the child and the child then can tell her own story, write it or draw it, if possible. Again, these methods help the child develop coping strategies that can be tapped later in life when confronted with new challenges. [Heiney]

The use of books to support therapeutic work, bibliotherapy, is especially helpful as works written by people who have transcended similar experiences help to model for patients that these experiences are indeed survivable. [Cohen] Especially those books which have pictures depicting people with apparent variations in their physical appearances engaged in active and worthwhile pursuits can provide the impetus for patients to see that there are options open to them post-treatment. [Sabolich]

Certainly, body image programs like the Look Good, Feel Better program of the American Cancer Society (ACS) which focus on improving the physical appearance of patients, are concrete ways of helping patients feel more acceptable. This program, which teaches women how to use cosmetics and accessories to maximize their appearance during active treatment, often leaves such patients stating that they feel "pampered."

Social support is critical since body image is a function of how acceptable one feels in society. Reactions of "the other" certainly register and are translated into varying degrees of self-acceptance. In the cancer community for example, the ACS One to One program matches volunteer survivors with newly-diagnosed patients who learn that indeed there is life after treatment. Programs like the Lost Chord Club and Reach to Recovery have helped thousands of people come to terms with a new body image. [Chamorro]

For patients able to tolerate group exposure, support groups in which they have an opportunity to encounter others coping with similar challenges, have long been a mainstay of introducing them to the possibilities of life after illness and treatment. The Wellness Community, for example, hosts support groups, many of which address body image changes explicitly. [Benjamin]

The rest of this chapter is devoted to describing the conceptual frameworks and techniques illustrated by case review of three clinical interventions which the practitioner can use to assist patients to adjust to changes in their physical appearance and/or function. These modalities include interactive guided imagery, empty chair work, and therapeutic letter-writing. All are really variations on the theme of dis-identification from a body part in order to re-integrate the transformed part into a cohesive sense of personal wholeness once again. (To dis-identify from a part is akin to separating from it long enough to recognize that one is not the part, that one is larger than the part. From this point of detachment, one can more accurately perceive what is needed and meet the needs more effectively to contribute to the highest good of the person as a whole.)

These techniques tap non-logical (*not* illogical) ways of knowing which seek after patterns not readily discernible by logical methods of inquiry. Not that logic is to be avoided; it is just that logic alone does not provide patients with a complete picture of the depth and wealth of information available to them about their true natures.

Body image disturbances can often be vehicles for self-rejection. The purpose of these treatment modalities is to help the individual eventually transform the unacceptable body part into something not merely acceptable, but also forgivable, and then actively nurtured. One of the advantages of these techniques is that they minimize much of the transference issues that commonly occur in psychotherapy so that the patient's work remains largely focused on the body image disturbance at hand.

These techniques may also be used with other kinds of body image disturbances as well, such as eating disorders, work with abused individuals, or with those people who appear addicted to cosmetic alterations in order to make themselves "acceptable." The focus of this chapter, however, will be on their use with patients undergoing medical or surgical treatment for physical illnesses.

INTERACTIVE GUIDED IMAGERY: CONCEPTUAL FRAMEWORK

One only sees what one has grown an eye to see.
- Unknown-

Guided imagery is well-known in psychotherapeutic and wellness circles as a technique to induce the relaxation response. [Naparstek] Imagery is a spontaneous thought that has sensory qualities to it. It is an internal representation that conveys information. As an older form of knowing, it is information-dense, closely related to affect, and is deeply rooted in human physiology.

The technique as so practiced is a passive one on the part of the patient, the therapist usually coaching him/her into a state of relaxation. Deep breathing exercises, attendant music, and/or a script incorporating patient-engaged sensory images can be used to promote wellness and healing, facilitate sleep, improve pain management as an adjunct to analgesic treatment, and the like.

Interactive guided imagery, however, is a dynamic modality, based on the verbally active participation of the patient. It is the process whereby the therapist assists the individual to make active contact with a part of the individual's personality or body and to negotiate a more effective outcome for the good of the whole. [Rancour, 1991] Interactive guided imagery has been used successfully to assist individuals navigate through grief work, skill mastery, decision-making, working with resistance, to bridge to inner wisdom, stress management, psychotherapy, and other such purposes.

This strategy is rooted in the work of Roberto Assagioli and the Psychosynthesis school of therapy. [Assagioli] The conceptual framework of Psychosynthesis posits that each individual is born with a true self as the center of one's personality. As the individual develops through life, major character traits and roles emerge which help the individual survive whatever developmental or situational challenges are encountered. For example, such roles can include daughter, mother, wife, physician, etc. Character traits may include such qualities as "the critic" or "judge," "the martyr," "the victim," or "the rescuer," etc. Accordingly, each person may be seen as a walking cast of thousands as these traits and roles become refined into what are called sub-personalities.

Each sub-personality represents a legitimate need. The problem is never the need, but how one goes about getting the need met. For example, the patient legitimately needs acceptance, but if he is identified with a victim sub-personality, manipulation may be used to get it, and therefore is problematic. Or for example, the patient legitimately needs predictability in life, but if she identifies with a critic or judge sub-personality, the exhibited behavior may be controlling or bullying, also problematic. The difficulties come into play, therefore, when the individual forgets who he truly is (the centered self) and identifies with one of these sub-personalities. When this happens, it is hypothesized that there is a higher probability that pain and dysfunction can occur since identification with one of these parts means that the rest of the sub-personalities may not get what they need.

When one is centered, the self can negotiate for the needs of the whole. Ironically therefore, being "self-centered" is associated with the highest forms of spiritual maturity, a sense of peace and serenity, and self-actualization. Likewise, being "off-center" is relating to the world from the point of view of only one part of one's personality, the outcome of which is often painful or dysfunctional. [Ferrucci]

Integration, therefore, is accomplished when the patient understands that while she *has* a body, feelings, and thoughts, she is *not* the body, feelings and thoughts. In this way, the individual can recognize and detach (dis-identify) from these sub-personalities, learn more effective ways of meeting the needs, and become more self-identified, thereby enabling a more balanced and centered approach to living in the world. It is more functional to negotiate one's way through life by responding *to* the sub-personalities than *from* them. The basic premise here is that just because one never got what one needed from others earlier in life, doesn't necessarily mean one never will, as one learns to meet one's own needs in more effective ways.

Interactive guided imagery lends itself to applications with patients whose body image has become distorted by physical illness and/or its treatment. [Rancour, 1994] Especially in this culture, in which the physical appearance of bodies has been elevated to a multi-billion dollar a year cosmetic surgery industry, people who must undergo treatments that may be considered mutilating suffer from varying degree of social stigma. Such stigma can dramatically impact the integrity of their body image, self-esteem and self-concept. Often, these people are at risk for developing other debilitating conditions such as anxiety, depression and post-traumatic stress disorder if their body image alterations are not directly addressed. [National Cancer Institute] These co-morbidities can complicate recovery from treatment for serious illness and thus, interfere with healing. And of course, the individual can suffer from body image disturbances whether the person's physical alterations are perceptible to others or not.

The prospect of engaging in such treatment can be so daunting that some patients may decide to opt out of it because they cannot face the likelihood of such extreme body alterations. Psychotherapeutic approaches aside, sometimes there is no other way to deal with patient denial and refusal regarding treatment other than by engaging in more pragmatic measures. One patient refused treatment for a facial cancer because he could not cope with the expectation that he would be socially ostracized for undergoing such a radical change in his appearance. Accompanying him to an appointment with a plastic surgeon to review facial reconstruction options enabled him to sign the consent form and proceed with the life-saving surgery. This patient survived and experienced an acceptable quality of life post-treatment.

INTERACTIVE GUIDED IMAGERY: THE TECHNIQUE

Become a witness to the crossroads of people's lives.
-Unknown-

As with all such therapeutic encounters, the therapist begins by preparing one's self, by centering, and by operationalizing a caring intent towards the patient. The patient is then prepared by explaining the procedure and obtaining consent to proceed. The therapist assures the patient that he will retain conscious control during the entire procedure, and that the process can be slowed or stopped whenever it is wished. Paradoxical intention is primarily invoked during the first session in order to reduce unrealistic expectations. (e.g., "Don't expect that too much will happen during this session since this is the first time you are trying this.") Otherwise, performance anxiety can get the better of the patient (and sometimes the therapist!) and interfere with the process.

Some patients may report that they do not have much of an imagination and do not "see" images, and therefore insist that this modality will not be effective for them. Such patients can be asked how many windows there are in the house or apartment where they live. They will then stop a moment to consider, and when specifically asked what is happening, become aware that indeed they are visually counting the windows using their imagination. If resistance to using this technique is excessive, the options are to focus on where the resistance is coming from, or to simply move on to a different modality for the body image work. Certainly it is understood that no one modality is effective for everybody.

The patient is counseled that the purpose of the session is not to induce relaxation, but rather to induce a heightened state of alertness in order to focus on the intended work at hand. The initial relaxation exercise is used merely to help the patient become more inward-focused and to help her stay in the present as much as possible to maximize concentration. The patient's eyes are usually closed and she is sitting upright to avoid falling asleep.

The relaxation response can be accomplished by whatever method works best for the patient and in whatever way the therapist feels most accomplished. Some patients find selected music helps them center. Others prefer guided coaching from the therapist who can help them focus on their breathing, "take a trip through their bodies" relaxing various muscle groups (progressive relaxation), or simply "go to a safe place" using the patient's imagination.

Once the patient has reached the desired level of centered conscious awareness, the therapist asks him to allow an image to come to mind that represents or symbolizes the disease, body organ, or symptom which has been distressing to him Counseling the patient to remain inward-focused, she is then instructed to describe the image in detail out loud. Descriptions should be as multi-sensory as possible: how the image looks, if it makes a sound, if there is an accompanying smell or taste, what the texture of the image is like, etc.

As the patient is asked to investigate the phenomenon, oftentimes repulsion or disgust can eventually become transformed into curiosity.

The patient is then asked to describe out loud what it feels like to be with the image. The response is often negative, as in "I can't stand being with it," or even "I hate it." At such times when the patient finds proximity to the image so repugnant, it is often wise to slow the process down so as not to overwhelm him and inadvertently sabotage the work. The patient can be counseled to deep breathe at these points in order to build tolerance regarding staying focused on the task at hand, however difficult. Infrequently, the patient cannot tolerate it and the session is stopped with the suggestion being that until the next session, she merely keeps the image accessible and tries to begin to tolerate its presence in a conscious way for longer periods so that the work can resume later (desensitization). Or other variations on this theme can be suggested, such as the therapeutic letter-writing exercise described later in this chapter.

Once contact with the image has been established, the patient is directed to ask the image what it wants from her. As the answer is frequently negative, the patient is directed to ask the image why it wants this. The response is usually a legitimate unmet need which can be explored in greater detail. The patient and the image, thus, enter into a dialogue to determine more effective ways of getting the need met.

The role of the therapist in all of this is not one of interpreter, but that of facilitator and observer. If the therapist has an intuition about the contact being made, the therapist directs the patient to ask a question to seek further information. Observations, such as. "I am noticing a tear sliding down your cheek. What is happening?" or "Are you aware that you are clenching your fists right now?" serve to deepen self-awareness without assigning a meaning to the behavior for the patient to whom interpretation is always left. In this manner, the patient learns how to use the process for the purpose of developing self-awareness, and does not need to rely so much upon the therapist as the work progresses.

Once the patient becomes aware of the unmet need, he can negotiate with the sub-personality (body part or function) on more effective methods to get the need met which do not compromise meeting other competing needs as well. There are times when it makes sense for the patient to be directed to shift his conscious awareness into the image, to become the image itself. The therapist should expect initial resistance, but with encouragement, this exercise can allow the patient to experience the needs firsthand and allow an experience of the positive attributes of the image as well, qualities that may not have been readily so self-evident. The patient learns what the part needs from the point of view of the body part itself. For example, the patient may not relish the idea of "moving into" a painful limb, but it may enable her to become conscious of the anguish that body part might be feeling. This can lead to an opening of the heart so that forgiveness work and healing can proceed.

An exchange of information between the patient and the part ensues as they work towards resolution, if possible. This kind of discussion and intra-personal consensus–building may occur over several sessions or may take just one session before a paradigm shift in consciousness occurs. It is important not to rush the patient to conclusion prematurely since so much of this effort is fraught with active grief which must be simultaneously experienced and discharged.

When it appears that the patient has managed about as much work as is feasible for the session, he is directed to shift his conscious awareness back to the centered self again, by focusing on breathing, and returning to a more conventional state of awareness, into the present reality. The therapist can then encourage descriptions of any energy transformations or changes in resistance, awareness and perceptions. Again, the therapist is cautioned about not interpreting the patient's reported experiences, but simply making observations which help the patient debrief the process and use it as a launch pad for self-discovery and healing.

INTERACTIVE GUIDED IMAGERY: A CASE ILLUSTRATION

Sandra W. is a 34 year old woman who had been seen in a previous series of sessions for relationship counseling. She has now returned having since married. She and her husband have been trying for some time to have children with no success. Prior to consulting the therapist, she underwent diagnostic testing to determine the cause of her infertility and it was discovered that she had ovarian cancer. She is resisting the recommended surgery as it will preclude her ability to reproduce biologically. She is still holding out the hope that perhaps the cancer can be cured without jeopardizing her ability to become pregnant, carry a child to term and deliver a healthy baby. She is very angry at the disruption this has caused to her plans and the vision she holds for herself for her future. Her inability to let go of the dream for her own biological children is jeopardizing her own survival as she continues to delay seeking treatment.

Sandra: I can't believe that the only cure for me is a TAH (total abdominal hysterectomy). I have asked the doctor about radiation and chemotherapy, but she says the stage of the tumor requires the operation. And soon. Personally, I think there is way too much emphasis on the surgery. I see it more as a last resort.

Therapist: Did you discuss egg salvage procedures?

Sandra: She says there is already too much damage to my ovaries and the chance that the embryo wouldn't be viable isn't worth the risk.

Therapist: That must have been pretty hard to hear considering how hard you and Rick have been working on getting pregnant.

Sandra: I am not willing to give this up yet. I am so mad at Dr. Willis for not being willing to consider other options. I don't like being pressured. I am thinking of getting a second opinion.

Therapist: While I think getting a second opinion is always a good idea, do you think you might be killing the messenger?

Sandra: What do you mean?

Therapist: It could not have been easy to hear what she had to say to you.

Sandra: Oh yeah, right. Well, I *am* angry. It took me so long to find the right guy, and now this. I am not getting any younger. And I am tired of people telling me I can always adopt. I don't want to adopt. I want my own children. I am so angry that my body is not getting with the program.

Therapist: I am wondering if what you are really doing is grieving.

Sandra: What do you mean?

Therapist: You are being asked to lose a child you have already imagined into being. It may be hard to believe that there isn't something you could do to control all this or that you could somehow negotiate it differently. Or even be so angry you might not follow through with the recommended treatment.

Sandra: (Prolonged silence. Thinking. Eventually tears. Makes fists and pounds her legs.) It is just so unfair to come this far and then find out there is something wrong with me.

Therapist: So really you are angry with yourself more than anything else?

Sandra: (Pointing vaguely to her abdomen.) No, really more like angry at these. (Ovaries.)

Therapist: Would you like to explore this a bit more?

Sandra: You mean using the imagery? (Patient has used this technique successfully in the past.)

Therapist: Nodding.

Sandra: It's not going to change anything.

Therapist: Maybe not, but what have you got to lose?

Sandra: (Blowing her nose.) Nothing, I guess.

Therapist then directs the patient to close her eyes and get into a comfortable position, to begin to pay attention to her breathing and to use the breath as a means to enter into a state of heightened alertness. This takes but a matter of minutes. Once the patient and therapist are centered, the therapist begins:

Therapist: And now, staying very inward focused, allow an image to come to mind that represents your ovaries and project that image out into the room. Nothing to change, nothing to judge. Just allowing whatever first pops into your mind. And when you have it there, describe out loud what you are perceiving.

Sandra: (After some moments, frowning.) Two big black blobs – like big black amoebas.

Therapist: What else do you notice about them?

Sandra: They're just ugly. They keep shifting shapes, like amoebas would – blob-like.

Therapist: What's it like being around them?

Sandra: I hate them. I can't stand being with them. Actually I'd like to punish them for what they are doing to me right now.

Therapist: Ask them what they want from you.

Sandra: I'd really rather not. (But tilts her head to one side….) They say they want to get my attention.

Therapist: Ask them why they want your attention.

Sandra: They say because they are sick and tired.

Therapist: And what are they sick and tired of?

Sandra: (Sitting upright.) Of being sick and tired. (Said in a small voice.)

Therapist: What else do they have to say?

Sandra: They say they have been sick for a long time and didn't know how else to let me know other than by preventing pregnancy. Since I didn't seem to feel any pain, they've been trying to get my attention this way.

Therapist: Ask them what for?

Sandra: (Listening… then in a very small voice.) To save my life.

Therapist: Ask them if they understand that in order to save your life, they will have to be sacrificed.

Sandra: (Silently asks the question.) They understand quite well. They want to see me live and be happy. They think I will make someone a wonderful mother some day. (She begins to cry softly.)

Therapist: Ask them what they need from you right now.

Sandra: (Tearfully). Forgiveness. *They* are asking *me* for forgiveness.

Therapist: Can you give them what they are asking for?

Sandra: (Quietly.) It is me who should be asking them for forgiveness. I've been so angry with them.

Therapist: Well, how about it? Can you forgive them?

Sandra: (Silently nods her head and murmurs) I forgive you. (Pauses. A few moments later, she makes a cradle with her arms and begins to rock rhythmically back and forth for some time.)

Therapist: What is happening?

Sandra: They have asked me to comfort them like I would comfort crying babies. We are all crying together.

Therapist: Stay with what is happening for as long as it feels right to do so.

Sandra: (Several minutes later, stops rocking and puts her arms back in her lap.)

Therapist: What is happening now?

Sandra: With the rocking, they have changed into miniature babies.

Therapist: What does it feel like to be with them now?

Sandra: (Softly smiling, nodding.) Fine. Good.

Therapist: Is there anything else right now that feels unfinished for the time being?

Sandra: (Shakes her head 'no.')

Therapist: I'd like to suggest that you allow this image to remain available to you in your conscious awareness for the rest of the week so that if they need anything from you or if you need anything from them, you can work it out together. OK with that?

Sandra: (Nods.)

Therapist: Then bid the image farewell for now, realizing you can connect with it any time you wish and that you take that power with you everywhere you go. Take some deep breaths, and gradually, bring your conscious awareness back into the here and now, and when you are ready, you can stretch and open your eyes.

INTERACTIVE GUIDED IMAGERY: DISCUSSION

The world breaks everyone and afterward, many are strong in the broken places.

- Ernest Hemingway-

Once the session is over, the therapist is then free to debrief the patient using open-ended questions to stimulate further expressions of latent grief or the refinement of further insights. The above example is a good illustration of how with gentle examination, the "shadow side" of the sub-personality, in this case, a body part, is transformed when the light of investigation and imagination is shined upon it. This particular patient was well-versed in the modality from previous experience with it, and understood how to use it with minimal assistance.

The role of the therapist is to help the patient strive for understanding by detaching from the affected body part, thereby moving towards self- identification in order to investigate it. Projecting the part out into the room assists this process in a very concrete way. The patient then is freed to respond *to* the body part rather than *from* the body part. Being re-identified with her true self can help ensure that decision-making is in the highest interest of the whole person, and not just due to the pain being experienced by conflict with one part. The difficulty here is a complicated grief reaction. The healing process is that of forgiveness, and ultimately, transformation.

In this particular case, the patient decided to go ahead with the TAH, and several years later, asked the therapist to write a letter of recommendation for her to apply for adoption. This couple now has two adopted children. Interestingly, the patient returned for treatment years later to work through the shock of finally coming to terms with her life-threatening diagnosis: "I guess I was so mad about the baby thing, it didn't hit me until the kids had grown up enough and given me enough space to realize I could have died from all of that!"

EMPTY CHAIR WORK: CONCEPTUAL FRAMEWORK AND TECHNIQUE

Curing is about wanting things to return to the way they used to be. Healing is about using the present situation to bring us closer to God.

-Ram Dass-

Those familiar with the Gestalt school of therapy will remember that this form of psychotherapy has been pivotal in helping people shift their focus from "talking about" their problems as if they were in the past, the psychoanalytic approach, to "working with" their problems in the present. [Perls, 1998] The Gestaltists developed a number of therapeutic strategies designed to create more immediacy for patients, to interrupt the tendencies during therapy to "stay in one's head," to rationalize, and instead, to make more direct contact with their emotional experience. These techniques were seen as highly evocative and underpinned the emerging belief supporting the efficacy of brief psychotherapy over more conventional Freudian psychoanalytic approaches which often required long-term talk therapy. [Polster & Polster]

Empty chair work is a tool described by Fritz Perls in his classic *Gestalt Therapy Verbatim*. [Perls, 1980] Empty chair work is much like interactive guided imagery, in that the patient is asked to project the object of the problem to be dealt with outside of himself, this time "into the empty chair." For some, this could be a person with whom the patient might be having a conflict. For example, someone who has unfinished business with a deceased parent might be encouraged to "put Dad in the chair," and then subsequently dialogue with him towards resolution of the conflict, albeit posthumously. This approach is considered to have much more affective immediacy, and therefore is far more compelling in eliciting resolution of the presenting problem.

This technique can also be adapted for use to dialogue with a body part, symptom or function which is interfering with the patient's ability to move towards a wholly-integrated sense of self. As with all such therapeutic encounters, the therapist begins by preparing one's self, by centering, and by operationalizing a caring intent towards the patient. The patient is then prepared by explaining the procedure and obtaining consent to proceed.

The technique is reminiscent of interactive guided imagery in that the therapist directs the patient to use her imagination to project the troubling symptom or body part outside of herself. In this case, into an empty chair, and the patient conducts the dialogue with the image in order to come to terms with whatever intra-personal conflict the illness or its treatment is creating. The patient's eyes are usually open and he can even be asked to move back and forth from one chair to the other if this eases the process. The role of the therapist is the same, that is, one of facilitator.

EMPTY CHAIR WORK: CASE ILLUSTRATION

Marian G. is a very attractive 42 year old woman, mother of a 10 year old boy, and married to a highly successful business man. Marian was diagnosed with colon cancer and is facing surgery. She has made it explicitly clear that while she is willing to have surgery if the surgeon can remove the tumor and the affected colon and reanastamose the ends, she will *not* consent to a colostomy. The surgeon is reluctant to perform the surgery without keeping all options open once Marian is on the table. During an interdisciplinary clinical case conference, it is decided that body image work be started immediately in order to help the patient consider all options as she faces surgery for her cancer. (This work took place over two sessions but has been condensed here for the purpose of this chapter.)

Marian: (Suspiciously) Did Dr. Koffman send you in here to talk to me?

Therapist: He is worried about you.

Marian: Well, I've already made up my mind about this. I am not going to walk around with a bag on my belly, passing gas at dinner parties, and not be able to wear a bathing suit on vacation.

Therapist: It sounds like your physical appearance is pretty important to you.

Marian: I know it probably sounds vain - and maybe it is - but I find the whole notion of a colostomy bag unacceptable. Having to have bowel movements through my stomach...I certainly would never be able to entertain the notion of having sex with my husband again. The whole thing feels dirty to me. (She involuntarily shudders.)

Therapist: You're having a fairly visceral reaction to the whole thing.

Marian: (She sheepishly smiles at the pun.) Well, who wouldn't? I can't figure out how people let themselves get talked into these things. They sent someone up here from the Ostomy Club and I tried to be polite, but really, I just don't see it happening for me.

Therapist: What does your husband say about all this?

Marian: He wants me to go ahead with the surgery, and he says he will be okay with whatever happens. But there is something I haven't told anyone else about, and I think it enters a lot into this whole issue for me.

Therapist: Do you want to talk about it?

Marian: (Uncomfortable.) About three years ago, Dan had an affair with someone he works with. We almost divorced over it, but decided to stick it out for Michael's sake. I still have problems trusting him.

Therapist: Has he been unfaithful since then?

Marian: Not that I know of, but I have told him that if I ever find out that he is cheating on me again, I will leave him and take Michael with me.

Therapist: This must have been pretty painful for you.

Marian: (Tears up.) You have no idea.

Therapist: So the current decision has something to do with this past infidelity? Not wanting to be unattractive to Dan?

Marian: (Nods her head "yes.") I just don't think I could go through the other woman thing again. She was younger than me of course. The idea of wearing a bag on my belly makes me feel like I would just be pushing him into someone else's arms.

Therapist: So you and Dan have never really resolved the trust issue between you? Even before the cancer diagnosis?

Marian: No. It just sits there between us like the proverbial elephant in the room.

Therapist: I've talked to Dan. My sense of him is that he really loves you and is afraid to lose you.

Marian: (Weeping.) I want to believe that, but I guess I'm still nursing my wounds.

Therapist: Have you two talked this through at all?

Marian: We've tried, but we've just learned to live with it as best we can. And now this cancer thing has come up… You know it's funny. I'm sure people look at us as having it all. From the outside we always looked like we had everything going for us. People really don't know how miserable we are.

Therapist: How do you think this is affecting Michael?

Marian: He's a great kid. I think he's doing the best he can.

Therapist: I think so too, but my guess is he is also hurting. Would you and Dan be interested in discussing this together with me? It might be helpful to parse this out with a neutral party. What do you think?

Marian: I suppose it couldn't hurt. I just don't think right now it would help that much. It just feels like too much water over the dam.

Therapist: What have you got to lose?

Marian: (Shrugs.) It's OK by me if it's OK by him.

Therapist: I'll talk to him about it.

This was followed by several couple's counseling sessions during which Marian expressed her hurt, rage and unwillingness to forgive Dan for his faithlessness. He expressed his remorse and his fear about losing her to the cancer. He admitted that her illness had forced him to reevaluate his priorities and that he had no doubt about the fact that her welfare was of primary importance to him, no matter whether she had a colostomy or not. While she found this hard to believe, it was obvious that the current crisis was conspiring to allow her to suspend her previous disbelief so that she might be willing to consider working on *wanting* to forgive him. The next session was with Marian alone:

Therapist: How's it going with Dan?

Marian: We're making progress, but it's slow-going.

Therapist: It takes a lot of courage to work on trust when you've been hurt so badly. I'm wondering if it has given you a reason to reconsider the surgery.

Marian: How do you mean?

Therapist: In terms of the relationship you are trying to rebuild with Dan.

Marian: (Shrugs) I don't know.

Therapist: I'd like to offer a suggestion about how we can proceed from here, but it will most likely sound a little strange to you. You'll need to use your imagination a bit.

Marian: What did you have in mind?

Therapist: I'd like you to imagine you could project your colon outside of your body and put it in that chair over there.

Marian: (Incredulous.) You want me to do what?

Therapist: Indulge me. (Smiling.)

Marian: (Now that there has been some history together, she smiles back and shrugs.) Is this supposed to be some kind of wacko therapy thing?

Therapist: It is. Do you trust me?

Marian: (Nods and looks at the chair.) OK, it's sitting over there. (She involuntarily shudders.)

Therapist: What was that? (Referring to her nonverbal behavior.)

Marian: It's just that this is so bizarre, and let's face it, it's just a mass of quivering guts sitting over there. (She laughs nervously.)

Therapist: So describe your mass of quivering guts to me out loud.

Marian: (Staring intently at the chair.) Well, they're pink for the most part. Looks a lot like sausage casings if you know what those look like. They're sitting over there in a kind of jumbled mess, somewhat coiled like a rope but really just kind of dumped out on the chair. Also, they really stink.

Therapist: What's it like to be with them?

Marian: Well, despite the fact that it's gross, it's wonderful to have them sitting outside my body. I almost feel cancer-free.

Therapist: What does that feel like?

Marian: (Said in a small voice.) Clean, pure, fresh.

Therapist: Which makes what's sitting over in the chair dirty, impure, unclean?

Marian: I guess.

Therapist: Ask your guts what they want from you- you can ask them out loud or silently. Listen to what they tell you and then tell me what they say.

Marian: (Pausing) I'm not getting anything back from them.

Therapist: What's it like to get nothing back from them?

Marian: (Frustrated.) Predictable. I'm used to getting nothing back. I've tried to be a good wife and mother, so my husband cheats on me and I get cancer. I'm used to getting kicked in the teeth.

Therapist: Tell your guts you are angry with them, and ask them again what they want from you.

Marian: (Angry.) This is not getting us anywhere.

Therapist: I'd like you to take some nice deep breaths right now. Go on....And I want you to be prepared to resist this next suggestion. Keep breathing. I want you to shift your conscious awareness into the image and as best you can, become the image of your guts in the chair.

Marian: (Looking at therapist in disbelief.) Do I have to?

Therapist: No, of course you do not have to.

Marian: (Looking back at the chair, deep breathing, finally closing her eyes.) All right, I am the guts.

Therapist: What's it like to be your guts?

Marian (as the image): Not so bad, I guess. Maybe a little sad.

Therapist: Are you surprised?

Marian (as the image): A little.

Therapist: Can you see Marian from where you are?

Marian (as the image): Yes.

Therapist: How does Marian look to you?

Marian (as the image): She looks lonely, afraid, mad.

Therapist: Do you have anything you'd like to tell her?

Marian (as the image): Yes, I'd like to tell her to stop hating us.

Therapist: Tell her.

Marian (as the image): Stop hating us.

Therapist: What's she say back to you?

Marian (as the image): She says, "Why should I?"

Therapist: Tell her.

Marian (as the image): Because we're not worth dying over.

Therapist: Go on.

Marian (as the image): Because there are other ways of finding peace in this life other than dying.

Therapist: Say that out loud again, louder.

Marian: (Louder) There are other ways of finding peace in this life other than dying.

Therapist: Anything else?

Marian (as the image): No, not really.

Therapist: Ask Marian if she needs anything else from you.

Marian (as the image): She is just looking for some peace.

Therapist: Any sense how she can find peace?

Marian (as the image): Stop pushing all of us away.

Therapist: Who is "all of us?"

Marian (as the image): Us-her guts, her husband, her surgeon, just life in general.

Therapist: How does she react to that?

Marian (as the image): She says it had never occurred to her that she was pushing life away, but she'll consider it.

Therapist: Anything else for now?

Marian (as the image): Not right now.

Therapist: OK then, take a nice deep breath for now, and very gradually, when you are ready, begin to shift your conscious awareness back into Marian. So that slowly, but surely, you are filling up Marian's body and looking back at the image in the chair. Let me know when that has happened.

Marian: (Eventually, opening her eyes.) I'm back in my body again.

Therapist: What is it like to be back in your body again?

Marian: Strange, actually. I'm a little disoriented.

Therapist: How does it feel to be with your guts now?

Marian: Fine. No big deal, really.

Therapist: Anything you need to say further to them at this point?

Marian: I just want to thank them, that's all.

Therapist: Go ahead.

Marian: (Silently looks at the chair.)

Therapist: Bid them farewell for now knowing you can reconnect with them anytime you want and that you take that power with you everywhere you go.

Marian: (Pausing, then looking at the therapist.) That was weird.

Therapist: Learn anything?

Marian: Yes, that I don't have to die to find peace.

EMPTY CHAIR WORK: DISCUSSION

To cure sometimes, but to comfort always.
                                    -Dame Cicely Saunders-

Often during periods of physical illness, the illness is not the only stressor occurring in the patient's life. Life on other fronts also goes on and can have an impact on the patient's body image which is further potentiated by the illness. In this case, marital difficulties had created a fertile ground for Marian's body image issues which were only exacerbated by her cancer diagnosis. She was clearly identified with a victim sub-personality which had cultivated a sense of powerlessness, and a fatalistic self-fulfilling prophecy about her prognosis. The unresolved conflict with her husband had conspired to create a kind of "death wish."

Using these techniques with other approaches, such as couple's counseling, can synergize both efforts. Including intimate partners in the therapy increases the probability that both parties grow together through the crisis, rather than grow apart.

Transferring one's conscious awareness into the affected body part makes it possible for the patient to see things from the affected part's point of view as well as strengthens the notion that she is not merely her body. This sub-personality dis-identification forces her to move towards self-identification so that she can realize that her personal value comes from being more than just her body.

And as with the case used to illustrate interactive guided imagery, the underlying issue with Marian was an unresolved grief issue complicated by the current physical assault on her body. Forgiveness in such situations seems to be the antidote to fear. The therapist intentionally used the exercise to interject a "live" message into the patient's conscious awareness.

Marian ultimately decided to go ahead and have the surgery, giving consent to the surgeon for a colostomy if it was deemed necessary. Unfortunately, her disease had already metastasized to such an extent that it was decided that her tumor was basically inoperable. Post-operatively, she and her husband reconciled and decided to opt for hospice care to ensure a high quality of palliative care and that bereavement follow-up for their son would be available. The unfinished business between her husband and herself was resolved. Marian died with serenity and peace, apparently not requiring her body's physical appearance to play an important role in her healing after all. What is often true is that we frequently get what we need, and not necessarily what we want.

THERAPEUTIC LETTER-WRITING: CONCEPTUAL FRAMEWORK

The writer, Nuala O'Faolin, notes:

There is an idea current in the prevailing culture that writing about something that pains you heals the pain. I was not, when I began my life story, and am not, healed of my mother. But you do gain a small distance from anything by keeping it in suspension in your mind while you work at finding the words to fit it. The process is so slow and incremental that you don't notice its effect but the point is that it is a process. I found out when I was a little girl that if you're crying uncontrollably and want to stop, the thing is to do something useful with your tears – water a plant, say. They'll dry up of themselves. The same happens when you try to make sentences out of painful material: the material lightens as it is put to work. [O'Faolin]

Writing has long been incorporated into psychotherapy. Pennebaker was able to demonstrate that patients who journal about their health problems need less medical care for as long as up to six months post-treatment. [Pennebaker] Writing about health issues can provide a map of the therapeutic process and can reveal the hidden opportunities an illness can provide. [Day]

Especially for people who may feel stigmatized, patients who are reluctant to speak openly about their body image issues may find writing an acceptable means of communication. [Rosenberg] Other advantages of writing include the fact that patients become actively engaged in their own treatment [McGihon], it can be an economical way of continuing work between sessions [Jordan & L'Abate], and it becomes a tool that, once learned, can be useful when coping with future crises. [Day] Such story-making provides opportunities for personal growth by protecting the ego, allowing the unconscious mind to hear a therapeutic message. [Heiney]

However, as can be predicted from the previous discussions, writing "about" is never as effectively powerful as writing "to," or "from." Again, since the focus of this clinical work is the re-integration of an assaulted body image, the patient's relationship with that part or function remains the focal point of therapy. Therefore, writing letters to and from the affected body part is a means to elevate mere writing "about" to a therapy that is highly evocative. [Rancour & Brauer] This may be crucial since many patients may undergo treatments for which they do not feel especially prepared. The ongoing nature of therapeutic letter-writing helps such patients adjust incrementally to work which otherwise might feel too intense to confront all at once. Since the letter-writing taps into non-logical, non-linear ways of knowing, much like guided imagery and empty chair work, the patient has access to realms of information about self that are not readily apparent, but are even more deeply felt as true.

THERAPEUTIC LETTER-WRITING: THE TECHNIQUE

In the hearing is the learning, but in the telling is the healing.
-Alcoholics Anonymous-

As with all such therapeutic encounters, the therapist begins by preparing one's self, by centering, and by operationalizing a caring intent towards the patient. The patient is then prepared by explaining the procedure and obtaining consent to proceed. Once the patient has been able to identify the body part or function which is being lost or altered, he is encouraged to describe the reaction to this crisis in detail. This serves as a springboard into the homework assignments that continue between each session. These sessions, by the way, can be as formalized as psychotherapy or simply integrated into outpatient clinical appointments. The goal of the intervention strategy remains the same, which is to assist the patient to continue to elaborate a new relationship with the affected body part.

The patient is directed to write a letter to the affected body part. The letter can be written all in one sitting or as an open-ended exercise, more closely resembling stream of consciousness. This exercise may also be used to cope with periods of insomnia when the patient can be encouraged to get out of a sleepless bed, and write down feelings until once again overtaken by sleep.

The letter should be uncensored in that the patient should be instructed to write whatever initially comes to mind. At the following session, the patient is asked to read the letter out loud. This becomes another opportunity for catharsis and very often stimulates a high degree of emotional mourning. The patient is then debriefed in terms of what it was like to write the letter, and what was discovered about the self that was previously unknown.

This then is followed by the next homework assignment, in which the patient is instructed to write a response to the initial letter from the point of view of the affected body part. Once more, at the next session, the patient is encouraged to read the letter out loud, and is debriefed in a similar fashion. The effort of dis-identification from the part that this exercise stimulates helps the patient to assume a different perspective, to remember that he is more than just a body. At the same time, it allows for grieving for, and transformation of, what is being lost or changed.

Each subsequent session can be the springboard for the next letter in the dialogue between patient and body part until it appears that there is indeed a coming to terms with how the altered part will be reintegrated into the whole of the person. Often this involves negotiation, forgiveness – as we have seen before – and the impetus to make this work mean something to the individual for his future welfare, and even perhaps for the welfare of others.

THERAPEUTIC LETTER-WRITING: CASE ILLUSTRATION

Ted R. is a 25 year old young man who is finally emerging from having been in a coma for a month. The intensive care unit staff is concerned about his ability to recover once he is able to understand what has happened to him while he was unconscious.

Ted has been an athlete, having been on the golf team while in college. He is currently employed as a pro working at a local golf club. While jogging, he apparently injured ligaments in his knee, and was advised to have the knee arthroscopically repaired. Post-operatively, he unfortunately developed a massive infection within the knee joint and it progressed so aggressively that he quickly became septic and lost consciousness. In efforts to stabilize him, he was given massive doses of antibiotics and had to be artificially ventilated.

At one point, it was decided that unless his affected leg was removed, his infection would overwhelm him. While he was unconscious, his parents, acting as his health care proxy, authorized an above the knee amputation in efforts to save his life. He is now recovering not only from his septicemia, but is surfacing to learn that while the last thing he consciously remembered was a knee-repair, he is now discovering that his leg has been amputated.

Once the therapist introduces herself to him, she stays with him as he explores the palpable absence of where his leg used to be, and she sits with him while he cries. Pain management is a priority due to phantom limb syndrome, and over several days, the pain service uses a PCA (patient controlled analgesia) pump to titrate the correct dosage of opioids to ensure adequate pain management so that his physical rehabilitation and his psychological, emotional and spiritual recovery can proceed.

During one of a series of visits, Ted appears to be over his initial shock and denial about his experience and is still trying to come to terms with his anger about having consented to a "simple" procedure. The rehabilitation staff report that he is refusing his physical therapy and is having trouble performing activities of daily living.

Therapist: Ted, you look particularly blue today.
Ted: I feel like my life is over.
Therapist: Can you say more about that?
Ted: My whole career has been built around golf, and now I feel like a gimp. What am I going to do for the rest of my life like this? (He gestures to his missing limb.)
Therapist: You sound like you're feeling pretty hopeless about the future.
Ted: (Angry) Wouldn't you feel that way? (Immediately contrite.) I'm sorry. When I think about the future, I just don't see one for someone like me. I don't know anything else except golf. And I don't want to learn anything else for that matter either.

Therapist: I know this is how you feel right now, but you will not always feel this way.

Ted: How can you be so sure?

Therapist: Because everything changes. Especially people.

Ted: Maybe other people do, but I don't see it for myself.

Therapist: Well would you mind my believing it for you until you can believe it for yourself?

Ted: Suit yourself.

Therapist: Ted, I'd like to make a suggestion. Would you humor me?

Ted: Whatever.

Therapist: Between now and the next time I see you, I'd like you to write a letter. This is a letter you are not going to send, but you are going to read it to me the next time I come to visit you.

Ted: Who is the letter to?

Therapist: Your lost leg.

Ted: You have got to be kidding, right?

Therapist: I told you you would have to humor me, Ted.

Ted: What is writing a letter to my leg going to accomplish?

Therapist: Your legs have always played an important role in your life. It was easy to take them for granted when you didn't have to think about them. Now you can't think of anything else. Working like this can be a way of helping you feel you are making progress so that you don't feel so paralyzed. You know: The journey of a thousand miles begins with the first step.

Ted: What's with all the walking metaphors?

Therapist: Seems to be the issue at hand, doesn't it?

Ted: So what do I say in this crazy letter?

Therapist: Whatever comes to mind. You could tell your leg what it has been like to lose it, what life has been like ever since you woke up. Things like that.

Ted: I guess I can do that. It just sort of creeps me out.

Therapist: Humor me.

Next session, Ted hands the therapist his letter.

Therapist: (Hands the letter back to him.) Read it to me out loud.

Ted: (Somewhat hesitantly, he begins to read out loud:) Dear Left Leg, I can't believe I am writing this to you. My counselor says I have to humor her, so I guess I am. (He stops and begins to choke up.) I cannot believe I am in this situation. I never really thought about you – pretty much took you for granted. Thought I'd always have you with me. Waking up without you has been so surreal. I am no longer a whole man. I feel like a cripple. I look like a cripple. This is robbing me of a way of life I have spent the past ten years preparing for. Ever since I was a kid, I've had a club in my hands. This pretty much takes it out of my hands-for good. (Momentarily stops, tearing up again.) I don't have a back-up plan. I have no other skills I can come up with at this time to earn my own living. I never thought of myself as a street person or someone who would have to live with his parents for the rest of his life. Now I'm thinking that way. I also look at this stump and wonder who will want a freak show like me. I am repulsed by my own body. How can I ever expect someone else to feel attracted to this? When I think about the future, I see myself growing old, unemployed and alone. I wish I had never consented to the surgery. I would have been in pain, but at least I would still have had you with me. I only have myself to blame. Signed, Don't Have a Leg to Stand On (Ted looks up.)

Therapist: What was it like to write that letter?

Ted: I only wrote it late last night because I knew you were coming in today. It was harder to do than it sounded when we first talked about it. I really didn't want to write it.

Therapist: Because…

Ted: (Crying.) I just wish I could go back in time and do this whole thing over. Last night, I had this dream that I was running across the greens at work. I don't know why I was running. I just was. Flying, so that my feet hardly touched the ground. It felt so real. It was just incredible. And then I woke up this morning, and had to remember all over again that I will never be able to run like that again. Never.

Therapist: (Sitting quietly with him while he cries. When the tears subside.) It is intense to realize that one cannot go back. That there is no "do over." Someone once told me that we never really get over our losses; we merely learn to live with them.

Ted: (Wiping his nose, nodding.) You got that right.

Therapist: But Ted, there are all sorts of ways we take flight in our lives. The vividness of your dream is a message from deep inside yourself.

Ted: I don't know what you mean.

Therapist: Are you ready for the next homework assignment?

Ted: I didn't know there was going to be all this homework when I met you.

Therapist: Your next assignment – should you choose to accept it – is that I want you to write a letter from your leg back to your self, responding to your first letter.

Ted: You've got to be kidding.

Therapist: No. I am not kidding. Would you be willing to do that?

Ted: I know – to humor you.

Therapist: (Smiles.)

Next session:

Ted: I wrote my letter right after our last session. The words just came flying out.

Therapist: (Smiles at the imagery of his language.) Can you read it to me?

Ted: Dear Don't Have a Leg to Stand On, Of course you have a leg to stand on – my mirror image. Hope you don't take him for granted because one leg is better than no legs. And remember, Ted, you are more than just a leg. You have got to stop blaming yourself for what happened to me. It was not your fault. You were doing the best you could by me. I know you are still in a state of shock over this, but trust me – better to be alive than the alternative. I am so sorry that you are feeling so hopeless. But the fact is just because you lost me doesn't mean your life is over. You have worked hard all your life. You will get over this. I do not hold anything against you. It is time you stopped doing that to yourself as well. If you do not get going with regard to your therapy, you may just as well lay down and die. Is that what you really want? I don't think so. If you can't do it for yourself, do it for me. Don't make the loss of me your excuse for quitting. That makes me responsible and I won't take that lying down! If you do that, then my having been with you while I was becomes pointless. If we have learned anything together, it has been to stand up and move ahead. And that is what I expect you to do now. Stand up and move ahead. Signed, Your Left Leg Ted: (Looking up, expectantly.)

Therapist: What was that like to write?

Ted: Like I said, it kinda creeps me out, but I feel like it is a voice from beyond the grave, kicking me in the butt.

Therapist: Literally. (Laughs with patient.)

Ted: Funny, that it was all just lying there, kinda right beneath the surface. If I hadn't seen all this in black and white, I don't think any of this would have occurred to me.

Therapist: Oh, I think it would have eventually. Putting it down on paper just bubbled it up to the surface faster.

Ted: You may be right, but I really don't know. I showed the letter to my parents and a couple of my friends. They thought it was weird, but interesting.

Therapist: And what do you think?

Ted: Same thing.

Therapist: Think you could write another letter back to your leg?

Ted: I suppose.

Next Session:

Ted: (Reading his letter.) Dear Left Leg, Thank you for the kick in the butt. And thank you too for forgiving me. I didn't realize how guilty I was feeling about all this. But seeing it on paper kind of laid it all out for me more clearly. I am rethinking a lot of my previous assumptions. I still really don't have any ideas about my future, but I seem to feel less sure that I will be living out of a homeless shelter or sleeping on a piece of cardboard under a bridge. It has been hard to go from living a life feeling secure in my future to living a life that seems pretty uncertain at this point. But I feel like you are right. I am going to give it a shot. One step at a time. I hope you will keep in touch. I like hearing from you. Helps me put up with the phantom pain if you seem less like a phantom. Just know I will never forget you. As long as I live. Signed, Ted

Therapist: What was that like to write?

Ted: Still very sad to write, and to read, but not near so painful. So where do we go from here?

Therapist: I have some further ideas about that.

Ted: Not more letters!

Therapist: No something different.

Ted: Thank God. I'm feeling crazy enough already with the letters.

THERAPEUTIC LETTER-WRITING: DISCUSSION

But what are our stories if not the mirrors we hold up to our fears?

-Wally Lamb-

Ted's latent humor comes through as an aid in helping him cope with his situation. His process became engaged as the exercise compelled him to experience not only his grief, but also provided him with a concrete way to express it, something that some young men may have difficulty putting into words. What is notable is that the language in Ted's letters comes alive with all sorts of walking and moving symbols: "kicked in the butt," "stand up and get moving," "one step at a time." The unconscious, if not intentional, use of such metaphors and dream work is the voice of Ted's inner wisdom to which the letters help him bridge in a non-linear, non-logical way. And the imagery all predicts movement (change).

Expressing confidence in the patient's ability to recover even when the patient can't feel it as yet is a legitimate role of the therapist. This is functionally "place-holding" for the patient's ego strength, until such time as the patient is sufficiently restored to be able to once again do that for himself. By not pushing Ted past the place where his grief has left him, the therapist creates a sacred space for him to be able to safely feel what he feels, and makes no demands that he be other than where he is. This gives him nothing to resist, and with that lack of transference, he can focus on his own process, rather than projecting it onto the therapeutic relationship.

Oftentimes, the forgiveness work can begin with the affected body part expressing its own grief over the experience, something the person may not be able to perceive from his own vantage point. Letter-writing can help the person dis-identify with the body part to once again experience self as being more than just a body. As the despondency recedes, the certainty about a dashed future can also recede with it.

Ted's ability to move past his psychospiritual "immobility" made him more receptive to other integrative therapeutic techniques. For example, the therapist showed him Kirlian photographs of leaves missing parts. Kirlian photography is a technique which captures the radiated energy of matter. Experiments in which leaves have been stripped or torn of their matter, demonstrate that their bioenergetic essence remains whole, despite the injury to their denser physical matter. (For examples, see the phantom leaf experiment at: *http://www.innergies.com/auras/photography.html*) This exercise helped Ted perceive himself as whole no matter what happened to his parts.

This paradigm shift was then followed with books, depicting in both word and image, stories of people who had lost limbs and still competed in sports, led purposeful work lives, had relationships and children. [Sabolich] Basically, this was an effort to assist Ted to see that he may still be able to retain his golf pro ambitions, albeit within a new paradigm of high level wellness. He was also receptive to meeting another person with an amputated leg who was engaged in a physically active job. The ability to see that this was still possible injected a new degree of hope into Ted's capacity to create a meaningful future for himself.

The therapist also asked for permission to contact his employer for conversations about how his job could be modified so that he could keep it. The Bureau of Vocational Rehabilitation was helpful, but as it turned out, Ted did not need to modify his job that much in order to eventually return to a productive career with the full cooperation of his employer. With the help of a newly-engineered prosthetic, Ted was still a remarkable teacher – and role model - on the greens. He also became a trained volunteer to help others adjust to amputations, hosting an annual golf event to benefit disabled veterans.

CONCLUSION

That which was lost and found again, that made more precious by restoration.
-The Eye of Horus-

Patients experiencing serious illness and its treatment often undergo alterations in body image. Such body image disturbances can be addressed with a number of effective treatment modalities, among them interactive guided imagery, empty chair work, and therapeutic letter-writing. The use of these interventions can help patients grieve the losses experienced when body parts or functions are surgically or medically altered, transform the relationships with their bodies, and help them re-integrate new identities. The process of rehabilitation can often be facilitated by this work and the quality of the patient's life can once more be restored, and sometimes, even transcended.

REFERENCES

Assagioli, R. (1980). *The act of will.* New York: Penguin Books.

Benjamin, H. (1995). *The wellness community guide to fighting for recovery from cancer.* New York: Tarcher-Putnam.

Bolen, J. Shinoda. (1996). *Close to the bone: Life-threatening illness and the search for meaning.* New York: Simon and Schuster.

Campbell, J. (1973). *The hero with a thousand faces.* Princeton, New Jersey: Princeton University Press.

Chamorro, T. (2005). Cancer and sexuality. In S. B. Baird (Ed.), *A cancer source book for nurses.* Boston: Jones and Barlett Publishers.

Cohen, L.J. (1994). Bibliotherapy: A valid treatment modality. *Journal of Psychosocial Nursing, 32 9,* pp. 40-44.

Day, A. L. (2001). The journal as a guide for the healing journey. *Nursing Clinics of North America, 36,* pp.131-142.

Doore, G. (1980). *Shaman's Path: Healing, personal growth and empowerment.* Boston: Shambhala Publications, Inc.

Ferrucci, P. (1982). *What we may be: Techniques for psychological and spiritual growth.* Los Angeles: J.P. Tarcher, Inc.

Frankl, V. (1997). *Man's search for meaning: An introduction to logotherapy.* New York: Washington Square Press.

Goffman, E. (1963). *Stigma: Notes on the management of spoiled identity.* Englewood, New Jersey: Prentice-Hall, Inc.

Heiney, S. (1995). The healing power of story. *Oncology Nursing Forum, 22 ,6,* pp.899–904.

James, O. (1997). *Play therapy: A comprehensive guide.* Northvale, New Jersey: Jason Aronson.

Jordan, K.B., & L'Abate, L. (1995). Programmed writing and therapy with symbiotically enmeshed patients. *American Journal of Psychotherapy, 49*, pp. 225-236.

Leshan, L. (1999). *Cancer as a turning point: A handbook for people with cancer, their families, and health professionals.* New York: Plume Press.

Malchiodi, C. (Ed.). (1999). *Medical art therapy with children.* Philadelphia: Jessica Kingsley.

McGihon, N.N. (1996). Writing as a therapeutic modality. *Journal of Psychosocial Nursing and Mental Health Services, 34*, 6, pp. 31-35.

Naperstek, B. (1995). *Staying well with guided imagery.* New York: Warner Books.

National Cancer Institute. (2005) Post-traumatic stress disorder. *http://www.cancer.gov/ cancertopics/pdq/supportivecare/post-traumatic-stress/HealthProfessional.*

O'Faolin, Nuala. (2003). *Almost There: The onward journey of a Dublin woman.* New Jersey: Riverhead Books.

Pennebaker, J.W. (1993). Putting stress into words: Health, linguistics, and therapeutic implications. *Behavior Research and Therapy, 31*, pp. 539-548.

Perls, F. (1969). *Gestalt therapy verbatim.* New York: Real People Press.

Perls, F. (1998). *Toward a psychology of being. (Third Edition)* New York: Van Nostrand.

Polster, E., & Polster, M. (1974). *Gestalt therapy integrated.* New York: Vintage Books.

Rancour, P. (1991). Guided Imagery: A technique for healing when curing is out of the question. *Perspectives in Psychiatric Care, Vol. 27, No. 4*, pp. 30-33.

Rancour, P. (1994). Interactive guided imagery with oncology patients: A case illustration. *Journal of Holistic Nursing, Vol. 12, No. 2*, pp. 148-154.

Rancour, P., & Brauer, K. (2003). A matched set: A case study in the use of letter-writing as a means of integrating an altered body image in a patient with recurrent breast cancer. Oncology Nursing Forum, pp. 841-846.

Rosenberg, L. (1990). The use of therapeutic correspondence: Creative approaches in psychotherapy. *Journal of Psychosocial Nursing, 28*, 11, pp. 29-33.

Sabolich, J. (1995) *You're not alone. Oklahoma City*, Oklahoma: Sabolich Prosthetic and Research Center.

Schneider, J. (1980). Clinically significant differences between grief, pathological grief and depression. *Patient Counseling and Health Education, 2*, pp. 267-275.

In: Body Image: New Research
Editor: Marlene V. Kindes, pp. 291-307

ISBN 1-60021-059-7
© 2006 Nova Science Publishers, Inc.

Chapter XIII

IMPACT OF VITILIGO ON BODY IMAGE: AN OVERVIEW

*Shahin Aghaei**

Department of Dermatology, Jahrom Medical School, Jahrom, Iran.

ABSTRACT

A healthy normal skin is essential for a person's physical and mental well being. It is an important aspect of their sexual attractiveness, a sense of well being and a sense of self confidence. The skin is the largest and most visible organ of the human body. Hence any discoloration on the skin visibly affects the witness and thus the person affected extremely.

Vitiligo is an important skin disease having major impact on the quality of life of sufferers. Although the disease does not produce direct physical impairment, it may considerably influence the psychological well-being of the patients. It has been suggested that patients suffer from low self-esteem, poor body image and a poor quality of life. A negative body image is directly related to self esteem. The more negative the perception of our bodies, the more negative we feel about ourselves. Vitiligo can also result in problems in interpersonal relations particularly as a result of depression and dissatisfaction. The men and women with vitiligo do not promote self- esteem or positive self image.

In this chapter, the impact of vitiligo on patient's body image in consideration of interpersonal relationship, psychological, and social aspects regarding cultural and geographical differences is reviewed.

---

* Correspondence concerning this article should be addressed to Shahin Aghaei, MD, Department of Dermatology, Jahrom Medical School, Jahrom, Iran. Tel.: +98 (791) 3331682; Fax: +98 (711) 2296439; shahinaghaei@yahoo.com.

INTRODUCTION

As Medansky and Handler [1] noted over 20 years ago, 'the skin is both the shelter which protects us and the façade which displays us.' Thus, 'just as the eyes are the mirror of the soul, the skin may reflect the psychosomatic personality and its struggles with life, conflict, and tension. Both the skin and the central nervous system emerge embriologically from the ectoderm. This provides some basis for the assumption that the skin and the brain may influence each other [2]. The skin situated in the interface between the body and the outside world, is a zone privileged by the interactions between the individual and the society [3].

Interest in the psychologic and social effects of various skin diseases has been increasing [4]. Studies have indicated that persons with a cutaneous disease experience a heightened level of distress, as measured by the General Health Questionnaire (GHQ) [5,6] and structured diagnostic interviews [7-9]. Attempts have been made to measure the ways that cutaneous disorders are disabling [10]. There are several scales to measure the extent of disability, some of which apply to particular conditions such as psoriasis [11,12] or acne [13,14] and others that can be used for a variety of conditions, such as the Dermatology Life Quality Index (DLQI) [15,16].. Weiss et al [9] compared the difficulties faced by patients who have vitiligo with leprosy in India; Porter et al [17-19] described the ways that vitiligo can affect social and sexual relationships in America. In these studies, a majority of patients reported that they experienced anxiety and embarrassment when meeting strangers or beginning a new sexual relationship, most experienced staring by others, and many believed they had been the victims of rude remarks. Similarly, Salzer and Schallruter [20] reported that 75% of patients attending a vitiligo clinic found their disfigurement moderately or severely intolerable.

In this chapter, the impact of vitiligo on patient's body image and quality of life in consideration of interpersonal relationship, psychological, and social aspects is reviewed.

BODY IMAGE & QUALITY OF LIFE

Body image is the way people perceive themselves and, equally important, the way they think others see them. Body image is constantly changing, continuously modified by biological growth, trauma, or decline; it is significantly influenced and molded by life circumstances -- accentuated by pleasure or pain [21].

Body image refers to our beliefs and feelings about how our bodies look and function. Our body image is influenced by our family, our friends, the media and society in general. It's heavily influenced by what we think we "should" look like in order to be attractive and how we think our bodies should "perform." Many of us-both males and females-are not satisfied with our bodies, and our body image is often not a true reflection of how our bodies actually are [22].

Persons' body image is their perception of their physical appearance. It is more than what a person thinks they will see in a mirror, but is inextricably tied to their self-esteem and acceptance by peers. Persons with a poor body image will perceive their own body as being unattractive or even repulsive to others. While a person with good body image, or positive "body acceptance", will either see themselves as attractive to others, or will at least accept it as is [23].

Body image is based on everyone thoughts and feelings about the way one's body looks. Sometimes the way she/he thinks other people are judging her/his appearance can influence her/his body image. Poor body image comes from negative thoughts and feelings about the appearance, and a healthy body image is made up of thoughts and feelings that are positive. Body image is a major factor in self-esteem; which is the way she/he thinks and feels about her/himself as a person. Self-esteem relates to how much one person like her/himself, and how she/he recognizes or appreciates her/his individual character, qualities, skills, and accomplishments. As with body image, self-esteem can also be based on how she/he thinks other people look at her/him as a person. People who have low self-esteem may not feel confident about themselves or how they look. It is often hard for them to see that they are an important and capable person. People with good self-esteem have a positive and confident attitude about their body and mind, and can recognize their strengths as well as personal value and worth. Good self-esteem is important for everyone because it helps she/he keeps a positive outlook on life and makes she/he feels proud of the person she/he is, both inside and out. Most teens with good self-esteem find life much more enjoyable. They tend to have better relationships with peers and adults, find it easier to deal with mistakes or disappointments, and are more likely to stick with a task until they succeed. Good self-esteem gives her/him the: *courage* to try new things, *power* to believe in her/himself, *confidence* to make healthy choices for her/his mind and body now and throughout the life. They may also have trouble dealing with people who stare, question, or make comments about their appearance. Anyone (with or without a facial difference) often feels uncomfortable if they are being stared at. These situations can make it difficult to meet new people, make friends, try out for sports teams, join clubs, and even apply for a job. It is hard to have pride and confidence if they feel like most social interactions leave they feeling bad about themselves. [24]

Overall quality of life (QOL) is an all inclusive concept incorporating all factors that impact upon an individual's life, whereas health-related QOL is more narrowly defined relating only to health aspects [25]. Good QOL is present when 'the hopes of an individual are matched by experience' [26]. QOL in dermatology is measured for clinical, research, audit and for political and financial purposes [25].

All clinicians use an intuitive view of how much the skin disease is affecting their patients when taking management decisions, but patients may assess QOL differently from their doctors [27]. When there are data to interpret the scores, more accurate measurement of QOL might be helpful in guiding management decisions, for example where expensive or hazardous therapy is being started. The use of simple QOL measures is usually welcomed by patients who wish to express their concerns.

CUTANEOUS DISEASE AND BODY IMAGE

A person's skin is one of the most important features of body image. Cutaneous disease may have severe detrimental effects on body image. In childhood and, especially adolescence, these effects are amplified by psycho-social pressures and influences. So childhood and adolescence cutaneous disease is recognized as an important factor in the development of a modified self image and poor self esteem. Individuals may develop coping mechanisms in order to manage their daily activities. This often includes avoidance techniques, covering up affected areas, and a reticence to leave the family home. Some individuals will develop somatisation with unusual symptoms to avoid school attendance, or even develop habits of self –harm and dermatitis artefacta [28].

Obvious skin disease may be inherited (such as dystrophic epidermolysis bullosa, ichthyosiform erythrodermas and others), or acquired (such as vitiligo). Disease extent does not necessarily correlate with psychological morbidity, and relatively mild disease may cause severe mental health problems [28,29].

Major differences in appearance due to burns, birth defects or other diseases and disorders can contribute to a poor body image and low self-esteem. The effects of body image on self-esteem can be especially powerful during the teenage years. Although it's perfectly normal to have negative thoughts and feelings towards the facial difference, finding ways to be positive is the key to building a healthy body image and good self-esteem. [24]

The physical or perceived disfigurement of the integument itself can become a source of significant stress, with a considerable impact on an individual's psychological, social, and physical well being. This is often overlooked or underestimated by the general public, many health insurers, and the medical community, including dermatologists. Although dermatologic conditions are responsible for a significant source of social stigmatization in many human societies and cultures, it is only recently that we have begun to quantitate the effect of skin disease on an individual's quality of life (QOL). Psoriasis, for example, impairs the social life of 40 percent of patients and 64 percent feel that their disease significantly impacts their socioeconomic functioning [11]. The impairment of QOL correlates with disease severity in patients with atopic dermatitis, which is also associated with high levels of anxiety, sleep, and mood disturbances [30]. Urticaria patients suffer QOL impairments similar to that of patients with coronary artery disease waiting for bypass surgery [31]. Melasma was found to have a significant impact on women's QOL. The increased health-related QOL burden of melasma was a composite of many factors, with a clearly greater impact of psychosocial factors on the QOL outcome [32]. Acne patients, with fewer symptoms than those with conditions such as psoriasis or eczema, have similar levels of deleterious emotional states [13,14]. The Dermatology Life Quality Index (DLQI) [15] and the Skindex-16 [33] are simple and practical validated instruments that can be used both in the office setting and for research purposes to quickly evaluating QOL. Specific instruments are also available for patients with psoriasis [11], eczema [34], acne [14], and urticaria [31] among others. These tests are helpful tools that can assess improvement in both the physical and the psychosocial aspects of a patient's disease. The sum of observations, studies, and therapeutic interventions suggests that stress plays a significant role in the biology and clinical expression of skin diseases, and supports the notion that therapies that address this issue may have a positive impact on the well-being of patients with dermatologic diseases.

Although many psychological studies of the physically handicapped have been conducted in recent years, less attention has given to the victims of skin disorders. Skin disfigurement, however, may be a barrier to privileges and opportunities because of the profound social significance of appearance and the attitudes and prejudices of society toward one whose appearance is atypical. The cosmetic disfigurement which accompanies skin disease may have profound effects on a patient's self-esteem and social relationships, and vitiligo is no exception [35].

The social effects of skin diseases may cause more hardship than the physical limitations. Physical disfigurements affect the nature of the impressions we form of individuals, the causes we assign to their behavior, and whether we choose to affiliate with them. Physically attractive people are believed to have more socially desirable traits than others. Individuals are more likely to attribute traits of kindness and intelligence to good-looking people, and better-looking people are thought to have more self-control, competence, and be better adjusted [36]. Although sometimes traits attributed to those who are physically disfigured may be positive [37] for the most part physically disfigured individuals are likely to provoke negative emotions [38].

Physically attractive people are not only evaluated more positively research have also shown that they treated better by peers, teachers, friends, strangers, and employers. Visibly disfigured people face special obstacles in efforts to maintain satisfying social relationships. Interactions between the physically disfigured and colleagues are often strained and tension-producing, and marked by stilted and artificial communication, both verbal and nonverbal [34]. In response to these pressures, impaired individuals may exhibit discomfort and strain in social relationships and may anticipate discriminatory interaction with the nonhandicapped [37]. Because of the social significance of the skin and face, the stigmatization of the cosmetically impaired may equal or exceed that of those with other body afflictions [39].

Beauty presupposes a blemish-free skin. Literature dealing directly with skin disease agrees that the victims of such disorders do indeed experience the same problems in social interaction that are faced by individuals with other types of visible disfigurements [40].

VITILIGO

Vitiligo, derivative of *vitium* (Latin) means flaw or blemish, is a specific type of leukoderma (white skin) manifested characteristically by depigmentation of the epidermis. Occasionally the loss of melanin is partial, i.e. hypopigmentation. Vitiligo is best defined as an acquired, progressive disorder that selectively destroys (or that results in the selective disappearance) of some or all melanocytes residing in the interfollicular epidermis and occasionally in the hair follicles as well.

Vitiligo affects all races and has a long history [41]. It is stated that it occurs in 1% to 2% of the world's population [42,43]. There is a preponderance of female in most series based on outpatient attendances, but the frequency in the population is probably the same in both sexes [44], the female prevalence in some studies probably can be attributed to greater concern (and greater willingness to express concern) about a cosmetic defect. Between 30 and 40% of patients have a positive family history [42], and a genetic factor is undoubtedly involved. Inheritance may be polygenic or determined by an autosomal dominant gene of variable penetrance. The condition is seen in monozygotic twins [45].

Vitiligo can begin at any age, but in 50% of cases it develops before the age of 20 years. The condition is slowly progressive [42,46].

Hypomelanotic macules are usually first noted on the sun-exposed areas of skin, on the face (Fig. 1) or dorsa of hands (Fig. 2). These areas are prone to sunburn. Rarely, itching in the absence of sunburn may occur. Damage to the 'normal' skin frequently results in an area of depigmentation. The amelanotic macules in vitiligo are found particularly in areas that are normally hyperpigmented, for example the face, axillae, groins, areolae and genitalia. Areas subjected to repeated friction and trauma are also likely to be affected, for example the dorsa of hands, feet, elbows, knees and ankles. The distribution of the lesions is usually symmetrical, although sometimes it is unilateral and may have a dermatomal arrangement. Rarely, there is complete vitiligo, but a few pigmented areas always remain [42,46].

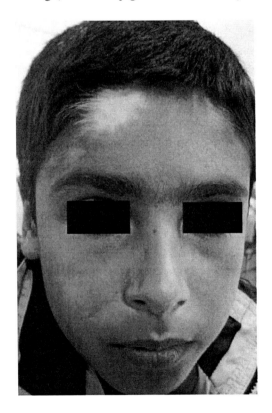

Fig. 1. Vitiligo on face.

The pigment loss may be partial or complete or both may occur in the same areas (trichrome vitiligo). The macules have a convex outline, increase irregularly in size and fuse with neighboring lesions to form complex patterns. The hairs in the patches frequently remain normally pigmented, but in older lesions the hairs too are often amelanotic. The margins of the lesions may become hyperpigmented. The main symptom is the cosmetic disability, although some patients present because of sunburn in the amelanotic areas [42,46].

The mechanism(s) by which the melanocytes are lost is not yet identified unequivocally. Various theories are suggested for the etiology of vitiligo; the same mechanism may not apply to all cases.

Current reviews of its etiology suggest that vitiligo is probably a heterogeneous disorder encompassing multiple etiologies. Potential mechanisms include genetic defects, neural and neuropeptide defects, biochemical, self-destruction, and viral and autoimmune mechanisms [43,47].

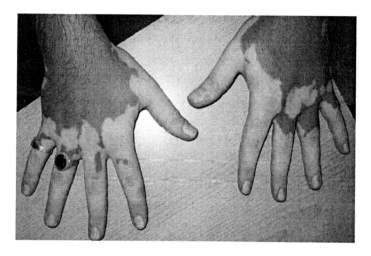

Fig. 2. Vitiligo on back of hands.

The most popular candidate is an immune-mediated pathogenesis. The *autoimmune hypothesis* is based on the clinical association of vitiligo with a number of disorders considered to be also autoimmune (Table 1) [48]. Organ-specific autoantibodies to thyroid, gastric parietal cells and adrenal tissue are found in the serum more frequently in patients with vitiligo than in the general population [49,50].

Table1. Disorders associated with vitiligo [48].

1-	Thyroid disease (hypo/hyperthyroidism [79])
2-	Pernicious anemia
3-	Addison's disease [80]
4-	Diabetes mellitus [81]
5-	Hypoparathyroidism
6-	Myasthenia gravis
7-	Alopecia areata
8-	Morphea and lichen sclerosis
9-	Halo nevus
10-	Malignant melanoma [82]
11-	Rheumatoid arthritis [43]

The *neurogenic hypothesis* [51] suggests that a compound is released at peripheral nerve endings in the skin that may inhibit melanogenesis and could have a toxic effect on melanocytes. There is little support for this hypothesis.

The *self-destruct theory* of Lerner [42] suggests that melanocytes destroy themselves due to a defect of a natural protective mechanism that removes toxic melanin precursors.

It has been suggested that defective keratinocyte metabolism plays a major role with catalase levels in the epidermis of vitiligo [52]. A new hypothesis has been put forward for the pathogenesis of this disorder [53].

The typical vitiligo macule has a chalk- or milk-white color, is round to oval in shape, has slightly brushed to fairly distinct, often scalloped margins, measures from several millimeters or many centimeters in diameter, and usually lacks other epidermal changes. There may be one, several, or up to hundreds of macules that may be small to large in size, even in a single patient. As vitiligo naturally evolves over time, the macules enlarge, coalesce, and impart a scalloped appearance to the interface of the normal and vitiligo skin. [46]

Vitiligo patients often can attribute the onset of their disease to a specific life event, crisis, or illness. Many can relate it to loss of a job, death of a close family member, an accident, or a severe systemic disease. In some, the onset follows a physical injury such as a cut or abrasion; this development of vitiligo congruent with a site of injury is referred to as the *Koebner phenomenon* and is characteristic of at least a third of vitiligo patients. Many patients related onset to sun exposure; this may cause koebnerization in predisposed individuals [46,54,55].

There are several clinical types of vitiligo. The *unilateral (segmental)* form usually does not cross the midline and does not have a classical dermatomal distribution but affects one segment of the integument. The segment might be composed of several or parts of several adjacent dermatomes or have no relationship to dermatomes at all. The progression is usually limited to months or a few years [56,57].

The *bilateral (non-segmental)* form is characterized by bilateral, usually symmetrical, depigmented macules. It is further subdivided into a localized form (*focal vitiligo*), limited to small areas of the integument, and into the *generalized type*. The latter is the most common type of vitiligo characterized by widespread extensive depigmentation that most commonly spread throughout the life of the individual. These macules are often symmetrically placed and involve extensor surfaces; the most common extensor surfaces include interphalangeal joints, metacarpal/metatarsal interphalangeal joints, elbows, and knees. Other surfaces involved include volar wrists, malleoli, umbilicus, lumbosacral area, anterior tibia, and axillae. Vitiligo macules may be periorificial and involve the skin around the eyes, nose, ears, mouth, and anus. Periungual involvement may occur alone or with certain mucosal surfaces (lips, distal penis, nipples); the latter is lip-tip vitiligo. In addition there is a very rare variety of generalized vitiligo, *universal vitiligo*, that seems to be a manifestation of a systemic autoimmune disease. This disorder is manifested by vitiligo, as well as multiple endocrine failures such as diabetes mellitus, adrenal insufficiency, thyroid dysfunction and gonadal dysfunction. All of the latter endocrine abnormalities seem to be caused by autoantibodies but the cause of the loss of melanocytes remains unidentified [46,54,55].

The diagnosis of generalized vitiligo in a patient with progressive, acquired chalk-white macules in typical sites is normally straightforward. Few such acquired conditions are as patterned and symmetric as vitiligo can be. Wood's lamp examination may be required to visualize macules in patients with lighter *skin phototype* (SPT) and to identify macules in sun-protected areas. The natural course of vitiligo is unpredictable. The most common course is one of gradual evolution of existing macules and periodic development of new ones.

Vitiligo, particularly in brown and black peoples and in Caucasian persons who can tan deeply SPT III, IV may be a psychosocial disaster [46,54,55].

Therapies for vitiligo include topical and systemic steroids, topical and systemic psoralen photochemotherapy, narrowband and broadband ultraviolet B (UVB), antioxidants and vitamins, khelin, phenylalanine, immunomodulators and immunosuppressants, depigmentation therapy, and a variety of surgical approaches [58,59].

VITILIGO IMPACT ON QUALITY OF LIFE AND BODY IMAGE

Last decade has witnessed an increasing interest in psychological effects of various skin diseases and quality of life in patients suffering from these diseases. A healthy normal skin is essential for a person's physical and mental well-being. It is an important aspect of their sexual attractiveness, a sense of well-being and a sense of self confidence. The skin is the largest and most visible organ of the human body. Hence any blemish on the skin visibly affects the witness and thus the person affected profoundly [60].

Vitiligo is an important skin disease having major impact on the quality of life of patients suffering from vitiligo. Appearance of skin can condition an individual self-image, and any pathological alteration can have psychological consequences [60,61].

Although the disease does not produce direct physical impairment, it may considerably influence the psychological well-being of the patients. It has been suggested that patients suffer from low self-esteem, poor body image and a poor quality of life [62].

Many vitiligo patients feel distressed and stigmatized by their condition. These patients often develop negative feeling about it, which are reinforced by their experiences over a number of years. Most patients of vitiligo report feelings of embarrassment, which can lead to a low self-esteem and social isolation [63].

In one study, over half of individuals with vitiligo said that people stare at them, 20% said that they have been the recipients of rude remarks by strangers, one-third said that interaction with strangers is especially stressful, and that vitiligo interfered with their relationships with the opposites sex [18]. Embarrassment during sexual relationships was especially frequent for men with vitiligo [17].

A questionnaire and interview study of 326 vitiligo patients treated in two major hospitals illustrates these points about the importance of appearance in psychological adjustment, the impact of the physical disfigurement caused by depigmentation of vitiligo, and the variation in response to a physically disfiguring condition. Over two-thirds of these patients described themselves as worried about vitiligo, primarily about its spread, whether their children would inherit the disease, whether new cures would be found, and other general carcinophobic fears. Many patients felt stigmatized by their condition [18].

Vitiligo on the face, head and neck substantially affects the quality of life, independently of degree of involvement [3,16,64].

In Iran and perhaps elsewhere also men, women and children with vitiligo face severe psychological and social problems. It is more acute in the case of young women and children. In Iran vitiligo is unfortunately associated with some religious beliefs. In some religious texts, it is said that a person who suffers from vitiligo should not become as a Mullah (a person versed in theology and sacred law). Thus people suffering from vitiligo in Iran and perhaps in other developing countries have more social problems than in developed countries. This is seriously felt among young unmarried women. This is so because of arranged marriages. Thus a young woman with vitiligo in Iran has little chance of getting married. A married women developing vitiligo after marriage shall have marital problems perhaps ending in divorce due to religious beliefs and civil rules.

Vitiligo is thus an important skin disease having major impact on the quality of life of patients suffering from vitiligo. Appearance of skin can condition an individual self-image, and any pathological alteration can have psychological consequences [63]. Many vitiligo patients feel distressed and stigmatized by their condition. They attract undue attention from the general public some times whispered comments, antagonism and ostrisisam. The self image of the vitiligo patients drops considerably and may lead to depression. These patients often develop negative feeling about it, which are reinforced by their experiences over a number of years. Most patients of vitiligo report feelings of embarrassment, which can lead to a low self-esteem and social isolation [61]. Vitiligo lesions over face may be particularly embarrassing and the frustration of resistant lesions over exposed part of hands and feet can lead to anger and disillusionment. Particularly in teenagers, mood disturbances including irritability and depression are common. Patients with vitiligo are very sensitive to the way other perceives them and they will often withdraw, because they anticipate being rejected. Sometimes, strangers and even close friends can make extremely hurtful and humiliating comments. The impact of such factors is profound subjecting them to emotional distress, interference with their employment, or use tension-lessoning, oblivion-producing substances such as alcohol [65]. Severe depression has been known to lead to suicide attempts [66].

Patients with vitiligo often suffer financial loss because they often have to take time off work to attend hospital appointments like PUVA appointment. Vitiligo lesions over exposed sites can adversely affect a person's chances of getting a job at interview and so restrict career choices. Vitiligo beginning in childhood can be associated with significant psychological trauma that may have long lasting effects on the personal self-esteem of these children. Children with vitiligo usually avoid sport or restrict such activities. Children often lose vital days from school. Parents of children with vitiligo may have to take time off their work to regularly accompany them for hospital appointments. Children with vitiligo deal with the disease well or be devastated by it, often depending on the attitude of their parents, siblings, relatives, teachers, friends, baby sitters etc [67]. Vitiligo can also result in problems in interpersonal relations particularly as a result of depression and frustration. Patients often feel that their family members are not supportive or lack understanding. The chronic nature of disease, long term treatment, lack of uniform effective therapy and unpredictable course of disease is usually very demoralizing for patients suffering from vitiligo. Compliance for regular long term visits for PUVA/narrow band UVB therapy; side effects of immunosuppressive therapies, long term risk of photoaging and carcinogenesis with phototherapy are other limitations for vitiligo patients.

Some workers have studied various factors influencing quality of life in patients with vitiligo in past [15,29]. Porter et al [17] reported that majority of vitiligo patients experienced anxiety and embarrassment when meeting strangers or beginning a new sexual relationship and many felt that they had been the victims of rude remarks. Salzer and Schallreuter [20] reported that 75% of vitiligo patients found their disfigurement moderately or severly intolerable. A possible relationship between stress and the development of vitiligo is under investigation. Al-Abadie et al [68] indicated that psychological stress increases level of neuroendocrine hormones which affects the immune system and alters the level of neuropeptides. The increase in the level of neuropeptides may be the initiating event in pathogenesis of vitiligo. In a study of 150 vitiligo patients, the nature and extent of the social and psychological difficulties associated with the disease and their impact on treatment outcome by using Dermatology Life Quality Index [DLQI] was assessed. The results clearly demonstrated that patients with high DLQI scores responded less favorably to a given therapeutic modality thereby suggesting that additional psychological approaches may be particularly helpful in these patients [69]. Papadopoulos et al [70] have shown that counseling can help to improve body image, self esteem and quality of life of patients with vitiligo, also having positive effect on course of the disease. It is important to recognize and deal with psychological components of this disease to improve their quality of life and to obtain a better treatment response.

Self-esteem, or favorable attitude toward the self, is associated with positive reaction to stress, and those with a positive self-image are better able to cope with the effect of physical disabilities. Vitiligo patients with low self-esteem manifested considerably more psychological disturbance due to the disease than did those whose self-esteem was high. Visibility of vitiligo and discrimination from others also were related to degree of disturbance caused by vitiligo, but severity of the condition was not the most important factor predicting poor adjustment. Someone with low self-esteem may react with depression to even a mild case of vitiligo, while someone with good self-esteem may be relatively unperturbed by more severe manifestations of vitiligo [71].

WHAT CAN WE DO?

Because there may be a connection between stress and exacerbation of vitiligo [72], psychologic interventions such as training in relaxation skills and other psychotherapeutic interventions [73,74] may be helpful. Others would argue that a more basic dimension of assertiveness and self-confidence are crucial and that when persons are able to adjust the reality of their disfigurement they are more able to form new relationships and be less distressed by others' reactions [75].

Children and adolescents with cutaneous disease have a higher prevalence of suicidal ideation, and attempted suicide when compared to their unaffected peers [28]. Organisations such as *Changing Faces,* and support groups such as *The Vitiligo Society* have provided invaluable leadership, support and advice for patients with skin disease. Individual and group liaison may greatly improve individuals' body image and self esteem [28]. Patients with a disfiguring or obvious skin disease can learn appropriate management not only of their skin disease, but of the disease's impact on their esteem, and on the impact of their skin disease on the general public. Dermatologists are increasingly aware that this important aspect of dermatological care is necessary for the well-being of their patients. Also training departments are increasingly aware that medical students need training in their approach to and management of patients with disfiguring skin conditions [28]. Being told that vitiligo is 'only a cosmetic disorder' is small comfort to the majority of patients who experience some degree of psychological stress due to the disease. Vitiligo must not be ignored by the physician. The psychological effect of skin disease should not be trivialized. Skin conditions are not 'only cosmetic disorders', but may have profound psychological effects on the lives of those whom they afflict because of the importance of appearance in how we evaluate and interact with others.

For those patients who manifest psychological ill effects due to vitiligo, it often helps to conceal the condition so that it is not so visible. There are several concealment strategies. Vitiligo is most noticeable when normal skin is tanned, since the contrast between the tanned skin and the vitiligo makes the depigmentation more visible. Patients can be advised to stay out of the sun at peak periods except during treatment time or use a strong sunscreen. Sun protection products are numbered according to the sun protection factor (SPF), with the higher numbers giving more protection. Patients with vitiligo should use a sunscreen with an SPF of 15 or higher. During treatment, an SPF of 8-10 protects against sunburn but dose not block the UVA needed for treatment.

Another helpful strategy is to conceal the vitiligo with clothing, if it is possible to do so. In one study, more than half the patients reported that they wore special clothing, often using a combination of hats, gloves, long stockings, and long sleeves in order to conceal effectively the depigmented skin and avoid negative reactions from others [76].

Concealment of the depigmented areas by cosmetics is another common strategy utilized by patients. Although appearance is a central part of the feminine role definition, studies of patients with vitiligo show no significant gender differences with regard to degree of disturbance by vitiligo. This is due in part to the fact that women are more likely than men in psychological adjustment, however, have been found in psoriasis patients, where the disorder cannot be disguised cosmetically [76,77].

The use of decorative cosmetics in disfiguring skin diseases is an effective, well-tolerated measure increasing the patients' quality of life [78]. Patients with more profound psychological reactions should be referred for counseling. Vitiligo patients can benefit from cognitive behavioral therapy in terms of coping and living with vitiligo [70].

Adjuvant psychosocial interventions could also mediate an increased adherence to medical treatments, provide social support, decrease stress or alter the response to stress, ameliorate anxiety, aid patients to develop better coping mechanisms, improve depression, and help with self image or distorted body perception.

CONCLUSION

To conclude vitiligo has a profound effect on the quality of life and body image of vitiligo patients and so the patients go to any extent in getting it treated although it is not life threatening. The dermatologists should treat it as serious disease with the various treatment modes now available and not dismiss simply because of not having a completely successful treatment. Improving the physician's interpersonal skills with the vitiligo patients increases patient's satisfaction and consequently may have a positive effect on adherence to treatment protocol and better out come of treatments.

REFERENCES

[1]   Medansky RS, Handler RM. Dermatopsychosomatics: classification, physiology and the therapeutic approach. *J Am Acad Dermatol* 1981; 5: 125-136.
[2]   Folks DG, Warnock JK. Psychocutaneous disorders. *Current Psychiatry Reports* 2001; 3: 219-25.
[3]   Zghal A, Zeglaoui F, Kallel L, Karmous R, Ben Ammar H, Lebbane R, Kammoun MR. Quality of life in dermatology: Tunisian version of the skindex-29. *Tunis Med.* 2003; 81(1): 34-7.
[4]   Rasmussen J. Psychosomatic dermatology. *Arch Dermatol* 1990: 126: 90-3.
[5]   Hughes J, Barraclough B, Hamblin L, et al. Psychiatric symptoms in dermatology patients. *Br J Psychiatry* 1983: 143: 51-4.
[6]   Root S, Kent G, Al-Abadie M. The relationship between disease severity, disability, and psychological distress in patients undergoing PUVA treatment for psoriasis. *Dermatology* 1994; 189: 234-7.
[7]   Rauch P, Jellinek M, Murphy J, et al. Screening for psychosocial dysfunction in pediatric dermatology practice. *Clin Pediatr* 1991; 30: 493-7.
[8]   Wessely S, Lewis H. The classification of psychiatric morbidity in attenders at a dermatology clinic. *Br J Psychiatry* 1989; 155: 686-91.
[9]   Weiss M, Doongaji D, Siddarha S, et al. The explanatory model interview catalogue (EMIC). *Br J Psychiatry* 1992; 160: 819-30.
[10]   Ryan T. Disability in dermatology. *Br J Hosp Med* 1991; 46: 33-6.
[11]   Finlay A, Coles E. The effect of psoriasis on quality of life of 369 patients. *Br J Dermatol* 1995; 132: 236-44.
[12]   Finlay A, Khan G, Luscombe D, et al. Validation of sickness impact profile and psoriasis disability index in psoriasid. *Br J Dermatology* 1990; 123: 751-56.
[13]   Motley R, Finlay AY. Practical use of a disability index in the routine management of acne. *Clin Exp Dermatol* 1992; 17: 1-3.
[14]   Aghaei S, Mazharinia N, Jafari P, Abbasfard Z. The Persian version of Cardiff Acne Disability Index: reliability and validity study. *Saudi Med J* 2006; 27(1): 447-9.
[15]   Finlay A, Khan G. Dermatology Life Quality Index (DLQI): a simple practical measure for routine clinical use. *Clin Exp Dermatol* 1994; 19: 210-6.

[16] Aghaei S, Sodaifi M, Jafari P, Mazharinia N, Finlay A. DLQI scores in vitiligo: reliability and validity study of the Persian version. *BMC Dermatol* 2004; 4: 8.

[17] Porter J, Beuf A, Lerner A, et al. The effect of vitiligo on sexual relationships. *J Am Acad Dermatol* 1990; 22: 221-2.

[18] Porter J, Beuf A, Lerner A, et al. Response to cosmetic disfigurement: patients with vitiligo. *Cutis* 1987; 39: 493-4.

[19] Porter J, Beuf A. Response of older people to impaired appearance: the effect of age on disturbance by vitiligo. *J Aging Stud* 1988; 2: 167-81.

[20] Salzer B Schallreuter K. Investigation of the personality structure in patients with vitiligo and a possible association with catecholamine metabolism. *Dermatology* 1995; 190: 109-15.

[21] Cash & Pruzinsky (1990). Journal article unknown, 80.

[22] *www.ualberta.ca/dept/health/public_html/ healthinfo/Decisions/bodyimage.*

[23] *www.en.wikipedia.org/wiki/Body_image.*

[24] www.youngwomenshealth.org/facial_difference.html

[25] Finlay AY. Quality of life measurement in dermatology: a practical guide. *Br J Dermatol* 1997; 136: 305-14.

[26] Calman KC. Quality of life in cancer patients – hypothesis. *J Med Ethics* 1984; 10: 124-7.

[27] Slevin ML, Plant H, Lynch D, et al. Who should measure quality of life, the doctor or the patient? *Br J Cancer* 1988; 57: 109-12.

[28] Bewley A. Skin disease and its impact on body image. *www.eadv2005.com/scientific /courses/C5.11.doc*

[29] Kent G, Al-abadie M. Factors affecting responses on dermatology life quality index among vitiligo sufferers. *Clin Exp Dermatol* 1996;21:330–333.

[30] Eun HC, Finlay AY. Measurement of atopic dermatitis disability. *Ann Dermatol* 1990; 2: 9-12.

[31] O'Donnell BF, Lawlor F, Simpson J, et al. Chronic urticaria: impact on quality of life. *Br J Dermatol* 1995; 133 (Suppl. 45): 27.

[32] Balkrishnan R, McMichael AJ, Camacho FT, et al. Development and validation of a health-related quality of life instrument for women with melasma. *Br J Dermatol* 2003; 149: 572-7.

[33] Chren MM et al: Measurement properties of Skindex-16: A brief quality-of-life measure for patients with skin diseases. *J Cutan Med Surg* 2001; 5:105.

[34] Salek MS, Finlay AY, Luscombe DK, et al. Cyclosporin greatly improves the quality of life of adults with severe atopic dermatitis. *Br J Dermatol* 1993; 129: 422-30.

[35] Porter J. The psychological effects of vitiligo: response to impaired appearance. In: Hann SK, Nordlund JJ. *Vitiligo*, 2000, Blackwell Science Ltd, Oxford, UK, pp: 97-100.

[36] Jones E, Farina A, Hastorf A, Markus H, Miller D, Scott R. *Social Stigma: the Psychology of Marked Relationships.* 1984, W. H. Freeman, New York.

[37] Comer R. Piliavin J. The effects of physical deviance on face to face interaction: the other side. *J Personality and Social Psychol* 1972; 23: 33-9.

[38] Goffman E. Stigma. 1963; Prentice Hall, Englewood Cliffs, NJ.

[39] Cassileth B, Lusk B, Tenaglia A. A psychological comparison of patients with malignant melanoma and other dermatological disorders. *J Am Acad Dermatol* 1982; 7: 742-46.

[40] Shuster S, Fisher G, Harris E, Binnell D. The effects of skin diseases on self image. *Br J Dermatol* 1978; 99: 18-19.

[41] Koranue RV Sachdeva KG. Vitiligo. *Int J Dermatol* 1988; 27: 676-81.

[42] Lerner AB. On the etiology of vitiligo and gray hair. *Am J Med* 1971; 51: 141-7.

[43] Grimes PE. Therapeutic trends for the treatment of vitiligo. *Cosmetic Dermatol* 2002; 15(6): 21-5.

[44] Howitz J, Brodthagen H, Schwartz M, et al. Prevalence of vitiligo. *Arch Dermatol* 1977; 113: 47-52.

[45] Cunliffe WJ, Hall R, Newell DJ, et al. Vitiligo, thyroid disease and autoimmunity. *Br J Dermatol* 1968; 80: 135-9.

[46] Ortonne JP, Mosher DB, Fitzpatrick TB, eds. In: *Vitiligo and Other Hypomelanosis of Hair and Skin.* New York, Plenum Medical, 1983: 129-310.

[47] Adiloglu AK, Basak PY, Can R, et al. Vitiligo and human herpesvirus 6. Is there a relationship? *Saudi Med J* 2005; 26(3): 492-4.

[48] Bleehen SS. Disorders of skin colors. In: Champion RH, Burton JL, Burns DA, Breathnach SM, eds. *Textbook of Dermatology.* London, Blackwell Science Ltd. 1988: 1802-5.

[49] Betterle C, Peserico A, Bersani G. Vitiligo and autoimmune polyendocrine deficiencies with autoantibodies to melanin-producing cells. *Arch Dermatol* 1979; 115: 364.

[50] Woolfson H, Finn OA, Mackie RM, et al. Serum anti-tumor antibodies and autoantibodies in vitiligo. *Br J Dermatol* 1975; 92: 395-400.

[51] Lerner AB. Vitiligo. *J Inves Dermatol* 1959; 32: 285.

[52] Schallreuter KU, Wood JM, Berger J. Low catalase levels in epidermis of patients with vitiligo. *J Invest Dermatol* 1991; 97: 1081-5.

[53] Schallreuter KU, Wood JM, Ziegler I, et al. Defective tetrahydrobiopterin and catecholamine biosynthesis in the depigmentation disorder vitiligo. *Biochem Biophys Acta* 1994; 1226: 181-92.

[54] Hann SK, Nordlund JJ: Definition of vitiligo, in *Vitiligo,* edited by SK Hann, JJ Nordlund. London, Blackwell Science, 2000, p:3.

[55] Nordlund JJ, Ortonne JP: Vitiligo and depigmentation, in *Current Problems in Dermatology,* St Louis, edited by WL Weston et al. Mosby–Year Book, 1992.

[56] Barona MI, Arrunategui A, Falabella R, Alzate A. An epidemiological case control study in a population with vitiligo. *J Am Acad Dermatol* 1995; 33: 621-25.

[57] Hann SK, Lee HJ. Segmental vitiligo: clinical findings in 208 patients. *J Am Acad Dermatol* 1996; 35: 671-74.

[58] Grimes PE. Vitiligo: an overview of therapeutic approaches. *Clin Dermatol* 1993; 11: 325-37.

[59] Grimes PE. Psoralen photochemotherapy for vitiligo. *Clin Dermatol* 1997; 15: 921-6.

[60] Parsad D, Dogra S, Kanwar AJ. Quality of life in patients with vitiligo. *Health Qual Life Outcomes.* 2003; 1: 58.

[61] Mattoo SK, Handa S, Kaur I, Gupta N, Malhotra R. Psychiatric morbidity in vitiligo: prevalence and correlates in India. *J Eur Acad Dermatol Venereol* 2002;16:573–578.

[62] Ongenae K, Van Geel N, De Schepper S, Naeyaert JM. Effect of vitiligo on self-reported health-related quality of life. *Br J Dermatol.* 2005 Jun; 152(6):1165-72.

[63] Savin J. The hidden face of dermatology. *Clin Exp Dermatol* 1993;18:393–395.

[64] Ongenae K, Dierckxsens L, Brochez L, van Geel N, Naeyaert JM. Quality of life and stigmatization profile in a cohort of vitiligo patients and effect of the use of camouflage. *Dermatology* 2005; 210(4): 279-85.

[65] Ginsburg IH. The psychological impact of skin diseases: An overview. *Clin* 1996;14:473–484.

[66] Cotterill JA, Cunliffe WJ. Suicide in dermatological patients. *Br J Dermatol* 1997;137:246–250.

[67] Hill-Beuf A, Porter JDR. Children coping with impared appearance. Social and psychologic influences. *Gen Hosp Psychiatry* 1984;6: 294–300.

[68] Al-Abadie MSK, Kent G, Gawkrodger DJ. The relationship between stress and the onset and exacerbation of psoriasis and other skin conditions. *Br J Dermatol* 1994;130:199–203.

[69] Parsad D, Pandhi R, Dogra S, Kanwar AJ, Kumar B. Dermatology Life Quality Index score in vitiligo and its impact on the treatment outcome. *Br J Dermatol* 2003;148: 373–374.

[70] Papadopoulos L, Bor R, Legg C. Coping with the disfiguring effects of vitiligo: A preliminary investigation into the effects of cognitive-behaviour therapy. *Br J Med Psych* 1999; 72:385–396.

[71] Porter J, Beuf A, Lerner A, Nordlund J. Children coping with impaired appearance: social and psychological influences. *General Hospital Psychiatry* 1984; 6: 294-301.

[72] Mozzanica N, Villa M, Foppa S, et al. Plasma α-melanocyte-stimulating hormone, β-endorphin, met-enkephalin, and natural killer cell activity in vitiligo. *J Am Acad Dermatol* 1992; 26: 693-700.

[73] Price M, Mottahedin I, Mayo P. Can psychotherapy help patients with psoriasis? *Clin Exp Dermatol* 1990; 16: 114-17.

[74] Winchell S, Watts R. Relaxation therapies in the treatment of psoriasis and possible pathophysiological mechanisms. *J Am Acad Dermatol* 1988; 18: 101-4.

[75] Partridge J. Changing faces. *The challenge of facial disfigurement*. London: Changing Faces, 1994.

[76] Porter J, Beuf A, Lerner A, Nordlund J. The psychological effect of vitiligo: a comparison of vitiligo patients with 'normal' controls, with psoriasis patients, and with patients with other pigmentary disorders. *J Am Acad Dermatol* 1986; 15(1): 220-25.

[77] Roengik R, Roengik H. Sex differences in the psychological effects of psoriasis. *Cutis* 1978; 21: 529-33.

[78] Boehncke WH, Ochsendorf F, Paeslack I, Kaufmann R, Zollner TM. Decorative cosmetics improve the quality of life in patients with disfiguring skin diseases. *Eur J Dermatol.* 2002 Nov-Dec; 12(6): 577-80.

[79] Cunliffe WJ, Hall R, Newell DJ, et al. Vitiligo, thyroid disease and autoimmunity. *Br J Dermatol* 1968; 80: 135-9.

[80] Dunlop D. Eighty-six cases of Addison's disease. *Br Med J* 1963; ii: 887-91.

[81] Moellmann G, Klein-Angerer S, Scollay DA, et al. Extracellular granular material and degeneration of keratinocytes in the normally pigmented epidermis of patients with vitiligo. *J Invest Dermatol* 1982; 79: 321-30.

[82] Frenk E. Depigmentations vitiligineuses chez des patients atteints de melanomas malins. *Dermatologica* 1969; 139: 84-91.

INDEX

B

C

E

149, 152, 154, 172, 174, 180, 183, 193, 218, 224, 230

evolution, 31, 56, 76, 81, 139, 140, 221, 260, 299

exclusion, 25, 176, 177, 178, 179, 197, 205

excuse, 286

exercise, vii, 16, 25, 27, 30, 65, 66, 67, 68, 70, 73, 74, 75, 230, 235, 240, 241, 242, 245, 246, 258, 259, 260, 261, 270, 271, 281, 282, 287

expectation, 236, 269

explicit memory, 106

exposure, viii, 9, 15, 16, 25, 26, 28, 30, 43, 50, 56, 63, 64, 66, 67, 73, 74, 76, 77, 117, 137, 238, 267, 298

expression, 20, 27, 111, 112, 113, 117, 119, 125, 127, 128, 174, 247, 248, 295

extensor, 298

extraction, 9

extrapolation, 43

F

face validity, 4

factor analysis, 4, 5, 7, 10, 29, 30, 31, 33, 156, 160, 163, 164, 179, 248

failure, 8, 121, 125, 142, 144, 170

family, 12, 16, 17, 21, 110, 111, 112, 115, 121, 122, 124, 126, 134, 135, 137, 139, 172, 173, 206, 208, 210, 213, 221, 292, 294, 296, 298, 300

family environment, 122

family history, 213, 296

family members, 300

family support, 137, 139

family system, 121

family therapy, 110, 112

fat, 13, 14, 17, 23, 24, 25, 31, 36, 37, 38, 42, 45, 48, 49, 52, 53, 54, 55, 56, 57, 58, 76, 84, 85, 86, 87, 88, 89, 90, 91, 93, 94, 95, 96, 97, 107, 118, 159, 204, 216, 217, 218, 225, 226, 230, 231, 232, 233, 234, 239, 241

fatigue, 265

fear, 24, 25, 49, 65, 88, 94, 95, 97, 102, 149, 170, 173, 181, 206, 278

feedback, 34, 118, 120, 123, 148, 180, 207

feelings, 21, 23, 25, 26, 51, 65, 73, 80, 119, 126, 132, 135, 138, 146, 147, 152, 153, 155, 164, 172, 173, 244, 267, 269, 282, 292, 293, 294, 299, 300

feet, 13, 152, 188, 248, 249, 250, 253, 256, 285, 296, 300

females, viii, 5, 26, 36, 42, 44, 45, 46, 60, 63, 64, 65, 66, 67, 69, 71, 72, 73, 74, 84, 87, 88, 89, 90, 92,

93, 95, 99, 108, 117, 137, 142, 143, 205, 226, 235, 236, 237, 241, 292

femininity, 48, 50

Fiji, 52

fitness, 15, 19, 31, 46, 50, 54, 68, 70, 74, 136, 235, 238, 240, 241, 260, 262

fixation, 26

flexibility, xi, 231, 243, 248

flight, 285

fluctuations, 114

fluid, 27, 128

focusing, 8, 9, 15, 18, 19, 98, 113, 116, 151, 238, 257, 272

foils, 85, 93

follicles, 295

food, ix, 24, 26, 42, 43, 48, 57, 59, 88, 106, 109, 111, 112, 113, 121, 122, 125, 126, 127, 133, 171, 221

food intake, 125

foreign language, 135

forgiveness, 271, 274, 275, 283, 287

fragility, 157

France, 2

free recall, 85, 87, 90, 93, 94, 95, 103

freedom, 122

friction, 296

friends, 25, 33, 172, 206, 286, 292, 293, 295, 300

friendship, 123

frontal lobe, 180, 189, 190

frustration, 11, 300

fulfillment, 84

funding, 129

G

gambling, 132

gay men, 4, 7, 9, 20

gender, xi, 2, 3, 5, 12, 21, 23, 32, 34, 44, 47, 49, 50, 56, 59, 60, 108, 115, 117, 121, 132, 201, 203, 204, 221, 224, 225, 226, 229, 230, 232, 233, 235, 236, 237, 241, 248, 302

gender differences, 23, 49, 56, 132, 241, 302

gender identity, 204

gender role, 21, 115, 236

gene, 83, 296

General Health Questionnaire, 153, 156, 177, 186, 292

generalized anxiety disorder, 202, 206, 207

generation, xi, 8, 9, 44, 88, 106, 226, 229

genetic defect, 297

H

I

K

keratinocyte, 298
kindergarten, 246, 260, 262
knees, 296, 298
knowledge, vii, viii, ix, 1, 14, 22, 79, 82, 83, 84, 88, 91, 99, 102, 103, 109, 110, 115, 118, 185

L

labour, 50
laceration, 150
lactation, 38, 42, 43
land, 265
language, 99, 114, 125, 126, 175, 180, 245, 246, 247, 261, 285, 287
latency, 83, 85, 100
laxatives, 134
lead, 64, 65, 66, 120, 125, 139, 146, 148, 149, 170, 179, 236, 258, 264, 271, 299, 300
leadership, 46, 301
learning, 48, 188, 191, 282
leisure, 50
leisure time, 50
lens, 116, 125
leprosy, 292
lesions, 190, 296, 300
liability, 225
liberalisation, 49
lichen, 297
life experiences, 244
life quality, 304
life satisfaction, 105
lifespan, 65, 76, 77, 129
lifestyle, xi, 27, 55, 112, 229
lifetime, 25, 205, 206, 207, 208, 209
likelihood, 18, 74, 208, 269
limitation, 17, 88, 104, 111
linkage, 164, 170
links, 74, 153, 164, 180, 182
listening, 125
living arrangements, 163
location, 37, 55, 149, 249, 252
locus, xii, 14, 27, 260, 264
longevity, 45
longitudinal study, 31, 183
love, 121, 122
low-density lipoprotein, 26
lying, 125, 151, 172, 174, 286

M

magazines, vii, 4, 12, 13, 14, 15, 16, 18, 30, 31, 49, 50, 52, 64, 65, 66, 68, 70, 73, 236, 241
major depression, 26, 141, 183, 205, 210, 212, 213
major depressive disorder, x, 200, 202
Malaysia, 45, 47, 59
males, viii, 15, 16, 18, 26, 27, 31, 32, 36, 38, 44, 46, 47, 49, 57, 63, 64, 65, 67, 69, 71, 72, 73, 74, 76, 108, 137, 142, 178, 205, 237, 245, 248, 292
malignant melanoma, 305
malnutrition, 216
management, 8, 11, 143, 268, 283, 288, 293, 302, 303
mania, 32, 184
manic, 26, 202
manic symptoms, 26
manipulation, 241, 269
market, 74, 201
marriage, 300
married women, 37, 300
masculinity, 3, 8, 22, 32, 46, 50
mass, x, 12, 13, 14, 15, 16, 17, 34, 40, 43, 48, 49, 58, 60, 64, 85, 92, 146, 170, 171, 172, 173, 174, 175, 176, 177, 178, 179, 181, 197, 234, 235, 237, 278
mass communication, 49
mass media, 12, 13, 14, 15, 16, 17, 34, 48, 49, 64, 234, 235, 237
mastery, 120
materialism, 264
matrix, 2
maturation, 114, 234, 237
maturation process, 237
MBI, 6, 7, 8, 11, 21
meanings, 89, 182
measurement, vii, 1, 10, 18, 20, 23, 27, 29, 75, 118, 151, 152, 231, 246, 247, 260, 262, 293, 304
measures, vii, viii, 1, 3, 4, 5, 7, 8, 9, 11, 17, 19, 20, 25, 26, 28, 29, 30, 44, 63, 68, 69, 75, 83, 85, 90, 92, 93, 96, 97, 98, 100, 101, 110, 115, 116, 119, 124, 127, 134, 135, 137, 146, 152, 155, 175, 207, 216, 217, 225, 238, 245, 261, 264, 269, 293, 298
media, 12, 13, 14, 15, 16, 17, 18, 28, 29, 30, 33, 43, 48, 49, 50, 52, 53, 55, 57, 64, 65, 66, 74, 75, 76, 77, 114, 123, 124, 234, 236, 238, 264, 292
median, 86, 95, 100
medication, x, 111, 131, 142, 146, 149, 154, 167, 172, 173, 179, 181, 187, 192, 266
melanin, 295, 298, 305
melanoma, 297, 307

Q

R

S

T

U

V